History and Theory of Early Childhood Education

Samuel J. Braun

Cambridge-Somerville
Mental Health and
Retardation Center

Esther P. Edwards

Tufts University

Charles A. Jones Publishing Company

Worthington, Ohio

1 2 3 4 5 6 7 8 9 10 / 76 75 74 73 72

Library of Congress Catalog Card Number: 79-181374

International Standard Book Number: 0-8396-0012-7

Printed in the United States of America

Photograph on jacket and page 10 from Clifton Johnson, *The Country School in New England,* New York: D. Appleton & Co., 1893.

Photograph on page 1 from *Eliot-Pearson News,* Medford, Mass.: Tufts University, Eliot-Pearson Department of Child Study, August 1967.

Photograph on page 45 from Don Denevi, "The Education of a Genius: Analyzing Major Influences on the Life of America's Greatest Architect," *Young Children* 23 (1968): 234.

Photograph on page 80 from Clifton Johnson, *The Country School in New England,* New York: D. Appleton & Co., 1893.

Photograph on page 110 from Maria Montessori, *Gelbsttatige Erziehung im Fruhen Kindesalter,* 1913.

Photograph on page 147 from Harriet M. Johnson, *Children in the Nursery School,* New York: John Day Co., 1928.

Photograph on page 180 from E. Stevinson, *The Open-Air Nursery,* London: J.M. Dent & Sons, Ltd., n.d.

Photograph on page 207 from Margaret McMillen, *The Nursery School,* London: J.M. Dent & Sons, Ltd., n.d.

Photograph on page 264 from Harriet M. Johnson, *Children in the Nursery School,* New York: John Day Co., 1928.

Photograph on page 342 from Wolff and Phillips, "Designed for 24-Hour Child Care," *Architectural Record,* March, 1944.

Dedication

To Abigail Adams Eliot, an early pioneer in early childhood education, who for over fifty years, has contributed her crisp, forthright, New England disposition and her considerable energy and humanity. The authors are particularly indebted to her excellent memory and willingness to share early experiences in the field. She describes herself as a doer. Having begun the Ruggles Street Nursery School and Nursery Training School of Boston, she helped guide the training school in 1951 to an eventual home, the Eliot-Pearson Department of Child Study at Tufts University. One year later she moved to Pasadena, California to help establish Pacific Oaks College. Upon her return at the age of 62 she taught a group of four-year-olds at the Brooks School in Concord for three years. She is indefatigable and continues to lend herself to community activities.

The Charles A. Jones Publishing Company International Series in Education

Adams, *Simulation Games*

Allen/Barnes/Reece/Roberson, *Teacher Self-Appraisal: A Way of Looking Over Your Own Shoulder*

Armstrong/Cornell/Kraner/Roberson, *The Development and Evaluation of Behavioral Objectives*

Braun/Edwards, *History and Theory of Early Childhood Education*

Carlton/Goodwin, *The Collective Dilemma: Negotiations in Education*

Criscuolo, *Improving Classroom Reading Instruction*

Crosswhite/Higgins/Osborne/Shumway, *Teaching Mathematics: Psychological Foundations*

Denues, *Career Perspective: Your Choice of Work*

DeStefano, *Understanding the Language of the Culturally Different*

Doll, *Leadership to Improve Schools*

Elashoff/Snow, PYGMALION *Reconsidered*

Frymier/Hawn, *Curriculum Improvement for Better Schools*

Goodlad/Klein, *Behind the Classroom Door*

Hauenstein, *Curriculum Planning for Behavioral Development*

Havighurst/Levine, *Farewell to Schools???*

Higgins, *Mathematics Teaching and Learning*

Hitt, *Education as a Human Enterprise*

Leland/Smith, *Mental Retardation: Perspectives for the Future*

Lessinger/Tyler, *Accountability in Education*

Levine, *Models for Integrated Education*

Lutz, *Toward Improved Urban Education*

Meyer, *A Statistical Analysis of Behavior*

Nerbovig, *Unit Planning: A Model for Curriculum Development*

Overly/Kinghorn/Preston, *The Middle School: Humanizing Education for Youth*

Passow, *Reactions to Silberman's* CRISIS IN THE CLASSROOM

Perry/Wildman, *The Impact of Negotiations in Public Education: The Evidence from the Schools*

Pula/Goff, *Technology in Education: Challenge and Change*

Rich, *Humanistic Foundations of Education*

Shane/Shane/Gibson/Munger, *Guiding Human Development: The Counselor and the Teacher in the Elementary School*

Thiagarajan, *The Programing Process: A Practical Guide*

VonHaden/King, *Innovations in Education: Their Pros and Cons*

Weber, *Early Childhood Education: Perspectives on Change*

Wernick, *Career Education Through Teacher Planning and Performance*

Wiles, *Changing Perspectives in Educational Research*

Wiman, *Instructional Materials*

Preface

An increasing interest in early childhood education during the decade ahead is inevitable. The application of research findings about the disadvantaged and about early enrichment programs are stimulating a more encompassing and sustaining national interest in helping young children. These developments are enhanced greatly by full understanding of a broader historical framework upon which vast advances can and will be made.

In order to put this mounting interest in more useful educational perspective to those responsible for advancing programs for the young, we trace the evolution of concepts about early childhood education in Western civilization and place those major concepts in the context of the economic, political, and religious beliefs of the times in which each arose. Major events of the past century are making great impact on today's educational thought; programs for young children are no exception. In fact, the industrial and techno-logical revolutions are contributing greatly to the development of programs for the young. Tenement living in engorged cities, two world wars, the depression, and poverty all have made their marks on our ideas about the young, their families, and the role of early education in improving the quality of life.

To provide additional perspective, *History and Theory of Early Childhood Education* begins with significant excerpts from the writ-ings of early educational theorists (parts 1-3). We frequently ob-serve that early childhood educators appreciate and benefit from a broader knowledge of early ideas and practices. An understanding of the larger issues inherent in the education of all children can be promoted through an acquaintance with the educational theories of Plato and Aristotle, the learned men of the Middle Ages, as well as philosophers of the seventeenth, eighteenth, and nineteenth cen-turies. Part 4 describes the formation of the American public school system, and parts 5 and 6 discuss the evolution of early childhood education in Europe and the United States.

In parts 7-10, some of the most important theoretical bases for early childhood education are traced to the behavioral sciences; in particular, child development. Because the field has many people advocating different curricula and methods, we present some larger guideposts to help the reader adapt the varied approaches which leading educators expound and practice successfully.

Throughout the book, materials from original sources of lasting value are included. The most relevant original articles appear in the text, and other important sources in the appendix will be of help to teachers, counselors, and administrators. To build the reader's enthusiasm for further exploration on his own is one of the major purposes of this book. *History and Theory of Early Childhood Education* is an introduction to a field whose roots are still young, a field of great potential for generations ahead.

In the midst of our collaboration, Esther met an untimely death in an automobile accident. I have attempted to finish preparing the book in what has seemed like a lonely but necessary task. Esther's contribution remains a significant one, for she brings to this book many unique and varied experiences and interests in the field of early childhood education.

I am indebted to the encouragement given me by Dr. Evelyn Pitcher, chairman of the Child Study Department, Tufts University, in urging that the work be completed. I wish to thank Bettye M. Caldwell, Roger W. Coulson, Eileen M. Earhart, James L. Hymes, Jr., Betty H. Landsberger, Evelyn Weber, and Doris Williams for their helpful comments and suggestions. My colleague, Miriam Lasher, must take a great deal of the credit for helping with the tedious details of securing permissions from various publishers. Her work is much appreciated. The editorial help of Harriet Avery contributed to smoothing out and condensing the material. Louise Clancy, Sandra Stadtlander, and, especially, Johanna Larsen struggled to type a manuscript from copy which bore the inevitable multicolored scribbles in the margins signifying corrections. Miriam Lasher proofread various sections of the book. Sally Braun also proofread but, most of all, showed patience and tolerance; she nurtured our children during moments of my preoccupation.

All these people helped to fill a void which still lingers. I trust that the book remains faithful to what Esther and I originally began together.

Cambridge, Mass.   **Samuel J. Braun, M.D.**

Contents

part 1

Introduction

Anthropologists number the societies of man in the hundreds. Yet only a few have ever evolved *formal* systems of education: ancient Sumeria, ancient Egypt, traditional China, India, Persia, Islam; the lost American cultures of the Maya, the Aztec, and the Inca. And, of course, most complex of them all is our own still evolving tradition, call it either European or Western, which originated in Greece and Judea and today spreads over much of the world.

The number is astonishingly small—only nine formal systems of education in the whole rich history of man. How have human cultures continued intact through time? Quite outside any formal system of schooling, man has handed on from one generation to the next his customs, skills, concepts, and values in the most fundamental way: through example and imitation, ritual and legend, tribal custom and unwritten law. *Informal* teaching and learning

1

which take place in the shelter, on the warpath or the hunt, in yam patch or around the fire is education of the most basic sort. It exists wherever groups of people share a continuing identity. Even in the most advanced societies something like it must underlie whatever happens in schools and universities.

While at least nine *formal* systems of education can be recognized,* informal education goes on and must go on continuously, wherever a human society bridges the gap from one generation to the next. Without it, no enduring society has ever existed. So education has been present wherever a father has taught his son to fish from the reef, to shoot with bow and arrow, to drive a dog team, to placate the gods, wherever a mother has taught her daughter to cook, to plant and harvest, to chew hides to make them supple, to decorate her face with tattoo or with kohl. The skills of the home, of the war hunt, and of exploration were learned by children in the context of family and tribe. Words and ideas were absorbed unselfconsciously day by day. The wise old men, the *ingakook*, and the witch doctor shared with the boy and sometimes with the girl the ritualized wisdom of the group, the standards whereby good might be distinguished from evil. For millenia every human group passed on to its young its increment of knowledge with no need to designate a special place where this ought to happen or special people to do it. What every adult taught was simply what it was to be an Eskimo, a Dyak, Yoruba, Crow, Bedouin, Hellene, Celt.

In certain societies, after thousands of years, this informal imparting of knowledge became inadequate. How can this need to develop new ways of educating the young be accounted for? The oral tradition was not at fault; it proved reliable and durable as a means for preserving myth and history. Through it the *Iliad* and the *Odyssey* were transmitted for centuries and much of the Bible for comparably long periods. From medieval Europe to the invention of the printing press, bards and troubadours did as much to keep information alive as did the scribes.

Land use and the amassing of goods beyond the subsistence level give a clue. When men began to live in settled communities, as farmers rather than wanderers after game, they needed to measure and to record their tilled fields. When they began to live along the river valleys, in India, in China, in Sumeria, in Egypt, they needed to measure flood and low water. Gathered into permanent groups, they required laws and systems of government and had to create ways to preserve and record these, whether on sun-baked

---

*In the sense that trained teachers impart whatever knowledge is considered crucial.

brick, papyrus, silk scroll, or palm-leaf book. In some societies, such as the Inca, symbols indicating numbers evolved before those for words.

To measure, to count the bags of grain, to know when the next flood would sweep down the Nile with life-giving silt were all-important. To do these things required groups of people with a special function and discipline. Sometimes these groups acquired a special mystique, as did the magi of Zoroastrianism, the priests and scribes of Egypt, the mandarins of imperial China. They possessed the key to the number system. On their tablets or scrolls, they worked out the eclipses of sun and moon, the cycles of rich harvests, the dynasties of kings. They had the obligation of imparting their esoteric knowledge to a select few of the next generation who in their proper turn would possess it, would possibly enrich it, and of necessity would hand it on to their own successors. These were the first teachers in any formal sense.

Their knowledge became in time a source of stability in states where the learned élite had a stake in the *status quo* and united with king and nobles to maintain it. Ancient Egypt exemplifies this system. Beginning as many petty groupings along a river, then as a pair of rival states, and finally forming a single great state, Egypt always resembled a thousand-mile long string of settlements between deserts. The problem of gaining unity, and maintaining it once achieved, was gradually solved. The enormously long history of ancient Egypt, which endured two and a half millenia before it was conquered by Alexander, attests to the stability of the state. Although the Pharoah was "Child of the Sun," with religious sanctions and great wealth, who could stop a chieftain, weeks away beyond the cataracts, from setting up his own small copy of the court of Thebes or of Memphis? Who could keep him and his children and his children's children loyal and subservient to what might have been only an idea or a fading, far-off memory of the ruler? Precisely, it was the training that he had received at the Pharoah's court. Every great noble, every ruler of a district, was in a true sense a "child of the palace." When his son was seven, each chieftain brought him miles and days and left him to grow and learn in the shadow of the Pharoah, until the child had absorbed not only writing and numeration, the laws, etiquette, the science of war, but also the more basic value of loyalty. So, imbued with his role vis-à-vis the Pharoah's majesty, he returned to his own district as a young man to uphold the unity of Egypt.

Formal education was associated with a privileged and powerful few. For everyone else education was encompassed by family and apprentice training. Even today, traditional skills and the folk wisdom have continued outside the structure of the school while formal education often has provided a direct route to political and economic power. As in the past, education has set its possessors apart—lending them prestige and power.

In some nations, however, it has been open to a larger segment of the people, even (ideally, though perhaps not in practice) to everyone who can benefit from it. Historically, these educational gains have come about through the efforts of one or another group to meet the obligations of a personal religion. For the Jews, in particular, it became important very early for every man to know the Word of God. Islam has always classed together Jews, Christians, and themselves (Muslims) as "the people of the Book." One main strand of formal education in our own Western society (in Northern Europe as well as Puritan New England) has sprung from a belief in every man's need to be acquainted with the Bible. The religious ideas of personal goodness and individual responsibility led directly to attempts to insure every man the opportunity to read the sacred texts. It was no longer sufficient that a few leaders possess the essential learnings; every man must do so. Formal education, then, became something that every man needed. This development is unique to Western society.

The strand of educational thought and practice which flowed from ancient Judea could blend into, enrich, and be enriched by another similar strand from Greece. Plato and Aristotle reflected a deep belief in Greek intellectual society in their emphasis on man seen as noble and good, beautiful and useful in body and mind, gaining personal fulfillment by learning and adhering to the laws of life within the context of the good society. In Judea, man's relationship to God was seen as outweighing the practical necessities of food, profit, power, and property; in Greece, Aristotle warned that "to seek for utility everywhere is entirely unsuited to men that are great-souled and free." (2)*

Historically, the need for formal education stems from two sources: one, to preserve order in communities of men and to maintain a stable society and a viable state; two, to help man to become more fully and completely himself, more attuned to God, the possessor of greater personal fullness of being.

So far this chapter has not focused on the education of the young child as a special case in education. Two main points ought to be made about the education of young children. First, today, as in the past, the basic socialization of the infant and little child in every

---

*Numbers within parentheses refer to References at the end of each part.

society is seen as the function of mother and family. The child of the Australian aborigine, the Bedouin, the infant in Paris, Rome, London, and New York are nurtured by their mothers within the supportive concentric rings of family, community, and society. In this fashion, before we possess any words, each of us is initiated into a world of expected behaviors. We are taught the language of our people and, through the medium of that language, the pace of our learning accelerates in a kind of increasing geometric ratio. Long before school intervenes, even school at the level of the three-year-old nursery group, the small child already has become a member of his society. He can use language and ideas and is aware of many family, social, and sex roles. He possesses innumerable ways of perceiving and responding to his environment which will permanently shape the tenor of his life. All the most important learnings are well underway before a child enters his first schoolroom. Through a totally informal education he has gained his sense of himself, of his world and the other people in it, and of the whole complex network of relationships by which he is bound. Such education is still the most basic. Without it, no human child becomes, in any real sense, a human being.

Second, with the advent of an industrial, technologically complicated society, some of what parents used to teach their children in the old traditional fashion of example and shared work can no longer be taught, or taught well enough, for a long enough time, to enough children. The father as worker has vanished from the home. Sometimes the mother works outside it as well. Even if both parents were available to their young children, the old traditional skills and occupations have inexorably left home and farm and craftsman's shop. Cloth and thread are spun in a factory rather than by grandmother at the humming wheel in the corner. Clothes come ready-made. Similarly, children see less of the basic processes of food preparation. Breakfast, lunch, and supper come from cans and premixed packages. Even the warm, friendly, understandable beasts of the country child's life have been superseded by immense and complex tractors, harvesters, and mowers. In every area of life, specialization has increased, and meaning has diminished for children. What was once rich and stimulating aliment for their understanding has become remote and incomprehensible. Imagine what is implied to the literal mind of childhood by the casual statement: "Daddy is in the office making money!" In a true sense, *modern early childhood education is itself a child of the industrial revolution.* It was born of the need to create for small children a milieu in which life could come to have meaning analogous to the meaning it had in an earlier time when the child played around his mother's feet in the kitchen or stumbled after his father down the plowed furrows as he sowed seeds.

Early childhood education programs in the industrialized countries of the West were either a fruit of social welfare efforts (as in Montessori's *casa dei bambini* in Rome) or a result of the attempt to provide life-enhancing experiences for privileged children in preparation for regular school. Now educators are formulating ways to insure every child's right to such an education. The first years of a child's life are crucial. His earliest experiences open doors of possibility which, without them, might be forever shut. To create a more brotherly society in which man can more fully become man, all children must be provided with the essential food for enhancing life, a diet rich both in material necessities and in perceptual and cognitive stimulus.

Our society has arrived at a degree of complexity in which cues are too intricate for children to decipher. Major demands are made on everyone. Once only rulers, wise men, priests, and scribes needed formal education; now everyone needs it. But we cannot make use of it unless our early experience prepares us to do so. For some children, the home is the best possible medium for such preparation, but only if it contains adults who are loving, articulate, educated, reasonably stable emotionally, and able to attend to the child, to teach him the skills, information, and values that will allow him to utilize the school experience. For children who lack such a setting, the society must act *in loco parentis* and provide it in substitute form. The intricate and demanding question is how to make this provision. Head Start is an attempt; Day Care, another. Such an undertaking requires time, money, well-trained teachers, and a concerned citizenry. The education of young children has become a need and an obligation that reaches beyond the institution of the family.

Still on whatever age level extrafamilial education begins, there will always be at the beginning of life the human interaction of mother and child. Further experience can only be built on this foundation. The one-to-one duality of mother and child comes first.

Appreciation of young children and their education is recent. During much of the long span of Western society, there was little recognition that childhood was a unique period. Philippe Ariès, in his provocative book, *Centuries of Childhood*, has specifically shown that during the largest part of the Christian era, in a Europe where war and hunger were commonplace, and the fate of the newborn was more likely death than long life, the typical man or woman emerged straight out of his babyhood into a sort of junior adult status. (1) He was obviously not as strong, as competent, as important as the full adults about him, but he was not thought to be in a different stage of life. Rather, he was simply inferior. The seven-year-old apprentice articled to his master, filing links for chain mail, dipping candles, carding wool, was a member of the working population. Portraits of children, which began to appear at the very end of the Middle Ages, show children in their small suits of armor, their boned stomachers and starched ruffs, captured by the artists as stiff and staring premature adults. The very idea of childhood as a special time of life had to precede any conception of early childhood education.

Such an awareness had existed in classic times. The tender, child-like bas-reliefs on monuments to a few deceased boys or girls of Greece and Rome are reminders of this fact. But any such luxury of an especially protected time of life for the young was lost in the decline and distintegration of the ancient world. As Rome was overturned by barbarian hordes, children had to grow up rapidly in order to survive. On mosaics of the first millenium even the Christ child is adult in form. Small in stature, he stands on his mother's knee, but he is a majestic, stately, totally unchildlike figure all the same.

But from about 1200 A.D., there is a shift toward depicting the Christ child as a child. Slowly the God-king-priest figure relaxed and became a true child. Europe began to acquire a sense of structure and security to see its children as young beings whose unfolding lives deserved to be fostered and nurtured, not merely hurried along. Yet five hundred years later people were shocked to hear Rousseau proclaim in *Émile* that the child is not "the adult writ small." (4) So slowly do man's ideas unfold, so much are his expectations chained to the conventions of the day, that a hundred generations of children were forced into the mold of premature adulthood. They, in turn, did the same to those who came after them without noticing that the mold was, at the very least, an awkward fit.

Today we have a far more developed sense of the stages of growth: infancy, early childhood (for which there are as yet no comfortable terms—toddlerhood? preschooler?), childhood itself—with the term preadolescence increasingly used for its later portion, adolescence, young adulthood, and maturity. We have become used to all these terms without fully understanding their implications. Most of them are very new. They reflect the new sensitivity to sequences of growth which the very existence of these words indicates.

It would be false, of course, to claim that men such as Plato and Aristotle, or even the much later Comenius, Locke, and Rousseau, dealt with an educational specialty called *early childhood education* or even recognized it as a possible subcategory; clearly they did not. When they wrote about education they dealt with its total sweep, and they saw it as an inseparable part of the society as a whole. To understand their thoughts completely, one must read the whole body of their works. We have cited here small segments which relate to our particular theme, with the realization that lifting them out of context distorts them somewhat.

Early childhood education has its own concerns. However, this entity did not spring full-grown from the forehead of Froebel. In fact, we would serve no purpose by separating ourselves from the currents of educational thought. Lawrence Cremin comments in similar fashion:

We tend to think of popular education as a relatively recent phenomenon in the history of the West, associating it with the sweeping seventeenth- and eighteenth-century revolutions that ushered in the modern world. Actually, the idea itself is much older, dating as it does, from the earliest systematic speculations on the nature of human polity. The classic treatise, of course, is Plato's *Republic*, which remains to this day the most penetrating analysis of education and politics ever undertaken. Recall Plato's argument: In order to talk about the good life, we have to talk about the good society; and in order to talk about the good society, we have to talk about the kind of education that will bring that society into existence and sustain it. Hence, there is no vision of the good life that does not imply a set of educational policies; and conversely, every educational policy has implicit in it a vision of the good life. . . . Alfred North Whitehead once quipped that all of Western philosophy has been a series of footnotes to Plato, and certainly in education this has been the case. Every major philosopher since Plato has written on education, and every one of them has been governed in some way or other by Plato's insights. (3)

We draw on the insights of the past, but we must ask our own relevant questions about them. After reading the selections presented you might attempt to answer the following questions: 1) What are the goals of this educational policy? What does it hope to achieve, and for whom? What needs, dilemmas, values in the greater society does it consciously or unconsciously reflect? What sort of society does it hope to form? 2) Who shall be educated? 3) Who shall do the educating? How will he be chosen and how trained for the task? 4) What will be the basic teaching methods? How shall the learner be motivated? What is considered an appropriate reward or an effective sanction? 5) What is held to be the nature of learning? Is it habit-formation or the gaining of rational understanding? Development of character? Preparation for a vocation? Is it training the body, or the mind, or both, or something beyond any of these? Does it come chiefly from the impact of society on learner, or from the learner himself, or through what relationships, forces, obligations? 6) What kind of person is conceived of as the outcome of this educational policy? What sort of human being is the ideal man whose formation is the *raison d'être* of the system?

These are the underlying questions implicit in the examination of each selection offered. In presenting excerpts from some germinal minds in the mainstream of educational development, we hope their "answers" in their time will help the reader to insights he can use as touchstones of his own. It is clear that each of us, today as in the past, must find his own solutions. These must be forged from two possibly conflicting strands: the needs of the individual and the needs of the society. This enduring dilemma is not always easily resolved. Our task is to help the reader see that there are choices to be made.

References to Part 1

1. Ariés, Phillippe, *Centuries of Childhood: A Social History of Family Life*, trans. Robert Baldick (New York: Alfred A. Knopf, 1962).
2. Aristotle, *Politics*, trans. H. Rackham, Loeb Classical Library (Cambridge: Harvard University Press, 1939). In Robert Ulich, *Three Thousand Years of Educational Wisdom* (Cambridge: Harvard University Press, 1954), p. 68. Copyright 1947, 1954 by the President and Fellows of Harvard College.
3. Cremin, Lawrence A., *The Genius of American Education* (New York: Random House, Vintage Books, 1965), pp. 3-5.
4. Rousseau, Jean Jacques, *Emile, Julie, and Other Writings*, ed. S. E. Frost, Jr.; trans. R. L. Archer (Woodbury, N. Y.: Barron's Educational Series, 1964).

part 2

Early
Educational
Theorists

Plato (c. 428–348 B.C.)

G. Lowes Dickinson suggests that the political theory and practice of Athens gave "form to all later political thinking" in Europe. (5) Politics was the very breath of life in Athens. In the ruling class of citizens, everybody knew everybody else, at the very least by reputation. Information passed from man to man by word of mouth, and teaching went on in a social context in the open air. Men lived in their city rather than in their homes. A large segment of life was public life, and an Athenian felt himself basically identified with Athens, her customs, her gods, and her history. He shared the conviction that a man could be a lover of the arts, an athlete, a convivial and generous friend to his friends, and still play an effective role in the winning of wars and the governing of states.

In Plato's boyhood, the disastrous Peloponnesian War (431-404 B.C.) ended in the crushing of Athens by Sparta and her allies, those other Greek cities for whom Athens had long been the envied model. Left standing only through sudden charity of the Spartans, Athens was shamed and powerless. Her politics were in turmoil; her population bitter, suspicious, and ready to search for scapegoats. In this atmosphere of a querulous police state, Socrates was condemned and killed in 399 B.C. by the ruling oligarchs, some of whom were Plato's kinsmen.

Plato was still a relatively young man when these events occurred, but the profound impact his teacher, Socrates, had had upon him is shown in his *Dialogues*, written years later. Socrates is nonetheless the focal personality and the source of insight. In normal times, Plato's life would have been one of involvement in Athenian politics. After Socrates' death, however, he felt compelled to leave the unjust government and the disintegration he saw around him. He traveled for some years through the Mediterranean world, returning from his self-exile only in middle age, circa 380 B.C.

Plato founded the Academy shortly after his return and taught there for the rest of his life, with the exception of the unfortunate attempt to enter into active political life in Sicily as counsellor to the young ruler, Dionysius II. He taught and he wrote. This activity seems normal for an intellectual, but for an Athenian intellectual, it was not normal. Only a generation before, Socrates had made no attempt to record his teaching. Athenians were talkers rather than writers — poetry, drama, yes; discussion, philosophy, no — not until the world of actuality had become an impossible one in which the citizen could no longer act upon his beliefs. Plato had been reduced by the tenor of the times to the role of spectator of affairs, whereas his predecessors had shaped them. Out of protest against his enforced passivity grew the *Dialogues* (his embodiment of the values that had been Socrates'), the *Republic*, and *Laws* (his effort to shape in the world of the mind a utopian state that would improve upon reality).

It is chiefly in the *Republic* that Plato's thought bears upon education. Living in a state where venality and privilege were swallowing up the values that Athens had once fought to preserve, Plato felt the need to create a class of guardians who would live not for themselves but for the body politic. They were to be above personal interest and gain. They willingly sacrificed family life for their role as arbiters of the life of Athens. "How to train them to act in this way?" Plato queried, and gave as his answer the step-by-step education of a philosopher-king, a man at once spirited and gentle, learned and brave. Such men must stem from good stock, and for this reason Plato would have marriage and procreation regulated. All children were to be taken away from their parents at birth and reared by the state, for the citizen's obligation to live and work for the public good could not be fulfilled if his time was taken up with the care of offspring. Instead, the citizen should feel that all the children were his to protect and foster, while state-supplied nurses did the actual upbringing. Women as well as men were to be occupied with the concerns of government (an extraordinary idea for the ancient world); therefore, boys and girls alike would be educated.

To train a wise, ethical ruling caste, even the earliest experience could not be vulgar or irrational. Plato forbade the ancient myths and legends: tales of gods in love and at war (often lascivious or terrifying) which had been traditionally told to children by their mothers and their nurses. He was wrestling with educational problems still with us today — how to develop the moral man out of the premoral child, how to train for reliability, trustworthiness, courage? With the rational man's hatred of the instinctual and the disorderly in life, Plato banned violence and pornography from childhood experience in his theoretical state, believing they would lead the child to either too lustful or timid an adulthood.

We still argue the question. What are "redeeming cultural elements" that separate the creative work from the obscene? What about violence in works for adults, and for children? Ought the wolf in *Little Red Riding Hood* actually eat grandmother? What kind of television programs should be aired? Who shall decide? What about sex in comic books, in movies, in ads? What is the effect of viewing violence on a child's behavior? Plato's answer involved strict censorship by the state, as does our own; ours, however, is a far less complete censorship with a wider segment of the population having more to say about it. The question of whether the earthy, elemental aspects of life ever can or ought to be banned from the young is a profound one. Many post-Freudians feel that these aspects of life well up inexorably in each human being; to try to ban them is to try to stop the tide from flowing. But Plato was a long time pre-Freud, and in a utopia, one can do as one pleases with the population — provided one is the author. In the

Republic, Book II, Section XVII, Socrates and Glaucon talk; Socrates speaks first.

from **Republic**

Plato

You know also that the beginning is the most important part of any work, especially in the case of a young and tender thing; for that is the time at which the character is being formed and the desired impression is more readily taken.

Quite true.

And shall we just carelessly allow children to hear any casual tales which may be devised by casual persons, and to receive into their minds ideas for the most part the very opposite of those which we shall wish them to have when they are grown up?

We cannot.

Then the first thing will be to establish a censorship of the writers of fiction, and let the censors receive any tale of fiction which is good, and reject the bad; and we will persuade mothers and nurses to tell their children the authorized ones only. Let them fashion the mind with such tales, even more fondly than they mould the body with their hands; but most of those which are now in use must be discarded. (7:221)

...if we mean our future guardians to regard the habit of lightly quarrelling among themselves as of all things the basest, should any word be said to them of the wars in heaven, and of the plots and fightings of the gods against one another, for they are not true. No, we shall never mention the battles of the giants, or let them be embroidered on garments; and we shall be silent about the innumerable other quarrels of gods and heroes with their friends and relatives. If we intend to persuade them that quarrelling is unholy, and that never up to this time has there been any hatred between citizens, then the stories which old men and old women tell them as children should be in this strain; and when they grow up, the poets also should be obliged to compose for them in a similar spirit. But the narrative of Hephaestus binding Hera his mother, or how on another occasion his father sent him flying for taking her part when she was being beaten, and all the battles of the gods in Homer — these tales must not be admitted into our State, whether they are supposed to have an allegorical meaning or not. For a young person cannot judge what is allegorical and what is literal; anything that he receives into his mind at that age is likely to become indelible and unalterable; and therefore it is most important that the tales which the young first hear should be models of virtuous thoughts. (7:222-223)

From *The Dialogues of Plato*, translated by Benjamin Jowett, 4th ed., vol. 2 (Oxford, England: The Clarendon Press, 1953), by permission of The Clarendon Press.

It is tempting to see direct parallels here between Plato's educational system and modern education, and there are some. But
what about the differences? Plato was secure in his belief that the
Guardians of the State could rightly act to obliterate beliefs that
had long been held, that were even considered part of the religious
heritage by the ordinary people. There is an element of "managing
the news" in Plato which even those people who most dislike the
tastelessness and excessive violence of some of current writing,
cinema, and television may like even less. Plato's solution cannot be
ours, but his recognition of the problem underlies the fact that we,
too, must deal with it and try to solve it. As long as there is any
appropriate limitation in the materials to which small children are
exposed, the basis of selection must be defined. To choose what is
good for children is not to be repressive, but it is to limit. Limitation may be most appropriate and necessary: but it is still limitation, and it raises difficult questions.

How did Plato answer the basic questions posed about any system of education? The purpose of his plan was to create the good
man in the good State, the Guardians being those most truly fit
to wield power for public benefit. They were by nature, designed
for the task, chosen not because of family influences but because of
innate aptitude:

> ... While all of you in the city are brothers, ... yet God in fashioning
> those of you who are fitted to hold rule mingled gold in their generation,
> for which reason they are the most precious — but in the helpers silver,
> and iron and brass in the farmers and other craftsmen. And as you are
> all skin, though for the most part you will breed after your kinds, it may
> sometimes happen that a golden father would beget a silver son and that
> a golden offspring would come from a silver sire and that the rest would
> in like manner be born of one another. So that the first and chief in-
> junction that the god lays upon the rulers is that of nothing else are
> they to be such careful guardians and so intently observant as of the
> intermixture of these metals in the souls of their offspring, and if sons
> are born to them with an infusion of brass or iron they shall by no means
> give way to pity in their treatment of them, but shall assign to each the
> status due to his nature and thrust them out among the artisans or the
> farmers. And again, if from these there is born a son with unexpected
> gold or silver in his composition they shall honor such and bid them go
> up higher, some to the office of guardian, some to the assistanceship,
> alleging that there is an oracle that the state shall then be overcome
> when the man of iron or brass is its guardian. (13:38)

Those children to be educated were the "men of gold or silver,"
fitted by birth to respond to their training and so work for the

good of the state. No one was to be banned from such education because of social class or sex, for as Plato explicitly states: ". . . you must not suppose that my words apply to the men more than to the women who arise among them endowed with the requisite qualities." (13:61) The artisans and farmers were to be trained through apprenticeship, the learning of crafts and trades but they would never share the full educational experience. However, the entire society, in actuality as well as in Plato's thought, was built on slavery. Slaves fulfilled the function of modern machines and have been estimated to number about two-thirds of the population. That a civilized country could exist without slaves, that the life of the Athenian gentleman, devoted to the well-being of the state, could have been otherwise supported was inconceivable to men of Plato's time. The slave was to receive no education other than that which he picked up in the course of performing his tasks since he was considered a nonperson.

Since only the Guardians partook of wisdom, they alone could teach. Part of their task was to recognize and to initiate their successors. Socrates, talking with Glaucon, outlines the steps of the "curriculum" which will train a Guardian (Book VII):

And surely you would not have the children of your imaginary State, whom you are nurturing and educating — if your imagination ever becomes a reality — you would not allow the future rulers to be mere irrational quantities, and yet to be set in authority over the highest matters?

Certainly not.

Then you will make a law that they shall have such an education as will enable them to attain the greatest skill in asking and answering questions?

Yes, he said, you and I together will make it.

Dialectic, then, as you will agree, is the coping-stone of the sciences, and is set over them; no other study can rightly be built on and above this, and our treatment of the studies required has now reached its end?

I agree, he said. (7:400)

. . . And, therefore, calculation and geometry and all the other elements of instruction, which are to be a preparation for dialectic, should be presented to the mind in childhood; not, however, under any notion of forcing our system of education.

Why not?

Because a freeman ought not to acquire knowledge of any kind like a slave. Bodily exercise, when compulsory, does no harm to the body; but the knowledge which is acquired under compulsion obtains no hold on the mind.

Very true.

Then, my good friend, I said, do not use compulsion, but let early education be a sort of amusement; you will then also be better able to find out the natural bent.

There is reason in your remark, he said.

Do you remember that the children were even to be taken to see the battle on horseback; and that if there were no danger they were to be brought close up and, like young hounds, have a taste of blood given them?

Yes, I remember.

The same practice may be followed, I said, in all these things — labours, lessons, dangers — and he who is most at home in all of them ought to be enrolled in a select number.

At what age?

At the age when the necessary gymnastics are over: the period whether of two or three years which passes in this sort of training is useless for any other purpose, for sleep and tiring exercise are unpropitious to learning. Moreover the trial of their quality in gymnastic exercises is one of the most important tests to which our youth are subjected. (7:402-403)

Each generation brings the next through a planned series of tasks and trials alternating between active service to the state in peace and in war and periods devoted to "continuous and strenuous" study — life in the world of the spirit. The true Guardian fulfills himself in both realms, but chooses philosophy over practical affairs when circumstances give him free choice.

Because Plato's "men of silver and gold" were defined as innately educable, he rid himself of having to motivate them to learn. Nor did Plato discuss method. A "right education," he suggested, "will make them reasonable men," but he did not attempt to specify what that method of teaching ought to be. One gathers that for young children Plato thought of it as the usual regimen then extant: instruction in literature and gymnastics with its content purified and strictly regulated. Later in life, the method probably was to be that which he actually employed in the Academy: conversation, discussion, and contemplation.

His ultimate objective was the good of the State, and he saw the Guardians as trained to sacrifice material gain and ease, even individual fulfillment, for its sake. Beautiful, idealistic, yet answering none of the hard practical questions of method, Plato's Utopia has gone on shaping men's thought, despite its never having been implemented. In all times, men have reached for a vision of the ideal good, and for his vision, Plato's thought is treasured. But for the practical concerns of life, a more individual and diverse kind of education has had to evolve.

Aristotle (384–322 B.C.)

Plato was intuitive and theoretical, transcending everyday concerns in pursuit of the ideal. By contrast, Aristotle's thought was firmly based on observed reality from which he created logical structures which organized the world of nature into a coherent whole. Robert Ulich writes of him:

Aristotle is the first giant orderer of the universe of thought. If one considers how germinal the knowledge of his time was in comparison with ours, then one can appreciate the creativeness of his mind. For it is no exaggeration to say that he laid the basis of our scholarly vocabulary in the whole broad field of the humanities, and that from his work issued the development of the higher curriculum as was customary from the times of the university of Alexandria up to the beginning of the 19th century; even the essential categories of natural philosophy have sprung from his mind. (19:62)

Born in Stagira, a little town in remote Thrace, more than forty years after Plato's birth, Aristotle was sent to Athens at eighteen and was associated with the Academy for twenty years. He was acquainted with the thought of Plato; but Plato was away from Athens for considerable stretches of time in those years, and how much direct contact there was between the two men is not known. During Aristotle's time at the Academy, he probably was involved in biological research, a lifelong interest. Aristotle's most famous pupil was Alexander; but his period of tutorship lasted only three years (343/2–340 B.C), and Aristotle seems neither to have fostered his pupil's urge toward world domination nor shared his views on government. Observing the later progress of that pupil, one might wonder how effective a teacher Aristotle was. When Alexander died in 323 B.C., Aristotle left Athens, having been accused of impiety as Socrates had been before him. He died the next year in exile in Asia Minor.

His writings are interesting to contrast with those of Plato. They resulted from direct observation and a citing of the habits of diverse peoples which anticipated the modern anthropologist's cross-cultural studies. His guidelines for the upbringing of small children can actually be followed. They are eminently concrete and practical. Those children to be educated were not seen as "golden" or "silver," but were the ordinary male offspring of the free citizens of the city state, as was the actual custom at the time. Aristotle held as self-evident that because the citizens belonged to the state and were its chief strength and support, education ought to be a matter of public policy, and the state should regulate children's up-bringing and should provide the same education for all (meaning all *free men*). Children up to the age of seven were to be nurtured at home by their mothers or nurses, but even for these small ones there was to be the children's tutor listening in on the tales told and the games played, making sure that these were fitting for future citizens who must be both liberal and moral. There are overtones of Plato throughout, of course, but Aristotle did not go as far beyond the mores of the day. Girls were not to be educated, for example, nor did he expect the able parent of the dull son to voluntarily assign his child to a lower social role.

It was in his vision of education as liberating that Aristotle rose above the merely mundane. He exceeded Plato in grounding his system on what actually existed, but his objectives went beyond the utilitarian. The young ought to be taught "those useful arts that are indisputably necessary," yet not "all the useful arts"; and they ought not to be taught anything, however useful, which would "render the person participating in them vulgar." Any pursuit which injured or deformed the body was forbidden, reflecting the Greek sense that the sound and beautiful body was the outward expression of the sound and beautiful mind. Earning wages was considered degrading. The free man was to give himself fully to the pursuit of learning and the tasks of the state.

Yet a balance of interests, "a liberal education," was crucial to Aristotle. Indeed, his own life was an example of the range and breadth he advocated — not an easy accomplishment at any time. For any individual to possess the wholeness or grasp of all the fields of knowledge which Aristotle was able to encompass is now impossible. While we face a dilemma he could not imagine, we accept his premise that "to seek for utility everywhere is entirely unsuited to men that are great-souled and free." It is our puzzle, rather than our loss, that the bulk of knowledge and demands made on professionals for expertise in each particular specialty preclude the kind of unity that was possible for Aristotle and possible for the educated minority up to about 150 years ago. How to weave science and technology into humanity is a problem we grimly face as a society and as educators. As C.P. Snow observed almost twenty years ago in *The Two Societies*, we must resolve how to remain "great-souled and free" in our knowing and thinking, and how to communicate, how to share ideas and insights from one discipline to another, even though the quantity of material we deal with has increased enormously.

Aristotle's *Politics* presents his own case for the good man within the good state:

from **Politics**

Aristotle

Book VII, section XV. When the children have been born, the particular mode of rearing adopted must be deemed an important determining influence in regard to their power of body. It appears from examining the other animals, and is also shown by the foreign races that make it their aim to keep up the military habit of body, that a diet giving an abundance of milk is most suited to the bodies of children, and one that allows rather little wine because of the diseases it causes. Moreover it is advantageous to subject them to as many movements as are practicable with children of that age.... And it is also advantageous to accustom them at once from early childhood to cold, for this is most useful both for health and with a view to military service. Hence among many non-Greek races it is customary in the case of some peoples to wash the children at birth by dipping them in a cold river, and with others, for instance the Celts, to give them scanty covering. For it is better to inure them at the very start to everything possible, but to inure them gradually; and the bodily habit of children is naturally well-fitted by warmth to be trained to bear cold. In the earliest period of life then it is expedient to employ this or a similar method of nursing; and the next period to this, up to the age of five, which is well not to direct as yet to any study nor to compulsory labours, in order that they may not hinder the growth, should nevertheless be allowed enough movement to avoid bodily inactivity; and this exercise should be obtained by means of various pursuits, particularly play. But even the games must not be unfit for freemen, nor laborious, nor undisciplined. Also the question of the kinds of tales and stories that should be told to children of this age must be attended to by officials called Children's Tutors. For all such amusements should prepare the way for their later pursuits; hence, most children's games should be imitations of the serious occupations of later life.... The tutors must supervise the children's pastimes, and in particular must see that they associate as little as possible with slaves. For children of this age, and up to seven years of age, must necessarily be reared at home; so it is reasonable to suppose that even at this age they may acquire a taint of illiberality from that they hear and see. The lawgiver ought, therefore, to banish indecent talk, as much as anything else, out of the state altogether (for light talk about anything disgrace-

From Robert Ulich, *Three Thousand Years of Educational Wisdom* (Cambridge, Mass.: Harvard University Press, 1954). Copyright 1947, 1954 by the President and Fellows of Harvard College.

ful soon passes into action) — so most of all from among the young, so that they may not say or hear anything of the sort; and anybody found saying or doing any of the things prohibited, if he is of free station but not yet promoted to reclining at the public meals, must be punished with marks of dishonor and with beating, and an older offender must be punished with marks of dishonor degrading to a free man, because of his slavish behavior. . . . But the younger ones must not be allowed in the audience at lampoons and at comedy, before they reach the age at which they will now have the right to recline at table in company and to drink deeply, and at which their education will render all of them immune to the harmful effects of such things. . . . Audiences are attracted by what they hear first; and this happens alike in regard to our dealings with people and to our dealings with things — all that comes first we like better. On this account we ought to make all base things unfamiliar to the young, and especially those that involve either depravity or malignity.

Book VIII, section I. Now nobody would dispute that the education of the young requires the special attention of the lawgiver. Indeed, the neglect of this in states is injurious to their constitutions; for education ought to be adapted to the particular form of constitution, since the particular character belonging to each constitution both guards the constitution generally and originally establishes it — for instance, the democratic spirit promotes democracy and the oligarchic spirit oligarchy; and the best spirit always causes a better constitution. Moreover in regard to all the facilities and crafts certain forms of preliminary education and training in their various operations are necessary, so that manifestly this is also requisite in regard to the actions of virtue. And inasmuch as the whole end for the state is one, it is manifest that education also must necessarily be one and the same for all and that the superintendance of this must be public, and not on private lines, in the way in which at present each man superintends the education of his own children, teaching them privately, and whatever special branch of knowledge he thinks fit. But matters of public interest ought to be under public supervision; . . .

Book VIII, section II. It is therefore not difficult to see that the young must be taught those useful arts that are indispensably necessary; but it is clear that they should not be taught all the useful arts, those pursuits that are liberal being kept distinct from those that are illiberal, and that they must participate in such among the useful arts as will not render the person who participates in them vulgar. A task and also an art or a science must be deemed vulgar if it renders the body or soul or mind of free men useless for the employments or actions of virtue. Hence we entitle vulgar all arts as deteriorate the condition of the body, and also the industries that earn wages; they make the mind preoccupied and degraded. And even with the liberal sciences, although it is not illiberal to take part in some of them up to a point, to devote oneself to them too assiduously and carefully is liable to have the injurious result specified. . . .

Book VIII, section III. It is clear therefore that there is a form of education in which boys should be trained not because it is useful or necessary but as being liberal and noble; though whether there is one such subject of education or several, and what these are and how they are to be pursued, must be discussed later. . . . To seek for utility everywhere is entirely unsuited to men that are great-souled and free. And since it is plain that education by habit must come before education by reason, and training of the body before training of the mind, it is clear from these considerations that the boys must be handed over to the care of the wrestling-master and the trainer; for the latter imparts a certain quality to the habit of the body and the former to its actions. (5)

Rome to the Middle Ages:
Mankind and Education
Await the Renaissance

Nothing really new was added by the Romans to the educational thought of Plato and Aristotle. Their system of education was based on that of Athens. It has been said that in conquering Greece by military means, Rome was conquered intellectually by it. Plutarch (c. 46–120 A.D.), in his *Moralis,* a compendium of good advice on almost everything including education, gives a kind of "Handy Manual of Child Care" for the first century. His emphasis, writes Ulich, is on "good breeding, good habits, and an all-round liberal training; in other words, just the right kind of education for a young gentleman from a privileged family." (19:90) Plutarch's writing does not contain Plato's profound discontent with society or Aristotle's judging, weighing, and ordering. Plutarch is a man wholly of his moment, accepting it and handing out maxims to parents.

Plutarch wrote of motivating children in a way which seems humane — and was more so than the beatings administered by the average unenlightened school master. Yet he bent the truth in his endeavor to win control over the child, to manipulate, to propagandize:

This also I assert, that children ought to be led to honorable practices by means of encouragement and reasoning, and most certainly not by blows or ill-treatment, for it surely is agreed that these are fitting rather for slaves than for the free-born; for so they grow numb and shudder at their tasks, partly from the pain of the blows, partly from the degradation. Praise and reproof are more helpful for the free-born than any sort of ill-usage, since the praise incites them toward what is honorable, and reproof keeps them from what is disgraceful.

But rebukes and praise should be used alternately and in a variety of ways; it is well to choose some time when the children are full of confidence to put them to shame by rebuke, and then in turn to cheer them

up by praises, and to imitate the nurses, who, when they have made
their babies cry, in turn offer them the breast for comfort. Moreover in
praising them it is essential not to excite and puff them up, for they are
made conceited and spoiled by excess of praise. (14)

He showed no concern about whether the child had merited
praise or blame. Plutarch spoke as a manipulator of behavior to an
audience made up of a worldly class who valued success above all
else. The great Greeks, Plutarch's supposed models, would have
scorned the falsity of this approach. Nonetheless, his place in educational thought gained an essentially unmerited importance
through its impact on a much later time, the Renaissance.

Fifteen hundred years intervened which marked the Roman decline, the wanderings of the barbarian tribes across Europe, the
growth of feudal society and town life in small walled cities, and,
finally, the return of a neoclassical view of life with the Renaissance
in Italy. When Plutarch emerged again as educational mentor, it
was to a very different group of men in a world altered to the core.

The first change, which was already manifest in a small way when
Plutarch was writing, was the advent of Christianity. Originally a
minute sect, many of whom were slaves, the earliest Christians
were too beset by more compelling problems to find a great concern for education. To *listen* to the Gospel took no learning. Later,
Christianity became established, growing in power as Rome declined, and the leaders of educational thought were religious leaders — Basil, Augustine, Jerome. Their concern was not to train
young minds and bodies for life in the world, but rather to nurture
souls for a future world. "We Christians, young men, hold that this
human life is not a supremely precious thing . . ." wrote Basil in his
Address to Young Men on the Right Use of Greek Literature. "We
place our hopes upon the things which are beyond, and in preparation for the life eternal do we all things that we do." (4) There
are letters from this period which give detailed instruction as to
how this preparation may be carried on. Jerome wrote to Laeta, a
Roman matron who had promised that her infant daughter would
be brought up as a virgin dedicated to Christ. The year was 403:

Thus must a soul be educated which is to be a temple of God. It must
learn to hear nothing and say nothing but what belongs to the fear of
God. It must have no understanding of unclean words, and no knowledge
of the world's songs. Its tongue must be steeped while still tender in
the sweetness of the psalms. Boys with their wanton thoughts must be
kept from Paula: even her maids and female attendants must be separated from worldly associates. For if they have learned some mischief
they may teach more. Get for her a set of letters made of boxwood or of
ivory and called each by its proper name. Let her play with these, so

that even her play may teach her something. . . . The very words which she tries bit by bit to put together and to pronounce ought not to be chance ones, but names specially fixed upon and heaped together for the purpose, those, for example, of the prophets or the apostles or the list of patriarchs from Adam downwards as it is given by Matthew and Luke. . . .

Let her very dress and garb remind her to Whom she is promised. Do not pierce her ears or paint her face consecrated to Christ with white lead or rouge. Do not hang gold or pearls about her neck or load her head with jewels, or by reddening her hair make it suggest the fires of ghenna. Let her pearls be of another kind and such that she may sell them hereafter and buy in their place the pearl that is "of great price." . . . (17:164-166)

Education for those children set aside for the religious life was intensely focused and individualized, but the usual form of instruction became the teaching of Church dogmas, history, and laws to adults who were to become religious. Much of the knowledge of the ancient Greeks and the Romans was lost as libraries were burned, cities sacked, and manuscripts scattered. In 413 A.D., ten years after Jerome wrote to Laeta, he wrote a letter on a similar theme to one Gaudentius. He described the upheaval:

The world sinks into ruin: yes! but shameful to say our sins still live and flourish. The renowned city, the capital of the Roman Empire, is swallowed up in one tremendous fire; and there is no part of the earth where Romans are not in exile. Churches once held sacred are now but heaps of dust and ashes. . . .

Such are the times in which our little Pacatula is born. Such are the swaddling clothes in which she draws her first breath; she is destined to know of tears before laughter and to feel sorrow sooner than joy. And hardly does she come upon the stage when she is called on to make her exit. Let her then suppose that the world has always been what it is now. Let her know nothing of the past, let her shun the present, and let her long for the future. . . . (17:171)

In time, the very idea of childhood became lost. The small child was dressed as an adult and took part in the activities of adults as soon as he was able. The children of serfs tended geese or pigs; they beat the moat at night to frighten the frogs so that the lord might sleep, and worked the land beside their parents. As soon as he could hold weapons, the boy who was to be a warrior began his training with sword, shield, helmet, and spear. Europe was school-less for a thousand years. Few people read or wrote, and all but a handful were churchmen. A man of the vision and political acumen of Charlemagne learned to read only as an adult, and to write hardly at all, keeping his wax tablet under his pillow and taking it out when he woke early to practice forming letters with his war-stiffened fingers. Skills, values, and some knowledge were passed on, but informally and unself-consciously for the most part, in the home and through the relationship of master and apprentice. Life was difficult and brief. The individual imagined himself set by God into a framework predetermined from eternity. Within that framework his duty was to fulfill his role without complaint in a world he conceived of as unchanging and unchangeable. The goal of every act, the great equalizer for those whose earthly lives were spent in cold, hunger, poverty, and disease, was the life to come. Toward it king and serf alike moved by means of worship and ritual, conformity and patience. For men living in such a world, an education which stimulated thought and inquiry, even if possible, would have been a meaningless luxury.

When the notion of individuality finally re-awoke in the Renaissance, the Ancients became the model for education again. The intensely personal mood of the fifteenth and sixteenth centuries in Italy, the almost frantic grasping for glory, power, and the beauty of the world, deformed the thought of the Greek and Roman sages. While their writings were the basic texts, attention was diverted from what Plato and Aristotle meant to what they *said*. As they had educated an elite of free men, so the Renaissance education was for the nobility alone. The young child of noble rank was seen as precious since he was scion of the family and held the promise of the future. However, the child as such was of little concern. Though the serious, charming portraits — a young de'Medici, a small Sforza, Prince Juan Balthasar on his fat pony — portray children who were cherished, they show children very much in the role of adults. The pride and magnificence that characterized the Renaissance view of man's part in the drama of social and political life left little place for the tenderness, the quiet imagination about the capacities and needs of children — in short, the very concerns education of the very young demand.

Luther (1483–1546)

The religion of towering, frescoed churches, of prelates in silk wielding immense power, of indulgences sold for money, left much room for spiritual inwardness, Luther thought. So the Alps Reformation began. The era was one of struggle and upheaval: congregations turned against their clergy, townsmen against the restrictive guilds, small landholders against their feudal overlords, peasants against the landed classes — all moving chaotically, without awareness of how deep the groundswell went, toward an overturned

world. If the upheaval eventually resulted in a more humane structure for European society, the outcome was unimaginable for a
long time.

In early sixteenth century Germany, Luther moved both nobles
and ordinary burghers to turn away from the Church and toward
a more personal road to God and to salvation. With his translation
of the Bible, Luther set the spoken language in permanent form
and provided the essential reading matter of German Protestantism. If the ordinary man must find his own way to God with the
Bible as light and guidebook, then read he must for his soul's sake.
A new concern for education began as a need for the population in
general.

Much of Luther's theology was medievally obsessed with the
devil as temptor and opponent of the soul, but his educational ideas
were surprisingly liberal. In a letter to Margrave George of Bran-
denburg, Luther suggested a plan which anticipated genuine democracy of opportunity:

It is well that in all towns and villages good primary schools should
be established out of which could be picked and chosen those who are
fit for the universities, out of which then the men can be taken who are
to serve your land and people. If the towns or their citizens cannot do
this, then it would be well to establish new stipends for the support of
a few bright fellows in the deserted monasteries, so that every town
might have one or two students. In the course of time, when the common
people see that their sons can become pastors and preachers, and get
other offices, many of those who now think that a scholar cannot get a
living will again keep their sons in school. (10)

Luther bluntly charged the authorities with the duty under God
of seeing that a Christian life was possible for each citizen, no
matter how humble. Girls as well as boys were to be instructed.
The schools were to foster a whole range of development in the
child: intellectual and religious, of course, but also physical, emotional (in which Luther saw music as basic), and social, in the sense
that the educated person became the good citizen. Nor did education stop with childhood. Luther believed the adult capable of
educating himself, and to this end he advocated libraries. In many
ways, his thinking was astonishingly modern, dealing factually with
a range of practical problems. His educational writings had enormous impact. For once, the authorities listened and acted. To think
that the princes and potentates who joined Luther's cause did so
out of religious conviction alone would be naive. Religious conviction did exist and was real, but political expediency also existed.
However motivated, they did join, and the most complete public

school system to exist in any country before the nineteenth century was set up in Germany.

The events of the relatively recent past have obscured the image of Germany as educational mecca of the world. (Until the First World War, Germany was where the aspiring young doctor, scientist, scholar went to study.) German higher education flowered from a long tradition of general literacy, which went back to Luther. An inevitable fact of life in his time, however, was that an education embodying true freedom of inquiry and individual choice in areas where state interests were in opposition was not possible. The best that men of that period could hope for was relative freedom under enlightened princes who were no less absolute for being benevolent. When some princes appeared who were not benevolent, there was no tradition of individual resistance. But they appeared far beyond Luther's time.

from **Letters to the Mayors
and Aldermen of all
the Cities of Germany
in Behalf of Christian Schools**
Martin Luther

It is indeed a sin and shame that we must be aroused and incited to the duty of educating our children and of considering their highest interests, whereas nature itself should move us thereto, and the example of the heathen affords us varied instruction. There is no irrational animal that does not care for and instruct its young in what they should know, except the ostrich, of which God says: "She leaveth her eggs in the earth, and warmeth them in the dust; and is hardened against her young ones, as though they were not hers." (Job, xxxix, 14, 15) And what would it avail if we possessed and performed all else, and became perfect saints, if we neglect that for which we chiefly live, namely, to care for the young? In my judgment there is no other outward offense that in the sight of God so heavily burdens the world, and deserves such heavy chastisement, as the neglect to educate children. . . .

But all that, you say, is addressed to parents; what does it concern the members of the council and the mayors? That is true; but how, if parents neglect it? Who shall attend to it then? Shall we therefore let it alone, and suffer the children to be neglected? How will the mayors and council excuse themselves, and prove that such a duty does not belong to them?

Parents neglect this duty from various causes.

In the first place, there are some who are so lacking in piety and up-rightness that they would not do it if they could, but like the ostrich, harden themselves against their own offspring and do nothing for them. Nevertheless these children must live among us and with us. How then can reason and, above all, Christian charity, suffer them to grow up ill-bred, and to infect other children, till at last the whole city be destroyed, like Sodom, Gomorrah, and some other cities?

In the second place, the great majority of parents are unqualified for it, and do not understand how children should be brought up and taught. For they have learned nothing but to provide for their bodily wants; and in order to teach and train children thoroughly, a separate class is needed.

In the third place, even if parents were qualified and willing to do it themselves, yet on account of other employments and household duties they have no time for it, so that necessity requires us to have teachers for public schools, unless each parent employ a private in-structor. But that would be too expensive for persons of ordinary means, and many a bright boy, on account of poverty, would be neglected. . . .

Therefore it will be the duty of the mayors and council to exercise the greatest care over the young. For since the happiness, honor, and life of the city are committed to their hands, they would be held recreant before God and the world, if they did not, day and night, with all their power, seek its welfare and improvement. Now the welfare of a city does not consist alone in great treasures, firm walls, beautiful houses, and munitions of war: indeed, where all these are found, and reckless fools come to power, the city sustains the greater injury. But the highest welfare, safety, and power of a city consists in able, learned, wise, up-right, cultivated citizens, who can secure, preserve, and utilize every treasure and advantage. . . .

But, you say again, if we shall and must have schools, what is the use to teach Latin, Greek, Hebrew, and the other liberal arts? Is it not enough to teach the Scriptures, which are necessary to salvation, in the mother tongue? To which I answer: I know, alas! that we Germans must always remain irrational brutes, as we are deservedly called by surrounding nations. But I wonder why we do not also say: of what use to us are silk, wine, spices, and other foreign articles, since we our-selves have an abundance of wine, corn, wool, flax, wood, and stone in the German states, not only for our necessities, but also for embellish-ment and ornament? The languages and other liberal arts, which are not only harmless, but even a greater ornament, benefit, and honor than these things, both for understanding the Holy Scriptures and carrying on the Civil government, we are disposed to despise; and the foreign articles which are neither necessary nor useful, and which besides greatly impoverish us, we are unwilling to dispense with. . . . (11:222-225)

Even if there were no soul . . . and men did not need schools and the languages for the sake of Christianity and the Scriptures, still, for the establishment of the best schools everywhere, both for boys and girls, this consideration is of itself sufficient, namely, that society, for the maintenance of civil order and the proper regulation of the household, needs accomplished and well-trained men and women. Now such men are to come from boys, and such women from girls; hence it is necessary that boys and girls be properly taught and brought up. . . . (11:232)

My idea is that boys should spend an hour or two a day in school, and the rest of the time work at home, learn some trade and do whatever is desired, so that study and work may go on together, while the children are young and can attend to both. (11:233)

Luther gives the following advice to the mayors and aldermen about the care that needs to be taken when they select books for libraries, an essential companion to schools:

In the first place, a library should contain the Holy Scriptures in Latin, Greek, Hebrew, German, and other languages. Then the best and most ancient commentators in Greek, Hebrew, and Latin.

Secondly, such books as are useful in acquiring the languages, as the poets and orators, without considering whether they are heathen or Christian, Greek or Latin. For it is from such works that grammar must be learned.

Thirdly, books treating of all the arts and sciences.

Lastly, books on jurisprudence and medicine, though here discrimination is necessary.

A prominent place should be given to chronicles and histories, in whatever languages they may be obtained; for they are wonderfully useful in understanding and regulating the course of the world and in disclosing the marvelous works of God. . . . (11:237)

"Here I stand. I can do nothing else. God help me. Amen." So spoke the young Luther at Worms, refusing to retract any of his doctrines, and the intransigent strength of the statement was characteristic of his personality: Luther was filled with conviction and total faith in God as he conceived of Him, and he turned that faith into action. He was intemperate, even fierce, in his allegiances, a man of enormous vitality, vigor, and emotional drive. He preached education as he preached religion and made a permanent mark on his country's life.

Erasmus (c. 1466–1536)

Luther's great contemporary, Erasmus of Rotterdam, was the rational man *par excellence*. Not lacking in conviction, but lacking in the partisanship that underlay the polarization of good and evil, he could never take sides in the Reformation, for he saw the excesses of both protagonists with deadly clarity. Humanist and savant,

Erasmus seems closer in some ways to modern times than to his own: he was objective with the critical acumen which foretold the scientific mind; yet he also had a tolerance rare in any time, particularly in his own. Such men are not likely to be popular with their embroiled contemporaries, and Erasmus was not. Luther, who had initially considered him an ally, held him in the end a bitter enemy. Yet Erasmus, too, had worked for the reform of the Church, and churchmen widely regarded him with suspicion. In spite of this, his superb mind won him universal respect, and his writings on education, though not his major works, had some impact on the growth of humanistic ways of instructing children.

While in England from 1509 to 1514, he was professor of divinity at Cambridge, and a friend of Thomas More. There he became interested in the nature of good schooling, and in 1511 wrote *Upon the Method of Right Instruction*, in which he advocated orderly planning both for teaching pupils and for training their teachers. In *On Christian Matrimony* (1526), he devoted a chapter to the education of girls. His great work in education was *Liberal Education of Boys* (1529) in which he advocated the value of education in terms which could be upheld almost unchanged by a modern man who believes that human beings must develop within the context of a human culture in order to develop in any adequate fashion.

Three conditions ... determine individual progress. They are Nature, Training, and Practice. By *Nature* I mean, partly, innate capacity for being trained, partly, native bent toward excellence. By *Training*, I mean the skilled application of instruction and guidance. By *Practice*, the free exercise on our own part of that activity which has been implanted by Nature and is furthered by Training. Nature without skilled Training must be imperfect, and Practice without the method which Training supplies leads to hopeless confusion. (6)

Erasmus' work marked one step in the changed view of human life brought about by the Humanist evolution of thought. The Middle Ages had seen man as in exile from paradise, enduring existence on this earth in the hope of attaining eternal life. The better the man, the less relevant to his interest was the "here and now." But for Humanism, "here and now" was important, engrossing, central. The obsession with preparation for eternity faded, and preparation for life in the world became important in its own right. Erasmus, Bacon, Montaigne, and others laid the groundwork between the fifteenth and the seventeenth centuries for a new attitude about humanity which was to flower in the Enlightenment of the eighteenth century. Secular concerns and satisfactions flourished. Men dared to turn from exclusive concern with religion.

The Church, too, met the challenge of Reformation with Counter-reformation, its own house-cleaning, up-grading, spiritualizing movement within the orthodox establishment. The Jesuit Order, founded by Ignatius of Loyola (Spain) in 1539, soon became one of the foundation stones of Catholicism in its struggle against Protestantism, and Jesuit schools became recognized throughout Europe as outstanding educational institutions. Even those who opposed the Jesuits admired the efficacy of their teaching. In fact, their existence stimulated other religious sects to establish their own schools.

Comenius (1592–1670)

John Amos Comenius brings educational thought across the divide into modernity. One may wonder whether the deeply religious Moravian bishop would have considered himself in any formal sense a Humanist, but humane he was, in a marked degree and concerned about the education of all children rich and poor, male and female, bright and dull. He saw them all as precious in the sight of God.

Caught in the swirling currents of the Thirty Years War, that peculiarly vicious combat which set brother against brother across Europe, he refused to hate either the Catholics who were persecuting his people, or the Lutherans and Calvinists who scorned them. Pietist, mystic, almost a lifelong refugee, Comenius became, in a true sense, a citizen of the world, while retaining a deep oneness with his own national and religious group. He was a rare spirit, a warm, serene, and generous man in a harsh time.

As a young man he was driven out of Bohemia after the Battle of the White Mountain in 1626. He became schoolmaster, writer, and bishop of the Moravian communities which had found refuge in Poland. He was invited to Sweden in 1638 to work out a plan for reorganizing its school system, and to England in 1641, from which he was driven by the Civil War to Amsterdam. He returned to Sweden, then again to Amsterdam where he died. "His manuscripts and books were lost in besieged cities and burning houses." (18) Yet, he left a body of educational writings which combines his deeply ethical philosophy with the injunctions to look outward with care and study everything in the world. Indeed, since the world is to Comenius the expression of God the Creator, man ought to honor Him by coming to know His work. Learning morality, and piety were to Comenius the three foundation stones of the good life and education.

from **Didactica Magna**

John Comenius

The Great Didactic in which is presented a generally valid art of teaching everything to everyone, or, reliable and perfect directions for erecting schools in all communities, towns, and villages of any Christian state. In these schools all youth of both sexes, without exception, can be instructed in the sciences, improved in their morals, filled with piety, and, in suchwise, be equipped in early years for all that belongs to the life here and beyond. This will be done by a concise, agreeable, and thorough form of instruction which:

derives its reasons from the genuine nature of things,

proves its truth by dint of adequate examples taken from the mechanical arts,

arranges the sequence of instruction by years, months, days, and hours, and finally, shows an easy and safe way for the happy pursuit of all these suggestions.

The Beginning and End of our Didactic will be: To seek and find a method by which the teachers teach less and the learners learn more, by which the schools have less noise, obstinancy, and frustrated endeavor, but more leisure, pleasantness, and definite progress, and by which the Christian State will suffer less under obscurity, confusion, and conflict, and will enjoy a greater amount of light, order, peace, and quiet. . . .

Chapter 6:–If Man Is To Be Man He Must Be Educated.   Nature gives the germinal capacities for knowledge, morality, and religion, but it does not give knowledge, morality, and religion themselves. Rather these are acquired through learning, acting, and praying. Therefore, somebody has rightly defined man as an educable animal since he cannot become man unless he is educated.

Chapter 7:–The Education of Man Is Best Done In His Early Youth, and Only Then Will It Succeed.   It is a property of all things becoming that they can easily be bent and formed as long as they are tender, but that they refuse to obey when they have hardened. Soft wax can be modeled and remodeled, hard wax will crumble. The young tree can be planted, replanted, trimmed, and bent to any shape; not so the grown. So also the hands and limbs of man can be trained for art and craft only during childhood, as long as the sinews are soft. If someone is to become a good scribe, painter, tailor, smith, musician, etc., he must devote himself to his vocation as long as his imagination is still flexible

From Robert Ulich, *Three Thousand Years of Educational Wisdom* (Cambridge, Mass.: Harvard University Press, 1954). Copyright 1947, 1954 by the President and Fellows of Harvard College.

and his fingers still elastic. In the same way piety must be implanted into the hearts during infancy lest it not root. If we want to educate a person in virtue, we must polish him at a tender age. And if someone is to advance toward wisdom, he must be opened up for it in the first years of his life when his industriousness is still burning, his mind is malleable, and his memory still strong. . . .

Chapter 9:–All Youth of Both Sexes Must Be Entrusted to the Schools. Not only the children of the rich and noble but all children ought to be educated in the same way whether they are nobles or commoners, rich or poor, boys or girls, or whether they come from cities, towns, or villages. That is evident for the following reasons: First, all men are born for the same main purpose: they are to be human beings, i.e., rational creatures, masters over the other creatures, and images of the Creator. . . . God Himself often testifies that before Him all things are equal. . . .

Second, we do not know for which calling divine dispensation has destined one or the other of us. So much at least is known that God has chosen the most perfect tools of his glory out of the poorest, humblest, and unknown people. . . .

Third, it is no contradiction that some are by nature feeble and dull; this fact but commends, and calls for, the universal cultivation of the minds. . . . Also it is difficult to find a person so defective that he could not be helped in one or the other direction; and if dull people may achieve nothing in scholarship their morals can be improved. . . .

Fourth, nor can there be given sufficient reason why the female sex should be excluded from studying. For also girls are images of God; they participate in His Grace and in the future kingdom of God, and they are equipped with the same industriousness and capacity for wisdom. . . .

*Chapter 16:–General Postulates of Teaching and Learning.** First postulate: Nature follows a well-ordered time plan. . . . Hence, all material of learning must be so divided according to age levels that only is assigned to the child which is within the compass of his capacity. Second postulate: Nature prepares the material before it begins to form it. . . . Schools fail in this principle very often. . . . Hence, in order to improve teaching the following have to be done: 1) One has to have books and other adequate tools ready. 2) Perception must come before language. 3) Language must be learned not from grammar but from fitting authors.

---

*Up to the nineteenth century, Comenius was remembered by people who were unaware of his educational or religious ideas, but knew him only as a writer of textbooks. His "readers" do not embody his principles very well. The best known, *Orbis Sensualium Pictus*, is an attempt to combine the learning of Latin vocabulary with visual aids and cultural education. Each section is headed by a picture; the words taught are described in the content, despite the fact that the pictures do not much resemble any of the child's known and concrete reality. It is an attempt to add an image to totally abstract verbalism.

4) Observation has to precede analysis. 5) Examples have to precede the rules.

Third postulate: Nature chooses fitting materials for its activity. . . . Therefore, in the future: first, each child entrusted to a school ought to stay in it. Second, the minds of the pupils should be made susceptible to the subject chosen for treatment. Third, all obstacles ought to be removed from the pupil.

Fourth postulate: Nature does not get confused, but proceeds by carefully distinguishing the single objects. . . . Therefore, pupils in school ought to be occupied with only one subject at any one time.

Fifth postulate: Nature begins its activities from within. . . . Therefore, in the future: first one ought to train the knowledge of things, second the memory, and third the language and the hand. . . .

Chapter 17:–Requisites for Fast Teaching and Learning. . . . It will be evident that . . . we will succeed if we follow in the steps of nature. This means that instruction 1) Must begin early and before the mind is corrupted. 2) The minds must be made ready for it. 3) It must proceed from the general to the particular, and 4) From the easier to the more difficult. 5) Progress must not be rushed. 6) The minds must not be forced to do anything but that to which they aspire according to their age and motivation. 7) Everything must be related through sense impression, if possible. 8) Everything must be applied immediately, and, 9) Everything must be taught consistently according to one and the same method. (3)

The pervasive democratic view of man held by the Pietists (all men were erring children of God, whatever their earthly rank) comes through in these excerpts. The idea that all youth ought to be educated in common will not be echoed so completely again until Horace Mann in the mid-nineteenth century preaches the common school. Comenius was extraordinary in his vision of education as a social concern, existing for the good of everyone. Yet, within this group instruction, the individual was not ignored or suppressed. The good of the group *and* the good of the unique person were equally essential. To an unprecedented degree in his time, he created a balance between both values.

Comenius's ideas on universal education were formulated in the early seventeenth century but forgotten for many years. That there is any connection between his writings and the thought of the early settlers of New England is not known, but during his lifetime, those remote little colonies of Puritans and Separatists, clinging to the scruff of an unsettled continent, put into practice educational procedures remarkably like those he avocated. Of course, the Separatists (Pilgrims) were akin in thought to the Pietists. More probably, it was a case of similar viewpoints leading to similar behavior.

The Commonwealth Educators

England has had a long tradition of concern with education. In the first half of the sixteenth century, Sir Thomas Elyot wrote in his *Boke Named the Governour* (1531) that to rule, the noble classes must be trained in social responsibility such as those who instructed the young Tudors. Sir Thomas More, Sir Francis Bacon, and Roger Ascham were among the Elisabethans who wrote and thought deeply on educational issues. During Comenius's brief stay in England, they played a role in helping him formulate his beliefs. While Cromwell was in power, a brilliant group now called the Commonwealth Educators tried to apply to the reformation of the schools the ideas that flowed from Bacon's empirical philosophy, embodied in his dictum that "knowledge and human power are synonymous." (2) Of these men, John Milton (*Of Education,* 1644) is best known. They were a brilliant lot, and their humanism took on a new hue — republican concern for the education of the citizen, made responsible not by cause of gentle birth but through brains, bearing, and character.

In 1648, Sir William Petty published *W.P.'s Advice to Mr. Samuel Hartlib for the Advancement of some Particular Parts of Learning.* Of all the circle of Commonwealth Educators, Petty's educational ideas were the most progressive and daring. He proposes that schools be founded for all children. "*Ergastula Literaria,* Literary-workhouses, where children may be taught as well to doe something toward their living, as to read and write," (12:349) and "that the business of Education be not (as now) committed to the worst and unworthiest of men, but that it be seriously studied by the best and abler persons." (12:350) Like Comenius before him, Petty advocated universal education:

That all children of above seven yeares old may be presented to this kind of Education, none being to be excluded by reason of the poverty and inability of their Parents, for hereby it hath come to passe, that many are now holding the plough, which might have been made fit to steere the state. Wherefore let such poor children be imployed on works whereby they may earne their living, equall to their strength and understanding. . . . And if they cannot get their whole living, and their Parents can contribute nothing at all to make it up, let them stay somewhat the longer in the workhouses. (12:350)

Like the Deweyites long after him, he believes in the primacy of direct experience over verbal learning:

That since few children have need of reading before they know, or can be acquainted with the things they read of, or of writing, before their thoughts are worth the recording, or they are able to put them into any forms—much lesse of learning languages, when there bee Books enough for their present use in their owne mother tongue; our opinion is, that those things being with all somewhat above their capacity . . . be deferred awhile, and others more needfull for them, such as are in the order of Nature before those afore mentioned, and are attainable by the help of Memory, which is either most strong or unpreoccupied in children, be studied before them. We wish, therefore, that the Educands be taught to observe and remember all sensible Objects and Actions, whether they be Naturall or Artificiall, which the Educators must upon all occasions expound unto them. (12:350)

His other specific suggestions are eminently reasonable, humane, and built on sensible understanding of children's powers and needs. To make learning as easy and as useful as possible is his basic purpose: encourage individual talents, allow for the intellectual goals of some without demanding theoretical aptitude of all. This world is one with a democratic, workaday flavor doomed to disappear along with the Puritan Commonwealth and not to revive for many years. From 1640 to 1660 there was a concept (even if unrealized) of startling newness: a more universal, a more ethical yet more practical manner of educating the young, so that in maturity a far wider, more inclusive group of Englishmen would be fit to think, to work, and to govern.

It was ironic, but understandable, that Petty's ideas and those of the general circle of Commonwealth Educators were forgotten while John Locke's *Some Thoughts Concerning Education* (1693) became famous. Locke's ideas are, in fact, more conventional, less revolutionary, less of the future and more expressive of the current than those of his predecessors.

John Locke (1632–1704)

The Commonwealth fell and monarchy returned in Charles II and James II, reviving the last of feudal absolutions and the divinity of kings. As the Stuarts were brushed aside by the Glorious Revolution and William and Mary, the monarchy became limited, with power shared within the narrow bounds of the political alliance of the aristocracy with the wealthy. Both groups tacitly agreed that in their hands and those of their heirs should rest the government. To this England John Locke directed his book.

After civil war and the successive violent upheavals of the century moving to its close, peace and a time of prosperous stability had come at last. The country gentleman, the urban man of means, that "small class of man — at most four to five percent of the population — who enjoyed the rank, title, and privileges of 'Gentlemen' or above" had leisure now to direct attention and energy to the upbringing of their children. "This tiny minority owned most of the wealth, wielded the power, and made all the decisions — political, social, economic — for the whole nation; to all intents and purposes it *was* England in the seventeenth century. (8:51)

The "gentlemen" were the opinion makers. They knew Locke as philosopher (*Of Human Understanding*), as defender of religious liberty (*Letter Concerning Toleration*), and as political theorist who denied the absolute rights of kings (*Two Treatises of Government* — written from political exile in Holland). They respected Locke as a prime spokesman for a philosophy which assured them their influential place in their society, their relative freedom of action, their power and security; in short, they could subscribe to Locke's educational advice.

In Holland in 1684, Locke began the series of letters to his friend, Edward Clarke, a Somerset landowner and father of a large family, which later became *Some Thoughts on Education*. Clarke's eldest son, also named Edward, was then a boy of eight. Asked by the parents to provide a guide to the upbringing of this child and his sisters, Locke addressed himself first to questions about the development of a healthy physical constitution, and then to a general method of education for a young gentleman. This method emphasized:

... the efficacy of right habits formed early in life, of the twin principles of esteem and disgrace to discipline children, and of good parental example rather than colorless and hardly remembered rules and admonitions; the self-defeating nature of excessive corporal punishment; the necessity of allowing children their own amusements and frivolities, that is, letting them be children when they actually are; and, perhaps most importantly, the wisdom of paying close attention to their different temperaments and rhythms of development, and thereby accommodating the educational program to the child, not the child to the program. These sections are devoted to the formation of character and the implementation of the most effective methods of discipline; they are not, be it noted, limited in any way to a particular class of wealth, socially prominent, or highly privileged members of society. Potentially they apply to everyone. (8:52-53)

Locke formulated a remarkably broad point of view about the nature and the value of education in this long series of letters written until at least 1688. Indeed, for the rest of his life, Locke continued to be concerned with educational ideas. The first edition of *Some Thoughts on Education* appeared anonymously in the spring of 1693.* In this case, the first two printings remained anonymous. In 1695 the third edition contained a signed dedication, although the title page still lacked an author's name. Locke continued to work over the *Education* until his death in 1704. In 1705 the fifth and definitive edition was published.

Locke has long been associated with the idea of the newborn child as *tabula rasa*, empty slate, to be written on by training and circumstance in any way that these dictate. "I imagine the minds of children to be as easily turned this or that way as water itself," wrote Locke in *Some Thoughts on Education*. (9:356) Yet, to feel that he had no respect for individual temperament is to overstate the case. He advises parents and tutors to study the child, to pay attention to his moods, his interests, his innate capacities, and to shape the plan of education in terms of their understanding of him. The formation of good habits is essential, but it is not sufficient. Reason enters in, too, and good human relations. The careless, self-indulgent parent will have only himself to blame for the careless, self-indulgent child.

By turning to Locke himself, one can see why this treatise was republished in the eighteenth century in English (twenty-one times), in Dutch, French, Swedish, German, and Italian, and later in Czech and Spanish. (8:17) Would a child brought up as Locke suggests have thrived?

from **Some Thoughts
on Education**

John Locke

(27) As the strength of the body lies chiefly in being able to endure hardship so also does that of the mind. And the great principle and foundation of all virtue and worth is placed in this, that a man is able to deny himself his own desires, cross his own inclinations, and purely follow what reason directs as best, though the appetite lean the other way.

(28) The great mistake I have observed in people's breeding their children has been, that this has not been taken care enough of in its due season; that the mind has not been made obedient to discipline,

---

*To venture into publication without signature was a custom of Locke's due to modesty and a timid need to test the direction of the intellectual and political wind.

From Robert Ulich, *Three Thousand Years of Educational Wisdom* (Cambridge, Mass.: Harvard University Press, 1954). Copyright 1947, 1954 by the President and Fellows of Harvard College.

and pliant to reason, when at first it was most tender, most easy to be bowed. Parents being wisely ordained by nature to love their children, are very apt, if reason watch not that natural affection very warily; are apt, I say, to let it run into fondness. They love their little ones, and it is their duty: but they often with them cherish their faults too. . . . (9:356-357)

(60) But pray remember, children are not to be taught by rules, which will be always slipping out of their memories. What you think necessary for them to do, settle in them by an indispensable practice, as often as the occasion returns; and, if it be possible, make occasions. This will beget habits in them, which, being once established, operate of themselves easily and naturally, without the assistance of the memory. But here let me give two cautions: 1. The one is, that you keep them to the practice of what you would have grow into a habit in them, by kind words and gentle admonitions, rather as minding them of what they forgot, than by harsh rebukes and chiding, as if they were wilfully guilty. 2ndly. Another thing you are to take care of, is, not to endeavor to settle too many habits at once, lest by a variety you confound them, and so perfect none. When constant custom has made any one thing easy and natural to them, and they practice it without reflection, you may then go on to another.

This method of teaching children by a repeated practice, and the same action done over and over again, under the eye and direction of the tutor, till they have got the habit of doing it well, and not by relying on rules entrusted to their memories; has so many advantages, which way soever we consider it, that I cannot but wonder . . . how it could possibly be so neglected. I shall name one more that comes now in my way. By this method we shall see, whether what be required of him be adapted to his capacity, and any way suited to the child's natural genius and constitution: for that, too, must be considered in a right education. We must not hope wholly to change their original tempers, nor make the gay pensive and grave, nor the melancholy sportive, without spoiling them. God has stamped certain characters upon men's minds, which, like their shapes, may perhaps be a little mended; but can hardly be totally altered and transformed into the contrary. . . . (9:359-360)

(65) Having under consideration how great the influence of company is, and how prone we are all, especially children, to imitation; I must here take the liberty to mind parents of this one thing, vis. that he that will have his son have a respect for him and his orders, must himself have a great reverence for his son. . . . You must do nothing before him, which you would not have him imitate.

(67) . . . None of the things they are to learn should ever be made a burden to them, or imposed on them as a task. Whatever is so proposed presently becomes irksome: the mind takes an aversion to it, though before it were a thing of delight or indifference. Let a child be

but ordered to whip his top at a certain time every day, whether he has or has not a mind to it; let this be required of him as a duty, wherein he must spend so many hours morning and afternoon, and see whether he will not soon be weary of any play at this rate.

(68) ... As a consequence of this, they should seldom be put about doing even those things you have got an inclination in them to, but when they have a mind and disposition to it. ... (9:362-363)

(161) The great skill of a teacher is to get and keep the attention of his scholar: whilst he has that, he is sure to advance as fast as the learner's abilities will carry him; and without that, all his bustle and bother will be to little or no purpose. To attain this, he should make the child comprehend, (as much as may be,) the usefulness of what he teaches him; and let him see, by what he has learned, that can do something he could not do before; something which gives him some power and real advantage above others, who are ignorant of it. To this he should add sweetness in all his instructions; and by a certain tenderness in his whole carriage, make the child sensible that he loves him, and designs nothing but his good; the only way to beget love in the child, which will make him hearken to his lessons, and relish what he teaches him. (9:378)

Jean Jacques Rousseau
(1712–1778)

Locke was the reasoned, balanced, forward-looking voice of his time; Jean Jacques Rousseau was like a torrent of lava sweeping across his. The France he knew in the early and mid-eighteenth century was world-weary and corrupt. Denied useful occupation by royal fiat, and ordered to dance attendance at Versailles, a top-heavy structure of nobles formed a froth over the hungry, ignorant, embittered peasants who made possible the nobles' silk and jewels, horses and carriages and elegant estates. The society was rotted with injustice and ready to crumble, and among those who urged the debacle of the French Revolution was Jean Jacques Rousseau.

Before the Revolution, Rousseau played out his strange, distorted, undisciplined life. His books burn with the fire of his intensity even though his ideas were seldom consistent with the way he lived his life. *Discours sur les arts et sciences*, written for a prize offered by the academy of Dijon, proclaimed the doctrine of the noble savage, the superiority of the uncorrupted natural state of man over the civilized, and with this one stroke, Rousseau made his reputation throughout Europe. He was thirty-seven years old; he had lived a floating, even subterranean life. Suddenly he was famous. *Julie, où La Nouvelle Heloise*, a novel written in letter form, appeared in 1760. It described the love of a low-born man and a girl of rank, his anguish when she marries a free-thinker of her own class, and the eventual resolution of distress by noble sentiment. Love is glorified, the conventions of the time excoriated (although Rousseau himself was anything but a reliable or steadfast lover). In 1762, both *Émile, où de l'Education* and the *Contrat Social* were published, the latter in Amsterdam (its obviously antimonarchic viewpoint made printing impossible in France). Rousseau ingeniously attempted to base all legal government on the consent, real or implied, of the governed. Although far from a workable prescription for the governing of a state, it does carry powerful sentiments *pro* individual freedom and *anti* autocracy. It was enough to bring about Rousseau's banishment from France in June of the same year.

Émile, où de l'Education was in the form of a novel, but it was, in fact, a treatise on wide-ranging facets of child-rearing and education, from the value of breast feeding by an infant's own mother to the role of the father as natural mentor, tutor, and guide (Rousseau abandoned his own children to a foundling hospital). He had opinions about everything: the genesis of language as well as the development of egocentric child into responsible, humane youth. Convinced of the inherent corruption of society, Rousseau isolated his hero. Émile was brought up on an island, seeing only his tutor. Until the age of twelve, his education was to be "negative"; books were forbidden. He learned everything he knew from his immediate contact with a world of nature, developing his senses and forming his personality. Under such a regime, declared Rousseau, the innate goodness of uncorrupted humanity would flower in Émile, and he would grow up whole, free, able to set his hand to whatever is necessary for his life.

To much of it our common sense raises objections. But the force of Rousseau's conviction influenced men of his time. "All things are good as they come out of the hands of their Creator," he proclaimed:

from **Émile, où
de l'Education**

Jean Jacques Rousseau

... but every thing degenerates in the hands of man. He compels one soil to nourish the productions of another, and one tree to bear the fruits of another. He blends and confounds elements, climates, and seasons: he mutilates his dogs, his horses, and his slaves: he defaces, he confounds every thing: he delights in deformity and monsters. He is not content with any thing in its natural state, not even with his own species. His very offspring must be trained up for him, like a horse in the menage, and be taught to grow after his own fancy, like a tree in his garden.

Without this, matters would be still worse than they are, and our species would not be civilized but by halves. Should a man, in a state of society, be given up, from the cradle, to his own notions and conduct, he would certainly turn out the most preposterous of human beings. The influence of prejudice, authority, necessity, example, and all those social institutions in which we are immersed, would stifle in him the emotions of nature, and substitute nothing in their place. His humanity would resemble a shrub, growing by accident in the highway, which would soon be destroyed by the casual injuries it must receive from the frequent passenger. . . .

We are born weak, we have need of help; we are born destitute of every thing, we stand in need of assistance; we are born stupid, we have need of understanding. All that we are not possessed of at our birth, and which we require when grown up, is bestowed on us by education.

This education we receive from nature, from men, or from circumstances. The constitutional exertion of our organs and faculties is the education of nature; the uses we are taught to make of that exertion, constitute the education given us by men; and in the acquisitions made by our own experience, on the objects that surround us, consists our education from circumstances. . . . (16:383-384)

According to the order of nature, all men being equal, their common vocation is the profession of humanity; and whoever is well educated to discharge the duties of a man, cannot be badly prepared to fill up any of those offices that have a relation to him. . . . (16:387)

This material was heady stuff to men who had never thought in these terms, never read anything like it, and who were reaching for something better than the society around them. Something within them vibrated to the passionate conviction with which Rousseau expressed his remarkably insightful but sometimes improbable ideas on education:

. . . A man truly free, wills only what he is able to perform, and performs what he pleases. This is my fundamental maxim. It need only be applied to a state of infancy, and all the rules of education will naturally flow from it. . . .

[A child] should be neither treated as an irrational animal, nor as a man; but simply as a child; he should be made sensible of his weakness, but not abandoned to suffer by it; he should be taught dependence, and not merely obedience; he should be instructed to ask, and not to command. He is in a state of submission to others, only because of his wants, and because they know better than himself what is good or hurtful for him. . . .

Nature requires children to be children before they are men. By endeavoring to pervert this order, we produce forward fruits, that have neither maturity nor taste, and will not fail soon to wither or corrupt. . . .

Treat your pupil according to his years. Put him first into his place, and keep him there so strictly, that he may never afterwards be tempted to go from it. . . . Never command him to do anything in the world. Let him not even imagine you pretend to have any authority over him. Let him only be made sensible that he is weak, and you are strong; that, from your situation and his, he lies necessarily at your mercy: . . . let him early feel on his aspiring crest the hard yoke nature hath imposed on man, the heavy yoke of necessity under which every finite being must bow; let him see that necessity in the nature and constitution of things, and not in the caprices of mankind. . . .

Almost every method has been tried but one, and that the only one which can succeed, natural liberty duly regulated. . . . *Give your pupil no kind of verbal instructions; he should receive none but from experience:* inflict on him no kind of punishment, for he knows not what it is to be at fault: require him never to ask pardon, for he cannot offend you. As he is insensible of all moral obligation, he cannot do anything morally evil, or that is deserving of punishment or reprimand. . . .

May I venture here to lay down the greatest, most important, and most useful rule of education? It is this, Not to gain time, but to lose it. . . .

The first part of education, therefore, ought to be purely negative. It consists, neither in teaching virtue nor truth; but in guarding the heart from vice, and the mind from error. If you could be content to do nothing yourself, and could prevent any thing being done by others; if you could bring your pupil healthy and robust to the age of twelve years, without his being able to distinguish his right hand from his left, the eyes of his understanding would be open to reason at your first lesson; void both of habit and prejudice, his passions would not operate against your endeavors, attempting nothing in the beginning, you might produce a prodigy of education. (16:396-400)

Locke's great maxim was to reason with children: and it is the most popular method at the present day. Its success does not appear to recommend it; for my own part, I have never seen anyone so silly as those children with whom they reason so much. Of all man's faculties, Reason, which is a combination of the rest, is developed last and with greatest difficulty; yet this is the faculty which we are asked to use for the development of the earlier. It is the climax of a good education to form a man who is capable of reason; and we propose to educate a young child by means of his reason! This is beginning where we ought to end, and making of the finished product an instrument in its own manufacture.... (15)

Of the five books which make up *Émile*, the first deals specifically with the first five years of life. Rousseau dignifies these years as a stage in child development. It is one of the first depictions of this stage in life distinguishing young children from miniature adults or the embodiment of original sin. While much of what he says is true and sensitive, his writings are a passionate rush of feeling, unsubstantiated assertion, and hypothesis, probably colored by his own haphazard childhood. His mother died at birth and as a result, he passed from relative to relative.

The spirit of Rousseau may have been interpreted variously over the years, but certainly *Émile* has had an incalculable impact on education. In the move of teachers and students toward greater freedom and individuality, Rousseau's doctrine has taken root — though it has taken a multitude of different embodiments. No thinker after Rousseau could escape dealing with the ideas he set awing with a flurry of feeling.

In harmony with Rousseau's belief in nature and the right of the child to grow untrammeled by society, a Swiss teacher, Johann Heinrich Pestalozzi, was to express the counterpart of Rousseau's freshness of spirit in his own life one generation later. A compassion for humanity pervaded an early work, *The Evening Hour of a Hermit*, and continued to infuse his personal and professional life. Rousseau's work prepared the mind of Europe to accept and to respect a man like Pestalozzi, and Pestalozzi, in his turn, gave substance to what had been before him only hypothetical notions.

References to Part 2

1. Aristotle, *Politics*, trans. H. Rackham, Loeb Classical Library (Cambridge, Mass.: Harvard University Press, 1939). In Robert Ulich, *Three Thousand Years of Educational Wisdom*. (Cambridge: Harvard University Press), 1954, pp. 62-68. Copyright 1947, 1954 by the President and Fellows of Harvard College.
2. Bacon, Francis, *Novum Organum and Advancement of Learning*, trans. Joseph Devey (New York: Macmillan Co., n.d.).
3. Comenius, *Didactica magna*, trans. Robert Ulich, from German ed. In Robert Ulich, *Three Thousand Years*.
4. Cook, Albert S., ed., *Essays on the Study and Use of Poetry by Plutarch and Basil the Great*, Yale Studies in English, vol. 15 (New York: Henry Holt & Co., 1902). In Robert Ulich, *Three Thousand Years*, p. 153.

5. Dickinson, G. Lowes, *Plato and His Dialogues* (Baltimore, Md.: Penguin Books, 1931), p. 13.

6. Erasmus, "De pueris statim ac liberaliter instituendis" [The argument . . . that children should straight away from their earliest years be trained in virtue and sound learning], in *Desiderius Erasmus Concerning the Aim and Method of Education,* William H. Woodward (Cambridge, England: At the University Press, 1904). In Robert Ulich, *History of Educational Thought,* rev. ed. (New York: Van Nostrand Reinhold Co., 1968), p. 145.

7. Jowett, Benjamin, trans., *Dialogues of Plato,* 4th ed. (Oxford, England: Clarendon Press, 1953), vol. 2. By permission of The Clarendon Press, Oxford.

8. Locke, John, *The Educational Writings: A Critical Edition,* ed. James L. Axtell (Cambridge, England: At the University Press, 1968).

9. _____, *Some Thoughts on Education* (Boston, 1830). In Robert Ulich, *Three Thousand Years.*

10. Luther, Martin, *Luther's Correspondence and Other Contemporary Letters,* trans. and ed. Preserved Smith, vol. 2 (Philadelphia: United Lutheran Publication House, 1913-1918), pp. 487-488.

11. Painter, F. V. N., *Luther on Education* (Philadelphia: Concordia Publishing House, 1890). In Robert Ulich, *Three Thousand Years.*

12. Petty, William, *Advice to Mr. Samuel Hartlib for the Advancement of Some Particular Parts of Learning* (London, 1648). In Robert Ulich, *Three Thousand Years.*

13. Plato, *Republic,* trans. Paul Shorey, Loeb Classical Library (Cambridge, Mass.: Harvard University Press, 1930-1935). In Robert Ulich, *Three Thousand Years.*

14. Plutarch, *Moralia,* trans. F. C. Babbittt, Loeb Classical Library (Cambridge, Mass.: Harvard University Press, 1927). In Robert Ulich, *Three Thousand Years,* p. 96.

15. Rousseau, Jean Jacques, *Emile, Julie and Other Writings,* ed. S. E. Frost, Jr.; trans. R. L. Archer (Woodbury, N.Y.: Barron's Educational Series, 1964), p. 95.

16. _____, *Emilius or A Treatise on Education* (Edinburgh, 1773). In Robert Ulich, *Three Thousand Years.*

17. St. Jerome, *Principle Works of St. Jerome,* trans. W. H. Freemantle (New York: Charles Scribner's Sons, 1893). In Robert Ulich, *Three Thousand Years.*

18. Ulich, Robert, *History of Educational Thought,* p. 190.

19. _____, *Three Thousand Years.*

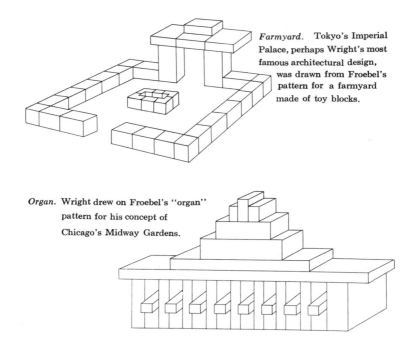

Farmyard. Tokyo's Imperial Palace, perhaps Wright's most famous architectural design, was drawn from Froebel's pattern for a farmyard made of toy blocks.

Organ. Wright drew on Froebel's "organ" pattern for his concept of Chicago's Midway Gardens.

part 3

Pestalozzi, Froebel, and Kindergarten Education

Pestalozzi represents a beginning point for early childhood education. He actually taught young children. Froebel studied with him as well. Pestalozzi marks the beginning of the kindergarten movement, i.e., more formalized thought devoted to the education of young children. In the Introduction, a distinction was made between *socialization* (the basic humanization of the child by parents and other close adults) and *early education.* Although socialization is an essential process, it was clearly an unconscious one until the dawn of anthropological insight in the twentieth century. Early childhood education was also uncontrived until Froebel began to

45

devote his efforts towards a cogent plan and analysis of activities for young children.

Johann Pestalozzi (1746-1827)

Johann Heinrich Pestalozzi was one of those great teachers whose method is nothing, whose force, power, charm, and influence stem, not from his theories but from something emanating from his innermost self. A badly educated, poor country boy, Pestalozzi, nonetheless, became the very embodiment of the educational ideal for many cultured men of his time. His whole life was an expression of tender concern for the unfortunate — the poor villagers or farmers of the rural Switzerland of his day, the beggar children, the orphans of the Napoleonic adventure whom he took in and cared for with his own meager allotments. His own words and those of a former pupil describe what he did and his educational goals better than volumes written by others.

from **Pestalozzi's Letter to Heinrich Gessner about his orphanage at Stanz, Switzerland (1799)**

My friend, once more I awake from a dream; once more I see my work destroyed, and my failing strength wasted.

But, however weak and unfortunate my attempt may have been, a friend of humanity will not grudge a few moments to consider the reasons which convince me that some day a more fortunate posterity will certainly take up the thread of my hopes at the place where it is now broken.

From its very beginning I looked on the Revolution as a simple consequence of the corruption of human nature, and on the evils which it produced as a necessary means of bringing men back to a sense of the conditions which are essential to their happiness.

Although I was by no means prepared to accept all the political forms that a body of such men as the revolutionists might make for themselves, I was inclined to look upon certain points of their Constitution not only as useful measures protecting important interests, but as suggesting the principles upon which all true progress of humanity must be based. . . .

As I have explained my plan for the public education of the poor in the third and fourth parts of *Leonard and Gertrude*, I need not repeat it here. I submitted it to the director Stapfer, with all the enthusiasm of

From Roger de Guimps, *Pestalozzi, His Life and Work* (New York: Appleton, 1890).

a man who felt that his hopes were about to be realized, and he encouraged me with an earnestness which showed how thoroughly he understood the needs of popular education. It was the same with the minister Rengger.

It was my intention to try to find near Zurich or in Aargau a place where I should be able to join industry and agriculture to the other means of instruction, and so give my establishment all the development necessary to its complete success. But the Unterwalden disaster (September, 1798) left me no further choice in the matter. The Government felt the urgent need of sending help to this unfortunate district, and begged me for this once to make an attempt to put my plans into execution in a place where almost everything that could have made it a success was wanting.

I went there gladly. I felt that the innocence of the people would make up for what was wanting, and that their distress would, at any rate, make them grateful.

My eagerness to realize at last the great dream of my life would have led me to work on the very highest peaks of the Alps, and, so to speak, without fire or water.

For a house, the Government made over to me the new part of the Ursuline convent at Stanz, but when I arrived it was still uncompleted, and not in any way fitted to receive a large number of children. Before anything else could be done, then, the house itself had to be got ready. The Government gave the necessary orders, and Rengger pushed on the work with much zeal and useful activity. I was never indeed allowed to want for money.

In spite, however, of the admirable support I received, all this preparation took time, and time was precisely what we could least afford, since it was of the highest importance that a number of children, whom the war had left homeless and destitute, should be received at once.

I was still without everything but money when the children arrived; neither kitchen, rooms, nor beds were ready to receive them. At first this was a source of inconceivable confusion. For the first few weeks I was shut up in a very small room; the weather was bad, and the alterations, which made a great dust and filled the corridors with rubbish, rendered the air very unhealthy.

The want of beds compelled me at first to send some of the poor children home at night; these children generally came back the next day covered with vermin. Most of them on their arrival were very degenerated specimens of humanity. Many of them had a sort of chronic skin-disease, which almost prevented their walking, or sores on their heads, or rags full of vermin; many were almost skeletons, with haggard, careworn faces, and shrinking looks; some brazen, accustomed to begging, hypocrisy, and all sorts of deceit; others broken by misfortune, patient, suspicious, timid, and entirely devoid of affection. There were also some spoilt children amongst them who had known the sweets of comfort, and were therefore full of pretensions. These kept to themselves, affected to despise the little beggars their comrades, and to suffer from this equality, and seemed to find it impossible to adapt themselves to the ways of the house, which differed too much from their old habits. But what was common to them all was a persistent idleness, resulting from their want of physical and mental activity. Out of every ten children there was hardly one who knew his A B C; as for any other knowledge, it was, of course, out of the question.

This complete ignorance was what troubled me least, for I trusted in the natural powers that God bestows on even the poorest and most neglected children. I had observed for a long time that behind their coarseness, shyness, and apparent incapacity, are hidden the finest faculties, the most precious powers; and now, even amongst these poor creatures by whom I was surrounded at Stanz, marked natural abilities soon began to show themselves. I knew how useful the common needs of life are in teaching men the relations of things, in bringing out their natural intelligence, in forming their judgment, and in arousing faculties which, buried, as it were, beneath the coarser elements of their nature, cannot become active and useful till they are set free. It was my object then to arouse these faculties, and bring them to bear on the pure and simple circumstances of domestic life, for I was convinced that in this way I should be able to form the hearts and minds of children almost as I wished.

Now that I had an opportunity of carrying out this object, I felt sure that my affection would change the nature of my children as quickly as the sun changes the frozen earth in spring; nor was I wrong, for before the snow of our mountains had melted the children were no longer the same.

But I must not anticipate. Just as in the evening I often mark the quick growth of the gourd by the side of the house, so I want you to mark the growth of my plant; and, my friend, I will not hide from you the worm which sometimes eats into its leaves, sometimes even into its heart.

I opened the establishment with no other helper but a woman-servant. I had not only to teach the children, but to look after their physical needs. I preferred being alone, and, indeed, it was the only way to reach my end. No one in the world would have cared to fall in with my views for the education of children, and at that time I knew scarcely any one capable even of understanding them. The better the education of the men who might have helped me, the less their power of understanding me and of confining themselves, even in theory, to the simple beginnings to which I sought to return. All their views as to the organization and needs of the enterprise were entirely different from mine. What they especially disagreed with was the idea that such an undertaking could be carried out without the help of any artificial means, but simply by the influence exercised on the children by Nature, and by the activity to which they were aroused by the needs of their daily life.

And yet it was precisely upon this idea that I based my chief hope of success; it was, as it were, a basis for innumerable other points of view.

Experienced teachers, then, could not help me; still less boorish, ignorant men. I had nothing to put into the hands of assistants to guide them, nor any results or apparatus by which I could make my ideas clearer to them.

Thus, whether I would or no, I had first to make my experiment alone, and collect facts to illustrate the essential features of my system before I could venture to look for outside help. Indeed, in my then position, nobody could help me. I knew that I must help myself and shaped my plans accordingly.

I wanted to prove by my experiment that *if public education is to have any real value, it must imitate the methods which make the merit of domestic education*; for it is my opinion that *if public education does not take into consideration the circumstances of family life, and everything else that bears on a man's general education, it can only lead to an artificial and methodical dwarfing of humanity* [italics added].

In any good education, the mother must be able to judge daily, nay hourly, from the child's eyes, lips, and face, of the slightest change in his soul. The power of the educator, too, must be that of a father, quickened by the general circumstances of domestic life.

Such was the foundation upon which I built. I determined that there should not be a minute in the day when my children should not be aware from my face and my lips that my heart was theirs, that their happiness was my happiness, and their pleasures my pleasures. . . .

Whenever he does anything gladly, anything that brings him honour, anything that helps to realize any of his great hopes, or stimulates his powers, and enables him to say with truth, *I can*, then he is exercising his will.

The will, however, cannot be stimulated by mere words; its action must depend upon those feelings and powers which are the result of general culture. Words alone cannot give us a knowledge of things; they are only useful for giving expression to what we have in our mind.

The first thing to be done was to win the confidence and affection of the children. I was sure that if I succeeded in doing that, all the rest would follow of itself. Think for a moment of the prejudices of the people, and even of the children, and you will understand the difficulties with which I had to contend.

The unfortunate country had suffered all the horrors of war. Most of the inhabitants detested the new constitution, and were not only exasperated with the Government, but suspicious of its offered help. Opposed by the natural melancholy of their character to anything new coming from outside, they held fast, with bitter and defiant obstinacy, to everything connected with their former condition, wretched as it was in many respects. To these people I was simply an agent of the new order of things. They looked on me as a mere instrument, working not for them, but for the men who were the cause of their misfortunes, and whose opinions, views, and plans were entirely opposed to their own. This political distrust was strengthened by a no less deep religious distrust. I was a heretic, and so all my efforts to do good could only imperil their children's souls. Amongst them no Protestant had ever held the smallest public office; what must they have felt, then, on seeing one made a teacher of children? To make matters worse, religious and political passion in Stanz was just then excited to an unusually high degree.

Think, my friend, of this temper of the people, of my weakness, of my poor appearance, of the ill-will to which I was almost publicly exposed, and then judge how much I had to endure for the sake of carrying on my work.

And yet, however painful this want of help and support was to me, it was favourable to the success of my undertaking, for it compelled me to be always everything for my children. I was alone with them from morning till night. It was my hand that supplied all their wants, both of body and soul. All needful help, consolation, and instruction they received direct from me. Their hands were in mine, my eyes were fixed on theirs.

We wept and smiled together. They forgot the world and Stanz; they only knew that they were with me and I with them. We shared our food and drink. I had neither family, friends, nor servants; nothing but them. I was with them in sickness, and in health, and when they slept, I was the last to go to bed, and the first to get up. In the bedroom I prayed with them, and, at their own request, taught them till they fell asleep. Their clothes and bodies were intolerably filthy, but I looked after both myself, and was thus constantly exposed to the risk of contagion.

This is how it was that these children gradually became so attached to me, some indeed so deeply that they contradicted their parents and friends when they heard evil things said about me. . . .

The children did not always understand my love. Accustomed to idleness, unbounded liberty, and the fortuitous and lawless pleasures of an almost wild life, they had come to the convent in the expectation of being well fed, and of having nothing to do. Some of them soon discovered that they had been there long enough, and wanted to go away again; they talked of the school fever that attacks children when they are kept employed all day long. This dissatisfaction, which showed itself during the first months, resulted principally from the fact that many of them were ill, the consequence either of the sudden change of diet and habits, or of the severity of the weather and the dampness of the building in which we lived. We all coughed a great deal, and several children were seized with a peculiar sort of fever. . . .

On the return of spring it was evident to everybody that the children were all doing well, growing rapidly, and gaining colour. Certain magistrates and ecclesiastics, who saw them some time afterwards, stated that they had improved almost beyond recognition.

A few of the children, however, continued in ill-health for some time, and the influence of the parents was not favourable to their recovery.

"Poor child, how ill you look! I am sure I could look after you at home as well as you are looked after here. Come away with me." That was the sort of thing said by women who were in the habit of begging from door to door. On Sundays, especially, numbers of parents used to come and openly pity their children till they made them cry, and then urge them to go away. I lost a great many in this way; and though their places were soon filled by others, you can understand how bad these constant changes were for an establishment that was only just beginning.

Many parents thought they were doing me a personal favour by leaving the children with me, and even asked the Capuchins [friars at a nearby monastery] whether it was because I had no other means of subsistence that I was so anxious to have pupils. It was the general opinion amongst these people that poverty alone could have induced me to give myself so much trouble, an opinion which came out in their behaviour towards me.

Some asked me for money to make up for what they had lost by their children being no longer able to beg; others, hat on head, informed me that they did not mind trying a few days longer; others, again, laid down their own conditions.

Months passed in this way before I had the satisfaction of having my hand grasped by a single grateful parent. But the children were won over much sooner. . . .

Those who ran away were the worst in character and the least capable. But they were not incited to go till they were free of their vermin and their rags. Several were sent to me with no other purpose than that of being taken away again as soon as they were clean and well clothed.

But after a time their better judgment overcame the defiant hostility with which they arrived. In 1799 I had nearly eighty children. Most of them were bright and intelligent, some even remarkably so.

For most of them study was something entirely new. As soon as they found that they could learn, their zeal was indefatigable, and in a few weeks children who had never before opened a book, and could hardly repeat a *Pater Noster* or an *Ave*, would study the whole day long with the keenest interest. Even after supper, when I used to say to them, "Children, will you go to bed, or learn something?" they would generally answer, especially in the first month or two, "Learn something." It is true that afterwards, when they had to get up very early, it was not quite the same.

But this first eagerness did much towards starting the establishment on the right lines, and making the studies the success they ultimately were, a success, indeed, which far surpassed my expectations. And yet the difficulties in the way of introducing a well-ordered system of studies were at that time almost insurmountable.

Neither my trust nor my zeal had as yet been able to overcome either the intractability of individuals or the want of coherence in the whole experiment. The general order of the establishment, I felt, must be based upon order of a higher character. As this higher order did not yet exist, I had to attempt to create it; for without this foundation I could not hope to organize properly either the teaching or the general management of the place, nor should I have wished to do so. I wanted everything to result not from a preconceived plan, but from my relations with the children. The high principles and educating forces I was seeking, I looked for from the harmonious common life of my children, from their attention, activity, and needs. It was not, then, from any external organization that I looked for the regeneration of which they stood so much in need. If I had employed constraint, regulations and lectures, I should, instead of winning and ennobling my children's hearts, have repelled them and made them bitter, and thus been farther than ever from my aim. First of all, I had to arouse in them pure, moral, and noble feelings, so that afterwards, in external things, I might be sure of their ready attention, activity, and obedience. I had, in short, to follow the high precept of Jesus Christ, "Cleanse first that which is within, that the outside may be clean also"; and if ever the truth of this precept was made manifest, it was made manifest then.

My one aim was to make their new life in common, and their new powers, awaken a feeling of brotherhood amongst the children, and make them affectionate, just, and considerate.

I reached this end without much difficulty. Amongst these seventy wild beggar-children there soon existed such peace, friendship, and cordial relations as are rare even between actual brothers and sisters.

The principle to which I endeavoured to conform all my conduct was as follows: Endeavour, first, to broaden your children's sympathies, and, by satisfying their daily needs, to bring love and kindness into such unceasing contact with their impressions and their activity, that these sentiments may be engrafted in their hearts; then try to give them such judgment and tact as will enable them to make a wise, sure, and abundant use of these virtues in the circle which surrounds them. In the last place, do not hesitate to touch on the difficult questions of good and evil, and the words connected with them. And you must do this especially in connection with the ordinary events of every day, upon which your whole teaching in these matters must be founded, so that the children may be reminded of their own feelings, and supplied, as it were, with solid facts upon which to base their conception of the beauty and justice of the moral life. Even though you should have to spend whole nights in trying to express in two words what others say in twenty, never regret the loss of sleep.

I gave my children very few explanations; I taught them neither morality nor religion. But sometimes, when they were perfectly quiet, I used to say to them, "Do you not think that you are better and more reasonable when you are like this than when you are making a noise?" When they clung round my neck and called me their father, I used to say, "My children, would it be right to deceive your father? After kissing me like this, would you like to do anything behind my back to vex me?" When our talk turned on the misery of the country, and they were feeling glad at the thought of their own happier lot, I would say, "How good

God is to have given man a compassionate heart!" Sometimes, too, I asked them if they did not see a great difference between a Government that cares for the poor and teaches them to earn a livelihood, and one that leaves them to their idleness and vice, with beggary and the workhouse for sole resource.

Often I drew them a picture of the happiness of a simple, peaceful household, that by economy and hard work has provided for all its wants, and put itself in a position to give advice to the ignorant, and help to the unfortunate. When they pressed round me, I used to ask the best of them, even during the first few months, whether they would not like to live like me, and have a number of unfortunate children about them to take care of and turn into useful men. The depth of their feelings would even bring tears to their eyes, as they answered, "Ah, if I could only do that!"

What encouraged them most was the thought of not always remaining poor, but of some day taking their place again amongst their fellows, with knowledge and talents that should make them useful, and win them the esteem of other men. . . . It was not possible to organize any system of discipline for the establishment; that could only come slowly, as the general work developed.

Silence, as an aid to application, is perhaps the great secret of such an institution. I found it very useful to insist on silence when I was teaching, and also to pay particular attention to the attitude of my children. The result was that the moment I asked for silence, I could teach in quite a low voice. The children repeated my words all together; and as there was no other sound, I was able to detect the slightest mistakes of pronunciation. It is true that this was not always so. Sometimes, whilst they repeated sentences after me, I would ask them half in fun to keep their eyes fixed on their middle fingers. It is hardly credible how useful simple things of this sort sometimes are as means to the very highest ends.

One young girl, for instance, who had been little better than a savage, by keeping her head and body upright, and not looking about, made more progress in her moral education than any one would have believed possible.

These experiences have shown me that the mere habit of carrying oneself well does much more for the education of the moral sentiments than any amount of teaching and lectures in which this simple fact is ignored.

Thanks to the application of these principles, my children soon became more open, more contented, and more susceptible to every good and noble influence than any one could possibly have foreseen when they first came to me, so utterly devoid were they of ideas, good feelings, and moral principles. As a matter of fact, this lack of previous instruction was not a serious obstacle to me; indeed, it hardly troubled me at all. I am inclined even to say that, in the simple method I was following, it was often an advantage, for I had incomparably less trouble to develop those children whose minds were still blank, than those who had already acquired a few more or less correct ideas. The former, too, were much more open than the latter to the influence of all pure and simple sentiments.

But when the children were obdurate and churlish, then I was severe, and made use of corporal punishment.

My dear friend, the pedagogical principle which says that we must win the hearts and minds of our children by words alone, without having recourse to corporal punishment, is certainly good, and applicable under favourable conditions and circumstances; but with children of such widely different ages as mine, children for the most part beggars, and all full of deeply-rooted faults, a certain amount of corporal punishment was inevitable, especially as I was anxious to arrive surely, speedily, and by the simplest means, at gaining an influence over them all, for the sake of putting them all in the right road. I was compelled to punish them, but it would be a mistake to suppose that I thereby, in any way, lost the confidence of my pupils.

It is not the rare and isolated actions that form the opinions and feelings of children, but the impressions of every day and every hour. From such impressions they judge whether we are kindly disposed towards them or not, and this settles their general attitude towards us. Their judgment of isolated actions depends upon this general attitude.

This is how it is that punishments inflicted by parents rarely make a bad impression. But it is quite different with schoolmasters and teachers who are not with their children night and day, and have none of those relations with them which result from life in common. . . .

Many things that make no difference in a small household could not be tolerated where the numbers were so great. I tried to make my children feel this, always leaving them to decide what could or could not be allowed. It is true that, in my intercourse with them, I never spoke of liberty or equality; but, at the same time, I encouraged them as far as possible to be free and unconstrained in my presence, with the result that every day I marked more and more that clear, open look in their eyes which, in my experience, is the sign of a really liberal education. I could not bear the thought of betraying the trust I read in their faces, and was always seeking to encourage it, as well as the free development of their individuality, that nothing might cloud their angel eyes, the mere sight of which gave me such deep pleasure. . . .

I believe that the first development of thought in the child is very much disturbed by a wordy system of teaching, which is not adapted either to his faculties or the circumstances of his life.

According to my experience, success depends upon whether what is taught to children commends itself to them as true, through being closely connected with their own personal observation and experience. . . .

I have now put before you my views as to the family spirit which ought to prevail in an educational establishment, and I have told you of my attempts to carry them out. I have still to explain the essential principles upon which all my teaching was based.

I knew no other order, method, or art, but that which resulted naturally from my children's conviction of my love for them, nor did I care to know any other.

Thus I subordinated the instruction of my children to a higher aim, which was to arouse and strengthen their best sentiments by the relations of every-day life as they existed between themselves and me.

I had Gedicke's reading-book, but it was of no more use to me than any other school-book; for I felt that, with all these children of such different ages, I had an admirable opportunity for carrying out my own views on early education. I was well aware, too, how impossible it would be to organize my teaching according to the ordinary system in use in the best schools.

As a general rule I attached little importance to the study of words, even when explanations of the ideas they represented were given.

I tried to connect study with manual labour, the school with the workshop, and make one thing of them. . . .

I hold it to be extremely important that men should be encouraged to learn by themselves and allowed to develop freely. It is in this way alone that the diversity of individual talent is produced and made evident.

I always made the children learn perfectly even the least important things, and I never allowed them to lose ground; a word once learnt, for instance, was never to be forgotten, and a letter once well written never to be written badly again. I was very patient with all who were weak or slow, but very severe with those who did anything less well than they had done it before.

The number and inequality of my children rendered my task easier. Just as in a family the eldest and cleverest child readily shows what he knows to his younger brothers and sisters, and feels proud and happy to be able to take his mother's place for a moment, so my children were delighted when they knew something that they could teach others. A sentiment of honour awoke in them, and they learned twice as well by making the younger ones repeat their words. In this way I soon had helpers and collaborators amongst the children themselves. When I was teaching them to spell difficult words by heart, I used to allow any child who succeeded in saying one properly to teach it to the others. These child-helpers, whom I had formed from the very outset, and who had followed my method step by step, were certainly much more useful to me than any regular schoolmasters could have been.

I myself learned with the children. Our whole system was so simple and so natural that I should have had difficulty in finding a master who would not have thought it undignified to learn and teach as I was doing.

My aim was so to simplify the means of instruction that it should be quite possible for even the most ordinary man to teach his children himself; thus schools would gradually almost cease to be necessary, so far as the first elements are concerned. Just as the mother gives her child its first material food, so is she ordained by God to give it its first spiritual food, and I consider that very great harm is done to the child by taking it away from home too soon and submitting it to artificial school methods. The time is drawing near when methods of teaching will be so simplified that each mother will be able not only to teach her children without help, but continue her own education at the same time. . . .

I have proved two things which will be of considerable use to us in bringing about this desirable improvement. The first is that it is possible and even easy to teach many children of different ages at once and well; the second, that many things can be taught to such children even whilst they are engaged in manual labour. This sort of teaching will appear little more than an exercise of memory, as indeed it is; but when the memory is applied to a series of psychologically graduated ideas, it brings all the other faculties into play. Thus, by making children learn at one time spelling, at another exercises on numbers, at another simple songs, we exercise not only their memory, but their power of combination, their judgment, their taste, and many of the best feelings of their hearts. In this way it is possible to stimulate all a child's faculties, even when one seems to be exercising his memory only.

These exercises not only gave my children an ever-increasing power of attention and discernment, but did very much for their general mental and moral development, and gave that balance to their natures which is the foundation of human wisdom. . . .

Such were my dreams; but at the very moment that I seemed to be on the point of realizing them, I had to leave Stanz. (4:149–163, 165–171)

from **Reminiscence
of L. Vuillemin, an
historian, about Pestalozzi
his former teacher, n.d.**

Imagine, my children, a very ugly man, with rough, bristling hair, his face scarred with small-pox and covered with freckles, a pointed, untidy beard, no neck-tie, ill-fitting trousers, stockings down, and enormous shoes; add to this a breathless, shuffling gait, eyes either large and flashing, or half-closed as though turned within, features expressing either a profound sadness or the most peaceful happiness, speech now slow and musical, now thundering and hurried, and you will have some idea of the man we called "Father Pestalozzi."

Such as I have described him to you, we loved him; yes, we all loved him, for he loved us all; we loved him so much that when we lost sight

---

From Roger de Guimps, *Pestalozzi, His Life and Work* (New York, Appleton, 1890).

of him for a time we felt sad and lonely, and when he came back to us again we could not turn our eyes away from him.

We knew that at the time when the wars of the Swiss Revolution had so largely increased the number of poor and orphan children, he had taken a great number of them into his house and cared for them as a father, and we felt that he was the true friend of children, and of all who were in trouble or misfortune.

My fellow-citizens of Yverdun, my native town, had generously placed at his disposal the old Castle. It was built in the shape of a huge square, and its great rooms and courts were admirably adapted for the games as well as the studies of a large school. Within its walls were assembled from a hundred and fifty to two hundred children of all nations, who divided their time between lessons and happy play. It often happened that a game of prisoner's base, begun in the Castle court, would be finished on the grass near the lake. In winter we used to make a mighty snow-fortress, which was attacked and defended with equal heroism. Sickness was hardly known among us.

Early every morning we went in turns and had a shower of cold water thrown over us. We were generally bareheaded, but once, when a bitterly cold wind was blowing, my father took pity upon me, and gave me a hat. My companions had no sooner perceived it than a hue and cry was raised: "A hat, a hat!" It was soon knocked off my head and a hundred hands sent it flying about the playground and corridors, till at last it went spinning through a window, and fell into the river that flows under the walls of the Castle. It was carried away to the lake and I never saw it again.

Our masters were for the most part young men, and nearly all children of the revolutionary period, who had grown up round Pestalozzi, their father and ours. There were, indeed, a few educated men and scholars who had come to share his task; but, taken altogether, there was not much learning. I myself have heard Pestalozzi boast, when an old man, of not having read anything for forty years. Nor did our masters, his first pupils, read much more than Pestalozzi himself. Their teaching was addressed to the understanding rather than the memory, and had for its aim the harmonious cultivation of the germs implanted in us by Providence. "Make it your aim to develop the child," Pestalozzi was never tired of repeating, "and do not merely train him as you would train a dog, and as so many children in our schools often are trained."

Our studies were almost entirely based on number, form, and language. Language was taught us by the help of sense-impression; we were taught to see correctly, and in that way to form for ourselves a just idea of the relations of things. What we had thoroughly understood we had no trouble to express clearly.

The first elements of geography were taught us from the land itself. We were first taken to a narrow valley not far from Yverdun, where the river Buron runs. After taking a general view of the valley, we were made to examine the details, until we had obtained an exact and complete idea of it. We were then told to take some of the clay which lay in beds on one side of the valley, and fill the baskets which we had brought for the purpose. On our return to the Castle, we took our places at the long tables, and reproduced in relief the valley we had just studied, each one doing the part which had been allotted to him. In the course of the next few days more walks and more explorations, each day on higher ground and each time with a further extension of our work. Only when our relief was finished were we shown the map, which by this means we did not see till we were in a position to understand it.

We had to discover the truths of geometry for ourselves. After being once put in the way of it, the end to be reached was pointed out to us. and we were left to work alone. It was the same with arithmetic, which we did aloud, without paper. Some of us became wonderfully quick at this, and as charlatanism penetrates everywhere, these only were brought before the numerous strangers that the name of Pestalozzi daily attracted to Yverdun. We were told over and over again that a great work was going on in our midst, that the eyes of the world were upon us, and we readily believed it.

The Pestalozzian Method, as it was somewhat ostentatiously called, was, it is true, an enigma, not only to us but to our teachers, who, like the disciples of Socrates, each interpreted the master's doctrine in his own way. But we were still far from the time when these divergencies resulted in discord, and when the chief masters, after each claiming to be the only one who had understood Pestalozzi, ended by declaring that Pestalozzi had not understood himself. (4:253–256)

A brief timetable of Pestalozzi's life adds form to these personal accounts. He was still young when his father died and left his widow dependent upon the struggles of her son. Pestalozzi settled at Neuhof, near Zurich, as a young adult and attempted to earn a living as a farmer while teaching the children of the poor peasants who lived nearby. He was unable to keep either farm or school afloat, and in 1780 he went bankrupt. Discouraged, uncertain of his future, and under great emotional stress, he wrote the brief and poignant *Evening Hour of a Hermit*, a document profoundly modern in its psychological insight, i.e., man at one with nature and man's values and relationships as the deep core of his life. *The Evening Hour of a Hermit* was little noted and only read widely after other writings and Pestalozzi's fame as a teacher had made him well-known throughout Western Europe. In 1781 he wrote *Leonard and Gertrude*, an account of how first a household, then a village, are reformed by the simplicity, honesty, and warmth of a country woman. A sequel followed in 1801 called *How Gertrude Teaches her Children*, in which Pestalozzi described more explicitly the method he advocated: observation leads to heightened awareness, which in turn leads to speech and the academic skills. The basic

vocational skills—spinning, weaving, housekeeping, and husbandry
are tied into the educational plan and motivate learning (from
Leonard and Gertrude).

The instruction she gave them in the rudiments of arithmetic was
intimately connected with the realities of life. She taught them to count
the number of steps from one end of the room to the other, and two
of the rows of five panes each, in one of the windows, gave her an opportunity to unfold the decimal relations of numbers. She also made them
count their threads while spinning, and the number of turns on the reel,
when they wound the yarn into skeins. Above all, in every occupation
of life she taught them an accurate and intelligent observation of common objects and the forces of nature.

All that Gertrude's children knew, they knew so thoroughly that they
were able to teach it to the younger ones; and this they often begged
permission to do. On this day, while the visitors were present, Jonas
sat with each arm around the neck of a smaller child, and made the little
ones pronounce the syllables of the A-B-C book after him; while Lizzie
placed herself with her wheel between two of the others, and while all
three spun, taught them the words of a hymn with the utmost patience.

When the guests took their departure, they told Gertrude they would
come again on the morrow. "Why?" she returned; "You will only see
the same thing over again." But Glülphi said: "That is the best praise
you could possibly give yourself." Gertrude blushed at this compliment,
and stood confused when the gentlemen kindly pressed her hand in
taking leave.

The three could not sufficiently admire what they had seen at the
mason's house, and Glülphi was so overcome by the powerful impression
made upon him, that he longed to be alone and seek counsel of his own
thoughts. He hastened to his room, and as he crossed the threshold, the
words broke from his lips: "*I* must be schoolmaster in Bonnal!" All
night visions of Gertrude's schoolroom floated through his mind, and he
only fell asleep toward morning. Before his eyes were fairly open, he
murmured: "I will be schoolmaster!" — and hastened to Arner to acquaint him with his resolution. (8)

But before the second book appeared, Pestalozzi had had further
chances to actually try out his ideas. In 1798, he had taken the
children of Canton Unterwalden who had been orphaned by the
French invasion into a deserted convent where he cared for and
educated them for a year, at which point the French government
requisitioned the convent as a hospital, forcing the children to be
dispersed. Pestalozzi then established a school at Burgdorf, where
he remained for the next five years. From 1805 to 1825 he labored
at his final school in the castle at Yverdun on Lake Neuchatel.
Dissension among his teachers made his last ten years unhappy,

and in 1825 he retired to Neuhof, where he had lived in his youth, and there he wrote until his death in 1827.

His life was devoted to human relationships, a life of the mind but more a life of feeling and of service. More than what he said or wrote, what Pestalozzi *did* was his doctrine. His educational doctrine is not an easy one to follow for it must be followed with devotion, self-forgetfulness, deep and loving concern for children and for the essence of childhood. He could not make his approach clear; in the setting of Yverdun, contention and disunity rose out of his inability to formulate what he believed. But when he dealt with children, his magnetism, the gravitational effect of his goodness and love, involved them in an almost mystical way in an experience that profoundly shaped their lives.

Among the many visitors who came to Yverdun was the young Friedrich Froebel, who sought out Pestalozzi. Froebel wrote later in his *Autobiography* of his brief stay at Yverdun:

Now to return to the new life which I had begun. It was only to be expected that each thing and all things I heard of Pestalozzi seized powerfully upon me; and this more especially applies to a sketchy narrative of his life, his aims, and his struggles, which I found in a literary newspaper, where also was stated Pestalozzi's well-known desire and endeavor — namely, in some nook or corner of the world, no matter where, to build up an institution for the education of the poor, after his own heart. This narrative, especially the last point of it, was to my heart like oil poured on fire. There and then the resolution was taken to go and look upon this man who could so think and so endeavor to act, and to study his life and its work.

Three days afterwards (it was towards the end of August, 1805) I was already on the road to Yverdun, where Pestalozzi had not long before established himself. Once arrived there, and having met with the friendliest reception by Pestalozzi and his teachers . . . I was taken, like every other visitor, to the class-rooms, and there left more or less to my own devices. I was still very inexperienced, both in the theory and the practice of teaching, relying chiefly in such things upon my memory of my own school-time, and I was therefore very little fitted for a rigorous examination into details of methods and into the way they were connected to make a whole system. The latter point, indeed, was neither clearly thought out, nor was it worked out in practice. What I saw was to me at once elevating and depressing, arousing and bewildering. My visit lasted only a fortnight. I worked away and tried to take in as much as I could. . . . Nevertheless, I soon felt that heart and mind would alike come to grief in a man of my disposition if I were to stay longer with Pestalozzi, much as I desired to do so. (3:536–537)

In 1808 Froebel returned and spent a longer time at Yverdun. He was always sympathetic to Pestalozzi's goals and to the man himself, whom he loved and revered, yet could not help but criticize him for his inability to explain what he was trying to do educationally. Froebel made this comment: "... he [Pestalozzi] could never give any definite account of his idea, his plan, his intention. He always said, 'Go and see for yourself' (very good for him who knew *how* to look, how to hear, how to perceive); 'it works splendidly!' " (3:539)

Since he could not accept as the ideal educational practice the procedure of the best-known teacher in Europe, young Froebel dared to find for himself a method still more valid and more useful. The result of his work was the kindergarten, the true beginning of modern preschool education, created not only out of love and concern for children, but also out of a recognition that, with industrialization, the world was radically changing. Pestalozzi had created a school suited to a timeless, traditional, rural and village setting; his school could have functioned four hundred years earlier with no real changes. Psychologically modern, it was, nevertheless, academically allied to a way of life that was breaking up in Europe.

Froebel was an urban man, a man who saw and could understand what factories, life in crowded cities, the employment of parents out of the home, were doing to small children. His educational system was an answer to these problems, problems not in the ken of Locke, Rousseau, or Pestalozzi. With Froebel, preschool education as a planned, organized portion of the school system begins. With Froebel, modern teaching of young children becomes an entity in its own right. There is a strand that links the modern kindergarten to Pestalozzi and to the spirit of the great educators and educational theoreticians of the past. It is in the affection and concern for children, and in the attempt to protect as well as to instruct them. But when Froebel left Yverdun to make his own intellectual way, one may say that a long era of educational history came to an end. When Froebel opened his first kindergarten, something genuinely new was added to the very concept of schooling.

Friedrich Wilhelm Froebel
(1782-1852)

Friedrich Wilhelm August Froebel was born on April 21, 1782, in Oberweissbach, a village in what is now the central portion of East Germany. Steeped in the religious beliefs of his father, a hard working pastor, Froebel had to contend with the politics and times of a divided Prussia, where in the early nineteenth century, waves of reaction to the ideas embodied in the French Revolution swept unpredictably across its various principalities. Yet Froebel's work and educational thought was most intimately a product of his inner life and his own personal development. A biography from F. Seidel's edition of the *Menschen-erziehung* written in 1883 highlights his experiences and life struggles.

from **Die**
Erziehung der Menscheit
Friedrich Froebel

Losing his mother within his first year, having kind elder brothers but no sister, the child was left much to himself, with few playmates and little outdoor freedom. His father tried to teach him his "rudiments," and failed. He found the boy dull, and placed him in the *Girls'* division of the village school, of which he was official superintendent. For this irregularity, Friedrich was always grateful, and he repeated to his dying-day the hymns he had learnt there. In a short account of his own life, he says: "I came to school on a Monday morning while the girls were repeating aloud the best of Sunday's sermon, "Seek ye first the Kingdom of God," and to this day (forty years later) the tone of every word is fresh in my memory." At ten years of age, his mother's brother, Pastor Hofmann of Stadt Ilm, took Friedrich to live with him and attend the Town School. Here he learned *pretty* well; preferring the classes on Religion and Arithmetic: evincing certainly no precocious wisdom or goodness, as we judge by his illustrations of boyish mischief, told with a gravity most unconsciously comic. When fifteen (1797) Friedrich returned home, and was placed for two years, as pupil in Wood-craft, with a Forester, whose neglect of the instruction due from him left the lad of rare gifts and character to unfold his own powers, unimpeded. Good books his master had; so Friedrich worked at Botany, studied Mathematic, and made a map of the neighbourhood. Near the end of 1799, a messenger being wanted to bring to his brother Traugott, Student of Medicine at Jena, the half-yearly allowance, Friedrich, having left the Forester, volunteered on this service. When at Jena he begged leave to stay till the Easter vacation; afterwards returned for a year, and devoted himself to hearing lectures. The two brothers lived most frugally, but found that an allowance, spare for one, was not enough for two. After his brother's departure, Friedrich, unable to pay their joint debts of some £5, or less, was committed to the University's prison, where he spent nine weeks: mending his Latin, with the help of a fellow-*prisoner*; studying Winckelmann's Letters on Art; and writing a Mathematical Essay. By pledging his small expectations, Friedrich was released and returned home. Next year he worked on a farm, but was recalled home by his father's failing health, and had the happiness

From William H. Herford, *The Student's Froebel: Adapted from Die Erziehung der Menscheit of F. Froebel, Part I, Theory of Education* (Boston: D. C. Heath & Co., 1900).

of ministering to his father's comfort, till his death, February 1802. Left wholly to his own resources, he worked for his bread, as clerk — secretary — book-keeper, during three years and more, when a small legacy from his fatherly uncle Hofmann made him think a settled profession possible. At mid-summer 1805 he set out for Frankfurt, hoping to make himself an Architect. On the way, he visited a farmer friend, who at parting begged from Froebel — in German fashion — a verse or motto for his album. "Not knowing what he said" — for no idea of becoming an Educator had then entered his mind! — Froebel wrote: *Gieb du den Menschen Brot: mein Streben sei, sie ihnen selbst zu geben,* "Be it yours to give men *bread*: mine, to give them — *themselves.*" His call was on the way!

When Froebel had already begun work with an architect, a Frankfurt friend introduced him to Gruner, Head of the new Model School, and formerly a pupil of Pestalozzi. Gruner said to him: "Let architecture alone; become a teacher." With hesitation, Froebel accepted a place with him; and, at once, with a class of children before him, felt he had found his life-work. Thenceforward all events became steps towards realizing that ideal Education of Man by the Harmonious Development of Body, Mind, and Heart, which Froebel conceived more completely and vividly than any of his precursors. In August 1805, Froebel visited Yverdun, where Pestalozzi had his Institute, was kindly received, and in three weeks learned enough to make him wish to come again. He taught under Gruner for two years, and made his class, of forty girls and boys, the model class of the Model School. In method, his great achievement was to lay the foundation of Geography in "Home-knowledge"; that is, points of the compass — forms of surface — courses of streams, roads, etc., learned in country-walks by his pupils' own observation. He finds his own knowledge, tried by use, defective, and to better it quits Frankfurt. Unable to afford the cost of University residence, Froebel accepts, and for three years retains, the post of tutor to three brothers; stipulating to have them entirely to himself, in the country. In 1808 he takes his pupils to Yverdun, where, for two years, he and they share meals and work with Pestalozzi, his teachers and pupils: learning, his biographer says, "to know both the good and the ill sides of Pestalozzi's theory and practice." In 1811 Froebel studied first at Göttingen, then at Berlin, eking out by private lessons his scanty means. In 1813 the War of liberation from France called every German patriot to arms. Among his fellow-volunteers, Froebel found two students of theology — Langethal and Middendorff — his first converts, and afterwards his chief fellow-workers. Their vows, to work together for the Education of humanity, were exchanged by the camp fire, under starry heaven; while discussion of Means and Methods, Finance and Philosophy, occupied the hours of weary waiting. When the war was over (1814), Froebel returned to Berlin, to be Assistant at the Museum of Mineralogy.

The summons to practical work came (1816) by the death of his brother Christopher, pastor at Griesheim, whose widow wrote for advice how to educate her three boys. Led as by the pointing of God's finger,

Froebel left Berlin, visiting on the way another brother, Christian, a manufacturer with moderate means, who gave him his two sons as pupils. So Froebel began school in the parsonage at Griesheim as teacher of his five nephews. Middendorff obeyed the summons to join his friend, bringing with him a younger brother of Langethal's as sixth recruit. The parsonage had to be vacated, so a small farm, Keilhau, was bought, and Froebel married (1818) Henrietta Hoffmeister, his true helpmeet for twenty-one years. Langethal coming to remove his brother, found his old enthusiasm so revived by what he saw that he stayed to throw in his lot with them. When new buildings were needed to house new pupils, brother Christian wound up his affairs and settled near them with family and means. In 1826, Keilhau held fifty-six pupils. Then came persecution about "Demagogical Intrigues." The German "people" were impatient that their Princes had not found the convenient season for granting Free Constitutions, promised when the Nation was summoned to arm against Napoleon, in 1813. Froebel was no conspirator; but his training, being humane, was suspected. Keilhau was inspected by State and Church, and reports were favourable. Parents, however, were alarmed, and (1829) the number of pupils fell from *sixty* to *five*. The storm was weathered, though the little band of brothers had often utmost difficulty in finding money for daily needs. In 1831, Froebel left the Saxon School to his friends, having been invited to form one at Willisau, near Lucerne. In 1833, he removed to Burgdorf, near Berne, where orphan children, aged from four to six years were received, and training-classes for Teachers held. Herein we recognize the rise of the Kindergarten, not yet so named. In 1839 his wife died. To commemorate the 400th anniversary of the Invention of Printing (1840) he commenced the "German Kindergarten": to consist of Classes, to train young women as Nurses and Teachers, in true methods of development; along with a school for little children whom they should teach. He travelled far to procure money for this undertaking, but his success was very modest, though at Hamburg, Dresden, and elsewhere, Child-gardens were set up. Now and then a "Schoolman" visited Froebel, and exchanged contempt for admiration. Diesterweg, for example, an excellent writer on Pedagogy, avows his complete conversion. A few great ones of the earth did themselves the honour to help and second Froebel's work; but he did not live to hear the chorus of praise, of himself and his system, that resounds today; which, like all voices of earth that rise above a whisper, contains many weak notes and false tones. In August 1850, Froebel then in his 69th year, directed games, songs and marches of a School festival, at which 300 children were entertained by the Duchess of Meiningen at her summer-place, Altenstein: Chateau Marienthal, was granted him for a training college: and success — by the world so called — seemed about to smile. Next year 7th August 1851, Prussia prohibits the Kindergarten in her States, on the ground that it taught children — Atheism! This blow, questionless, depressed Froebel, but did not *kill* either him of his cause. The German Teachers' Association, meeting at Gotha, Whitsuntide, 1852, invited his presence;

received and heard him with distinguished honour. A few days later he
fell ill, and on 21st June died. His last words were, "I am a Christian
Man."

Froebel was a Prophet and Apostle of the Kingdom of God, in the
true meaning of words. His are the *notes*: ceaseless toil, disappointment, conflict — waged, endured, nay! cheerfully supported, by the
consciousness of serving God. We are reminded of St. Paul: "Woe is me
if I preach not the Gospel," and Luther, "Here I stand! I can no other:
God help me!" A man of true genius, if we prefer the term; by three
acknowledged Hallmarks: 1. "Inward force of idea"; working like inspiration, mastering the whole man. 2. "Infinite power of taking pains":
— in bringing out this inward force to work on the world that heeds
reforming: he studies every science — toils at whatever comes to hand
— claims the hearing of every one — fails only to try gain. 3. "Turns
what it touches into gold." Cheapest, commonest materials, old-fashioned games and verses; not least the mother's baby-songs and finger-
plays: all are worked into a tissue of such strange power that, while
best, truly, if retained as a whole and used as Froebel meant it, yet
every morsel is precious: and even the travesty of Kindergarten, not
infrequent alas! in the educational market, takes the place of something
worse, viz. — the Rod and the Rote-learning of our ancestors. (5:xi–xvi)

This biography has a quality of innocence, a naive and uncrit-
ical acceptance of Froebel as master, which is significant because
it is true of the feeling he aroused in his many followers. For many
years, kindergarten procedures and attitudes toward children echoed his idealistic conception of the nature and function of education. He had hoped to remake the school from beginning to end.
He began with young children simply because he saw that later
progress was hampered if the six-year-olds coming into the classroom had already been so damaged by lack of attention, lack of
training, and sometimes by abuse as well. He viewed the kindergarten as an essential step in the whole ladder of educational experience, which would remake man, and, hence, the world closer
to the image of God.

That the kindergarten was criticized in Prussia on the grounds
of atheism is ironic, for Froebel's life and work consistently indicate
he was a deeply religious man. His "Introduction" to *The Education of Man*, the basic work of his maturity, published in 1826 expresses his intense faith in life as a religious experience with God:

1) In everything dwells and rules an eternal Law. This Law expresses
itself, distinctly and clearly alike in what is external to Man — Nature;
in what is internal to Man — the Soul; and in what unites these two —
Life. Human Minds of opposite types perceive this equally: those which
start from Faith, and are thoroughly possessed by the Feeling that

Nothing else can be (than what Faith tells;) and those which, with clear Intelligence, behold through the Outward that which is Within; and see that the External grows necessarily from the Internal. As Foundation of this all-ruling Law, exists of Necessity a conscious, almighty, and eternal Being. All this was recognized from the Beginning; is, and ever will be, recognized by every quietly heedful human Heart, and by every thoughtful Intellect of Man.

This Being is God. Every Thing came forth from God, and by God alone is governed; so that the sole Foundation of all Things is God. In Every Thing, God rules and lives. Every Thing rests and subsists in God. Things exist only because God acts in them. The Divine that acts in each Thing is the Essence of that Thing.

2) The Destination of all Things is by unfolding to set forth their Essence, which is the Divine that lives in them: thus, to reveal God in and by what is outward and transitory. The special Destination of *Man*, as a Being endowed with Perception and Reason, is to become fully and clearly conscious of his own Essence — the Divine that is in him, — and to make it manifest in his own Life. The *Education of Man* is the Awakening and Training of his *Humanity* to Consciousness and Reflection, so that his outward Life may be an Expression of this inward Law.

3) Recognition of this eternal Law, with Insight into its Foundation and the Variety of its Operations, is *Science — Science of Life*: and that Law, when applied in Practice by the thinking Creature on and by itself, is *Science of Education*.

A system of Rules issuing from Knowledge of that Law, designed to enable rational Beings to become conscious of their Destination, and to fulfill it, is *Doctrine of Education*.

Voluntary Application of this *Knowledge* (science, or doctrine) so as to develop and train rational Beings, in order to attain their true Destiny, is *Art of Teaching*.

4) The Aim of Education is to produce a pure, faithful, complete, and therefore holy, Life.

Knowledge and Practice united; Theory and Application coalescing into pure, faithful, and complete Living; this is *Life-wisdom*.

To be wise is the highest Endeavor possible to *Man*; it is also the highest Result of Man's self-determining Power.

To educate oneself and others, with conscious Purpose, is the two-fold work of Wisdom. . . .

Education should guide Man to the Understanding of himself; to Peace with Nature; and to Union with God. Education, therefore, has to raise the Human-being to a Knowledge of himself and of Humanity; to a Knowledge of God and of Nature; and to the pure and holy Life which follows from this Knowledge. (5:1–3)

This vision of an underlying oneness linking man, nature, and God significantly shaped Froebel's educational ideas. Ulich writes of it:

First, on the basis of his idea of the unity of all living things, Froebel derives a new conception of childhood. Childhood is not merely preparation for adulthood: it is a value in itself and possesses its own creativeness. It participates in the divine whole with the same rights of its own as adulthood, and, therefore, it can claim the same respect on the part of the educator. The adult has no right to feel himself superior and to interfere with the natural conditions of childhood; rather, he must combine guidance with the capacity of waiting and understanding. Here Froebel falls into line with Rousseau and Herbart.

The second postulate which Froebel derives from his idea of unity is that of the inner relatedness of all education. This means that the educator ought to lead the child through such situations as will help him to relate his experiences organically one with another. Only thus can the child realize his own personal unity and the unity inherent in the diversity of life. (9)

Therefore, Froebel had to build into his system both respect for the *individuality* of each child and an *organized, articulated* curriculum designed to insure the step by step progress of that child through the subjects necessary for his education.

An educator had to strike a *balance* between the *child's freedom* to be himself and to grow in his own way and the *society's obligation* to impart the skills, knowledge, and values which allow him to become a productive member of the larger whole. This balance characterizes Froebel's system. He taught that some part of each day ought to be spent by the child in each of these worlds. Play was the mode through which the child achieved equilibrium through harmonious development. His classes were not in *schoolrooms*, but *gardens for children* where every activity was designed to instruct through giving pleasure. In *The Education of Man* Froebel writes of play:

Play is the highest phase of child development — of human development at this period; for *it is self-active representation of the inner — representation of the inner from inner necessity and impulse.*

Play is the purest, most spiritual activity of man at this stage, and, at the same time, typical of human life as a whole — of the inner hidden natural life in man and all things. It gives, therefore, joy, freedom, contentment, inner and outer rest, peace with the world. It holds the sources of all that is good. A child that plays thoroughly, with self-active determination, perseveringly until physical fatigue forbids, will surely be a thorough, determined man, capable of self-sacrifice for the promotion of the welfare of himself and others. Is not the most beautiful expression of child-life at this time a playing child? — a child wholly absorbed in his play? — a child that has fallen asleep while so absorbed?

As already indicated, play at this time is not trivial, it is highly serious and of deep significance. Cultivate it and foster it, O mother; protect and guard it, O father! To the calm, keen vision of one who truly knows human nature, the spontaneous play of the child discloses the future inner life of the man.

The plays of childhood are the germinal leaves of all later life; for the whole man is developed and shown in these, in his tenderest dispositions, in his innermost tendencies. The whole later life of man, even to the moment when he shall leave it again, has its source in the period of childhood — be this later life pure or impure, gentle or violent, quiet or impulsive, industrious or indolent, rich or poor in deeds, passed in dull stupor or in keen creativeness, in stupid wonder or intelligent insight, producing or destroying, the bringer of harmony or discord, or war or peace. His future relations to father and mother, to the members of the family, to society and mankind, to nature and God — in accordance with the natural and individual disposition and tendencies of the child — depend chiefly upon his mode of life at this period; for the child's life in and with himself, his family, nature, and God, is as yet a unit. (3:573–574)

One begins to recognize that Froebel is merely asserting, not offering any proof that mature life flows from child's play. A modern child developmentalist would by no means deny Froebel's assertions though he might qualify them. He would agree that play can be more than pleasurable to a child; it can be instructive and even therapeutic. Since Froebel's time, however, *when, how, why, for whom, in what set of circumstances* have had to be figured out much more explicitly. Froebel does not answer these conditions. He states that play is the basis for growth, "the germinal leaves of all later life," a matter of quasi-gospel belief to be doubted at one's peril. Although the flow and content of his poetic language may have served to sentimentalize childhood, it washed over the sometimes naive and rather poorly educated maiden ladies of the last century. They were absorbed in the mission he set before them. So, a true start of early childhood education of a distinctive, widespread, and enduring variety was begun.

Committed to *play* as a mode of instruction for young children and a *curriculum* representative of the larger society, Froebel went about devising his educational plan. He designed *gifts* (objects) to be handled and examined by the child in order to lead him step by step to an orderly sense of reality and planned occupations to train the hand, eye, and mind. His kindergarten *occupations* are akin to present day crafts and table games. They were designed to synthesize and creatively express the impressions received through *gifts*. The latter were presented to a group of children by a teacher with the help of rhythmic songs and hand motions. Although greatly modified, a similar segment in today's early childhood education, known commonly as "circle time," can be found.

Hazel Lambert describes some of the content of the Froebelian kindergarten:

The "gifts" consisted of various materials used to teach the child the nature of form, number, and measurement. The first "gift" was six soft colored balls; the second included a cube, a cylinder, and a sphere; the third was a number of sections which together formed a cube. By manipulating these materials in prescribed fashion, the child learned to count, combine, divide, make fractions out of wholes, arrange in order, measure, and analyze.

The "occupations" consisted of the essentials for such activities as modeling, drawing, sewing, and coloring. Again the use of materials was prescribed. By following a carefully conceived and formulated plan, the child learned to manipulate clay, cut, string beads, sew, weave, fold paper, make cardboard designs, draw freehand, trace, paste, and so on. A minimum of free play was permitted. . . . (7)

A modern kindergarten teacher is apt to be startled by examining the extant collections of work done a hundred years ago in Froebelian classes. There are intricate abstract designs or complex pictures (a carriage and pair of horses, a pack of running dogs) pricked out with tiny, regular pin holes, a task which must have taken someone's five-year-old fingers hours to do. The coloring was done with pallid, hard-to-control water color paints on 4″ by 6″ sheets printed with extremely detailed pictures to be colored, e.g., a farmyard scene. Sewing cards also had complex patterns to be filled with many tiny and even stitches. Weaving involved the manipulation of slim strips of paper into other precut, fragile paper forms. Some children with excellent coordination may well have enjoyed it, but one wonders about all the little boys (and girls) whose hands were still "all thumbs," who must have torn their woven mats, spilled their water colors, pricked their fingers and bled onto their stitching. They may well have dreaded the daily "occupation" time.

Perspectives on the Froebelian Curriculum

Why were small motor skills emphasized in a program designed to free children to happily follow their own course of development? Perhaps, one can see the subtle influence of the industrial revolution. Parents were beginning to leave the home to work. Responsibility for the training of their children in necessary skills was slowly moving into the public sphere, as the home provided too little chance to acquire this dexterity. At the time when Froebel was founding the kindergarten and for nearly a hundred years thereafter, i.e., to the time of the Weimar Republic, after World War I, German working-class children generally went to school for only four years and were then apprenticed in a craft or trade. Further education could be pursued, but only after a long day of working for wages. Most occupations demanded great manual skill. Machines were only just beginning to play a part in carpentry, masonry, and metal work, the clothing trades, and all sorts of manufacture. The productions of the world were still carried on by men's own hands. Business correspondence and bookkeeping were done in script. The hand needed to be trained, and five did not seem too young to begin. It was to Froebel's credit that he attempted to make the training appropriate and pleasant for children. The child's point of view was insufficiently understood for educators to have been aware that he was consistently approached on an inappropriately adult level with adult materials and standards. The child was to be prepared for adult life. Why should children undertake to draw their own pictures when adults could do it better? Why should children freely use, or even misuse, materials when adults knew what they were for and how expensive they were? That sort of freedom of choice was still far in the future.

That the disciples of a great and creative innovator attempt to retain the spark of the original work too slavishly seems to be true. A certain orthodoxy and elaborateness becomes associated with "the method" or message they are attempting to convey. In the field of early childhood education, the followers of Froebel and Montessori come quickly to mind. Oversimplification and certain strains appear as the attempt is made to fit all of a child's reality to the educational philosophy. Some "lessons" from the notebook of a young trainee* in a kindergarten training school, established by Mrs. Quincy Adams Shaw in Boston (circa 1888) are reproduced to illustrate how Froebel's notions were translated to practice.

A recurring theme in these notes is Froebel's preoccupation with theology. His mission was to demonstrate the unity of God's creation in both the *gifts* and the *occupations*. The orderliness that he found in nature and in mathematics is evident. Without the appro-

---

*Evelyn Osgood Chandler. The authors are grateful to her daughter, Miss Martha Chandler, for giving them access to these materials as she has done for many whom she taught at Boston Nursery Training School and at Eliot-Pearson Child Study Department at Tufts University.

priate presentation by the teacher, both the child's impression and expression of this divine unity would be lacking. This conviction can be found in Mrs. Chandler's carefully hand-written notebook. The following was entitled *First Gift Analysis:*

I. The first gift consists of six soft worsted balls, each ball having one of the colors of the rainbow; blue, green, yellow, orange, red and violet. They are contained in a box in which are also six strings of different colors corresponding with the balls.

II. Contrast in the gift is color, resulting in the abstraction of color from form, and of form from color.

III. The salient characteristics of the ball are unity and moldability.

IV. Froebel considers it as the external counterpart of the child in the first stages of his development; its individual unity corresponding to his mental condition and its moldability corresponding to his instinctive activity. Through its recognition he is led to separate himself from the external world, and the external world from himself.

V. The objects of the gift are first to stimulate observation and second, to lead to self-expression. At its simplest and most general of normal types, the ball offers the first basis for the classification of external objects, while by its external indefiniteness and wide adaptability, it is the best medium for the expression of the child's indefinite ideas.

VI. The kindergarten gifts, being designed to lead to the mastery of material objects by the abstraction of general qualities, it follows they must form a sequence in which there is a progressive advance from an object which embodies, in their simplest form, the qualities common to all things, to objects which are more definite in their nature and more restricted in their powers. Hence, Froebel's choice of the balls with its simplicity and manifold adaptations as a starting point in his organically connected sequence of gifts. (1)

Songs were taught the children to insure that lessons were learned! Before reproducing the "songs for the first gift," a scene from a kindergarten prior to the turn of the century should be re-created. It is fortunate that Abigail Eliot, the founder of Boston's Ruggles Street Nursery School, maintains a vivid recollection of her own public kindergarten experience on top of Beacon Hill. Forty children sat at small tables arranged as a hollow square at the center of the room to receive the ten to twenty minutes of instruction during a three-hour session. To follow what the teacher did and said during these moments was important. Each child and teacher had a box containing the same *gift*. Miss Eliot recalls her own kindergarten teacher's remarks after they had lifted the boxes to the top of their desks. "Turn the box right side up. Put your finger in the niche. Now slowly pull the drawer towards you." At each step of the way the teacher would pause, look around, and quietly help those having difficulty. (2)

The songs may have sounded like the one below taken from Mrs. Chandler's notebook (verses from "Now Take This Little Ball"):

> Now take this little ball
>   And do not let it fall,
> Balls of yellow, red, and blue
>   Some for me and some for you.
> Now take this little ball
>   And do not let it fall,
>
> Hold it in your hand
>   Then quite still let it stand
> Balls of yellow, blue, and red
>   You are round just like my head
> Hold it in your hand
>   Then quite still let it stand.
>
> Now make your soft balls rise
>   Up, up towards the skies
> Trees and flowers, all things below
>   Upward, upward try to go
> Now make your soft ball rise
>   Up, up towards the skies
>
> You're tired little ball
>   So downward you must fall
> Like ripe apples from the tree
>   Some for you and some for me.
> You're tired little ball
>   Lo! downward you must fall
>
> Dear ball, you're tired of play
>   So "good-bye" for today.
> Into your nice little box now creep
>   And stay there till again I'll peep
> Dear ball you're tired of play
>   So "good-bye" for today.

An example of the orthodoxy referred to earlier is found in these notes about one of the *occupations*, weaving. "The slips [of paper] used in weaving indicate the transition from the line to the surface; therefore, in the sequence of the kindergarten occupations, the place of the mats is directly after the sewing and drawing. The special significance of the mats lies in the fact that they afford the clearest and most striking perception of number." (1) Other secondary advantages are listed including the fact that "they give employment to little hands; they require and reward care; they satisfy and develop the sense of color."(1)

These accounts and reminiscences of the Froebel kindergarten appear forbidding in contrast to much of today's practice. In the context of that era, they were not experienced that way. Today less attention is paid to demonstrating materials and lessons. Models of behavior and learning tend to be more diverse and individualized; consequently, expectations are not always clear. The responsibility for learning is delegated more to the child; the teacher is cast in the role of stimulating his learning. The question may well be asked if the child and his teacher did not have an easier task in Froebel's kindergarten.

History of Froebelian
Kindergarten in the U.S.A.

Kindergartens in the United States developed very early from the Froebelian kindergarten in Germany. Patty Smith Hill, Professor of education at Columbia University, and one of the great figures in the development of preschool education in America in the first decades of this century, wrote a brief history of the kindergarten in 1941. She recounts its beginnings in this country.

from **Kindergarten**
Patty Smith Hill

Mrs. Carl Schurz, who had studied in Germany under Froebel himself, opened a kindergarten in her own home in Watertown, Wis., in 1855, originally for the benefit of her own children. Later, in a visit to Boston, Mrs. Schurz met Elizabeth Peabody, a member of the famous Peabody family of Boston. The Peabodys were all noted for their rare ability as teachers, "making even Latin interesting."

Miss Peabody championed the new cause of the kindergarten, and endeavored to demonstrate Froebel's theories in her own kindergarten opened in Boston in 1860. Later, Miss Peabody studied in Germany, but unfortunately too late to come under the tutelage of Froebel himself. However, she returned to America and devoted a long life to spreading the gospel of a new education for young children. As a well-known and respected member of the Concord School of Philosophy and the Brook Farm experiment, Elizabeth Peabody and her two sisters, Mrs. Horace

From Patty Smith Hill, "Kindergarten," *American Educators' Encyclopedia* (Lake Bluff, Ill.: The United Educators, Inc., 1941), by permission.

Mann and Mrs. Nathaniel Hawthorne, won the interest of such intel-
lectual leaders of the day as Ralph Waldo Emerson, Horace Mann, the
Alcotts and William Ellery Channing. Also attending the Concord
School were William T. Harris, later United States Commissioner of
Education, and Susan E. Blow, who together were responsible for the
opening of the first public-school kindergarten in America, in Saint
Louis in 1873.

Unfortunately for the future of the kindergarten in America, some of
the contemporaries and immediate successors of Mrs. Schurz and Miss
Peabody studied under the more literal-minded followers of Froebel in
Germany, who, attempting to carry forward his work after his death in
1851, sent to America representatives with a far more fixed and inflex-
ible conception of kindergarten education than Froebel's. Some of the
immediate successors of Frobel, including his second wife, tended to
accept as final many aspects of the experiments originated by Froebel
which he, with a more critical attitude toward his own work, would undoubtedly have discarded. Had Froebel lived long enough to secure the
later psychological and scientific data which he so eagerly sought with
slight success in his university studies, many fixed and formal aspects
of his curricula would have been eliminated.

The Early Philanthropic
Kindergartens in America

Even though these literal and formal conceptions of kindergarten
practices were unfortunately transplanted to America, we must give full
credit to the work of these pioneers, whose formal interpretations of
Froebel were accompanied by other values which more than offset the
disadvantages of the traditional curricula they introduced. In the light
of their really great contributions we should not quibble over these mistakes, but remember that when the kindergarten was first introduced
into the United States it survived as a philanthropy long before it was
accepted as an organic member of the educational system. During this
long probation period it was eagerly sought by missions, institutional
churches and philanthropic organizations as the most hopeful form of
social regeneration.

This was a period of national social awakening and religious disillusionment in America. As a nation the people were then gradually
awakening to the new social problems resulting from enormous increases
in foreign populations. The tides of immigration brought to American
shores peoples difficult to assimiliate and slow to accept American
ideals and standards of living. Slums were in process of formation. They
became sources of disease, crime, delinquency and industrial disorders,
breeding centers of problems which America was unprepared to meet.

Religious disillusionment followed the efforts of churches to locate
missions in the city slums, for the purpose of converting the dwellers

therein. Thoughtful religious leaders with a new consciousness of the fact that an "overnight conversion," however sincere, might be only of temporary value, had to cope with the habits of character due to years of wrong living. The spirit might be willing, but the flesh was weak, and little could be accomplished through efforts to reconstruct adult society.

The kindergarten appeared on the horizon at the right moment for philanthropy, but at the wrong time for public education. Society turned to the young child as the one great hope, and kindergartens opened rapidly under religious and philanthropic influences all over America. They were located in the worst slums of the cities, and highly cultured and intelligent young women prepared themselves in normal schools supported by philanthropists. These young women entered upon the work with rare enthusiasm and consecration to the cause. No neighborhood was too criminal, no family too degenerate, no child too bad. Into Little Italy, Little Russia, Little Egypt and the Ghettos they went, offering daily care to humanity in its early years.

Both kindergartners and philanthropic boards soon saw the need of the ministrations of the physician, the nurse, the social worker or the visiting teacher. Funds were so low that the kindergartner taught in the morning and spent her afternoons as a social-welfare worker, eagerly seeking work for the unemployed parents, space in hospitals for ill mothers, sisters or brothers, searching for physicians who would remove adenoids and tonsils or dentists who would extract diseased teeth, free of charge. This was the most important contribution of the pioneer kindergartners, as at this period the kindergarten was frequently the only social agency offering a helping hand in the rapidly-increasing slums.

Education and philanthropy were widely removed in those days. Schools accepted no responsibility for the physical condition of the child, or for the home which sent the child to school ill-nourished and diseased in body and mind. Thus the kindergartner of that day came into daily contact with family life at its lowest ebb. She was trained by necessity to see the child she attempted to teach handicapped in his learning by the social conditions of the home and slum in which he lived.

Philanthropic boards, with financial problems which they could not solve, then turned to the public schools asking them to adopt the kindergarten as the foundation grade in the public-school system. As an entering wedge, these philanthropic boards requested the use of vacant rooms in public-school buildings—for there were such in those days—and the kindergartner was allowed to enter, although somewhat as a stepchild. The least attractive room, left unused for this reason, was turned over for her use rent free. Salaries and running expenses were still being defrayed by the philanthropic agencies, which were convinced through experience of the educational as well as the philanthropic value of the kindergarten. The next step was to persuade boards of education to accept full financial responsibility, and the kindergarten soon became an accepted member of the public-school system.

Troubles soon followed, however, as the kindergarten was something of a misfit in the public schools at this period and for many years afterwards. In the first place, the long experience under philanthropic influences greatly increased the inherent tendency of the kindergarten to include in education responsibility for all those conditions in the home which hindered the learning and general welfare of the child. When the kindergartner entered the public schools she found no opportunities to continue this welfare work. There was no medical inspection, no school nurse, no school luncheon, no school psychologist, no social case-worker, no visiting teacher. The kindergartner's previous training, which included such ministrations as these, struck a strange chord in a public-school system.

Soon after the public schools were induced to adopt these philanthropic kindergartens, assuming financial as well as administrative responsibility, the proportion of children to teacher was heavily increased, to the detriment of child and teacher. In order to reduce costs per capita and to reach large numbers of children, the double session was introduced, with different groups of children for each session. This plan of necessity eliminated all welfare work formerly done by the kindergartner in the afternoons, such as home visiting, medical and clinical cooperation and various other forms of parental guidance and assistance.

The Froebelian philosophy as interpreted by the kindergarten included the all-round care of the child — in the home as well as the school. Even as early as 1840, we are told that a noted visitor to Froebel's first kindergarten in Blankenburg found the room empty and was directed to the fountain on the village green, where he discovered Middendorf, one of Froebel's first co-workers, teaching the boys to wash their feet and the little girls to mend their clothes. Such social welfare and community work as this was the heritage of the kindergarten from its earliest establishment, and it is unfortunate that this birthright was relinquished and temporarily lost when the kindergarten, under public-school administration, had to conform to the traditional procedure of the school in order to survive.

Adjustment to public-school conditions came slowly, but as educators became more familiar with and more reconciled to the self-active playing, singing, dancing and talking kindergarten child, there grew up a consciousness on the part of both kindergarten and primary teachers that there were but slight differences in the nature and needs of the six-year-old primary child and the joyously-working kindergarten child as promoted into the primary grade the day or week before.

Until this happy adjustment took place, the promotion of the self-active kindergarten children into the grades had made it possible for the poorest and most formal first-grade teacher to criticize and condemn the work of the best kindergarten teacher as well as the kindergarten cause, because of the wide gap that existed between kindergarten and primary ideals at that time.

All the activities and subjects of the primary school have their foundations laid in the kindergarten. We regard a kindergartner as most unintelligent if she fails to see her opportunity and obligation to discover and utilize the beginnings of all the school subjects in the spontaneous work and play of children from four to six years old. In like manner, we are most critical of any primary teacher who is not prepared to build the achievements of the first-grade level upon those mastered in the child's previous experience in the kindergarten. While the majority of kindergartners still do not deem it wise to teach reading and writing as such in the kindergarten, the kindergartner fails as a teacher in her own field if she does not recognize and utilize the experiences in which the three R's originate. Standard tests have been created by which we may detect evidences of reading readiness for kindergarten use. If these can be used in the kindergarten, much positive information regarding the child's readiness for reading can be passed on to the first-grade teacher. This plan would save time in ascertaining the proper grouping of children in the first grade according to the level of reading achievements for which they are ready.

It must be granted that many children of six-year mentality are found in the kindergartens, and five-year mentalities in the first grades. These errors are easily located and should be corrected. It is also agreed that the kindergarten can greatly contribute to reading facility in the grades by: 1) broadening the kindergarten child's first-hand experience; 2) by helping the child to gain from these experiences clear images and ideas which may be easily recalled through the printed page; 3) by helping the child to deepen and clarify the ideas gained through varied modes of expression and by better organization of these ideas in his work and play, including oral language; 4) by encouraging the child to utilize these ideas in his play purposes and plans, improving these in both content and form through the application and use of ideas gained in contact with people and things. These are the backgrounds which will familiarize the child with the meanings found later in the printed page; but, when enthusiasts add to these normal backgrounds the reading activities of the first grade, some rightly protest.

Influence of the New Psychology and Philosophy

The new psychology, philosophy, and physical and social hygiene developed rapidly after this period, especially in American universities from 1890 on, under the leadership of such men as G. Stanley Hall, William James, William Burnham, John Dewey, Edward Lee Thorndike, Francis Parker, Luther Gulick, William Heard Kilpatrick and many others. As the next generation of kindergarten and primary teachers studied in these university classes, they began to discover the discrepancy between earlier and later conclusions regarding child development.

Convinced of this fact, a small group of kindergartners, under the influence of these thinkers, felt the necessity for a far more critical analysis of the traditional theory and practice of Froebel, as the basis for a reconstructive movement which they were determined to initiate. As a consequence of this effort to reconstruct kindergarten education as accepted by the majority of the pioneers in this field, marked differences of opinion inevitably arose, which later led to a decided schism within the fold.

These opposing views developed into two well-defined schools of kindergarten thought: the conservative group and the so-called progressive group, led by a younger group studying in university classes in psychology and philosophy.

Bitter criticism followed from the conservative wing, but it must be granted that each party was equally arduous in struggling to preserve the rights of the young child as each interpreted them.

These opposing views led to wholesome criticism, and a friendly but stiff battle lasting from about 1890 or 1895 to 1910. The controversy finally culminated in a happy adjustment with a truce called. From this time forward both groups united in studying under the direction of all recognized leaders who could illuminate their common problems and enable them to initiate a more scientific program for young children.

At the present time, nursery school, kindergarten and primary teachers are well-nigh unrivaled in the open-minded enthusiasm with which they are studying and altering their curricula. These modifications of both theory and practice have been effected not only by the child-study movement, but by a social philosophy growing out of conclusions drawn from a rapidly-changing family life in a rapidly-changing society. (6)

Summary

From various beginnings, the institution known as the kindergarten developed and became part of the educational experience of many children in many lands. Its greatest impetus came from the conviction and fervor of Friedrich Froebel; it was also the child of the industrial revolution. Without the shift of adult lives from home, farm, and village shop to mill, mine, factory, and city, there would not have been the need for a new sort of experience for young children.

Kindergartens arose outside of the schools of the day; therefore, they are still less than wholly integrated into the American educational system. Though public school systems now often run kindergartens, a chasm continues to exist in general attitude between kindergarten (which is preschool, for enjoyment and play, not obligatory, "easy on the kids") and first grade (which is school, the real world, the place where "you'd better behave or the teacher will make you"). Unfortunately, this chasm hampers the work of both. Perhaps Froebel chose the name kindergarten, too well. He wanted it to reflect the spirit of a place where children simply unfolded like flowers. But today many people do not believe that children simply unfold. They believe that even young children can learn from experience, that children must do so if they are to learn at all, and that there is much that can and ought to be taught before the three R's appropriately appear on the scene.

School for five-year-olds and school for six-year-olds should flow indistinguishably together, each offering whatever stimuli and learning the children are ready to receive. A closer union between kindergartens and first grade classes would be for the good of all. England has attained this integration in the Infant School, where five-, and six-, and seven-year-olds often mingle in the same classroom. It is lacking in most American schools and in most American thinking about schools, and the lack is a sore one.

References to Part 3

1. Chandler, Evelyn Osgood, "Notebooks" (Boston, circa 1888).
2. Eliot, Abigail Adams, personal communication, 1970.
3. Froebel, Friedrich, Autobiography, trans. Emile Michaelis and Keatley Moore (Syracuse, N.Y.: C. W. Bardeen, 1890). In Robert Ulich, Three Thousand Years of Educational Wisdom (Cambridge, Mass.: Harvard University Press, 1954). Copyright 1947, 1954 by the President and Fellows of Harvard College.
4. Guimps, Roger de, Pestalozzi, His Life and Work, trans. from 2nd French ed. by J. Russell (New York and London: Appleton, 1890).
5. Herford, William H., The Student's Froebel: Adapted from Die Erziehung der Menscheit of F. Froebel, Part I, Theory of Education (Boston: D. C. Heath & Co., 1900).
6. Hill, Patty Smith, "Kindergarten," American Educators' Encyclopedia (Lake Bluff, Ill.: The United Educators, 1941), pp. 1948-1972.
7. Lambert, Hazel M., Teaching the Kindergarten Child (New York: Harcourt, Brace & Co., 1958), p. 8
8. Pestalozzi, Johann Heinrich, Leonard and Gertrude, trans. Eva Channing (Boston: D. C. Heath & Co., 1907), pp. 156-157.
9. Ulich, Robert, History of Educational Thought, rev. ed. (New York: Van Nostrand Reinhold Co., 1968), p. 288.

part 4

Education
in America:
Colonial Roots
to Progressivism

The history of the kindergarten movement began outside the public school system. Although the system influenced kindergartens, the study of the evolution of the public school system in America may help in understanding why the "preschool" or early childhood education has remained separate from the primary grades. Its allegiance is more to the so-called "progressive movement," which grew as a reaction to public education at the turn of the century and the emergence of the science of child psychology.

A Colonial Education

Plantation owners of Virginia, Maryland, and the Carolinas established a classical and legal education for their sons because they felt that their sons needed to know the law and have the force of character to apply it. Tutors were imported from England for this small upper stratum of society to insure the education of gentlemen which Locke described.

However, in puritan Massachusetts and in Connecticut of the 1600's, education was passionately pursued. Required of everyone, schools were established in this area astonishingly early. Boston Latin School claims 1635 as its date of origin, though proof establishes it at 1643. (6) In a colony settled in 1630, Harvard College was founded in 1636. Bailyn suggests that this early interest stems from the impact of wilderness on settlers accustomed to an ordered, traditional community. (1) Schooling their children may have provided their single bailiwick against the encroachment of wilderness and the harsh, demanding climate.

The very ideas of democracy and upward mobility would have been an anathema to the Puritan founders of Massachusetts. To be saved from eternal damnation, however, a man must know and live by his Bible. All men must be able to read the Bible, the first and greatest arm of schooling. In a religious community, education had to be available to everyone: girls as well as boys, poor as well as rich. Moreover, men must obey the magistrates and; therefore, must be able to read the laws.

Knowing the letters and deciphering the Lord's Prayer and the catechism were taught in the first school all children attended. This school was the Dame School, usually held by an old woman in her kitchen. Between stirring the pot and turning the spindle, she heard little boys and girls struggle through their horn books and New England Primers. Writing was ordinarily taught by a schoolmaster, who could cut and shape the quill pens. It was a more advanced step; though later on, slates were used for practicing letters and numbers.

Only a few children went on to the Latin Grammar School, which was not free, nor was it liberal. Its purpose was the preparation necessary for the roles of magistrate and minister. For most boys, however, the next step in education was apprenticeship, i.e., carpenter, baker, printer, candlemaker, wheelwright. The Latin Grammar School led strictly to Harvard College, from which came the scholars and leaders of the Commonwealth. It offered Latin, rudiments of Greek, and a little arithmetic. The entrance requirements for Harvard in 1642 make its offerings plain:

When any scholar is able to understand Tully, or such like classical Latine author extempore, and make and speak true Latine in Verse and Prose . . . and decline perfectly the Paradigms of Nounes and Verbes in Greek Tongue: Let him then and not before be capable of admission into the College.

All sixty Harvard classes in the 1600's graduated only 465 members. Among them, however, were the leaders whose legislation established the principles upon which American public education rests to this day. In 1642 the Great and General Court (Capital laws of Massachusetts) held that parents and/or masters must train all their children to read in order to comprehend the Bible and the Capital Laws of the Commonwealth, for the *benefit of the Commonwealth* as well as the individual:

This Court, taking into consideration the great neglect of many parents and masters in training up their children in learning and labor, and other which may be profitable to the Commonwealth, do hereupon order and decree, that in every town the chosen men appointed for managing the prudential affairs of the same shall henceforth stand charged with the care of the redress of this evil, so as they shall be sufficiently punished by fines for the neglect thereof, upon presentment of the grand jury or other information or complaint in any court within this jurisdiction; and for this end, they or the greater number of them shall have power to take account from time to time of all parents and masters and of their children concerning the imployment of their children, especially of their ability to read and understand the principles of religion and the capital laws of this country, and to impose fines upon such as shall refuse to render such accounts to them when they shall be required; and they shall have power, with consent of any court of the magistrate, to put forth (as) apprentices the children of such as they shall find not fit and able to bring them up . . . They are to take care of such as are sett to keep cattle, (that they) be sett to some other imployment withal: as, spinning upon the rock, knitting, weaving tape; and that boys and girls be not suffered to converse together so as may occasion wanton, dishonest, or immodest behavior; and for their (the officials) better performance of this trust committed to them, they may divide the town amongst them, appointing to every of the said townsmen a certain number of families to have a special oversight of. (7)

The grammar is convoluted, but the intention is plain. By 1642 some families were more concerned that their children guard the cows well than learn their letters, and the Commonwealth set its power to remedy the situation. All during the century, in law after law, the legislators of Massachusetts and Connecticut struggled with recalcitrant human nature. Even the allure of salvation or the horrors of hell could not drive all parents and masters nor all villages and towns to take that concern for their children's instruction which the lawmakers felt they should.

The next significant step was the famous 1647 "Old Deluder Satan" law, from which is derived the district control of the American School system. The legislators wrote:

It being one chief project of that old deluder Satan to keep men from the knowledge of the Scriptures, as in former times by keeping them in an unknown tongue, so in these latter times by persuading from the use of tongues ... that learning may not be buried in the grave of our fathers in the church and commonwealth, the Lord assisting our endeavors:

It is therefore ordered, that every township in this jurisdiction, after the Lord hath increased them to the number of fifty householders, shall forthwith appoint one within their town to teach all such children as shall resort to him to read and write, whose wages shall be paid either by the parents or masters of such children, or by the inhabitants in general by way of supply, as the major part of those that order the prudentials of the town shall appoint; provided those that send their children be not oppressed by paying much more than they can have them taught for in other towns. And it is further ordered that where any town shall increase to the number of one hundred families or householders, they shall set up a grammer school, the master thereof being able to instruct youth so far as they may be fitted for the university. (7)

Towns neglecting these provisions were fined, and the records of the 1600's are filled with petitions by town after town to have the requirements waived, and with groans about the levying of penalties. This law was always honored more in the breach than the observance, but it was written on the books, and it subsequently provided a precedent for the resurrection of a school structure.

The word *resurrection* is used advisedly. The public schools of today by no means come down in unbroken succession from those Colonial institutions, although the seeds which much later were to sprout were engendered then. In 1692 the Privy Council in London, which could abrogate colonial laws, disallowed the Massachusetts law requiring universal compulsory education as part of the general withdrawal of educational opportunity for the lower classes in England in retribution for the Puritan rebellion. In earlier times the colonies would have railed against this arbitrariness; however, in the course of the eighteenth century, the New England of the Pilgrims had changed dramatically. Interest in education as a purely intellectual exercise diminished, as did religious zeal while the

Colonies developed into a mercantile power. The road to advancement was commerce and shipping. More than salt cod was carried across the seas on New England ship bottoms; the triangular trade — slaves, rum, sugar — flourished and merchant fortunes were made from it. The tangible gain of such profits and so many cargoes began to outweigh an eternity which was dreaded in the darkness of poverty but which was hardly felt in the daylight of wealth. The social solidarity of the small, narrow but homogeneous world of the Massachusetts and Connecticut towns began to crack as men sailed into the ports of the world and saw other nations and other values. The effect was to lessen the commitment to their own values and until another three or four generations had lived and died, no one would bother very much about education.

A new way of looking at life and death, God and man, time and the world, was coming in Europe; it was the Age of Reason. Although rural America was far removed from the intellectual currents of London, Paris, Amsterdam, the effect was eventually felt. First influenced were the landowners of the South, who were interested in law, government, and social order; second, the merchant gentry of the North. Finally, little by little, the farmer and apprentice, preacher and journeyman were subtly influenced.

Once man could shed the belief of a world fixed by God as a testing ground for the human soul, to do battle against Satan, he was free to think that God had given man the capacity and the duty to improve the conditions of his life and to work toward his own salvation. A new concept of humanity emerged: Man should be honored not because he is made in God's image, but because he is endowed with reason. He is not basically bad, sinful, in danger of hellfire and damnation, but good, perfectible, and of infinite personal worth. Man's goodness, his natural rights, ought to form the basis of the good society. The idea of progress dawned upon a world which had never thought in those terms, and it changed the whole concept of past, present, and future. The Enlightenment aroused an interest in science; with reason, man could build a better world for himself and his children.

In America, Ben Franklin was the very personification of what the Enlightenment could mean. A self-made man, he preached a practical education which might fit a man to do anything. In his *Proposals Relating to the Education of Youth in Pennsylvania* (1749), he asked support for a new Academy which would emphasize English and modern languages rather than Latin and Greek and would teach not only mathematics but also "natural and mechanic philosophy" (science and engineering). (10:226)

Franklin was not a major educational innovator, nor did he ever concern himself with the education of young children. Yet, through his writings in *Poor Richard's Almanack*, which Ulich calls "for years the friend and advisor of the American farmer and one of the greatest educational forces in America," (10:227) he colored the thinking of generations of men who were beginning to consider themselves Americans.

After the Revolutionary War, some changes occurred in education, but no advances were made. New academies deemphasized Latin, while they offered a more practical and palatable curriculum to boys destined for commerce. In 1779 Thomas Jefferson proposed to the Virginia legislature a "Bill for the More General Diffusion of Knowledge" which was defeated. Ulich writes:

Here, as in Jefferson's whole personality, we find the most interesting mixture of aristocratic and democratic elements: the idea of an intellectual elite is aristocratic; the insistence on recruiting this elite from the talented youth of the state, even from the poorest homes, is democratic. The bill proposes — we follow here closely the description given by Jefferson himself in his *Notes on Virginia:*

> ... to lay off every county into small districts of five or six miles square, called hundreds, and in each of them to establish a school for teaching reading, writing and arithmetic. The teacher has to be supported by the Hundred, and all parents have the right to send their children to this elementary school for three years without paying tuition, "and as much longer as they please, paying for it."

In each hundred a "visitor," to wit, a person of public merit and confidence, is entrusted with the general supervision of the elementary school and, in addition, with the task:

> ... to choose the boy of best genius in the school, of those whose parents are too poor to give them further education, and to send him forward to one of the grammar schools, of which twenty are proposed to be erected in different parts of the country, for teaching Greek, Latin, geography, and the higher branches of numerical arithmetic. (10:247–248)

Apart from Jefferson, the post-Revolution was not a proud moment in American education. The frontiers were being settled. Those dissatisfied with the *status quo* could climb the next mountain or settle another prairie where there was land for the taking, adventure, and freedom. Who needed schools on the frontier? Pioneer children typically went to a "blab school," such as Lincoln attended for six weeks, walking four miles in the morning to get there and four miles home at night. A log cabin, with a hide for a door, a smoky fire filling the windowless room, the half-wild hogs rooting underneath the floor boards, and the children reciting at the top of their lungs — one could hear such a school farther away than one could see it through the trees. Lincoln himself wrote:

There were some schools, so called; but no qualification was ever required of a teacher, beyond *readin', writin', and cipherin'* to the Rule of Three. If a straggler supposed to understand latin happened to sojourn in the neighborhood, he was looked upon as a wizard. (9)

School districts were, at best, fragmented, and teachers were commonly regarded as "social failures and vagabonds." Methods of teaching emphasized dogmatism, authoritarianism, and rote learning. Most teachers preferred the switch to explanations. Life went on outside the schoolhouse door; inside, children marked time until the dreary session was over.

Yet, the content of instruction was increasing as textbooks began to appear. Despite a teacher's ignorance, a child could learn for himself were a textbook available to him. From 1690, when it was first published in London, until well into the nineteenth century, the *New England Primer* had been the chief, and frequently the only, text available. A tiny book (three inches by four) with miniscule type, it offered: syllables; the famous theological A B C ("In Adam's fall / We sinned all"); the catechism; questions on salvation; an instructive woodcut of the Reverend Mr. Rogers being burned at the stake in Smithfield while his wife, nine children and a babe at the breast, looked on; "Now I Lay Me Down to Sleep"; and more. Totally religious, totally of the 1600's, it was still widely used in 1850. Between 1837 and 1849, more than 100,000 copies were sold in an America of approximately 25,000,000 inhabitants.

Patriotism gradually began to vie with religion for space in the post-Revolutionary books; woodcuts of Washington on his white horse, and of Bunker Hill and Yorktown took the place of the Reverend Mr. Rogers. The moral, rather than the theological, began to be emphasized, and the secular values of honesty, thrift, cleanliness, and modesty were preached or thinly disguised in little stories. In 1783, Noah Webster published his *Blue-backed Speller*, which by 1880 had sold 80,000,000 copies. It helped to unify the language, which had taken on area dialects, and it influenced people's opinions as well. Generations of school children learned not only to spell, but to read, to converse, and to think from its pages. It was less dogmatic than the *New England Primer*, but remained conservative, moralistic, and class conscious by modern standards. As late as 1848 it still taught: "God governed the world with infinite wisdom." "Pastors did not like to see vacant seats in church." "The devil is the great adversary of man." "It is man's duty to accept his place in the social scheme uncomplainingly."

The Industrial Revolution
Brings Public Schools

By the 1820's education for the common man was less available. Industrialization had begun with Eli Whitney's cotton gin. In New England and New York, factories were rising, country people were coming to live in mill towns, and children were tending spindles. By 1833, two-fifths of all persons employed in New England factories were children between the ages of seven and sixteen years old. At Hope Factory in Rhode Island, more than half the workers were children, and they spent fifteen to sixteen hours a day, six days a week in the factory. *Niles Weekly Register*, the *Wall Street Journal* of the time, calculated the wealth to be gained were *all* children put to work in factories. A survey in 1834 showed that 100,000 eligible voters in Pennsylvania were unable to read.

The spindle-tending children of the North and the cotton chopping children of the South were not attending school, nor were they learning a trade thus destroying the apprenticeship system as a carrier of cultural values. Although this system had offered little book learning, it *had* offered a possibility for advancement and even, as Franklin's own experience illustrated, self-education. It declined and no longer accentuated a stage in life but merely a specific way of learning a trade for an ever smaller portion of the population.

In the 1820's and 1830's those few states that gave any public aid to elementary education at all gave it as charity to the poor; therefore, many people refused it in order to conceal their poverty. When Horace Mann began his work in Massachusetts in 1837, he found that almost all the money spent on education in the Commonwealth was being paid by well-to-do parents to support their children in private schools. The majority of children were receiving none, even in the state which had been the fountainhead of education in America. Massachusetts was divided into over 3,000 school districts, but a full third of them did not even possess a schoolhouse. The town of Harwich, on Cape Cod, was split into nine school districts all of which shared a single schoolmaster when one could be found. It was customary for a schoolmaster to teach in one district for a term of six or eight weeks and in the next district for the following term. A given pupil, therefore, could find his school in session only every three and a half years or so.

In 1820, the 9 million populace of the United States was largely rural. In 1860, the number had swelled to 31 million and was becoming increasingly urban. Many of the people were immigrants and the children of immigrants flocking to the New World to escape the Irish potato famine of the late 1840's. They arrived in the cities, sharing the lot of poor Americans who had left the rural areas to work in the mills. Many lived in degradation and misery, lacking sanitation, sunshine, food, and privacy.

One positive factor resulted: proliferating evils were evident in the city. They rose up from crowded alleys and assaulted the sensibilities of the passersby. And so in the mid-nineteenth century, a crusading reform movement developed, which championed the cause of those imprisoned, insane, handicapped, and oppressed by poverty. By 1860, these socioeconomic conditions had also changed the whole direction, structure, and function of the American public school.

"Open a school and close a prison," Horace Mann was fond of saying. In the last decade, the view has taken shape that not all of the heritage of reform is considered beneficial to the schools today. But until recently, the American public schools have been strictly moralistic. The flag, the engravings of Washington crossing the Delaware and the young Lincoln with an ax, the exhortations to cleanliness, the quasi-moral tone are the result of what was a great crusade, a veritable holy war to establish the common school.

The men most deeply involved in it — Horace Mann, Henry Barnard, Calvin Stoddard, and others — were themselves the descendants of Calvinistic stock. The fervor of the Puritan forefathers had been transformed in them into a commitment to social betterment. Education seemed to them the vital foundation for a more humane national life, indeed, for the continuation of any national life at all.

In the beginning, those crusaders who wanted universal education had no legislative backing. They had to convince the rich and the legislatures, as reluctant then as now, to raise taxes. The convincing was accomplished through the judicious preaching of fear — a fear sown among the rich that a dispossessed majority might revolt, and a fear among the mill owners that their laborers would abandon them for the new lands of the prairies. More enlightened men of affairs began to accept the idea of public education as a way to maintain a stable work force by providing a chance for advancement in the East. In 1847 the secretary of the Maine Board of Education expressed this attitude bluntly when he said: "What surer guarantee can the capitalist find for the security of his investments, than is to be found in the sense of a community morally and intellectually enlightened?" So those who gradually did accept the ideas of the reformers were frequently motivated by nothing but self-interest — to maintain their investments, to keep their machinery humming, and to avoid riots, strikes, and revolutions. Economic realism began to strengthen idealism. Slowly men came to admit that public education had its benefits.

Of all the men who worked for the schools, Horace Mann is the paradigm. He had been chosen at the height of his political popularity in 1837 to serve as secretary to the newly created Massachusetts Board of Education. He had espoused many causes as a state legislator in years past, having left a thriving law practice to provide a moral leadership to a life of public enlightenment. The two great thrusts of Mann's platform were "public support and public control of the schools." (2:19)

In his twelfth year of office, Mann resigned to take the Congressional seat of former President John Quincy Adams. "There followed a stormy period in which his Abolitionist sympathies projected him into the forefront of national politics. In 1853 after having been defeated for the Massachusetts governorship a year before, he accepted the presidency of Antioch College in Ohio, a new institution founded by the Christian denomination and committed to co-education, nonsectarianism and equal opportunity for Negroes." (6:27) One senses his passionate commitment, as well as the imagination and intelligence which he brought to the struggle to establish the common school in Massachusetts. In his twelfth annual report (1848) as Secretary of the State Board of Education, Mann made his case:

Now surely nothing but Universal Education can counter-work this tendency to the domination of capital and the servility of labor. If one class possesses all the wealth and the education, while the residue of society is ignorant and poor, it matters not by what name the relation between them is called; the latter, in fact and in truth, will be servile dependents and subject of the former. . . . Education . . . beyond all other devices of human origin is the great equalizer of the conditions of men— the balance-wheel of the social machinery. (2:86–87)

In this same report he tackled the criticism received for excluding formal religious instruction from the public school system. "It is a system . . . which leaves open all other means of instruction — the pulpits, the Sunday Schools, the Bible classes, the catechisms, of all denominations — to be employed according to the preference of individual *parents* [italics added]. It is a system which restrains itself from teaching religious doctrine. . . . It knows no distinction of rich and poor, of bond and free, or between those who, in the imperfect light of this world, are seeking, through different avenues, to reach the gate of heaven." (2:111-112)

Common or public schools had been accepted in principle; in most parts of the country, however, they hardly existed in fact. There were no teachers, schoolhouses, books, chairs, desks, pens, paper, ink, slates, globes, fuel to keep the schoolhouse warm, water to slake the children's thirst. The overwhelming task of American educators for the rest of the 1800's was to transform the ideal into reality. To the everlasting credit of this nation, this task, too, was done and done repeatedly in every incorporated village, town, city, county, and state, for every single unit of government had to deliberate on the establishment of schools. Groan they might, but the propertied men across the country voted to tax themselves to educate the children of other people. This feat was no mean one for a democracy to pull off in a mere fifty years.

The essential preliminary step was the provision of adequate tax bases to make free common schools *possible*. The legislatures of all the states, one after the other, granted *permission* to communities to set up a school district and to tax for school support. Initially the sources of the tax moneys were undefined, but then legislation was drawn up to specifically permit the taxation of *property* in the school district to support the school. This step was the crucial one, and when it was approved, the communities had voted to undertake a permanent assessment of their own resources. Each property owner had deliberately decided on the issue of taxing himself, and the majority chose in favor of doing so ensuring public schools, town- and state-supported. The granting of aid to school districts by the state was decisive. Then the state could set standards: the school term had to be so long, the school day so many hours, the teachers trained, the building sound, the course of study adequate. Finally, the legislatures made it *compulsory* for school districts to tax themselves in order to qualify for state and county aid. Thus, reluctant communities were harnessed into a recognizable and effective system.

The *Kalamazoo Case* in 1874 pushed public support to the level of secondary schools. All legislation had concerned elementary grades, because secondary schools had been traditionally reserved for the tuition-paying elite, who were college bound. After the *Kalamazoo Case* was won, public high schools became a possibility and eventually a necessity. The school year was made longer and more consistent from community to community. Previously, it had comprised a summer and a winter term of six, eight, or ten weeks in length leaving the children free to work on the family farm in spring and fall. As family farms diminished, fall, winter, and spring became school time. Compulsory attendance began (only recently achieved in some rural states) and the total years in school length-ened. By the end of the century, the graded school had been estab-lished in place of the old ungraded village school in which all pupils studied in the same room. State-run normal schools provided the usual preparation for teachers. In the cities, the public schools would soon undergo their first great challenge: to educate the flood of immigrant children pouring into America.

The Progressive Movement

In the throes of an unprecedented effort to establish themselves and survive against economic and physical odds, American public schools of the latter half of the 1800's were little concerned with theory. The legislation was passed, the schoolhouses built, the books obtained, the teachers trained, and the children taught. Not only were the rural children lost in the city, but the Irish, Italian, Russian, and German children were lost in an English language environment. There was no time to analyze what was going on under the schoolhouse roof. Teachers taught, but no one asked what they taught, and how they taught it.

But the time came when voices raised precisely those questions, loudly, insistently, and critically. A new kind of reform came: pro-gressivism. People, particularly educated people, had begun to question whether the educational methods used were consistent with democratic ideals.

One of the earliest and most significant challenges was raised by Joseph Mayer Rice, through the medium of Walter Hines Page's revived magazine, *The Forum*. Lawrence A. Cremin writes of Rice:

from **The
Transformation of the School**
Lawrence A. Cremin

Astute, opinionated, and sharp in his judgements, Rice was a young New York pediatrician whose interest in prophylaxis had led him to some searching questions about the city's schools — questions so pressing that he spent the period between 1888 and 1890 studying pedagogy at Jena and Leipzig. He returned bearing some fairly definite ideas about a "science of education" — dangerous luggage for a young man of thirty-three — and spent 1891 looking for a means of publicizing them. A series

From Lawrence A. Cremin, *The Transformation of the School* (New York: Alfred A. Knopf, 1961). By permission of Random House, Inc.

of columns in *Epoch,* a small New York weekly, and a piece in the December *Forum* provided his first opportunities. His pungent writing inevitably attracted comment, and near the end of 1891 Page offered him a novel proposal.

On behalf of the *Forum* Rice was to prepare a firsthand appraisal of American public education. From Boston to Washington, from New York to St. Louis, he was to visit classrooms, talk with teachers, attend school board meetings, and interview parents. He was to place "no reliance whatever" on reports by school officials; his goal was to render an objective assessment for the public. The proposal could not have been more welcome. Rice left on January 7, 1892. His tour took him to thirty-six cities; he talked with some 1200 teachers; he returned late in June, his notes crammed with statistics, illustrations, and judgments. The summer was given to writing, and the first article appeared in October. Within a month he and Page both knew that they had taken an angry bull by the horns. By the time the final essay was published the following June, Rice's name had become a byword — frequently an epithet — to schoolmen across the nation.

Rice's story bore all the earmarks of the journalism destined to make "muckraking" a household word in America. In city after city public apathy, political interference, corruption, and incompetence were conspiring to ruin the schools. A teacher in Baltimore told him: "I formerly taught in the higher grades, but I had an attack of nervous prostration some time ago, and the doctor recommended rest. So I now teach in the primary, because teaching primary children does not tax the mind." . . . A Chicago teacher, rehearsing her pupils in a "concert drill," harangued them with the command: "Don't stop to think, tell me what you know!" In Philadelphia the "ward bosses" controlled the appointment of teachers and principals: in Buffalo the city superintendent was the single supervising officer for 700 teachers. . . .

But the picture was not uniformly black; here and there Rice found encouraging departures from the depressing rule. In Minneapolis " a very earnest and progressive corps of teachers" was broadening the school program around the three Rs and dealing sympathetically with children from "even the poorest immigrant homes." In Indianapolis, where politics had been firmly excluded from the management of schools, competent "progressive" teachers were attempting to introduce "the idea of unification" into the curriculum, combining the several subjects "so they may acquire more meaning by being seen in their relations to one another." . . . And finally, at Francis Parker's world-famous Cook County Normal School, . . . Rice found examples par excellence of the "all-side" education of children: nature study, art, social activities, and the three Rs all taught by an inspired, enthusiastic staff.

The final article in the June *Forum* was a call to action. All citizens could have the life and warmth of the "progressive school" for their children. The way was simple and clear: led by an aroused public, the school system would have to be "absolutely divorced from politics in every sense of the word"; direct, thorough, and scientific supervision would have to be introduced; and teachers would have to endeavor constantly to improve their professional and intellectual competence. "The general educational spirit of the country is progressive," Rice concluded; it remained only for the public in local communities throughout the nation to do the job. (3)

Rice's general introduction and his 1892 study of the schools bears a striking resemblance to present day criticism:

A General Consideration
of the American School System
Joseph Mayer Rice

As the character of the instruction which the child receives represents the result of the varied management of the schools, — the resultant, as it were, of the action of a number of forces, — to observe the teacher at her work without a knowledge of the whole school machinery would be observing in a very superficial manner. A brief analysis of the formation and action of the various elements that enter into the management of a school system will therefore be given at the outset. With this knowledge the reader will more readily perceive that the description of ludicrous teaching found from time to time in this volume is done not for the purpose of ridiculing the teacher, but for the purpose of showing the results of unscientific management. Besides, this analysis will be the means of showing clearly why the schools of different localities vary so much, and where the cause of all educational evils must be sought.

The elements that exert an influence on the condition of the schools of every city are four in number: The public at large, the board of education, the superintendent and his staff, and the teachers.

First. The public at large. As to the attitude of the public toward the schools, it must unfortunately be said that in the large majority of instances the people take absolutely no active interest in their schools.... I refer to an intelligent interest, an interest sufficiently deep to lead one to follow closely the actions of the board of education, the superintendent, and the teachers, and to seek some knowledge of the scientific development of children....

Second. The boards of education. These boards are selected according to whims. Some are elected by the people, others are appointed, the appointing power lying in the hands of mayors, judges, or councilmen; or a board of education (as at Buffalo) may consist simply of a committee of the common council.... The manner in which the boards conduct their affairs varies markedly. In some cities their actions are

From Joseph Mayer Rice, *The Public-School System of the United States,* (The Century Co., 1893).

governed to a considerable extent by selfish motives, whether political or other, while in other cities the members of the board are entirely unselfish in their official acts.

Third. The superintendent and his staff. The office of superintendent is, in my opinion, one the importance of which cannot be overestimated. Indeed, in the study of the educational conditions in any given locality, the superintendent may be regarded as the central figure.... However thorough and enthusiastic a superintendent may be, if the board be not in sympathy with his movements, he is hampered, and cannot do his best. If he is ever so diligent a worker, but not sufficiently conversant with the science of education, the teaching will be liable to retain a mechanical stamp.... And if he is the right man and does all in his power to raise the standard of his teachers, the extent to which his good influence will be felt will depend on the previous training, the general character, and the size of his corps of teachers....

Last. The teachers. This is, after all, the greatest problem. If all teachers were perfect, there would be little need to trouble with political corruption and superintendents. But as has already been intimated, this is far from the case. Indeed the professional weakness of the American teacher is the greatest sore spot of the American schools....

The graduate of a good city training school represents, generally speaking, the best this country produces in the way of teachers. When the training received at one of these institutions is compared with that received at a normal school in Germany, the limited extent of the former becomes apparent.... Of those teaching (besides normal-school graduates), most are high-school graduates....

The office of teacher in the average American school is perhaps the only one in the world that can be retained indefinitely in spite of the grossest negligence and incompetence....

The Old Education and the New

As my judgment concerning the degree of excellence of a school system is governed by the extent to which the teachers strive to abandon unscientific methods and to regulate their work according to the requirements of the new education, it may be well, before entering on the discussions of the schools of individual cities, to describe what is generally understood by scientific and unscientific schools — by the "old" and the "new" education — as well as to point out wherein they differ.

By an unscientific or mechanical school is meant one that is still conducted on the antiquated notion that the function of the school consists primarily, if not entirely, in crowding into the memory of the child a certain number of cut-and-dried facts — that is, that the school exists simply for the purpose of giving the child a certain amount of information. As, in such schools, the manner in which the mind acquires ideas is naturally disregarded, it follows that the teachers are held responsible for nothing beyond securing certain memoriter results. Consequently, the aim of the instruction is limited mainly to drilling facts into the minds of the children, and to hearing them recite lessons that they have learned by heart from textbooks. Such methods are termed antiquated, because they represent instruction as it was before the time of the great educators, when a science of education was unknown. Further, as the manner in which the mind acquires ideas is not taken into account, the teacher makes no attempt to study the needs of the child, and consequently no bond of sympathy forms between the pupil and the teacher. In these schools the attitude of the teacher toward the child is as a rule cold and unsympathetic, and at times actually cruel and barbarous.

The schools conducted on scientific principles differ widely from the mechanical schools. While the aim of the old education is mainly to give the child a certain amount of information, the aim of the new education is to lead the child to observe, to reason, and to acquire manual dexterity as well as to memorize facts — in a word, to develop the child naturally in all his faculties, intellectual, moral, and physical. As in these schools the teacher is guided in her work by the nature of the child mind, that is, by the laws of mental development, — she is constantly in search of such light as will guide her in giving the child the benefit of what is known of the nature of the mind and its mode of development. We find, therefore, widely distributed among the teachers a truly progressive spirit, much enthusiasm, and a desire to become conversant with the laws of psychology and the principles of education. It is almost exclusively in the cities where the teachers constantly pursue professional studies under the guidance of their superintendents that schools of this order are found.

As it is no longer the textbook or the arbitrary will of the superintendent, but the laws of psychology, that now become the ruling spirit of the school, the order of things becomes reversed and, in consequence, the atmosphere of the schoolroom entirely changed. The teacher who endeavors to instruct in accordance with the nature of the mind is of necessity obliged to study the child, so that she may understand him and know how to minister to his needs. In this manner a true bond of sympathy forms between the teacher and the child. The attitude of the teacher now changes from that of lord and master to that of friend and guide. She thus ceases to be cold and harsh, and becomes loving and sympathetic. The schoolroom loses its prison aspect and becomes characteristic of a refined and refining home. Further, when the teacher is guided in her work by the laws of psychology, there is a change in the methods of instruction as well as in the spirit of the classroom. While in the mechanical schools the recitation periods are devoted either to hearing children recite lessons that they have studied by heart, or to drilling the pupils in facts, in the schools conducted on scientific principles such procedures are not tolerated, the teachers being obliged to devote these periods to actual teaching, and — to the best of their ability — in accordance with methods approved by the educational scientists.

It may therefore be seen that the new education recognizes that there are elements aside from measurable results that require consideration in educating the child. The first and foremost among these elements is the child himself. The old system of education thinks only of the results, and with its eye upon the results, forgets the child. . . .

And, further, under the new system elements are brought into play which, by reason of their refining nature, can scarcely fail to exert a favorable influence on the moral character of the child. Among these are — first, the bond of sympathy that forms between the child and the teacher who strives to understand him, to interest him, and to make him happy. The atmosphere of the mechanical school is damp and chilly, while that of the progressive school is glowing with life and warmth. Second, the pursuit of studies that tend to develop the sympathetic and esthetic faculties of the child, among which are, 1) nature studies — the study of plants when regarded from the sympathetic and poetic sides, and the study of animals from the standpoint of sympathy; 2) the purely artistic studies — namely, music, poetry, drawing and painting from nature, the construction of beautiful forms (designing), and work with beautiful colors.

But why do the mechanical schools still exist in an enlightened age and in a country so progressive as ours? . . .

If facts should prove that the best results in the three R's are obtained in the primary schools that devote practically all the time to these subjects, and the poorest in the primary schools that spend the most time in leading pupils to observe, to reason, and to use their hands with facility, then the advocates of the reading, writing, and arithmetic schools would still have at least a crutch to lean upon. But it so happens that facts prove the contrary to be true; namely, that the pupils read and write better, and cipher at least as well, in the schools where the work is most thoughtful — that is, where most is done to lead the pupils to acquire ideas by being brought into relation with things instead of words, signs, and symbols. I found, with scarcely an exception, by far the best reading in the schools in which the pupils were taught to read through science lessons, and by far the best — not infrequently incredibly good — results in written language where the children began to express the results of their observations in their own words in writing, as early as the fifth or sixth month of school life. (8:9–26)

The Public School System
of New York City

In describing the schools of our cities, I begin with the discussion of the schools of New York City because they represent a condition that may be regarded, in many respects, as typical of the schools of all of our large cities. They show clearly the elements that lead to an inferior order of schools. . . .

Now, what is the character of the instruction that will be passed as satisfactory by the superintendents of the public schools of New York City? Surely no one can call me unjust when I answer this question by describing the work of a school whose principal has been marked uniformly "excellent" during the twenty-five years or more that she has held her present position. I cannot say that this school is a typical New York primary school; I shall describe typical work later. But I do most positively assert that the mere fact that a superintendent is permitted to give a school of this nature his warmest indorsement is sufficient to prove that the school system of New York is not conducted for the benefit of the child alone.

The principal of this school has pedagogical views and a maxim peculiarly her own. She believes that when a child enters upon school life his vocabulary is so small that it is practically worthless, and his power to think so feeble that his thoughts are worthless. She is consequently of the opinion that what the child knows and is able to do on coming to school should be entirely disregarded, that he should not be allowed to waste time, either in thinking or in finding his own words to express his thoughts, but that he should be supplied with ready-made thoughts as given in a ready-made vocabulary. She has therefore prepared sets of questions and answers, so that the child may be given in concise form most of the facts prescribed in the course of study for the three years of primary instruction. The instruction throughout the school consists principally of grinding these answers *verbatim* into the minds of the children. The principal's ideal lies in giving each child the ability to answer without hesitation, upon leaving her school, every one of the questions formulated by her. In order to reach the desired end, the school has been converted into the most dehumanizing institution that I have ever laid eyes upon, each child being treated as if he possessed a memory and the faculty of speech, but no individuality, no sensibilities, no soul.

So much concerning the pedagogical views on which this school is conducted; now as to the maxim. This maxim consists of three short words — "Save the minutes." The spirit of the school is, "do what you like with the child, immobilize him, automatize him, dehumanize him, but save, save the minutes." In many ways the minutes are saved. By giving the child ready-made thoughts, the minutes required in thinking are saved. By giving the child ready-made definitions, the minutes required in formulating them are saved. Everything is prohibited that is of no measurable advantage to the child, such as the movement of the head or a limb, when there is no logical reason why it should be moved at the time. I asked the principal whether the children were not allowed to move their heads. She answered, "Why should they look behind when the teacher is in front of them?" — words too logical to be refuted. . . .

When the teacher is the source of wisdom, all the children in the room stare fixedly in the direction of the teacher; when a word on the blackboard is the source of wisdom, all eyes stare fixedly at a point on the blackboard. There is one more peculiarity. When material, of whatever nature, is handed to the children, enough to supply a whole row is given to the end child. The material is then passed along sideways until each child in the row has been supplied. During this procedure the children are compelled to look straight in front of them, and to place their hands sidewise in order to receive the material, without looking whence it comes. The pupils are thus obliged to grope, as if they were blind, for the things passed to them...

Sense training is a special feature of the school, and at least a half-dozen different methods, nearly all of which are original, are used for the purpose. The first of these methods is one by means of which form and color are studied in combination. I witnessed such a lesson in the lowest primary grade. Before the lesson began there was passed to each child a little flag, on which had been pasted various forms and colors, such as a square piece of green paper, a triangular piece of red paper, etc. When each child had been supplied, a signal was given by the teacher. Upon receiving the signal, the first child sprang up, gave the name of the geometrical form upon his flag, loudly and rapidly defined the form, mentioned the name of the color, and fell back into his seat to make way for the second child, thus: "A square; a square has four equal sides and four corners; green" (down). Second child (up): "A triangle; a triangle has three sides and three corners; red" (down). Third child (up); "A trapezium; a trapezium has four sides, none of which are parallel, and four corners; yellow" (down). Fourth child (up): "A rhomb; a rhomb has four sides, two sharp corners and two blunt corners: blue." This process was continued until each child in the class had recited.... The children are drilled in these definitions as soon as they enter the school, and the definitions are repeated from week to week and from year to year, until the child has finished his primary-school education.... (8:29–35)

In the lowest grade of many of the New York primary schools the reading is exceptionally dry. In one of the schools I found seventy-five words written on a blackboard. I learned that these seventy-five words were those that the pupils had been taught to read prior to the time of my visit. Whenever a new word was learned it was added to the list and retained there, and the children were drilled daily both in reading and in spelling these words. I asked the principal, who had accompanied me to the class-room, whether the children never read sentences. I was informed that the teacher occasionally formed sentences by pointing with her stick to various words on the list. Of course, sentences so read in no way retain the spirit of letting the child read a sentence because it is the unity of thought....

I next asked the principal how the seventy-five words on the board had been selected. She told me that they represented words found in the reading-book the children would receive in the next higher grade.... In the lowest grade ... the children are ... simply to memorize a large number of word forms. Can instruction be made less scientific? ...

In the New York primary schools arithmetic is taught fully as unscientifically as the reading. It is mechanical and abstract from the very beginning. In the class of which I have just been speaking, I heard the pupils add a column of "ones" and "twos" that had been written on the blackboard. The children added thus: "One and one are two"; "two and two are four"; "four and one are five," and so on.

Now I asked the principal whether arithmetic was ever taught by a concrete method.

"They will have concrete arithmetic work when they are a little further along in their reading," she replied.

"Will you kindly inform me what connection there is between reading and concrete arithmetic?" I asked.

"You see," she answered, "when the children can read the word 'oranges' or 'apples,' at the top of the column of figures, and then the pupils, instead of saying, 'One and two are three,' 'three and two are five,' will say, 'One orange and two oranges are three oranges.' In that way the work in arithmetic is made concrete."...

It is not difficult to account for the low standard of the New York schools; indeed, under existing conditions, it would be surprising if the instruction were of a higher order. In the first place, there is absolutely no incentive to teach well. If mechanical teaching be in general deemed satisfactory, why should the teacher trouble with the preparation of lessons and the study of educational methods and principles, and then teach upon scientific principles at the risk of not covering the work of the grade? Further, a teacher scarcely imperils her position by doing exceedingly poor work, the only penalty being that an incompetent teacher cannot claim the maximum salary after she has taught the required fourteen years.... (8:39–46)

"Progressive" has become a synonym for "Deweyite", but the material just presented shows that the term precedes John Dewey. Progressive theories did mean much the same ones Dewey and his followers later embraced: a unified curriculum which featured handwork and self-directed activity, an interest in science, a respect for the child as a person. But the general reform movement in education for which progressivism initially stood (part of the nationwide, comprehensive reform movement of the 1890's) was soon given focus by Dewey, himself. His followers, however, were unreliable interpreters of the principles he advocated. Martin Dworkin writes of the movement:

In education, progressivism brought together several familiar tendencies — but with contemporary modifications. One tendency was a romantic emphasis upon the needs and interests of the child, in the tradition of Rousseau, Pestalozzi, and Froebel — but now colored and given scientific authority by the new psychology of learning and behavior. Another was the democratic faith in the instrument of the common or public school, inherited from Jefferson and Mann — but now applied to the problems of training the urban and rural citizenry for industrial and agricultural vocations, and of acculturating or Americanizing the swelling masses of immigrants. By the time Dewey moved to Columbia University in 1904, he was truly the leading theoretician and spokesman of the movement. But this leadership then — and, indeed, from then on — was largely that of a reverently misinterpreted prophet rather than a carefully obeyed commander. (5:9)

Dewey was chagrined about the direction the "progressive school movement" began to take. Too frequently, the movement was synonymous with permissiveness and unbridled license. Dworkin comments: "He frequently complained about what he considered evasions of educational responsibility in many so-called 'progressive' schools. Subject matter, for example, too often had been eliminated or minimized when the truly progressive approach called for creating the curriculum to develop new subject matter" (5:10)

Long before the progressive education movement in America warranted critical assessment, young John Dewey and his wife founded the Laboratory School at the University of Chicago in 1896 and continued to run it for eight years. The "Dewey School" had an impact that was "immediate and lasting, profound and world-wide." (5:33)

Dewey believed that education had to be integrated with life, not preparation for a remote future. Living in a time when increasing industrialization was separating children from the comprehensible roots of social life, he felt that education should especially preserve their basic skills, behavior, and insights. "My Pedagogic Creed" gives one a grounding in Dewey's beliefs about good education for young children. Not by any means consistently upheld by those who called themselves his followers, his principles, nonetheless, influenced educational thought. At the very least, the progressives were a fructifying influence on American education. Under their aegis, such varied trends as the testing movement, scientific educational practices and an interest in the teaching of science, the "project method," and problem solving as an educational approach began. The typical classroom at the turn of the century had rows of desks and chairs screwed immovably to the floor, and seated up front at a big, imposing desk was the teacher. The typical classroom today has chairs and tables that can be moved about for flexible grouping. If there is a teacher's desk, it is off to one side where the teacher can gather a few children around her for instruction while others work at various tasks. Even if a school today is not called "progressive," it has absorbed the impact of Dewey's thought.

My Pedagogic Creed
John Dewey

Article I — What Education Is

I believe that all education proceeds by the participation of the individual in the social consciousness of the race. This process begins unconsciously almost at birth, and is continually shaping the individual's powers, saturating his consciousness, forming his habits, training his ideas, and arousing his feelings and emotions. Through this unconscious education the individual gradually comes to share in the intellectual and moral resources which humanity has succeeded in getting together. He becomes an inheritor of the funded capital of civilization. The most formal and technical education in the world cannot safely depart from this general process. It can only organize it or differentiate it in some particular direction.

I believe that the only true education comes through the stimulation of the child's powers by the demands of the social situations in which he finds himself. Through these demands he is stimulated to act as a member of a unity, to emerge from his original narrowness of action and feeling, and to conceive of himself from the standpoint of the welfare of the group to which he belongs. Through the responses which others make to his own activities he comes to know what these mean in social terms. The value which they have is reflected back into them. For instance, through the response which is made to the child's instinctive babblings the child comes to know what those babblings mean; they are transformed into articulate language and thus the child is introduced into the consolidated wealth of ideas and emotions which are now summed up in language.

I believe that this educational process has two sides — one psychological and one sociological; and that neither can be subordinated to the other or neglected without evil results following. Of these two sides, the psychological is the basis. The child's own instincts and powers furnish the material and give the starting point for all education. Save as the efforts of the educator connect with some activity which the child is carrying on of his own initiative independent of the educator, education becomes reduced to a pressure from without. It may, indeed, give

John Dewey, "My Pedagogic Creed," *The School Journal,* 1897.

certain external results, but cannot truly be called educative. Without insight into the psychological structure and activities of the individual, the educative process will, therefore, be haphazard and arbitrary. If it chances to coincide with the child's activity it will get a leverage; if it does not, it will result in friction, or disintegration, or arrest of the child nature.

I believe that knowledge of social conditions, of the present state of civilization, is necessary in order properly to interpret the child's powers. The child has his own instincts and tendencies, but we do not know what these mean until we can translate them into their social equivalents. We must be able to carry them back into a social past and see them as the inheritance of previous race activities. We must also be able to project them into the future to see what their outcome and end will be. In the illustration just used, it is the ability to see in the child's babblings the promise and potency of a future social intercourse and conversation which enables one to deal in the proper way with that instinct.

I believe that the psychological and social sides are organically related and that education cannot be regarded as a compromise between the two, or a superimposition of one upon the other. We are told that the psychological definition of education is barren and formal — that it gives us only the idea of a development of all the mental powers without giving us any idea of the use to which these powers are put. On the other hand, it is urged that the social definition of education, as getting adjusted to civilization, makes of it a forced and external process, and results in subordinating the freedom of the individual to a preconceived social and political status.

I believe that each of these objections is true when urged against one side isolated from the other. In order to know what a power really is we must know what its end, use, or function is; and thus we cannot know save as we conceive of the individual as active in social relationships. But, on the other hand, the only possible adjustment which we can give to the child under existing conditions, is that which arises through putting him in complete possession of all his powers. With the advent of democracy and modern industrial conditions, it is impossible to foretell definitely just what civilization will be twenty years from now. Hence it is impossible to prepare the child for any precise set of conditions. To prepare him for the future life means to give him command of himself; it means so to train him that he will have the full and ready use of all his capacities; that his eye and ear and hand may be tools ready to command, that his judgment may be capable of grasping the conditions under which it has to work, and the executive forces be trained to act economically and efficiently. It is impossible to reach this sort of adjustment save as constant regard is had to the individual's own powers, tastes, and interests — say, that is, as education is continually converted into psychological terms.

In sum, I believe that the individual who is to be educated is a social individual and that society is an organic union of individuals. If we eliminate the social factor from the child we are left only with an abstraction; if we eliminate the individual factor from society, we are left only with an inert and lifeless mass. Education, therefore, must begin with a psychological insight into the child's capacties, interests, and habits. It must be controlled at every point by reference to these same considerations. These powers, interests, and habits must be continually interpreted — we must know what they mean. They must be translated into terms of their social equivalents — into terms of what they are capable of in the way of social service.

Article II — What the School Is

I believe that the school is primarily a social institution. Education being a social process, the school is simply that form of community life in which all those agencies are concentrated that will be most effective in bringing the child to share in the inherited resources of the race, and to use his own powers for social ends.

I believe that education, therefore, is a process of living and not a preparation for future living.

I believe that the school must represent present life — life as real and vital to the child as that which he carries on in the home, in the neighborhood, or on the playground.

I believe that education which does not occur through forms of life, or that are worth living for their own sake, is always a poor substitute for the genuine reality and tends to cramp and to deaden.

I believe that the school, as an institution, should simplify existing social life; should reduce it, as it were, to an embryonic form. Existing life is so complex that the child cannot be brought into contact with it without either confusion or distraction; he is either overwhelmed by the multiplicity of activities which are going on, so that he loses his own power of orderly reaction, or he is so stimulated by these various activities that his powers are prematurely called into play and he becomes either unduly specialized or else disintegrated.

I believe that as such simplified social life, the school life should grow gradually out of the home life; that it should take up and continue the activities with which the child is already familiar in the home.

I believe that it should exhibit these activities to the child, and reproduce them in such ways that the child will gradually learn the meaning of them, and be capable of playing his own part in relation to them.

I believe that this is a psychological necessity, because it is the only way of securing continuity in the child's growth, the only way of giving a back-ground of past experience to the new ideas given in school.

I believe that it is also a social necessity because the home is the form of social life in which the child has been nurtured and in connection with which he has had his moral training. It is the business of the school to deepen and extend his sense of the values bound up in his home life.

I believe that much of present education fails because it neglects this fundamental principle of the school as a form of community life. It conceives the school as a place where certain information is to be given, where certain lessons are to be learned, or where certain habits are to be formed. The value of these is conceived as lying largely in the remote future; the child must do these things for the sake of something else he is to do; they are mere preparation. As a result they do not become a part of the life experience of the child and so are not truly educative.

I believe that the moral education centers upon this conception of the school as a mode of social life, that the best and deepest moral training is precisely that which one gets through having to enter into proper relations with others in a unity of work and thought. The present educational systems, so far as they destroy or neglect this unity, render it difficult or impossible to get any genuine, regular moral training.

I believe that the child should be stimulated and controlled in his work through the life of the community.

I believe that under existing conditions far too much of the stimulus and control proceeds from the teacher, because of neglect of the idea of the school as a form of social life.

I believe that the teacher's place and work in the school is to be interpreted from this same basis. The teacher is not in the school to impose certain ideas or to form certain habits in the child, but is there as a member of the community to select the influences which shall affect the child and to assist him in properly responding to these influences.

I believe that the discipline of the school should proceed from the life of the school as a whole and not directly from the teacher.

I believe that the teacher's business is simply to determine on the basis of larger experience and riper wisdom, how the discipline of life shall come to the child.

I believe that all questions of the grading of the child and his promotion should be determined by reference to the same standard. Examinations are of use only so far as they test the child's fitness for social life and reveal the place in which he can be of the most service and where he can receive the most help.

Article III — The Subject-Matter of Education

I believe that the social life of the child is the basis of concentration, or correlation, in all his training or growth. The social life gives the unconscious unity and the background of all his efforts and of all his attainments.

I believe that the subject-matter of the school curriculum should mark a gradual differentiation out of the primitive unconscious unity of social life.

I believe that we violate the child's nature and render difficult the best ethical results, by introducing the child too abruptly to a number of special studies, of reading, writing, geography, etc. out of relation to this social life.

I believe, therefore, that the true center of correlation on the school subjects is not science, nor literature, nor history, nor geography, but the child's own social activities.

I believe that education cannot be unified in the study of science, or so called nature study, because apart from human activity, nature itself is not a unity; nature in itself is a number of diverse objects in space and time, and to attempt to make it the center of work by itself, is to introduce a principle of radiation rather than one of concentration.

I believe that literature is the reflex expression and interpretation of social experience; that hence it must follow upon and not precede such experience. It, therefore, cannot be made the basis, although it may be made the summary of unification.

I believe once more that history is of educative value in so far as it presents phases of social life and growth. It must be controlled by reference to social life. When taken simply as history it is thrown into the distant past and becomes dead and inert. Taken as the record of man's social life and progress it becomes full of meaning. I believe, however, that it cannot be so taken excepting as the child is also introduced directly into social life.

I believe accordingly that the primary basis of education is in the child's powers at work along the same general constructive lines as those which have brought civilization into being.

I believe that the only way to make the child conscious of his social heritage is to enable him to perform those fundamental types of activity which make civilization what it is.

I believe therefore, in the so-called expressive or constructive activities as the center of correlation.

I believe that this gives the standard for the place of cooking, sewing, manual training, etc. in the school.

I believe that they are not special studies which are to be introduced over and above a lot of others in the way of relaxation or relief, or as additional accomplishments. I believe rather that they represent, as types, fundamental forms of social activity; and that it is possible and desirable that the child's introduction into the more formal subjects of the curriculum be through the medium of these activities.

I believe that the study of science is educational in so far as it brings out the materials and processes which make social life what it is.

I believe that one of the greatest difficulties in the present teaching of science is that the material is presented in purely objective form, or is treated as a new peculiar kind of experience which the child can add to that which he has already had. In reality, science is of value because it gives the ability to interpret and control the experience already had. It should be introduced, not as so much new subject-matter, but as showing the factors already involved in previous experience and as furnishing tools by which that experience can be more easily and effectively regulated.

I believe that at present we lose much of the value of literature and language studies because of our elimination of the social element. Language is almost always treated in the books of pedagogy simply as the expression of thought. It is true that language is a logical instrument, but it is fundamentally and primarily a social instrument. Language is the device for communication; it is the tool through which one individual comes to share the ideas and feelings of others. When treated simply as a way of getting individual information, or as a means of showing off what one has learned, it loses its social motive and end.

I believe that there is, therefore, no succession of studies in the ideal school curriculum. If education is life, all life has, from the outset, a scientific aspect, an aspect of art and culture, and an aspect of communication. It cannot, therefore, be true that the proper studies for one grade are mere reading and writing, and that at a later grade, reading, or literature, or science, may be introduced. The progress is not in the succession of studies but in the development of new attitudes towards, and new interests in, experience.

I believe finally, that education must be conceived as a continuing reconstruction of experience; that the process and the goal of education are one and the same thing.

I believe that to set up any end outside of education, as furnishing its goal and standard, is to deprive the educational process of much of its meaning and tends to make us rely upon false and external stimuli in dealing with the child.

Article IV—The Nature of
Method

I believe that the question of method is ultimately reducible to the question of the order of development of the child's powers and interests. The law for presenting and treating material is the law implicit within the child's own nature. Because this is so I believe the following statements are of supreme importance as determining the spirit in which education is carried on:

1. I believe that the active side precedes the passive in the development of the child nature; that expression comes before conscious impression; that the muscular development precedes the sensory; that movements come before conscious sensations; I believe that consciousness is essentially motor or impulsive; that conscious states tend to project themelves in action.

I believe that the neglect of this principle is the cause of a large part of the waste of time and strength in school work. The child is thrown into a passive, receptive, or absorbing attitude. The conditions are such that he is not permitted to follow the law of his nature; the result is friction and waste.

I believe that ideas (intellectual and rational processes) also result from action and devolve for the sake of the better control of action.

What we term reason is primarily the law of orderly or effective action. To attempt to develop the reasoning powers, the powers of judgment, without reference to the selection and arrangement of means in action, is the fundamental fallacy in our present methods of dealing with this matter. As a result we present the child with arbitrary symbols. Symbols are a necessity in mental development, but they have their place as tools for economizing effort; presented by themselves they are a mass of meaningless and arbitrary ideas imposed from without.

2. I believe that the image is the great instrument of instruction. What a child gets out of any subject presented to him is simply the images which he himself forms with regard to it.

I believe that if nine tenths of the energy at present directed towards making the child learn certain things, were spent in seeing to it that the child was forming proper images, the work of instruction would be indefinitely facilitated.

I believe that much of the time and attention now given to the preparation and presentation of lessons might be more wisely and profitably expended in training the child's power of imagery and in seeing to it that he was continually forming definite, vivid, and growing images of the various subjects with which he comes in contact in his experience.

3. I believe that interests are the signs and symptoms of growing power. I believe that they represent dawning capacities. Accordingly the constant and careful observation of interests is of the utmost importance for the educator.

I believe that these interests are to be observed as showing the state of development which the child has reached.

I believe that they prophesy the stage upon which he is about to enter.

I believe that only through the continual and sympathetic observation of childhood's interests can the adult enter into the child's life and see what it is ready for, and upon what material it could work most readily and fruitfully.

I believe that these interests are neither to be humored nor repressed. To repress interest is to substitute the adult for the child, and so to weaken intellectual curiosity and alertness, to suppress initiative, and to deaden interest. To humor the interests is to substitute the transient for the permanent. The interest is always the sign of some power below; the important thing is to discover this power. To humor the interest is to fail to penetrate below the surface and its sure result is to substitute caprice and whim for genuine interest.

4. I believe that the emotions are the reflex of actions.

I believe that to endeavor to stimulate or arouse the emotions apart from their corresponding activities, is to introduce an unhealthy and morbid state of mind.

I believe that if we can only secure right habits of action and thought, with reference to the good, the true, and the beautiful, the emotions will for the most part take care of themselves.

I believe that next to deadness and dullness, formalism and routine, our education is threatened with no greater evil than sentimentalism.

I believe that this sentimentalism is the necessary result of the attempt to divorce feeling from action.

Article V—The School and Social Progress

I believe that education is the fundamental method of social progress and reform.

I believe that all reforms which rest simply upon the enactment of law, or the threatening of certain penalties, or upon changes in mechanical or outward arrangements, are transitory and futile.

I believe that education is a regulation of the process of coming to share in the social consciousness; and that the adjustment of individual activity on the basis of this social consciousness is the only sure method of social reconstruction.

I believe that this conception has due regard for both the individualistic and socialistic ideals. It is duly individual because it recognizes the formation of a certain character as the only genuine basis of right living. It is socialistic because it recognizes that this right character is not to be formed by merely individual precept, example, or exhortation, but rather by the influence of a certain form of institutional or community life upon the individual, and that the social organism through the school, as its organ, may determine ethical results.

I believe that in the ideal school we have the reconciliation of the individualistic and the institutional ideals.

I believe that the community's duty to education is, therefore, its paramount moral duty. By law and punishment, by social agitation and discussion, society can regulate and form itself in a more or less haphazard and chance way. But through education society can formulate its own purposes, can organize its own means and resources, and thus shape itself with definiteness and economy in the direction in which it wishes to move.

I believe that when society once recognizes the possibilities in this direction, and the obligations which these possibilities impose, it is impossible to conceive of the resources of time, attention, and money which will be put at the disposal of the educator.

I believe that it is the business of every one interested in education to insist upon the school as the primary and most effective interest of social progress and reform in order that society may be awakened to realize what the school stands for, and aroused to the necessity of endowing the educator with sufficient equipment properly to perform his task.

I believe that education thus conceived marks the most perfect and intimate union of science and art conceivable in human experience.

I believe that the art of thus giving shape to human powers and adapting them to social service, is the supreme art; one calling into its service the best of artists; that no insight, sympathy, tact, executive power, is too great for such service.

I believe that with the growth of psychological service, giving added insight into individual structure and laws of growth; and with growth of social science, adding to our knowledge of the right organization of individuals, all scientific resources can be utilized for the purposes of education.

I believe that when science and art thus join hands the most commanding motive for human action will be reached; the most genuine springs of human conduct aroused and the best service that human nature is capable of guaranteed.

I believe, finally, that the teacher is engaged, not simply in the training of individuals, but in the formation of the proper social life.

I believe that every teacher should realize the dignity of his calling; that he is a social servant set apart for the maintenance of proper social order and the securing of the right social growth.

I believe that in this way the teacher always is the prophet of the true God and the usherer in of the true kingdom of God. (4)

References to Part 4

1. Bailyn, Bernard, *Education in the Forming of American Society: Needs and Opportunities for Study* (New York: Vintage Books, 1960).

2. Cremin, Lawrence A., ed., *The Republic and the School: Horace Mann on the Education of Free Men* (New York: Teachers College Bureau of Publications, 1957).

3. _____, *The Transformation of the School: Progressivism in American Education, 1876–1957* (New York: Alfred Knopf, 1964), pp. 4–6.

4. Dewey, John, "My Pedagogic Creed," *The School Journal*, 54, no. 3 (January, 1897): 77–80.

5. Dworkin, Martin S., *Dewey on Education: Selections, with an Introduction and Notes* (New York: Teachers College Bureau of Publications, 1959).

6. Edwards, Newton, and Richey, Herman G., *The School in the American Social Order: The Dynamics of American Education* (Boston: Houghton Mifflin Co., 1947), p. 61.

7. Massachusetts, Capital Laws, 1642, 1647.

8. Rice, Joseph Mayer, *The Public-School System of the United States* (New York: The Century Co., 1893).

9. Sandburg, Carl, *Abraham Lincoln: The Prairie Years and The War Years, Volume I* (New York: Harcourt, Brace & Co., 1926), p. 36.

10. Ulich, Robert, *History of Educational Thought*, rev. ed. (New York: Van Nostrand Reinhold Co., 1968).

part 5

Europe in the
Twentieth Century

Major initiatives in early childhood education did not originate in America in the twentieth century. Programs and ideas began elsewhere but readily fell on receptive ears here. Early in the century two giants, Maria Montessori and Margaret McMillan, boldly experimented with the nursery school in a form still recognizable to this day. Both were influenced by the teaching materials and methods (especially those devoted to sense training) devised by Edouard Séguin during the mid-nineteenth century for mentally deficient children. (14) He, in turn, drew his inspiration from Jean Itard whose attempts to educate and socialize a true noble savage, *The Wild Boy of Aveyron*, kept the French intelligentsia in suspense at the turn of the eighteenth century. (5) Although obviously familiar with Pestalozzi and Froebel, both Montessori and McMillan preferred to claim their educational kinship elsewhere.

By the middle of the century, pioneering efforts were made in Israel and many of the European countries in government-sponsored quality programs for young children. Although early education programs in the Scandinavian countries, crèches in France, and day care in Germany or Yugoslavia existed, the day care experiences for *very* young children in Israel and Russia deeply influenced the beliefs and goals of early childhood educators in America. First looked upon with skepticism, no attempt was made to replicate their work here for many years; indeed, it was illegal.

Maria Montessori (1870–1952)

A late nineteenth century feminist and physician, Montessori became involved in the education of young children without any formal training in this field. The first woman to earn a degree in medicine in Italy, she developed an interest in "pedagogy" while working with retarded children as an intern at the psychiatric clinic of the University of Rome. At the age of twenty-eight she assumed the directorship of a tax-supported school for defective children.

Working thirteen hours a day with the children, she developed materials and methods which allowed them to perform reasonably well on school problems previously considered far beyond their capacity. Her great triumph, in reality and in the newspapers, came when she presented 'idiot' children from mental institutions at the public examinations for primary certificates, which was as far as the average Italian ever went in formal education, and her children passed the exam. (7:34)

In 1907 she was invited to organize a school within a tenement in the San Lorenzo quarter of Rome. The school was an attempt by the members of the Roman Association of Good Building to protect their property. Crowded living conditions and parents working long hours left many children unsupervised which resulted in destruction of buildings. Given a single room in one of the tenements and a single resident teacher, the *Dottoressa* designed her *casa dei bambini* or "Children's House" for fifty to sixty children between the ages of two-and-a-half to seven years. Open from 9 A.M. to 5 P.M. in the winter and from 8 A.M. to 6 P.M. in the summer, Dr. Montessori supervised the teacher closely and spent long hours there.

The school was considered communally owned by the parents whose rent partially covered the cost of the program. Montessori wrote about this arrangement: "The idea of collective ownership is new and very beautiful and profoundly educational." (4:63) It provided a doctor and governess to look after the children's growth and development in a manner which poor people could not otherwise afford. Clearly written rules and regulations had to be respected so that the parents and their children could be thought "deserving of the benefits" of the schools.

Montessori wrote about the conditions that she found and some of the objectives that she envisioned for the Children's Houses. They were by no means limited to educational "gains." At the opening of one of the Children's Houses, she delivered an Inaugural Address which describes the context in which she began her work.

from **Inaugural Address**

Maria Montessori

The Quarter of San Lorenzo is celebrated, for every newspaper in the city is filled with almost daily accounts of its wretched happenings. Yet there are many who are not familiar with the origin of this portion of our city.

It was never intended to build up here a tenement district for the people. And indeed San Lorenzo is not the *People's Quarter,* it is the Quarter of the *poor.* It is the Quarter where lives the underpaid, often unemployed workingman, a common type in a city which has no factory industries. It is the home of him who undergoes the period of surveillance to which he is condemned after his prison sentence is ended. They are all here, mingled, huddled together.

The district of San Lorenzo sprang into being between 1884 and 1888 at the time of the great building fever. No standards either social or hygienic guided these new constructions. The aim in building was simply to cover with walls square foot after square foot of ground. The more space covered, the greater the gain of the interested Banks and Companies. All this with a complete disregard of the disastrous future which they were preparing. It was natural that no one should concern himself with the stability of the building he was creating, since in no case would the property remain in the possession of him who built it.

When the storm burst, in the shape of the inevitable building panic of 1888 to 1890, these unfortunate houses remained for a long time untenanted. Then, little by little, the need of dwelling-places began to make itself felt, and these great houses began to fill. Now, those speculators who had been so unfortunate as to remain possessors of these buildings could not, and did not wish to, add fresh capital to that already lost, so the houses constructed in the first place in utter disregard of all laws of hygiene, and rendered still worse by having been used as temporary habitations, came to be occupied by the poorest class in the city....

From Maria Montessori, *The Montessori Method: Scientific Pedagogy as Applied to Child Education in Children's Houses,* Frederick A. Stokes, 1912.

Whoever enters, for the first time, one of these apartments is astonished and horrified. For this spectacle of genuine misery is not at all like the garish scene he has imagined. We enter here a world of shadows, and that which strikes us first is the darkness which, even though it be midday, makes it impossible to distinguish any of the details of the room.

When the eye has grown accustomed to the gloom, we perceive, within, the outlines of a bed upon which lies huddled a figure — someone ill and suffering. If we have come to bring money from some society for mutual aid, a candle must be lighted before the sum can be counted and the receipt signed. Oh, when we talk of social problems, how often we speak vaguely, drawing upon our fancy for details instead of preparing ourselves to judge intelligently through a personal investigation of facts and conditions.

We discuss earnestly the question of home study for school children, when for many of them home means a straw pallet thrown down in the corner of some dark hovel. We wish to establish circulating libraries that the poor may read at home. We plan to send among these people books which shall form their domestic literature — books through whose influence they shall come to higher standards of living. We hope through the printed page to educate these poor people in matters of hygiene, of morality, of culture, and in this we show ourselves profoundly ignorant of their most crying needs. For many of them have no light by which to read!

There lies before the social crusader of the present day a problem more profound than that of the intellectual elevation of the poor; the problem, indeed, of *life*. . . .

Conditions such as I have described make it more decorous, more hygienic, for these people to take refuge in the street and to let their children live there. But how often these streets are the scene of bloodshed, of quarrel, of sights so vile as to be almost inconceivable. The papers tell us of women pursued and killed by drunken husbands! Of young girls with the fear of worse than death, stoned by low men. Again, we see untellable things — a wretched woman thrown, by the drunken men who have preyed upon her, forth into the gutter. There, when day has come, the children of the neighbourhood crowd about her like scavengers about their dead prey, shouting and laughing at the sight of this wreck of womanhood, kicking her bruised and filthy body as it lies in the mud of the gutter!

Such spectacles of extreme brutality are possible here at the very gate of a cosmopolitan city, the mother of civilisation and queen of the fine arts, because of a new fact which was unknown to past centuries, namely, *the isolation of the masses of the poor.*

In the Middle Ages, leprosy was isolated: the Catholics isolated the Hebrews in the Ghetto; but poverty was never considered a peril and an infamy so great that it must be isolated. The homes of the poor were scattered among those of the rich and the contrast between these was a commonplace in literature up to our own times. Indeed, when I was a child in school, teachers, for the purpose of moral education, frequently resorted to the illustration of the kind princess who sends help to the poor cottage next door, or of the good children from the great house who carry food to the sick woman in the neighbouring attic.

To-day all this would be as unreal and artificial as a fairy tale. The poor may no longer learn from their more fortunate neighbours lessons in courtesy and good breeding, they no longer have the hope of help from them in cases of extreme need. We have herded them together far from us, without the walls, leaving them to learn of each other, in the abandon of desperation, the cruel lessons of brutality and vice. Anyone in whom the social conscience is awake must see that we have thus created infected regions that threaten with deadly peril the city which, wishing to make all beautiful and shining according to an æsthetic and aristocratic idea, has thrust without its walls whatever is ugly or diseased. . . .

Observing these streets with their deep holes, the doorsteps broken and tumbling, we might almost suppose that this disaster had been in the nature of a great inundation which had carried the very earth away; but looking about us at the houses stripped of all decorations, the walls broken and scarred, we are inclined to think that it was perhaps an earthquake which has afflicted this quarter. Then, looking still more closely, we see that in all this thickly settled neighbourhood there is not a shop to be found. So poor is the community that it has not been possible to establish even one of those popular bazars where necessary articles are sold at so low a price as to put them within the reach of anyone. The only shops of any sort are the low wine shops which open their evil-smelling doors to the passer-by. As we look upon all this, it is borne upon us that the disaster which has placed its weight of suffering upon these people is not a convulsion of nature, but poverty — poverty with its inseparable companion, vice. . . .

It is to meet this dire necessity that the great and kindly work of the Roman Association of Good Building has been undertaken. The advanced and highly modern way in which this work is being carried on is due to Edoardo Talamo, Director General of the Association. His plans, so original, so comprehensive, yet so practical, are without counterpart in Italy or elsewhere.

This Association was incorporated three years ago in Rome, its plan being to acquire city tenements, remodel them, put them into a productive condition, and administer them as a good father of a family would.

The first property acquired comprised a large portion of the Quarter of San Lorenzo, where to-day the Association possesses fifty-eight houses, occupying a ground space of about 30,000 square metres, and containing, independent of the ground floor, 1,600 small apartments. Thousands of people will in this way receive the beneficent influence of the protective reforms of the Good Building Association. Following its beneficent programme, the Association set about transforming these old houses, according to the most modern standards, paying as much attention to questions related to hygiene and morals as to those relating to buildings. The constructional changes would make the property of real and lasting value, while the hygienic and moral transformation would, through the improved condition of the inmates, make the rent from these apartments a more definite asset.

The Association of Good Building therefore decided upon a programme which would permit of a gradual attainment of their ideal. It is necessary to proceed slowly because it is not easy to empty a tenement house at a time when houses are scarce, and the humanitarian principles which govern the entire movement make it impossible to proceed more rapidly in this work of regeneration. . . .

The house which it offers to its tenants is not only sunny and airy, but in perfect order and repair, almost shining, and as if perfumed with purity and freshness. These good things, however, carry with them a responsibility which the tenant must assume if he wishes to enjoy them. He must pay an actual tax of *care* and *good will*. The tenant who receives a clean house must keep it so, must respect the walls from the big general entrance to the interior of his own little apartment. He who keeps his house in good condition receives the recognition and consideration due such a tenant. Thus all the tenants unite in an ennobling warfare for practical hygiene, an end made possible by the simple task of *conserving* the already perfect conditions.

Here indeed is something new! So far only our great national buildings have had a continued *maintenance fund*. Here, in these houses offered to the people, the maintenance is confided to a hundred or so workingmen, that is, to all the occupants of the building. This care is almost perfect. The people keep the house in perfect condition, without a single spot. The building in which we find ourselves to-day has been for two years under the sole protection of the tenants, and the work of maintenance has been left entirely to them. Yet few of our houses can compare in cleanliness and freshness with this home of the poor.

This first impulse has led to other reforms. From the clean home will come personal cleanliness. Dirty furniture cannot be tolerated in a clean house, and those persons living in a permanently clean house will come to desire personal cleanliness.

One of the most important hygienic reforms of the Association is that of *the baths*. Each remodeled tenement has a place set apart for bathrooms, furnished with tubs or shower, and having hot and cold water. All the tenants in regular turn may use these baths, as, for example, in various tenements the occupants go according to turn, to wash their clothes in the fountain in the court. This is a great convenience which invites the people to be clean. These hot and cold baths *within the house* are a great improvement upon the general public baths.

In this way we make possible to these people, at one and the same time, health and refinement, opening not only to the sun, but to progress, those dark habitations once the *vile caves* of misery.

But in striving to realise its ideal of a semi-gratuitous maintenance of its buildings, the Association met with a difficulty in regard to those children under school age, who must often be left alone during the entire day while their parents went out to work. These little ones, not being able to understand the educative motives which taught their parents to respect the house, became ignorant little vandals, defacing the walls and stairs. And here we have another reform the expense of which may be considered as indirectly assumed by the tenants as was the care of the building. This reform may be considered as the most brilliant transformation of a tax which progress and civilisation have as yet devised. The "Children's House" is earned by the parents through the care of the building. Its expenses are met by the sum that the Association would have otherwise been forced to spend upon repairs. A wonderful climax, this, of moral benefits received! Within the "Children's House," which belongs exclusively to those children under school age, working mothers may safely leave their little ones, and may proceed with a feeling of great relief and freedom to their own work. But this benefit, like that of the care of the house, is not conferred without a tax of care and of good will. The Regulations posted on the walls announce it thus: (12:49–61)

> The Roman Association of Good Building hereby establishes within its tenement house number   , a "Children's House," in which may be gathered together all children under common school age, belonging to the families of the tenants.
> The chief aim of the "Children's House" is to offer, free of charge, to the children of those parents who are obliged to absent themselves for their work, the personal care which the parents are not able to give.
> In the "Children's House" attention is given to the education, the health, the physical and moral development of the children. This work is carried on in a way suited to the age of the children.
> There shall be connected with the "Children's House" a Directress, a Physician, and a Caretaker.
> The programme and hours of the "Children's House" shall be fixed by the Directress.
> There may be admitted to the "Children's House" all the children in the tenement between the ages of three and seven.
> The parents who wish to avail themselves of the advantages of the "Children's House" pay nothing. They must, however, assume these binding obligations:
>> (a) To send their children to the "Children's House" at the appointed time, clean in body and clothing, and provided with a suitable apron.
>> (b) To show the greatest respect and deference toward the Directress and toward all persons connected with the "Children's House," and to co-operate with the Directress herself in the education of the children. Once a week, at least, the mothers may talk with the Directress, giving her information concerning the home life of the child, and receiving helpful advice from her.
> There shall be expelled from the "Children's House":
>> (a) Those children who present themselves unwashed, or in soiled clothing.

(b) Those who show themselves to be incorrigible.

(c) Those whose parents fail in respect to the persons connected with the "Children's House," or who destroy through bad conduct the educational work of the institution. (12:70–71)

The directress is always at the disposition of the mothers, and her life, as a cultured and educated person, is a constant example to the inhabitants of the house, for she is obliged to live in the tenement and to be therefore a co-habitant with the families of all her little pupils. This is a fact of immense importance. Among these almost savage people, into these houses where at night no one dared go about unarmed, there has come not only to teach, *but to live the very life they live*, a gentlewoman of culture, an educator by profession, who dedicates her time and her life to helping those about her! A true missionary, a moral queen among the people, she may, if she be possessed of sufficient tact and heart, reap an unheard-of harvest of good from her social work.

This house is verily *new*; it would seem a dream impossible of realisation, but it has been tried. It is true that there have been before this attempts made by generous persons to go and live among the poor to civilise them. But such work is not practical, unless the house of the poor is hygienic, making it possible for people of better standards to live there. Nor can such work succeed in its purpose unless some common advantage or interest unites all of the tenants in an effort toward better things.

This tenement is new also because of the pedagogical organisation of the "Children's House." This is not simply a place where the children are kept, not just an *asylum*, but a true school for their education, and its methods are inspired by the rational principles of scientific pedagogy.

The physical development of the children is followed, each child being studied from the anthropological standpoint. Linguistic exercises, a systematic sense-training, and exercises which directly fit the child for the duties of practical life, form the basis of the work done. . . .

This idea of the collective ownership of the school is new and very beautiful and profoundly educational.

The parents know that the "Childrens' House" is their property, and is maintained by a portion of the rent they pay. The mothers may go at any hour of the day to watch, to admire, or to meditate upon the life there. It is in every way a continual stimulus to reflection, and a fount of evident blessing and help to their own children. We may say that the mothers *adore* the "Children's House," and the directress. How many delicate and thoughtful attentions these good mothers show the teacher of their little ones! They often leave sweets or flowers upon the sill of the schoolroom window, as a silent token, reverently, almost religiously, given.

And when after three years of such a novitiate, the mothers send their children to the common schools, they will be excellently prepared to co-operate in the work of education, and will have acquired a sentiment, rarely found even among the best classes; namely, the idea that they must *merit* through their own conduct and with their own virtue, the possession of an educated son.

Another advance made by the "Children's House" as an institution is related to scientific pedagogy. This branch of pedagogy, heretofore, being based upon the anthropological study of the pupil whom it is to educate, has touched only a few of the positive questions which tend to transform education. For a man is not only a biological but a social product, and the social environment of individuals in the process of education, is the home. Scientific pedagogy will seek in vain to better the new generation if it does not succeed in influencing also the environment within which this new generation grows! I believe, therefore, that in opening the house to the light of new truths, and to the progress of civilisation we have solved the problem of being able to modify directly, the *environment* of the new generation, and have thus made it possible to apply, in a practical way, the fundamental principles of scientific pedagogy.

The "Children's House" marks still another triumph; it is the first step toward the *socialisation of the house.* The inmates find under their own roof the convenience of being able to leave their little ones in a place, not only safe, but where they have every advantage.

And let it be remembered that *all* the mothers in the tenement may enjoy this privilege, going away to their work with easy minds. Until the present time only one class in society might have this advantage. Rich women were able to go about their various occupations and amusements, leaving their children in the hands of a nurse or a governess. To-day the women of the people who live in these remodeled houses, may say, like the great lady, "I have left my son with the governess and the nurse." More than this, they may add, like the princess of the blood, "And the house physician watches over them and directs their sane and sturdy growth." These women, like the most advanced class of English and American mothers, possess a "Biographical Chart," which, filled for the mother by the directress and the doctor, gives her the most practical knowledge of her child's growth and condition.

We are all familiar with the ordinary advantages of the communistic transformation of the general environment. For example, the collective use of railway carriages, of street lights, of the telephone, all these are great advantages. The enormous production of useful articles, brought about by industrial progress, makes possible to all, clean clothes, carpets, curtains, table-delicacies, better tableware, etc. The making of such benefits generally tends to level social caste. All this we have seen in its reality. But the communising of *persons* is new. That the collectivity shall benefit from the services of the servant, the nurse, the teacher — this is a modern ideal. . . .

We are, then, communising a "maternal function," a feminine duty, within the house. We may see here in this practical act the solving of many of woman's problems which have seemed to many impossible of solution. What then will become of the home, one asks, if the woman goes away from it? The home will be transformed and will assume the functions of the woman.

I believe that in the future of society other forms of communistic life will come.

Take, for example, the infirmary; woman is the natural nurse for the dear ones of her household. But who does not know how often in these days she is obliged to tear herself unwillingly from the bedside of her sick to go to her work? Competition is great, and her absence from her post threatens the tenure of the position from which she draws the means of support. To be able to leave the sick one in a "house-infirmary," to which she may have access any free moments she may have, and where she is at liberty to watch during the night, would be an evident advantage to such a woman. . . .

Much more distant, but not impossible, is the communal kitchen, where the dinner ordered in the morning is sent at the proper time, by means of a dumb-waiter, to the family dining-room. Indeed, this has been successfully tried in America. Such a reform would be of the greatest advantage to those families of the middle-class who must confide their health and the pleasures of the table to the hands of an ignorant servant who ruins the food. At present, the only alternative in such cases is to go outside the home to some café where a cheap table d'hôte may be had.

Indeed, the transformation of the house must compensate for the loss in the family of the presence of the woman who has become a social wage-earner.

In this way the house will become a centre, drawing into itself all those good things which have hitherto been lacking: schools, public baths, hospitals, etc. . . .

We are, then, very far from the dreaded dissolution of the home and of the family, through the fact that woman has been forced by changed social and economic conditions to give her time and strength to remunerative work. The home itself assumes the gentle feminine attributes of the domestic housewife. The day may come when the tenant, having given to the proprietor of the house a certain sum, shall receive in exchange whatever is necessary to the *comfort* of life; in other words, the administration shall become the *steward* of the family. (12:61–68)

Montessori was best known for her design of materials for sense training. Committed to the idea that movement, manipulation, and the isolated training of the senses develop the capacity for thought, she developed materials that could be self-administered and that were self-correcting. The younger children practiced sensory discrimination of various graded stimuli, proceeding from a few which were strongly contrasted to many stimuli gradually and imperceptibly differentiated. When a particular sensory organ was involved, other sensory stimuli were isolated. Activities were developed for touch, thermal, visual, and auditory senses. No effort was made to acquaint the child with words. This introduction to words came later using Sequin's method to identify such things as color, thickness, and length. For example, the perception was associated with the name by presenting two colors: "This is red. This is blue." Then recognition of the name was associated with the object: "Give me red. Give me blue." Lastly, the teacher checked for memory by pointing to the object and asking, "What is this?" If the child should fail at any time in this sequence of steps, he was not corrected but the lesson was stopped. In this way Montessori felt sensory discrimination was translated into vocabulary. (12, 13)

The materials she developed for reading, writing, and arithmetic are similar to those for sense training. Graded wood cylinders, geometric insets which fit into variously shaped holes, sandpaper letters, and graded rods are some examples of her work. When self-correcting materials could not teach skills, Madame Montessori carefully taught the routines of "practical life": how to wash, sweep, prepare food, dress (e.g., buttoning, polishing shoes). Nothing was too mundane for the *Dottoressa's* attention. Children were encouraged to repeat these homely tasks in the prescribed way. Repetition, she observed, was enjoyable to young children. There was no part in her program for "imaginative" play. Playing house, dressing up, or painting was strictly "for keeps." A child's drawing that did not faithfully represent reality was quickly dismissed.

Martin Mayer calls attention to innovations in instruction and ideology for which she is responsible.

from **Schools,**
Slums, and Montessori
Martin Mayer

. . . Given a little dramatic instinct, the attention-getting device of the human voice, the stick of the examination, and the carrot of praise, a teacher can persuade the majority of a class to reproduce for her on demand whatever it is she has fed out. To organize a child's experiences in such a way that he comes out of them with what you want him to have is a far more complicated job. Most of what even a fairly young child knows and can do in Western society is beyond the innate equipment of the animal; as the biologist P. B. Medawar recently wrote, we are all born into the Old Stone Age, and in theory could stay there. Accepting the human need for knowledge — the drive to organize perceptions and secure an equilibrium of prediction — it still remains true that the organism is easily satisfied. All kinds of sympathetic magic will be accepted, by children or (to use an unfashionable word) by savages, as an appropriate and usable explanation of raw experience. Unaided, induction from life itself is likely to be misleading (Dewey points this up unusually well in *How We Think*), and the essence of the inductive approach is rigorous limitation of the aid to be given. Life must therefore be rearranged, very cleverly, to provide abstract experiences that start the mind on paths which actually go somewhere.

To achieve such results, the didactic materials must be:

1) simple — which does *not* mean "easy." The materials must be precisely denotative in terms of the discriminations to be learned, and not at all connotative. Teaching by an inductive approach, whether it involves concrete materials or words, rests first of all on the exclusion of irrelevancy. The lesson, Montessori writes, "must be stripped of all that is not absolute truth." Montessori reserves her greatest scorn for the teachers who complicate a lesson; and she disposes once and for all of the notion that there is some value to gaining a child's attention through the employment of a trick not directly related to the subject matter.

Didactic materials must also be:

2) inherently interesting. Montessori makes much of the children who go on and on with the same repetitive game, arranging and rearranging a set of the materials. Any nursery-school teacher knows how often a child left to himself will go back to the same puzzle he solved yesterday, simply for the pleasure of getting it right, though puzzles easier or harder than this one — or, apparently, to adult eyes, more interesting — are lying untouched upon the shelves. Generally speaking, the rule is that one does not know what will interest a child until one tries it. This difficulty (while real) is less severe than the others, because it can be met simply by quantity and liberty — if the teacher leaves enough stuff around the room, the child will find something that interests him. Boredom is most likely to arise when the teacher forces the situation, insisting that everybody must be interested in the same story or demonstration or lesson.

If the children are to be working largely on their own, however, it is also necessary that the materials be:

3) self-correcting. Montessori lays great stress on the idea that the teacher must not tell children they are wrong, but must rather put the materials away and try again later. Such actions may be frustrating for the child, who wants to know what is going on, and one imagines that the letter (if not the spirit) of the rule was often violated by Montessori herself as well as by her directresses. But the insight is certainly true: unless the child can see for himself whether an answer is right or wrong, didactic materials are likely to be ineffective. This self-correcting quality is what Montessori means by "objectivity," and it is most easily achieved when there are literal objects which the child has arranged either correctly or incorrectly, and which he can then step back to examine. The evanescence of words makes the spoken answer extremely

difficult to use for inductive purposes unless it can be instantly inserted into a written problem. Written answers to written questions may meet the specifications, if the lesson has been really imaginatively planned. There is no reason why a child cannot be confronted with a word correctly spelled, or a map correctly drawn, to enable him to compare his own work with better work; but in fact, unfortunately, teachers rarely do organize their classrooms or take the time to let the child correct himself. Mathematics is the most natural subject in which to achieve "objectivity," because written answers can be tried out in the written problem, and because concrete materials are convenient. It is worth noting, however, that neither the abacus nor the Montessori beads are wholly satisfactory for the inductive teaching of mathematics, because the beads once handled become part of memory just as quickly as words once spoken — it is usually necessary to start again, without evidence of the prior error, if a mistake is made.

Finally, if self-correcting materials are to be well used in a classroom, it is essential that they be:

4) thoroughly comprehensible to the teacher herself. For all Montessori's optimism, and the occasional euphoric statements by the modern reformers of math and science instruction, there are no "teacher-proof materials." However self-checking the puzzle may be, the teacher must know when to present it or to withhold it, how to verify what (if anything) has been learned from it—and, if possible, how to improve it to eliminate error-generating elements. In any event, the teacher is so important a personage in the child's life, even if she is merely a "directress," that she cannot avoid influencing what he perceives. Apart from certain bits of physical business, materials are usually self-correcting only when a teacher makes them so.

Another aspect of the Montessori materials, regarded as desirable for quite different theoretical reasons, is their attempt to involve muscles and tactile senses in fundamental learning operations. As Jerome Bruner has pointed out, there are a number of activities (Bruner's example is the tying of sailor's knots) which cannot be very well described in words or plainly presented in drawings—one gets the notion by watching someone do the job, and acquires an "understanding" through the process of duplicating what has been observed. The Montessori frames for buttoning clothes and tying shoelaces are lovely examples of this sort of thing, and their failure to become standard equipment in nursery schools and kindergartens is totally inexplicable. Think how much more nervous energy kindergarten and nursery teachers would have for important jobs if children could be got into their clothes at the end of the day by some technique less exhausting than force of will.

The most striking and famous example of Montessori's use of touch and muscle to approach abstraction comes, of course, in her prescriptions for the teaching of reading and writing. In the Montessori system, children learn the alphabet through the use of "sand letters"—sandpaper insets on smooth boards—over which they run their questing fingers. By the process of tracing the sand letters, the child acquires the basic movements which will enable him to write the letters when a pencil is placed in his hand. Here again, Montessori stresses the control of error, by the fact that the child's finger runs off the sandpaper onto the smooth wood; but now she insists, too, on the importance of "the *muscular memory* . . ." "Indeed," she adds, the child "sometimes recognizes the letters by touching them, when he cannot do so by looking at them."

Having learned the alphabet in this manner, the child is ready to move on to the construction of words, which is done in a straightforward manner through the use of alphabet cards. The child takes the cards from a storage box modeled on a printer's type-case, and spells out words which are dictated to him. Here, too, Montessori claims (though less convincingly) a self-checking feature: the child "will have the *proof* of the exact solution of his problem when he *rereads* the word." This process is easier in Italian than in English, though the gap in difficulty can be exaggerated—the difference between the sounds of the initial "e" in *fede* (faith) and *fedele* (faithful) is about as great as such differences are in English, and the fact that there is a logical adult explanation for it does not much help the child learning to read; moreover, there is no very logical reason for spelling differences like that between *obbligare* (to oblige) and *obliare* (to forget). Assuming this hurdle already topped, however, the next step is, as Montessori says, pure natural magic—the child, having learned to trace and write the letters, and then having put words together with pre-printed letter-cards, suddenly discovers he can write, all by himself. And despite the incredible blatherskite that passed for "science" among American reading experts during the last generation, Montessori was unquestionably correct in her statement that children as young as age four very much *want* to read and write, if they get the notion that they *can* read and write.

The didactic materials she describes in *The Montessori Method*, and at greater length in *Elementary Material* (which is volume two of *Advanced Montessori Method*), lie at the center of the *Dottoressa's* thought about education. And many of the materials are touched by genius. It is a great mistake, however, and one which too many Montessorians have made, to assume that *only* the materials developed by Montessori herself can be useful for her purposes, or that invention ceased when the old lady ran out of teaching ideas and shifted her attentions to Mankind at large. Toys like the Playskool postbox, with their requirement that the child find a two-dimensional figure (a hole in the box) matching in outline the shape of a three-dimensional figure (a block in his hand), point the way to games more interesting than Montessori's wafer-thin geometric shapes. The tying-shoe, which asks the child to lace a shape similar to the nuisance on his foot, is better than Montessori's tying frame. And it is possible that Omar Moore's electric typewriter, set in a "responsive environment" (the words used by Montessori herself), represents a true technological advance over Montessori's sand letters, though admittedly it does not yield the same advantages in terms of "muscular memory." In any event, one can certainly imagine a Montessori classroom, with booths at one end containing an electric typewriter and a computer programmed to calculate what response should be made to the child's explorations on it.

In mathematics, the Montessori materials have been clearly superseded. Centimeter rods (popularly, "Cuisenaire" rods, which is the brand name and pays tribute to the Belgian teacher who first systematized their use) are far more valuable mathematically than Montessori's rods. In the Montessori materials, the unit of length is greater than the unit of the cross-section of the rod, which means that only addition and subtraction problems can be managed—and not all of those. The centimeter rods, however, with a cube for the "1," offer opportunities to handle all the four rules of arithmetic (multiplication becomes the calculation of area, which is a useful notion later). Even if we decide not to teach more math in kindergarten, it is foolish to switch the child from one set of materials to another when he can start with the more valid. Montessori was by no means a mathematical illiterate (few others interested in elementary education before the year 1955 could have made her comment to the effect that a knowledge of the differential calculus is essential to an understanding of Newtonian astronomy), but we have advanced great distances in recent years in the teaching of mathematics. Montessori's willingness to teach "0" as "nothing" is totally unacceptable today, when the number line is available as didactic material for teaching the notion that "0" is also the balance point between positive and negative numbers or vectors—and when "arrays of number lines" will be used with seven-year-old (and perhaps even six-year-old) children to start them on work with Cartesian coordinates. There is good reason to suspect that very young children's mathematical sense is *much* more susceptible of development than Montessori or modern educators ever realized, and that appropriate mathematical games of a wholly Montessorian nature could further enliven the educational aspect of the kindergarten.

Finally, Montessori's views of art and music are pretty hopelessly those of the nineteenth century. She had both genius and spunk in deciding that musical instruments would have to be invented for her schools, but she was obviously too sure in her separation of musical sounds from "disordered and ugly noises." (In this connection, too, it might be observed that Martin Deutsch, working in New York nursery schools and kindergartens, has come to the conclusion that *for slum children today* the necessary aural-discrimination training lies in picking signals from a noisy background, not lowering the threshold of perception through systematic silence. Probably both are desirable. The point is that a Montessori school ought not to be stuck with its founder's outdated aesthetics and communication theories, but should expand its procedures with the growth of knowledge.) In art, too, Montessori was in our terms backward, demanding as her definition of beauty the literal portrayal of "reality." Though the Fauves were tearing Paris apart as she wrote, she insisted that the child who painted the tree-trunk red was demonstrating that he was not yet ready to advance in his abstract education. We have not progressed much in education since Montessori —but if her guidance is to be significant in the years to come, those who accept it must also be willing to reject those details which have lost their usefulness with the passage of fifty years.

Montessori's techniques were used first in mental institutions, then in the slums. Though her approach has values for the education of children from all backgrounds, many of the specific materials were designed to help children whose experience was desperately impoverished. In the years since, Montessori's inventions have had little impact on the schools, but they have been highly influential with the better toy manufacturers. There is something amusing about sophisticated parents, who have stocked their homes with Montessorian toys, spending up to fourteen hundred dollars a year to secure for their four-year-olds the values of exposure to Montessori's didactic materials in a schoolroom atmosphere. But it is not at all amusing to find that neither day-care centers nor kindergartens in the slums make use of the *only* systematic collection of educational devices designed for the sort of crippled children who are within their doors.

People who wish to plan Montessori schools for slum areas, however, should probably keep in mind that there were sociological as well as instructional innovations at the original *Case dei Bambini,* and that the Montessori approach might not work anywhere near so well in a "standard" school. The fact that Montessori's school was physically part of the model tenement where the children lived may have been quite important; the fact that the directress herself lived in the tenement was unquestionably quite important. There was, moreover, a certain toughness about Montessori's rules that will be difficult to recapture in the modern climate of opinion, which holds that a working-class child with dirty hands is insulted, alienated, and miserable whenever anyone tells him to wash up. Montessori's *Case* accepted only children whose parents were prepared to acknowledge "two obligations: namely, the physical and moral care of their own children. . . . The parents must learn to *deserve* the benefit of having within the house the great advantage of a school for their little ones. . . . The mother must go at least once a week, to confer with the directress, giving an account of her child, and accepting any helpful advice which the directress may be able to give." Children who showed up in a soiled shirt could be sent away, and all dialects (in which Italian is as rich as English) were to be stamped out.

Whether the directors of new Montessori schools wish to go this far or not, they would probably be wise to take two basic principles from the Roman experience: that the school and its personnel must be very intimately a part of the community, which accepts some direct responsibility for it; and that attendance must be a privilege earned by both parents and child, not a right. Many promising programs in the slums have been first handicapped and then gutted by an administrator's sentimental insistence that *everyone* must be part of them. At present, the schools succeed, more or less, with about twenty percent of the children in the slums; and it will take a near-miracle to raise this proportion to fifty percent within a generation. In all fairness to the children, we should measure our efforts by their contribution to this near-miracle, not by standards of utopian justice. (4:36-39)

Montessori's initial influence on American education was short lived. Although her experiments were popularized by writers like Dorothy Canfield Fisher in 1912, (2) her works did not receive wide attention again in this country until the 1950's. J. McVicker Hunt suggests that the resistance experienced by the Montessori movement here was attributable to its failure to capture the educational establishment which held prevalent beliefs about child development that have subsequently changed. He comments in a general way:

Most of Montessori's support had come from the elite of the political and educational progressives and through popular magazines; it had not come from those formulating the new psychological theories nor from those formulating the philosophy of education. Although Montessori got support from Howard C. Warren (1912), then president of the American Psychological Association, and from Lightner Witmer (1914), founder of the first Psychological Clinic at the University of Pennsylvania, she failed to get support from those psychologists of the functional school or of the emerging behavioristic school whose conceptions were shortly to become dominant. With such emerging theories, with the conceptions of the intelligence-testing movement, and with the psychoanalytic theory of psychosexual development, then just beginning to get a foothold in America following Freud's visit of 1909 at the invitation of G. Stanley Hall, Montessori's notions were too dissonant to hold their own. (4)

During the 'teens, Montessori's chief critic, William Kilpatrick, was at Columbia Teachers College. He compared her unfavorably to John Dewey, whom he claimed had a much broader view: "His [Dewey's] conception of the nature of the thinking process, together with his doctrines of interest and education as *life* [italics added] ... include all that is valid in Madame Montessori's doctrines of liberty and sense-training, afford the criteria for correcting her errors, and besides, go vastly further in the construction of the educational method." (6)

To this day, Montessori is considered a seer and lawgiver by some, and an anathema by others. Montessori teachers in many countries are trained to follow exactly what Madame Montessori wrote; the conflict continues, however, between those who follow her strictly, and those who deviate from her curriculum. Unquestionably, she was a woman of remarkable insight and sensitivity. Her theory of intellectual development was oversimplified, yet her materials transcended her explanations and are still enormously beneficial for children all over the world, but particularly for those in modern-day ghettos similar to her *ragazzi* of San Lorenzo.

Margaret McMillan
(1860–1931)

Margaret McMillan and her sister, Rachel, were crusaders who exerted considerable influence on educational legislation in Great Britain. Margaret had studied music in Frankfort. Returning to London where she took an occasional job as a governess and studied voice, she became deeply interested in socialism and the suffrage movement. Inspired by speakers such as George Bernard Shaw, she and Rachel went to the docks on Sundays to sell socialist pamphlets and address street corner meetings. Shortly after moving to Bradford with a group of socialists in 1893, she was elected to the Bradford School Board and used this position to fight for medical inspection of school children, school baths, and other causes. After moving to Deptford several years later, the sisters' interest in correcting the health problems of school children continued; they started a day and night camp school for neighborhood children who were ill. (3)

The McMillans were appalled by the celery-root complexions, the rickety legs, lice, scabies, and impetigo that they saw as evidence of neglect on the children growing up in Great Britain. Convinced the children's health problems were already too advanced by school age, the sisters began to work with a younger group. Determined to help these unfortunate youngsters, the sisters founded an open-air nursery school. The school was so named because it was similar to a lean-to having one side open to the elements to let the sun shine in. They were struggling to maintain it when Rachel died only three years later. Margaret continued their work, however, training teachers, promoting nursery schools, and writing political tracts until her own death in 1931.

The center served children from ages one to six and was intended to be primarily outdoors. Play was encouraged in the herb, vegetable, and flower gardens, in the sand box, and in the junk heap (piles of coal ashes, old nuts and bolts, etc.). Baths were provided in big waist-high tubs so that a teacher might scrub a dozen or more children without straining her back. Clean clothes, nourishing meals, and a learning experience were offered. (9)

To the Electors

THE OPEN-AIR NURSERY SCHOOL

UP to the present our national system of education has no foundation and no roof. Of the roof and towers this leaflet has nothing to say. But of the foundation—that is, of nurture and education for little children, we have new information and new figures.

The average of delicate and diseased children entering the Elementary School to-day at the age of five years is—*30 to 40 per cent.*

The average of Open-air Nursery School children (who have attended this type of school from two to five years old) is—*7 per cent.*

RICKETS

The average of ricketty children entering the Nursery School at the age of two years is enormous— Dr. Annis, of Greenwich, says 90 per cent., Dr. Thomson, Medical Officer of Health, says 80 per cent., in their respective boroughs. *Within one year* these cases of rickets are all *cured* in an Open-air Nursery School.

MEASLES

INFECTIOUS DISEASE.—Epidemics of measles are very fatal to young children. The Public Health Report of the L.C.C. states that of over 1000 children who died of measles in the epidemic of *1925-6* only 55 were over five years old. The death roll of infants was heavy, but not so heavy as was that of children of Nursery School age. *Over 700 children of 1 to 5 years old perished.*

The incidence of measles during the same period *in an Open-air Nursery School* was .7, *that is 2 out of 252 children* had measles. There was no death. The two recovered quickly, having good resistive powers, and were back in school in two weeks.

SKIN DISEASES

SCABIES, IMPETIGO, RINGWORM, etc. These diseases are very common in crowded areas, so common that Doctors and Nurses spend a great part of their time in treating them. They make up the enormous group known as *Minor Ailments*. *With proper treatment in Nursery Schools they should disappear* and be as rare as leprosy. They do not disappear. They persist from year to year in spite of the work of Nurses and School Nurses. *In the Open-air Nursery Schools, Scabies disappeared in 1925 and 1926.* No case was found. *Ringworm fell to .5. Impetigo rapidly disappeared.*

EDUCATIONAL VALUES

In Mr. Cyril Burt's tables, issued by the L.C.C. to Teachers, etc., the distribution of Intelligence is shown as follows: 46% of all school children are normal; 20% are bright or supe.-normal, and a very small number, viz.: one or two, stand even higher. This leaves 30% of dull or sub-normal children. *Of these, however, 39% are dull only through neglect in the first years.* Thus there are not more than 18% who can be classed as dull. This number might be found to be still lower, and *lessening* if nurture were the birthright of all.

COST OF THE NURSERY SCHOOL

The cost of such schools should average *£12 to £14 per annum. There is no added danger in large schools* (see L.C.C. Health Report issued in October, 1927, where the incidence of a School of over 200 was as low as that for schools of 20 to 40).

Parents in the North pay as much as 10/- per week to have children " minded." There is no need for such costly and unscientific treatment of the young.

Furthermore, *financial help is given by parents in the poorest areas.* One Nursery School alone has a steady income of £1,000. The full cost in large schools is £11 15s. per annum.

These facts are incontrovertible. They are more forcible than pleading or eloquent speech. The rate-payers have never before been put in possession of them. We believe that now publicity having been given to them *the case for Open-Air Nursery Schools is established.*

Issued by the Nursery School Association of Great Britain, 32 Bloomsbury Street, London, W.C.1

Printed by The William Morris Press Ltd., 41 Gartside Street, Manchester

To compensate for the neglect the children received at home, McMillan's concept of the nursery school included provision for medical and dental care, cognitive stimulation, and work with parents. She placed more emphasis on the emotional development of the child than did Montessori: "The little child learns to know his mother's face well, to recognize her quickly, and in this recognition, emotion plays so great a part that the familiar face becomes a kind of starting point of widening sympathy and interest of life. If early life gives little opportunity for the experience of preserving and stimulating emotions a remarkable mental apathy is the result." (8) Her greater emphasis on the child's emotional life and parent work are noticeable in the writings about the open-air nursery school. The following excerpt is taken from a chapter in *Montessori in Perspective* which reviewed McMillan's work:

from **Nursery Education**
for Disadvantaged Children

Samuel J. Braun

The initiation of monthly group meetings with the mothers proved to be "invaluable to both sides." (a) * Mothers talked about their children; teachers listened suggesting child rearing methods and games that the mother might introduce to the child. Visits to the home were not uncommon to "touch the parent" emotionally especially when child or parent attendance was sporadic. No child was excluded, no matter how difficult the situation.

Teachers-in-training were required to live in the neighborhood so that they might understand better the problems of the family: the housing conditions, the cost of food, the needs of the family who live always on "the brink of financial precipice." In their home visits the teachers were taught to be deeply interested in the roots and history of the family so that the child through conversing with his parents might feel the presence of past and future and not just live in a tenuous present. Often a dialogue between mother and child was noticed in the home which squelched his curiosity: "Where was you born, mother?" said a seven year old boy to his mother one day. "Me" she cried, startled. "I dunno what place 'twas exactly. Somewheres about Cross Street." "Was father born there too?" asked the boy. "Him? No. I dunno where he wur born. What strange questions you ask," cried the mother. His quick warm

---

From Samuel J. Braun, "Nursery Education for Disadvantaged Children: An Historical Review," *Montessori in Perspective*, ed., Lucille Perryman (Washington, D.C.: National Association for the Education of Young Children, 1966). By permission.
*Letters in parentheses refer to notes at the end of each article or extract.

interest served from that hour. He had met a blank wall and the past darkened as if a curtain had fallen. (b)

As the parents talked more of their grandfathers and great grandparents, they recalled many details; such as, how they parted their hair, how they smoked their pipes, how they planted trees, or how they had built ships. The child learned that he belonged to people who "are worth thinking about and being remembered for a long time at least by their own children." (b) Perhaps he learned that life was not trivial but had meaning and relationship to others.

McMillan hoped that the nursery might in another way serve the community flexibly. She hoped that during times of family crisis, illness or impending move that the nursery could be used as a residence. Actually in its original operation the nursery was residential but gradually this was modified to a day care center.

To staff the centers McMillan instituted a three year course for "freelance probationers." Of the first three girls trained for the job two had not attended any school after their fourteenth year. In fact McMillan felt strongly that the young girl had a natural gift with children that she might lose as a more mature woman. Any girl over the age of fourteen could be selected as a probationer so long as she was modestly bright and had a temperament that abounded in patience.

This was on-the-job training in the best tradition; trainees were paid while learning by doing. Four probationers were supervised by one trained teacher who in turn was responsible for thirty preschoolers. (c) Besides living in the community they served a part-time three month rotation in the medical and dental clinic in order to increase their observational skills and to enable them to refer the appropriate case from the nursery school. (b)

In the centers they learned to work with groups of six or seven preschoolers. (c) Much of the individual didactic material and curriculum developed by McMillan simulated that of Montessori; albeit she did not confine the materials to one individual but used them in the group as well. When Dr. Eliot visited McMillan and suggested that the material was similar to Montessori, McMillan became incensed. These ideas, McMillan stated, were not borrowed from Montessori but grew out of the work of Seguin. So intensely did she feel that the name of Montessori was not to be used in her school. (d) Yet McMillan's philosophical orientation was also based on the premise of sensory-motor learning as she likened the mind's processes into two movements, the inner regulatory and outer corrective movement. Without the use of the latter McMillan postulated madness for the inner world of illusion could not be checked with reality. In addition to her lack of conviction that the child must be worked with individually, she differed from Montessori in one other important way. She saw value in the child's spontaneous drawing of what had been remembered. In his abstraction she could note what was important enough to be remembered and what was left out; in other words she recognized the child's contribution and what impressed him as being important in its own right. (e)

The probationers received lectures on child development geared to practical application. They themselves were taught to train their own senses so that they could better appreciate the ways in which children learned. (b) As another important aspect of their apprenticeship McMillan hoped the probationers would add another dimension to their personality: "Now nature ordains that while a child can have only one mother, it can have a good many sisters to staff our nurseries and to receive there, under trained teachers, what we may call their technical education as women." (f) (1:17-19)

Notes

a. Newman, Evelyn S., "A Pioneer Undertaking," in *Nursery Schools: A Practical Handbook* (London: John Bale, Sons and Danielsson, Ltd., 1920), p. 17.
b. McMillan, Margaret, *The Nursery School* (New York: E. P. Dutton and Co., 1919).
c. Hawtrey, Freda, "The Training of Nursery School Teachers," in *Nursery Schools: A Practical Handbook*, p. 43.
d. Eliot, Abigail A., personal communication.
e. McMillan, Margaret, *Education through the Imagination* (London: Swan Sonnenschein, 1904).
f. _____, "Ideals for the School," in *Nursery Schools: A Practical Handbook*, p. 1.   (1:17-19)

Using her experiences in the nursery school, Margaret McMillan further publicized the plight of poor children and the need for prevention of health problems. The public became increasingly concerned when a high percentage of young men were found unfit for military service in World War I because of undiagnosed medical conditions and personal maladjustments; attention was directed to the first six years of life. Armed with data, McMillan fought hard for the passage of the Fisher Education Act of 1918, which provided tax money to communities requesting it for nursery services for children from ages two to five. Elected to the London County Council in 1919, she continued to press for greater subsidizing of this bill. "The Geddes Axe fell on it" in 1921. (10) There were no further appropriations because of debts incurred by the war, and she lost her Council seat in 1922. A pamphlet published by the Labour Party (page 350 of the appendix) illustrates her seemingly boundless energy to gain public support for nursery schools.

The American pioneers in early childhood education were influenced by McMillan's writings and many did visit the nursery schools. One of them, Dr. Abigail Eliot, actually studied and worked with McMillan. However, some of the Americans visiting the centers were astonished to discover that they had not multiplied all over London. In fact, very few people knew where they were located.

Israel's Attempt to Implement
a National Policy Towards
Young Children

While the early part of the twentieth century in Europe was characterized by individual achievement in early childhood education,
later policies with regard to the care and education of young children were developed by countries. Well articulated programs sponsored by the government dealt with the needs of a whole country's
preschool population. Such planning is not present in America.
Efforts have most recently been directed toward the disadvantaged;
there is no policy for the whole country.

Israel faced the extraordinary problem of an immense immigration of families from every part of the world and every level of
culture. Although bound together by religious ties, they came from
backgrounds as different as a cave dwelling in the Yemen desert
and a London apartment. Educated, illiterate, sophisticated, and
primitive — all had to learn to live together and all had to be
educated. Early education was considered essential; Abraham Minkovitch of the Hebrew University of Jerusalem gives a comprehensive picture of the task and its progress:

Early Childhood
Education in Israel
Abraham Minkovitch

Early childhood education in Israel can be described in terms of
the following aspects: a) scope and organization; b) pedagogical trends
and curricula; c) educational research; and d) future perspectives.

I. Scope and Organization

As far back as the period of the British Mandate, there was already
a well-established tradition of kindergartens within the Jewish community of the country. Shortly after the declaration of the State of Israel
in 1948, all five-year-olds were provided with free kindergartens as part
of the compulsory education law. No such tradition of early education
existed in the Arab sector of the country during the Mandate. For this
reason, the process of building up a system of kindergartens among
Israeli Arabs has been somewhat slower. However, at present, eighty-
five percent of Israeli-Arab five-year-olds attend kindergarten, while

Abraham Minkovitch, "Early Childhood Education in Israel," mimeographed 1968, reproduced by permission of the author.

government plans call for completing the absorption of all eligible children within the next few years.

The kindergarten in Israel is a one-year institution with no physical or administrative links to the elementary school. In most cases, it is also separate from nursery schools. The kindergartens have their own system of teacher training and supervision, together constituting a separate department in the Ministry of Education and Culture. Institutional education for ages younger than that of kindergarten (age five) was only in partial existence at the proclamation of the State, and was a characteristic feature among three particular segments of the population: the Kibbutz (collective settlement) movement, the wealthier and more educated families, and families with working mothers or those on welfare whose children were cared for in nursery schools maintained by the central labor union (Histadrut) and private welfare agencies.

The kibbutz movement has always provided semi-formal and formal education to its children from the earliest possible age. Up until the time of weaning (generally at around six months of age), the kibbutz child and its mother are together during all waking hours. From that point on, the amount of time the mother spends with the child becomes progressively smaller, but never less than three hours per day, generally after completing work. Most of the child's time is spent in a group of four or five other children under the care of a *M'tapelet* (mother surrogate). The latter performs what is essentially the role of the mother in the socialization process up to the age of three to three-and-one-half. At this point, the entire group, which has by now taken on the dimensions of a primary group, is combined with two additional primary groups into a nursery school class. During school hours, the children are under the supervision of a trained nursery school teacher. Outside of school and hours of contact with parents, each constituent group is under the care of another *M'tapelet*, one with special training in dealing not only with emotional, social, and developmental needs of the children, but with their cognitive growth as well.

We might point out that there are two approaches to preschool education in the kibbutz. In one system, three different age levels are combined within a single framework, i.e., twenty children in the range of ages three to six. Elementary school as a separate institution in this system starts at the second grade. Another approach involves homogeneous age-groups in three separate frameworks: a nursery school, a kindergarten, and a first grade with many preschool elements remaining.

A second framework for preschool education consists of a large number of private nursery schools, maintained solely through parent support. These schools are attended primarily by children of middle-class families, generally of European or American origin. There is little uniformity to the level at which these nurseries operate, since some are run by less than qualified teachers, and the supervision of the Ministry of Education is fairly loose. There are no accurate figures available on attendance in these nursery schools, although a conservative estimate would place sixty to seventy percent of the children on the particular population segment involved in these schools.

A third framework is the child care centers run by the central labor union (Histadrut) and private welfare agencies whose purpose is to aid the working mother or families on welfare and in need of special help. These centers accept children throughout the entire range of preschool education. In cases where there are sufficient numbers, a formal nursery school and kindergarten are established, under the supervision of the Ministry of Education and Culture.

Approximately ten years ago, the Ministry, in cooperation with local municipalities, began to set up a system of nursery schools for the children of new immigrants from Islamic countries of origin. This system has grown rapidly and today includes upwards of sixty percent of children from this population sector. Attendance in these schools is tuition-free, but not compulsory. All the teachers in these institutions are specially trained and under the supervision of the Ministry. Many of the teachers are young women in military service, especially assigned to this work. As implied above, children of ages of six to eight are taught in elementary school. However, we will consider this age range as well since the approach of the Ministry of Education is to perceive this group as being uniquely different from the rest of the elementary school age groups. This approach is reflected in teacher training: teacher's seminaries provide specialized instruction for grade one and two. It is also seen in curriculum construction, teacher guidance and inservice training. The latter is particularly true for those children designated as "culturally disadvantaged," since the Ministry has in recent years established a special institute for the problems of this population which we discuss later in more detail. We round out this part of the report by mentioning the system of teacher training for preschool and elementary education. Teacher training is carried out in special two or three year institutions that are similar to the American normal school. Admission to these institutions requires completion of an academic high school (similar to English Grammar school). In order to be trained as a nursery or kindergarten teacher, students are sometimes admitted after completing nonacademic high schools or occasionally after only three instead of four years of high school. These training institutions generally include three separate courses of study: one to prepare nursery and kindergarten teachers, a second for the teaching of the first two or three grades, and a third for the remaining grades.

II. Pedagogical Trends and Curricula

During the period of the Mandate, the tradition of the European kindergarten—a synthesis of the approaches of Froebel, Montessori, and Decroli—prevailed in preschool circles. An exception to this picture was the preschool education developed by the Kibbutz movement which was heavily influenced by psychoanalytic and paedocentric theories of Central European origin. As a result, preschool education in the Kibbutz focused on spontaneous activity and play as a means to catharsis, sublimation, and creativity, with a primary interest in emotional growth and social development. With the establishment of the State, a number of close cultural links were forged with the United States, as a result of which the influence of progressive education began to be felt in pedagogical circles. This made its mark on early childhood education, particularly its preschool aspects—more than anywhere else. As a result, the kindergartens throughout the country more and more began to resemble those of the Kibbutz movement. Didactic materials and directive instruction gradually disappeared in favor of spontaneous activity and free play. However, by the end of the 1950's, a gradual revision began to take place that saw a reemphasis on intellectual development and stimulation. In many respects, this development was being simultaneously reflected in many other countries, and can be seen as part of the educational *Zeitgeist* to which, of course, many factors contributed. Two factors, however, are worth mentioning: A) the problem of the culturally and socially disadvantaged, and B) new ideas in developmental psychology.

A. *The Problem of the Disadvantaged.*

When the State of Israel was established in 1948, there were living within its borders, besides 150,000 Arabs, approximately 600,000 Jews of primarily European origin. Within a period of less than ten years, there was an influx of close to 1,500,000 immigrants, comprised largely of families with many children from Islamic countries. The language spoken at home was, of course, not the language of Israel, most of the mothers were illiterate, while the literacy of many of the fathers consisted mainly of being able to read a prayer book. Thus was created in Israeli education a problem almost unknown to that time—the problem of the disadvantaged pupil. In comparison with other countries, the problem in Israel rapidly became more acute as such pupils currently constitute sixty percent of all preschoolers, while neither the parents nor the children spoke the prevailing language of the country.

It became quickly evident that since such children come to the elementary school seriously deficient in language and cognitive development, the task of preschool education is to provide training in just these areas. The problem of the disadvantaged also resulted in basic changes throughout the entire school system, both with respect to curriculum and methods of instruction. From the point of view of scope and organization, we need to emphasize two important facts: one, the inclusion of younger ages, and two, the establishment of an institute for the disadvantaged in the Ministry of Education. The task of the latter is to designate which schools are in need of special care and to devote special attention to the latter through special curricula, equipment, and appropriate textbooks. The most important function of the Institute, however, is intensive inservice training and preparation of teachers for those schools chosen to receive special attention. The impact of these developments on curriculum, particularly in the preschool area, is reflected in an emphasis on the upgrading of linguistic skills, the development of intellectual abilities, basic concept formation, and the imparting of basic information. Interestingly, many of the older structured didactic materials have now been brought back, new materials have been introduced and well-defined curricula have been developed in the areas of language, mathematics, natural and social sciences.

B. New Ideas in
Developmental Psychology.

The second factor that led to important changes in the preschool areas was the influx of new developments in psychology, particularly the notions of Piaget and his followers. A central idea that rapidly gained prominence was that in order for all children—not only the disadvantaged—to move from a level of infantile, intuitive intellectual functioning to a more abstract and logical way of thought, free play and spontaneous activity may not be enough, even for the more able. Education should provide the child with more structured materials and activities which can help accelerate the growth of logical operations and the development of basic concepts in various areas of knowledge, such as numbers, space, time, etc.

At the present time, there are two major educational trends in nursery schools and kindergartens in Israel, one labelled the intensive, the other, the directive method of instruction. The directive approach (which currently is to be found in a relatively small number of institutions) maintains that at least where the disadvantaged are concerned, the major, if not the sole aim of preschool education should be a combination of intellectual stimulation, language development, and the acquisition of information. This can best be done, from this point of view, completely through the use of structured materials, absolutely scheduled curricula, work with groups of children on predetermined tasks, habituating the child to persevere on a given task to which he has committed himself even if there is a waning of interest, and a great deal of teacher intervention into precisely those activities which up until now have been considered the private realm of the child, i.e., spontaneous play with toys and materials, and dramatic role-play.

The "intensive" approach, on the other hand, which is representative of most of the preschool institutions in Israel, attempts to arrive at a synthesis of the major elements of both directive and progressive approaches. Thus, three-quarters of the time in nursery schools and fifty percent of the time in kindergartens are still devoted to spontaneous and creative activity. The remaining time is utilized for semi-directive instruction. The adult's intervention is less-defined, less formal, and less binding than in the directive approach. Interventions are carried out either individually or in small groups, instead of gathering all children together for a formal learning task. Nevertheless, there is not a complete rejection of structured activity for larger groups or the entire class; one can find story-reading sessions, or discussions on various topics.

Until now we have discussed trends in curricula and methods of instruction at the preschool level. We turn to a consideration of these areas in the context of the first two grades of elementary school. Before the large immigration we spoke of previously, education in these grades was shaped by ideas from Gestalt psychology, the German-Austrian approach to topic-centered instruction, and the Dewey-Kilpatrick project methods. Some expressions of this approach were to be seen in the global method of reading instruction, and the centering of all subjects around topics of functional significance and immediate interest.

However, this approach, shaped as it was through the experience of teachers with children of a predominantly rich culturally background, did not prove appropriate to the needs of the disadvantaged. While there was widespread difficulty in all grades and subjects, the most prominent failure was in reading skills and arithmetic which showed up at the very beginning of school. By the end of the first grade, sixty to seventy percent of those children defined as disadvantaged did not acquire reading skills, while results in arithmetic were not much better. As might be expected, the failure in learning became progressively worse the longer the child remained in school, a phenomenon which Deutsch in the U.S. has termed "cumulative deficit."

These facts forced both the Ministry and the schools of education at Israel's universities to take drastic institutional and programmatic steps in the middle 1950's. We will briefly describe the most important steps taken that are still in existence today:

a. Reading instruction

The global method of instruction was dropped in favor of purely phonetic methods, or some combination of the global and phonetic. Some far reaching changes have also been introduced in instructional technique. Although all techniques strongly emphasize the acquisition of basic reading skills, they differ with respect to their relative emphasis on the importance of content during skill acquisition.

b. Textbooks

The Ministry of Education and Culture provided scholarships to a number of experienced teachers which enabled them to attend special courses at the Hebrew University. They were given training in the writing and preparation of textbooks in language and other subjects suitable for the culturally deprived. While this activity embraced all age levels, special emphasis was placed on the early grades.

c. Remedial instruction

Children in any grade who demonstrate difficulties in language or arithmetic are placed in special classes for these subjects. Each such remedial class consists of no more than eighteen children, while the teachers for these classes receive special training and supervision (one supervisor for twelve teachers). At any given time, the teacher works only with six or seven children, while the others in the class are given individual work assignments. Children admitted to these classes must be within a fairly normal range of intelligence, and in no case below seventy-five. Pupils may remain in such classes anywhere from six months to two years. If there is no progress during this period of time, he may be transferred to a special education institution. Experience shows that approximately sixty percent of children admitted to these classes return to their regular class after one year's remedial instruction. The Ministry has developed a number of tests which help select children for these classes, as well as help decide at what point they may return to their regular studies. At the present time, this system embraces only a small number of classes, in spite of its effectiveness.

d. Tutorial groups

Within each school designated as in need of special care, teachers in every class are allotted and paid for an additional three hours per week to provide tutorial instruction for children who are experiencing difficulties in their studies, particularly language and arithmetic. This is done in all schools where remedial instruction as described above is not feasible.

e. Extended school day

Over twenty percent of all elementary school classes (close to sixty percent of classes in schools designated as disadvantaged) have an extended school day. This is defined as eight additional hours of instruction per week devoted to remedial teaching, social activities and special interest groups. At one time this activity was also carried out in first grade, although for various reasons, it did not demonstrate its usefulness at this level. Currently, the extended school day begins in the second grade.

f. Institute for master teachers

Some ten years ago, the center for the disadvantaged in the Ministry established an institute for the training of teachers in specially designated schools who teach in grades one through three. This currently involves the training of seventy-five percent of all teachers of grades one through three in these schools. In this institute, a number of specially qualified teachers have been relieved of their regular teaching tasks and trained to guide and supervise other teachers, both individually and in groups, for work with the disadvantaged. The master teachers themselves are under the constant supervision and guidance of the Ministry, and attend regular study courses given by Hebrew University faculty members.

The institute also is charged with continuously following up and revising the program of studies in the early grades, publishing work books for the pupils as well as accompanying teacher's handbooks. In the near future, the Ministry plans to add to the Institute's functions the development of similar activities in kindergarten classes, and eventually, perhaps nursery schools as well.

g. Institute for
mathematics instruction

Under the influence of the "New Math" in the United States, as well as an extensive study of mathematics instruction with young children conducted by the Hebrew University, the Ministry of Education established an institute to foster the instruction of mathematics in the elementary school. A wide-ranging revision is currently being undertaken in the direction of emphasizing the development of mathematical thinking instead of mere skill acquisition. The scope of mathematical subject matter has been considerably widened, particularly in grades one and two. This is true of those schools designated as disadvantaged, but even more so in the regular schools. New text books are continuously being prepared and revised. We might point out that the "New Math" is represented by several different methods, some of them structured, others more environmental in approach. For each method, there is a separate group of master teachers (not connected to the institute for master teachers) who supervise teachers, both individually and in group in the new methods. Generally speaking, all the various methods emphasize the "spiral curriculum," the promotion of abstract thought and the formation of basic concepts through material manipulation, and the use of the "discovery method."

It should be clear from this presentation that a great many different kinds of activities are simultaneously being carried out in preschool and elementary grades. The amount and kind of evaluation being done varies from one activity to another which makes it difficult to obtain a clear picture as to the relative contribution of each method. The activity that has received the most extensive evaluation is reading, and here, the findings are quite clear, and highly encouraging. As we mentioned before, at one time sixty to seventy percent of disadvantaged children completed first grade without acquiring reading skills (among "normal" children, the figure was twenty-five). Today, only twenty-five percent of the disadvantaged and twelve percent of the "advantaged" are deficient in reading at the end of first grade. Since there are several opportunities for remedial instruction beyond first grade, the number of children so deficient is gradually diminishing. At the beginning of the 1950's, thirty to fifty percent of disadvantaged children completing the sixth grade were unable to read a third or fourth year text. Conservatively speaking, this figure has today been reduced to less than ten percent.

III. Educational Research

While the universities in Israel are engaged in educational research activities, sponsored either by the government and/or foreign funds, the Ministry also sponsors a special institute for educational research—the Szold Foundation. We will limit our discussion only to those studies conducted either by the universities or the Szold Foundation which have made some substantial impact on early childhood education, or those which are currently underway and are likely to make such an impact.

A. *Studies in Direct Effort*
to Promote Intellectual
Development in Preschool
Children.

Since the 1950's, a series of studies has been directed by Dr. Sara Smilanski (of the Szold Foundation), the major proponent of the directive approach mentioned above. The purpose of these studies was to explore the content and methods of promoting language, abstract thinking and concept formation in disadvantaged children of kindergarten and nursery school age. One of these studies (recently published in book form by Wiley) focused on the attempt to foster sociodramatic play in disadvantaged children of ages three to six—a type of play, according to the investigator, quite rare with these children and often even nonexistent. Through the medium of teaching the children how to engage in role-play, the investigator tried to achieve linguistic enrichment, to impart basic information about various social activities, and to develop the ability to symbolize experience. Dr. Smilanski is currently investigating the relative effects of developing reading readiness, including in some cases actual teaching of reading at the kindergarten level, followed or not followed by supportive instruction in the first two elementary grades. Approximately sixty classes of children who were taught reading skills in kindergarten are now in first grade where they continue to receive special attention. A number of additional kindergarten classes are now being taught, taking into account the experience already gained from the former groups. The philosophy that underlies these experiments has three important aspects. One, early introduction to reading may improve the child's symbolizing processes. Two, spreading the instruction of reading over a longer period of time may enable the very slow learners to achieve an optimal level of reading by the second grade. And three, the earlier a disadvantaged child learns to read, the more he will perhaps be able to acquire information that the "advantaged" child obtains from verbal interaction with his parents even before he is able to read.

B. *Diagnostic Tests*

In addition to standard intelligence tests (adapted from American tests or specifically constructed in Israel), the Ministry and universities have in recent years, begun to develop diagnostic tools for assessing readiness and achievement in young children in various areas of knowledge. Two examples will suffice. One is a readiness test for mathematical thinking based primarily on Piaget's ideas, which was standardized on a thousand children about to enter school in each of two populations —disadvantaged and "normal." A second is a revision and adaptation of the Caldwell inventory, constructed in the U.S.A. as part of the Headstart evaluation, which assesses language development, social behavior, and cognitive skills.

C. Heterogeneous Classes

The problem of integrating both advantaged and disadvantaged children within a single school framework, a problem evidently quite acute in many developed countries with heterogeneous populations, also exists in Israel. The difficulties that accompany such a problem are less of an ethnic nature, however, than they are issues of interclass relationships and educational methodology. Because of the egalitarian nature of Israeli society, as well as its special cultural and political circumstances, it is within the realm of possibility to overcome cultural and class differences and achieve gradual school integration. As a matter of fact, in those places where geography is not a factor, integration is gradually becoming more of a rule than an exception. Moreover, the upper grades of elementary school and the high schools in Israel are currently undergoing a drastic reform, one of the major purposes of which is to accelerate integration. Overt public opinion is generally unanimous in accepting the fact that integration is a social and cultural necessity. There is, however, some questioning among teachers and parents as to how to best accomplish integration without causing educational harm to both pupil populations. This involves such questions as: what is the best age to begin integrated education and what should be the proportion of students in each classroom, etc.

The elementary school is the place where integration is progressing at a rapid pace. Many difficulties are daily being encountered to which a number of different solutions are being supplied. One solution is the use of a grouping system from the sixth grade on in three subjects: mathematics, Hebrew, and a foreign language. Such a solution is not acceptable in Israel at younger age levels, so that other approaches have to be found. In preschool education, integration is relatively rare both for reasons of physical distance between neighborhoods (a more decisive factor at very young ages) and because the educational authorities are somewhat fearful of the possible negative educational results for all involved. This dilemma stimulated Dr. Dina Feitelson of the Hebrew University to put the issue of integration to an experimental test. She set up an intensive enrichment program for a number of nursery schools. Some of them consisted of only disadvantaged children, while others were composed of one third disadvantaged and two thirds highly gifted "advantaged" children. The research program is still not completed; tentative results, however, seem to indicate progress in the cognitive area in both types of nursery school, with no significant advantage to either type. We might also point out two more findings of interest in this study. In the homogeneous classes, a great deal of effort must be expended to raise the level of aspiration of the *teachers* so as to convince them that the children are capable of far greater achievement than in regular nursery school settings. In the heterogeneous classes, on the other hand, the major problem is that there is little social interaction between the two groups of children. The investigator is currently involved in exploring various approaches to overcome this problem.

D. Fostering Creativity
in the Disadvantaged

Dr. Feitelson is also engaged in another study which seeks to teach three and four year old disadvantaged children who do not attend nursery schools, how to engage in play activity. The children involved in the research come from severely disadvantaged families that usually have many children. Her observations on the children indicated that they rarely, if ever, engage in play, but spend most of their time running around aimlessly. Like Dr. Smilanski, Dr. Feitelson believes that disadvantaged children should be stimulated to learn how to play, and that the acquisition of play skills will contribute to cognitive development and growth of symbolization processes. The difference between the two is that Dr. Feitelson deals with a somewhat younger age, and instruction is done individually and through the medium of modelling rather than directive teaching. The actual play is based not only on previous experience, but is aided by structured and unstructured materials. A major purpose is to aid in the development of creative, divergent thinking.

E. Arithmetic Instruction
in the First and Second Grades.

In a study conducted at the Hebrew University, several problems in mathematics instruction were explored in one hundred classes of both advantaged and disadvantaged children. The study followed the same children through the second and third grades as well. Among the problems investigated were the efficiency of the spiral curriculum, the optimal range of subject matter, the possibility of overcoming initial deficiencies in readiness through appropriate methods of instruction, and the relative merits of the structural versus the environmental methods of instruction. Some of the findings from partial data analysis indicate that: the range of subject matter that advantaged children can assimilate by proper methods of instruction is much greater than previously held; the same holds true for the disadvantaged, although to a lesser extent; in contrasting the structural versus environmental approaches, there is little or no difference in effectiveness for the advantaged child, whereas for the disadvantaged child, extremes of either approach are less efficient than some combination of the two; and, when the curriculum and method of instruction are arranged so that the teacher, under systematic guidance, learns how to work slowly, patiently and gradually to habituate the pupils at first within a limited amount of subject matter to acquire basic concepts and principles through the manipulation of appropriate materials and through the method of discovery, it is possible to raise most disadvantaged children to a level of functioning in mathematical thinking higher than that of the advantaged child who has not had such special instruction.

F. Improving the Verbal Interaction Skills of Mothers of Disadvantaged Children

In light of the widely accepted belief that the primary factor in the later deficiencies of the disadvantaged child is the impoverished linguistic experience he receives at home, and the corollary belief that such experience may be crucial for intellectual development at a very early age, Dr. Gina Ortar of the Hebrew University is attempting to test these hypotheses more systematically and explore remedial methods. After a series of observations on the interactions among disadvantaged and advantaged mothers and their one and three year old children, Dr. Ortar became convinced that the major difference between the two groups of mothers was not so much a question of the amount of verbal interaction, as in its quality. Operationally, the most useful ways of dimensionalizing "quality" in her opinion were: length of mother's sentences; the use of proper connectives and prepositions; explanation of new difficult or ambiguous words; diverse and exact reflection of the situation about which verbal interaction takes place; and reflection to the child of internal states.

In assuming that defects in the quality of verbal interaction can be remedied through proper instruction, Dr. Ortar selected 120 disadvantaged mothers of both one and three year old children. The mothers are exposed to lectures, small group discussions and demonstrations utilizing slides accompanied by a taped example of proper and improper verbal interaction. In addition, half the mothers receive individual guidance by trained instructors who visit the home once or twice a week. One of the principles of this study is to avoid having the mothers feel inferior or guilty. Lecturers and instructors constantly emphasize that the education that the mothers are already giving their children is valuable and appropriate, with the only deficiency being that of verbal interaction which can be easily remedied. If the results of this research will indicate that such instruction of mothers is useful, the Ministry of Education will be favorably inclined towards turning it into a nationwide program.

G. Training Disadvantaged Nonprofessionals for Work in Education

Dr. Abraham Tannenbaum of Teacher's College, Columbia University, and currently a visiting professor at the Hebrew University, along with several other faculty members of the School of Education, is developing a demonstration project similar to one he carried out originally in New York City. It involves the training of parents and other adults from the disadvantaged community to provide tutorial and other assistance to children both in the classroom and at home.

We should point out that to the extent that the methods involved in the latter two research projects are adopted by the Ministry of Education for promoting the educational advancement of disadvantaged children, there is potentially a large manpower resource for their implementation—young women, ages eighteen to twenty, fulfilling their military service obligation in the Israeli army. Many of these young women have been active in educational activities of various kinds since the establishment of the state. Up until this past year, for example, the army maintained several teachers' seminaries where the young women received a concentrated course in education and were then sent out to newly established immigrant settlements where they served their military duty as teachers in elementary and nursery schools, or in the instruction of illiterate adults.

IV. Future Perspectives

As mentioned before, we are currently in the midst of a radical reform of the Israeli school system. The seventh and eighth grades are being separated from the elementary school to constitute, together with the first year of high school, a new educational unit which will exist either as an autonomous institution or as part of a larger, more comprehensive high school. Following on the heels of this development, the Ministry of Education is already beginning to sketch the outlines of a parallel reform in elementary education. The broad shape of the plan is as follows: preschool education will consist only of nursery schools (ages three to four). Kindergarten will become an integral part of the elementary school which will then consist of seven grades with an age range of five to eleven. Although geographically and administratively, this new institution will be a single unit, it will be composed of two subunits, the first three and the last four grades. From the point of view of educational atmosphere, curriculum and methods of instruction in the lower unit will be a combination of selected characteristics of the kindergarten and elementary school. In some respects, this subunit will resemble the British infant school, with the difference being that it will terminate one year later than in the latter.

The rationale for this new structure is three-fold. For one, the transition from the permissive atmosphere of the kindergarten to the structured demands of elementary school which in Israel is a rather abrupt one, can be made more gradual. This may help avoid untoward side-effects that take place with many children. Secondly, this will avoid many overlaps in programming which currently exist between the kindergarten and first grade. The impression of the educational authorities is that the current trend to increase intellectual content in the preschool years may become extreme if kindergartens remain as separate institutions. Combining them into an elementary school subunit may allow for the proper balancing of directive educational practice with opportunities for spontaneous and creative activity. Finally, the new structure can help avoid many of the excesses of reliance on books and teacher-centered verbal instruction at an inappropriately young age that frequently leads to empty "verbalism" and role learning. As a major source of information and learning, books begin to be appropriate, in the opinion of the planners, at the beginning of third grade. In the second grade, a more appropriate method for imparting knowledge and concept formation is to provide the child with concrete situations in which he can be active and engage in the manipulation of various structured and unstructured materials.

We emphasize again that these ideas for possible elementary school reform are highly tentative, may undergo considerable change over time, or even be put off for a long while. It is clear that the line of thinking evident in these plans stands somewhat in contradiction to current practice and policy, particularly that concerned with the rehabilitation of the disadvantaged at the early childhood level. For this in many ways typifies the problem of our times — on the one hand, a strong nostalgia for the progressive emphasis on freedom, spontaneity, and creativity which seems to wane from year to year, while on the other hand, the urgent necessity to train young people for the demands of a highly technological world and to bring the greatest number up to a level of maximal functioning. Unfortunately, educational and developmental psychology are not always helpful in solving this dilemma since findings in these fields can be used to reinforce either one approach or the other. (11)

Summary

Programs for young children have now proliferated in many countries. Paradoxically this century has brought with it much violence and turbulence; yet it has also lived up to its advance billing, *the century of the child.* Gone is the assumption that a child under the age of seven is taught at home by his parents who will show him whatever he needs to know.

References to Part 5

1.   Braun, Samuel J., "Nursery Education for Disadvantaged Children: An Historical Review," in *Montessori in Perspective,* ed. Lucile Perryman (Washington, D.C.: National Association for the Education of Young Children, 1966), pp. 7-24. Reproduced with permission. Copyright © 1966, National Association for the Education of Young Children, 1834 Connecticut Ave., N.W., Washington, D.C. 20009.

2. Fischer, Dorothy Canfield, *A Montessori Mother* (New York: Henry Holt & Co., 1912).

3. Greenwood, Rt. Hon. Arthur, "All Children Are Mine," Inaugural Margaret McMillan Lecture, mimeographed, Bradford, England, 1950.

4. Hunt, J. McVicker, "Revisiting Montessori: Introduction," in *The Montessori Method* (New York: Schocken Books, 1964), pp. xiii–xiv.

5. Itard, Jean, *The Wild Boy of Aveyron*, trans. George and Murial Humphrey (New York: Appleton-Century-Crofts, 1962).

6. Kilpatrick, W. H., *The Montessori System Examined* (Boston: Houghton-Mifflin Co., 1914), p. 66.

7. Mayer, Martin, "Schools, Slums, and Montessori," *Commentary*, June 1964, pp. 36–39. Reprinted by permission of Curtis Brown, Ltd. Copyright © 1964 by Martin Mayer.

8. McMillan, Margaret, *Education through the Imagination* (London: Swan Sonenschein, 1904), p. 76.

9. _____, *The Nursery School* (New York: E. P. Dutton and Co., 1919).

10. _____, *What the Open Air Nursery School Is* (London: The Labour Party, 1924), p. 3.

11. Minkovitch, Abraham, "Early Childhood Education in Israel," mimeographed, 1968.

12. Montessori, Maria, *The Montessori Method: Scientific Pedagogy as Applied to Child Education in "The Children's Houses" with Additions and Revisions by the Author*, trans. Anne E. George (New York: Frederick A. Stokes, 1912).

13. Rambusch, Nancy McCormick, *Learning How to Learn: An American Approach to Montessori* (Baltimore: Helicon Press, 1967).

14. Seguin, Edouard, *Idiocy: And Its Treatment by Physiological Method* (New York: Teachers College, Columbia University, 1907).

part 6

America in the
Twentieth Century

Though the Progressive Education Association did not survive the 1940's, the progressive viewpoint has been woven into the fabric of American education. In as diverse ways as the teaching of science in pre- and elementary schools, the typically American emphasis on tests and measures, the design of modern classrooms with flexible seating and the teacher's desk (if she has one) somewhere other than dead-center-in-front, progressive education has had a permanent, ongoing effect on the schools and teachers of the country, even though the pattern may have become a bit blurred with time. Progressive education is still very much with us, and so are the conservative trends as manifested by the emphasis on perpetuating the skills, knowledge, and values of the past. While these two positions are necessarily inimical, they are often complementary.

The twentieth century, therefore, marked no abrupt break with the tendencies that had gone before. The concern for social issues and the search for greater freedom and creativity, hallmarks of the progressivism of the 1890's, continued into the 1900's and flourished in the following decades, while conservatives continued to struggle for the values they held to be essential.

At the present time, both progressive and conservative attitudes have changed from those of the first half of the century. The impact of two world wars, the Depression, the cold war, the war in Southeast Asia, civil rights has altered educational approaches. As our national concerns have shifted, new issues, new needs, and new groups of children have come to the forefront.

Pioneers in the Field During the Early 1920's

When early childhood education tentatively began in the United States, there were only a handful of people who had had any experience in the field. Their backgrounds were diverse and unique, spanning many disciplines. Few knew one another; their interest in the preschooler sprouted quite independently, encouraged by the writings of Montessori and McMillan. When they did meet one another, it was often by accident. A formal meeting was called in 1925, when Patty Smith Hill invited twenty-five representatives to meet at Columbia Teachers College.

She selected the people to come to that meeting in N.Y.C. with great care, going over and over the list. She did not want a great big organization which would propagandize the idea of nursery schools before there were teachers adequately trained to conduct them. Actually, she thought the idea of having a nursery school organization at all was somewhat precipitate. She only called it because a "lay person" was bent to do something and Patty Hill wanted to have a finger (or a whole hand!) in directing the course. (25)

The group she brought together became the nucleus of the National Committee on Nursery Schools (1926), the forerunner of the National Association for Nursery Education (now the National Association for the Education of Young Children). The National Association for Nursery Education was formed in 1929 through a merging of early childhood educators on the west coast with the National Committee.

Of the early pioneers, Patty Smith Hill was most closely allied with the field of education, an elder statesman for the nursery school. Known as a strong advocate of progressive education in the kindergarten, she taught at Columbia Teachers College and helped to initiate a laboratory nursery school there in 1921, for which a nursery school teacher was brought from England. (23) However, this was not the first such school in New York City; in 1919, a nurse named Harriet Johnson established one in the City and Country School sponsored by the Bureau of Educational Experiments (later called Bank Street). "From the beginning the experiment was guided less by the past history of educational procedures and routines, than by certain fundamental scientific fact and principles out of which methods could be evolved and by which they could be judged." The "facts of growth and development" were considered the "best guide" to "educational procedure." (18)

The Merrill-Palmer Institute in Detroit was begun in 1922 by a home economist, Edna Noble White, who wrote:

The primary reason for the maintenance of our Nursery School is that we may have a laboratory for training young women in child care.... These students are sent to us by various institutions, receiving full credit for the work they do at the institution from which they come. The students carry a course with Mrs. Wooley in Child Care and Management, and do eight hours of laboratory work a week in the school. They carry a course in Child Health and Nutrition, and do laboratory work from that angle with the nursery school children, and in connection with the course in Social Problems relating to children in the home, they do a very limited amount of home visiting under supervision.... We feel that such courses should be made a part of the training of every young woman since they come in contact with children in many capacities — mothers, teachers, social workers, etc. (28)

In the same year Abigail Eliot, a social worker, began the Ruggles Street Nursery School in Boston. Miss White and Miss Eliot had met in 1921 while both were in England studying nursery schools. The influence of McMillan's philosophy on early childhood education in America was obviously considerable. Although Montessori's work was known here earlier, she did not enjoy so great an impact. The Child Education Foundation in New York City was organized to apply Montessori's teachings to the education of parents, young children, and prospective teachers. Eva McLin, its director, opened the first nursery school, a Montessori school, in 1915. The only other recorded nursery school in the United States in 1915 seems to have been a cooperative initiated by a group of faculty wives at the University of Chicago. (23)

Although it played no part in the organization of European nursery schools, interest in child development research was the motivation behind opening some such schools here. The preschool laboratory of the Iowa Child Welfare Research Station at the University of Iowa was such an example. Dr. Bird Baldwin began the six room "lab" in 1921 so that he might observe the same group of young children daily for a period of several years. "The children are occupied with a very simple, flexible schedule of singing, games, stories, rhythmic exercises and simple occupational projects. A graduate assistant keeps a detailed log book of observations made on the children and notes interesting reaction and the conditions under which new abilities develop." (8)

However, the name most closely associated with research and the young child was Arnold Gesell, a physician and former student of G. Stanley Hall. Even before he began collecting normative data on children at Yale, Gesell was calling attention to the intricacies of a child's sequential, unfolding development—the very expression and recapitulation of man's evolutionary history. While we today may criticize his tendency to view child development as only or wholly maturational, his writings helped teachers to concentrate on the child rather than pedagogical lessons. The following is from an early writing: "The primary child is in the expressive language period of development, and every opportunity for expression should be open to him. If we limit him to a line of a certain kind, or to blocked-out squares, or certain prescribed subjects, his drawings will become rigid, wooden, cramped, and expressionless. Give him a mood, something to say, something to illustrate; give him large undemarcated spaces, like the blackboard, so his expression may be full and free. He will flinch at nothing, and with fine abandon he will make the chalk tell his experience, even though they may be as complicated as a circus parade. Froebel would make the human figure the last aim; with the child it is the very first, for his interests and not his capacities determine what he will draw." (13)

Gesell spoke with conviction and force about the importance of the early years of life:

... The preschool period is biologically the most important period in the development of an individual for the simple but sufficient reason that *it comes first*. Coming first in a dynamic sequence, it inevitably influences all subsequent development.... (12:2) This remarkable velocity of mental development parallels the equal velocity of physical growth during these early years.

The character of this mental development is by no means purely or preeminently intellectual. Almost from the beginning it is social, emotional, moral and denotes the organization of a personality.... (12:7-8)

Man is neurologically a bundle of neuron patterns and psychologically a bundle of habit complexes and conditioned reflexes. The patterns and complexes which are first formed have a remarkable tendency to persist, particularly those which are highly colored emotionally and closely knit to instinctive tendencies. (12:9)

Embracing the new science of child study and interest in early childhood education, Lois Meek Stolz became an influential force by articulating the goals of both to an educated public. She left Columbia Teachers College and Miss Hill in 1924 to assume the newly created position of education secretary of the American Association of University Women. A seven-year matching grant with the Laura Spelman Rockefeller Fund had been negotiated just a year before to encourage the public to study the education of children, especially the preschooler and his relationship to his young mother. (26) Her office in Washington became a clearinghouse for information. She organized study topics for discussion, reading, and observation, as well as visiting extensively throughout the country. One notes her enthusiasm for the work in 1926: "... part of a large social movement in child study. . . . There has been phenomenal growth in the past three years in attention paid to the preschool period. . . . Education for parenthood has invaded the undergraduate work of universities." (19:17-18) However, it is well to remember that a list compiled in 1924 showed no more than twenty-eight nursery schools in eleven states. (23:137)

Abigail Eliot and
Ruggles Street

What influenced Abigail Eliot in Boston was a typical experience in America during the 1920's. Unlike her colleagues, however, she was more closely linked to the movement begun in England with a disadvantaged population and less toward child development research in a laboratory nursery school. The Woman's Education Association, which sponsored her early work, was founded in 1872 "for the purpose of promoting the better education of women." In its remarkable fifty-seven year history, it helped found Radcliffe College, the Marine Biological Laboratory in Woods Hole, Massachusetts, the Boston Children's Museum, and with Miss Eliot, the Ruggles Street Nursery School and Training Center. The organization had previously established a school in 1915 in cooperation with the Montessori Society. However, insufficient funds made it impossible to continue. (7) The nursery committee of the Woman's

Education Association headed by Mrs. Henry G. Pearson, who had sponsored the teacher, was also not enthusiastic about the efficacy of what they saw happening in the school. (13)

Later Margaret McMillan's work became known to this same committee which then raised money to send Miss Eliot, a trained social worker, to study for six months with Miss McMillan in 1921. The Ruggles Street Day Nursery, situated in a low income neighborhood in Boston, became, on her return in January of 1922, the Ruggles Street Nursery School. Its former purpose was that of group day care with no educational program at all; physical protection, sterile cleanliness, orderliness, and obedience had been stressed. The program, as devised by Miss Eliot, is well described in the report of the Ruggles Street Nursery School and Training Center (May 1924).

from **Report of the**
Ruggles Street Nursery
School and Training Center

[The main playroom contained low tables and chairs, blackboards, blossoming plants on low window sills, an aquarium containing goldfish, a sand box, packing box, boxes of "mighty blocks," piano and low shelves.] In the toilet rooms beyond low sinks containing basins with low faucets and low soap containers; the mirrors are low, and so are the hooks for towels, combs, cups, tooth brushes, each marked with a child's name and a small distinguishing picture. Upstairs two large sleeping rooms are full of little beds, mostly of the folding variety for use out-of-doors in good weather; each child has his own bed and blanket sleeping bag. [The yard is complete with flower garden, pool and sandbox.] What do they do all day? During the hour when they are arriving, there is in attendance every day a nurse from the Community Health Association who inspects each child for symptoms of contagious disease. She also talks with the mothers about health problems, and the mothers in turn consult her; she helps teach the children health habits. The steadily growing group of children plays about, each as he chooses, until the nurse is ready to wind up with a unanimous gargle of salt and water — a fascinating noise truly! The next half hour is spent partly in the kindergarten "circle," but chiefly in music, rhythm work, songs, dramatic games, and "the band." Preparations follow for the mid-morning lunch, — preparations all quite in the children's charge, from hand-washing to placing of tables and chairs, passing the cups and napkins, pouring milk and handing round crackers. Clearing up afterwards is also done by the children, in turn day by day: they wash and wipe the cups, clear the table, sweep the floor.

Next follows a period of "quiet" occupations at tables or on the floor. With a little wise guidance perhaps, each child selects what he wants from a special closet containing a variety of material — certain of the kindergarten gifts, some of the Montessori apparatus, and some of Miss McMillan's; also chalk, scissors, paste, plasticine, hammers and nails, and several kinds of blocks.

In this work he is guided as little as possible and is limited only in two ways: he must make a genuine attempt to use what he has taken, and he must put away one thing before taking another. Sometimes a child will remain busily engaged with one occupation for as much as three-quarters of an hour; another may in the same length of time try his hand at three different things. Often the older children like to be gathered in a group to work out some simple "project." In due season, everyone is seen putting away his occupation and, if it is an out-of-doors day, lugging his chair within and perhaps replacing it by some of the big playthings shown in the pictures, for this is the period of active play recorded in some of the best illustrations.

Dinner hour is approaching. The company swarms again into the toilet rooms and with immense pride and zest prepares itself, with an elaborate washing of faces and hands, combing of hair, drinking of water, and tying on of bibs. Even more than the luncheon, dinner gives scope for amazing baby achievements — patience in waiting, skill in passing, courtesy in giving and receiving — and all with perfect decorum yet perfect content.

Dinner over, they brush their teeth and clamber gaily upstairs, or trot out under the trees, take off their shoes, crawl into their bags, and sleep. After nearly two hours of sleep or quiet resting, they get up happy and fresh and are ready for a drink of orange juice and a romp or stories or games before going home.

Educational Aspects

Education begins at birth. Much that many people think of as inherited is learned in the earliest years. These years are the most fruitful time for teaching, since a little child learns at a greater speed than he ever will again, and the early associations have a permanence which none formed in later life can rival. Psychologists say that the fundamental bases of character and personality are established during this period when the brain is growing. Mental hygienists are finding that the roots of mental and nervous disorders lie in maladjustments formed at the beginning of life.

Educationally all this may be called "habit." In the early years habits are easily formed, and these habits may be kept all through life. Habits of manner, behavior, interest, attitude have their foundation in the response of the little child to his environment. So the education of the nursery school children is guidance into good habits. Such education can be accomplished only by studying the children individually, by discovering what habits should be changed or developed. The schools herein described aim to create an environment in which self-control, self-development, and self-expression are encouraged, and to let the children live in it. Freedom within law, self-dependence, orderliness, love of beauty is the standard set. (24)

The school was loosely affiliated with the Harvard Graduate School of Education, and Professor George E. Johnson acted as its educational advisor. One of his contributions was directed toward helping the school keep adequate records on each child. The following list was presented in greater detail in the 1924 report: 1) Control of Body, 2) Control of Matter [a statement attributed to Miss McMillan is offered in explanation: "... a two year old is primarily a physicist, discovering and learning to control the physical world"], 3) Speech, 4) Use of Senses, 5) Emotions, 6) Higher Mental Powers—curiosity, memory, imagination, reason, will, 7) Moral and Social Habits—self-assertion, pugnacity, sociability, ownership, nurture, worship.

Dr. Douglas Thom, a child psychiatrist, whom Miss Eliot met fortuitously in England two years previously, took great interest in the preschool child, his family, and the Ruggles Street Nursery School. As a psychiatrist during World War I, he had seen a number of soldiers suffer nervous breakdowns. Convinced that their cause could be traced to early childhood experiences, he embarked on a career in mental hygiene, a then burgeoning movement. His Habit Clinic, like the Judge Baker Guidance Center established earlier for the study of individual delinquents, was one of the first child guidance centers. The Habit Clinic, however, handled younger behavior problem children and their families. Thom also helped to organize the Play School for Habit Training in the North End of Boston in 1922 as a supplement to one of the Habit Clinics—the first experiment in using special nursery schools to treat preschoolers with behavior problems. (23) Many children in his care also attended Ruggles Street Nursery. The school not only followed his "direction" but helped and encouraged mothers to do so at home as well.

Although Margaret McMillan was skeptical of working with parents, Miss Eliot did not share her mentor's pessimism. Abigail Eliot's background in social work made work with parents a very natural part of her concept of the job of the early childhood educator. The profession from which she came, however, looked upon the Ruggles Street experiment with concern; were the children enrolled "guinea pigs?"

A similar reaction came from many of the primary educators who thought the nursery school was frought with serious dangers: the children were too young to be away from home and too susceptible to diseases. Lucy Wheelock was such a person. Founder of Wheelock College, she was one generation older than Miss Eliot, but one generation younger than the original Froebelian founders of the kindergarten. When she invited Miss Eliot to give a course about the nursery school to her students, it was several years after Ruggles Street and the Boston Nursery Training School had been established, and even then she was doubtful. While it was acceptable that her students know about nursery schools, there was no expectation they would start one; it was not practical and certainly not proven.

Yet, among middle-class parents there was interest and enthusiasm for early childhood education. A group of mothers formed a cooperative, the Cambridge Nursery School, one year after Ruggles Street, with guidance from Miss Eliot. They reported quite similar procedures and responses of the children. The Cambridge children "may come less able to take care of themselves and more self-conscious. But here, (as at Ruggles Street), they soon lose themselves in the common joy of using their powers of companionship, of service. And on the average they carry through the 'quiet occupations,' handle the big, active sports, act out nursery rhymes ... (and other activities) neither better nor worse than the Ruggles Street group." (24) Cooperative nursery schools, similar to the Cambridge Nursery School, were responsible for swelling the ranks to 262 schools by 1930. (2)

An educational philosophy for the Ruggles Street Nursery Training School of Boston did not fully emerge until 1944. The following were called "Fundamental Principles":

1) Children are persons.
2) Education should always be thought of as guidance (teaching) which influences the development of persons (personalities).
3) Maturing and learning must go hand in hand in the process of development.
4) It is important that personalities be well balanced. Therefore in guiding children, we should aim to help them develop balancing traits at the same time that we try to supply what they need for self-realization. Some of the balancing traits are:
     security and growing independence
     self-expression and self-control
     awareness of self and social awareness
     growth in freedom and growth in responsibility
     opportunity to create and ability to conform (21)

Underlying these "principles" was an abiding interest in and respect for the relationship between teacher and child. Lawrence Frank, in addition to his other contributions, emphasized the warmth of a teacher-child relationship as the single most important factor in a child's learning process. He opposed Watson's behaviorism which tended to develop teachers to stand apart from the child, attempting to manipulate the environment and watch children absorb knowledge. Abigail Eliot still shudders as she recalls the remark of one such teacher: "My ambition is to conduct my school so that I never have to touch a child." (3)

Lawrence Frank and
The Child Study Movement

University-based research in early childhood education and child development was stimulated by the efforts of one remarkable man, Lawrence Frank. His accomplishments were made through the administration of the Laura Spelman Rockefeller Fund. Known as the "midwife of projects in early childhood," he was a matter of curiosity to his fellow citizens in the early 1920's. He often spoke of the incredulity of the public at the very idea of early childhood education and told with delight of his overhearing people say of him in the elevator of his office building: "Can you imagine? He's interested in little children. He gives money away to people that study them!" (11)

Lawrence Frank recounted those days in a 1961 lecture at Merrill-Palmer Institute in Detroit, "The Beginnings of Child Development and Family Life Education in the Twentieth Century." He was very much a part of the early research; he shared the touch-and-go challenge of a new idea and struggled to make it survive. Some of his comments on the directions taken in child development are typical of his continual probing and questioning.

from **The Beginnings**
of Child Development and
Family Life Education
in the Twentieth Century

Lawrence Frank

. . . In 1923, the Laura Spelman Rockefeller Memorial, a new foundation, decided to support the fields of child study and parent education, making five-year grants to universities, which were later renewed and

From Lawrence Frank, "The Beginnings of Child Development and Family Life Education," *Merrill-Palmer Quarterly*, copyright 1962, by permission of Merrill-Palmer Institute.

enlarged, providing many fellowships to train research personnel and parent educators and supporting the National Research Council Committee on Child Development and also the National Council on Parent Education. Thus, over a period of years, the Memorial, which ceased operation in 1930, and the General Education Board, provided many millions to foster child development as a growing enterprise, through the leadership of the many individuals who entered this new field and gave it a definition and place in the scientific community. Later, the Josiah Macy, Jr. Foundation, on a smaller scale with limited resources, aided the studies of child personality development, especially at Sarah Lawrence College under Lois Murphy and Eugene Lerner, and at Vassar under Mary Fisher Langmuir, Joseph Stone, and others, where the new euthenics program with a nursery school had been recently started. . . .

As in almost every new field of investigation, the initial focus was upon collection of data and their statistical manipulation to establish correlations of variables and chronological age norms for structural, functional, behavioral, and intellectual growth and development, approached as more or less separate and unrelated events. Only later did students of child development begin to consider the intra-individual relations and intra-organic variability as contrasted with inter-individual comparisons and variations among children.

The increase in courses in child development in colleges and universities evoked many text books on child development which reflected the conception of child development that has largely prevailed over the years. These texts usually provide a succession of chapters — one on each principal topic such as physical growth, motor development, language development, intellectual development, social development, and other well-defined aspects of child development. Each chapter cites a selected list of the many published studies on that topic, giving an evaluation and interpretation of them, and then goes on to the next topic. Accordingly, those reading a text book on child development may never realize that each of the changes described in these different chapters occurs concurrently in every child, at different rates and magnitudes so that the norms quoted are rarely attributable to any single, identified child. This, of course, is recognized by child development specialists, but may be confusing to young students and parents, who are seeking to learn about children, and find only a series of discrete findings on different samples of children who have been observed or measured for one or more dimensions, but otherwise are unknown. In other words, much of the material presented under the general title of child development consists of a large number of cross-sectional studies which have used children as subjects for sources of data to study the problems of a discipline or of its specialized branches, and then, so to speak, have thrown the child away as no longer of interest. This is an entirely legitimate procedure, indeed, the preferred if not essential approach by which individual investigators can contribute to their discipline and win acceptance and promotion. It is not unfair, however, to say that these various scientific artifacts offer limited understanding of child development as an ongrowing process occurring in an identified child, who exhibits all of these dimensions in his own idiosyncratic fashion.

Two departures from the standard text book pattern should be noted. First are the publications by Gesell, who described the characteristic patterns of successive age groups in children and later adolescents. These were often criticized because they were not based on formal, statistical studies, but were largely clinical summations based on Gesell's observations of children in these different age groups. Second, and more recently, Joseph Stone and Joseph Church published their *Childhood and Adolescence, A Psychology of the Growing Person*, as a serial or longitudinal presentation of child development.... (9:14-16)

The term "child development" is now widely accepted, but we still lack a conceptual formulation that will embrace the development of the child from fertilization to old age, and recognize his multidimensionality, his persistence while changing. We are hindered in this, I believe, by the assumptions and techniques that are valid — indeed, indispensible — in the various disciplines, but are neither relevant nor adequate to the study of a multidimensional process such as development. The symposium at Minnesota a few years ago, published as *The Concept of Development*, indicates that we cannot easily free ourselves from these long-accepted and highly fruitful approaches of our analytic, scientific procedures.

Thus, as indicated, children have been repeatedly studied by different disciplines, although rarely do they focus on the same children. Each uses a child as the source of data for the specific problem he wishes to investigate, just as they have used rats or fruit flies as so many "anonymous units." The investigator is only rarely concerned with further information about children, except for purposes of describing his sample, according to age and sex composition, and sometimes the socio-economic class to which they belong. This approach may be regarded as reifying data, that is, making an observation of measurement into entity, and then relating that entity to other entities on a time, space and energy scale.

About 1800, the natural philosophers of that period had made many careful observations and numerous measurements of heat, light, electricity and magnetism, but they reified these observations into entities — heat was a substance; electricity, a fluid; light, a corpuscle; and, for each of these entities, a special theory was constructed. The unification of the physical sciences began, when it was realized that these supposed substances were different expressions of fundamental energy transformations and transmission, for which a single unified concept could be formulated to replace the variety of special *ad hoc* explanations. In the field of child growth and development we await a similar unification, which will come, when we recognize the organism-personality as a persistent but ever-changing configuration, which reveals, through these changing dimensions and functional activities, its essential unity, exhibited by the interrelations of all his structure-functions and his behavior. . . .

We might say, that we have been primarily concerned with snapshots — that is, the observation and measurement of a child at one moment of time — as contrasted with moving pictures, which record the sequence of changes occurring in an identified child as he grows and develops. Years ago, Woodger, in England, remarked that anatomy had focused on the cadaver as offering fruitful opportunities for study of the non-functioning organism in "timeless space"; it might be said, that many studies of children and youth are conducted in "spaceless time," insofar as the observations and measurements ignore the context in which they occur. Only recently have we begun to recognize how often the observer is in the picture, and that his observations may significantly alter the behavior he is attempting to study. . . . (9: 18-21)

A letter* from Erik Erikson to Larry Frank on the occasion of his 75th birthday captures the relationship he fostered among his colleagues in the child development field:

Once upon a time there was a wide-eyed young immigrant who regularly got cinders in his eyes when visiting New York. In that very condition he attended a meeting one day and sat beside a rosy, alert and amused-looking older man. The man, as if he had been waiting to be of help to somebody, guided him to a corner and deftly removed the cinder. Having done this, it seemed natural to him that he should also invite the stranger to drop in on him when in New Hampshire. His name sounded like Frank.

A few weeks later the young man and his wife were indeed, driving through New Hampshire. Noticing a sign "ASHLAND," they looked up Mr. Frank's telephone number and were promptly invited for dinner. After that it seemed quite natural to Mr. Frank to ask the couple to stay for the night—so natural, in fact, that they stayed for a week. Larry even sent for their children. After that it was surprising that the host found it natural also to arrange for a research position for the young man, so he could develop some notions he had. Thus started a friendship typical for Larry: a complete blend of the personal and the professional, of the intellectual and what can only be called joyful — a combination which has nurtured the work of the many who were likewise understood and encouraged by this rare man. (6)

Work Projects Administration

By 1933 there were 1700 nursery schools. The Work Projects Administration in Washington had endorsed a plan to employ

---

*By permission of Erik H. Erikson.

school teachers out of work and "to combat physical and mental handicaps being imposed upon young children by conditions incident to current economic and social difficulties" caused by the depression. (4)

Lois Meek Stolz had suggested the plan to Harry Hopkins, but insisted there be money for supervision. Begun in churches, cellars, any place there was space, almost any unemployed educated person was encouraged to become an early childhood educator. When news of this plan broke, the National Association for Nursery Education was holding a conference in Toronto. The membership was aghast lest the standards drop in the early childhood education movement in this country. They need not have feared; the Association took an active role in supervising the new personnel, joining with the Association for Childhood Education and the National Council on Parent Education in forming an "advisory committee to assist the Washington Office in developing needed guides, records, studies and field services." (1) The task was a huge one. Although federal funds had been authorized, the major responsibility was left to "state agencies and local groups, most of which had little or no knowledge of what was required, nor experience in organizing such activities." (9:26) Hastily arranged training sessions had to be started, and considerable effort was expended in reaching even out-of-the-way parts of the country. Abigail Eliot supervised the New England region, no small feat. She recalls advising state administrators to set at least one firm standard: "Don't take two-year-olds!" An earlier experience with two-year-olds in the McMillan nursery school influenced this remark; on a pea-soup foggy day, she had been left to reassure and to comfort thirty-two tearful two-year-olds whom she could not even see. Lawrence Frank assesses the W.P.A. nursery school movement:

Within a remarkably short period of time, the emergency nursery schools and parent education programs were operating all over the country, involving the participation of many individuals and using the premises and facilities of various organizations to house the nursery schools and provide for parent meetings. Looking back, and seeing all the limitations and often exasperating delays, handicaps, and resistance to programs, we can say that, nevertheless, something of great significance was achieved. Through this emergency program, nursery schools which had been limited in numbers and were but slightly known by the public generally, became widely recognized and were generally accepted all over the country. Likewise, parent education programs were started in many states and communities where they are still operating on a permanent basis. Moreover, the experience gained in this emergency program provided a basis for the further enlargement of nursery schools and day care centers in World War II, when so many nursery schools were established to assist mothers working in war industries or on local jobs, while their husbands were in the Army and Navy. Again, federal funds were made available to the local communities in which settlement houses, churches and other agencies provided space for nursery schools and for parent education meetings. . . . (9:27)

The greatest impact was undoubtedly the popularization of the nursery school movement. The "profession" had also helped to train many individuals who were unacquainted with early child-hood education. At the end of the second year a survey was taken of the 3,775 teachers employed. Only 158 had had previous nursery school experience; 290, kindergarten experience. 64.42 percent had previously taught. (5) An optimism developed about what was possible. A new role was assumed for early childhood education, psychology, anthropology.

A brave new world was being awakened through all the efforts of the early childhood educators. They shared a hope that the gen-eration they would educate under their ideal plans never before implemented would become a sort of angelic band: well-adjusted, free to be creative and expressive, happy, tolerant, and peaceful. Children so educated could realize any splendid future, better than the past had been. Frank expressed this pervasive, vital hope for the influence of the preschool in his 1937 speech, *The Fundamental Needs of the Child:* (Excerpts from this article appear in the Appendix.)

The nursery school, in close and cooperative relationship with the home and parents, is the primary agency for mental hygiene. The op-portunity in preschool education to build wholesome, sane, cooperative, and mature personalities, and to determine the future of our culture, is unlimited. The discharge of that responsibility lies in helping the young child to meet the persistent life tasks and to fulfill his insistent needs. (10:378)

Self-realization, personal growth, social adjustment were the key phrases. Freud's ideas were beginning to make themselves felt in America. Such concepts as infant sexuality, the unconscious, the effects of repression, the lifelong potency of physical drives shocked and frightened many people in an America where the Puritan ethic had perhaps gone underground but had never disappeared. To the more sophisticated and intellectual members, Freudian concepts came with the force of revelation. (19) Preschools would be an in-strument whereby the new generation of children, emerging rela-tively unscathed from their permissive and loving homes, would grow toward a full and free maturity never before seen. In some schools and for some teachers, early childhood education and psychiatry became fused.

The classroom experience was considered basic to emotional and social stability. Little was mentioned about teaching information to small children in school. The question of the intellectual content would have received disdainful comment that some old-fashioned types completely misunderstood what education for the young child was all about. Social, emotional, and physical growth were acceptable, but the fourth side of the square, intellectual growth, was temporarily erased from the concern of many preschool teachers.

Play's the Thing

This attitude had its roots in the thinking of Dewey and his followers, as well as Freudian tenet. Dewey and G. Stanley Hall would say, "the brain is handmade." They meant that a human being's capacity to think is based on his physical, manual, and manipulative experiences. Hence, the emphasis on handwork in the Dewey Laboratory School and in progressive schools while words were considered secondary; they had no meaning for children unless they followed tangible, first hand experiences. As though a child's mind were a larva in a cocoon, it might well sleep undisturbed while other aspects of the child's life were strengthened; the thinking creature would eventually emerge the better for having lain quiescent. Every approach to teaching has its myths which illustrate its ideal approach. For the Deweyites the apocryphal child who never picked up a book or learned a letter until he was ten, then painlessly and promptly commenced his reading career on *Moby Dick* expressed their ideal credo.*

---

*Cognitive psychologists today are not in agreement with this Dewey-Hall viewpoint, but not in total disagreement either. The difference is in the timing. Everyone, at least everyone who accepts Piaget's ideas about the sensory-motor period, believes that in young human beings a nonverbal, nonsymbolic period when all learning is physical does indeed come first. But presently it is believed that this period in the child's life covers only the first eighteen months to two years. By twenty-four months the normal child is spontaneously learning words, and symbolic processes are becoming of essential importance to his inner life. The linguists tell us now that the time when a child naturally becomes aware of the rules of language and begins teaching himself syntax is between the ages of two and three. Tangible experience, of course, is necessary, but so is symbolic; each variety interacts with and strengthens the other. Progressives wanted to wait too long. Years after children were using language, ready to benefit from language they were still being kept from it. We no longer believe it sinful to offer cognitive experiences in the preschool. Many of the progressives, however, did think sin and early instruction of a cognitive nature were synonymous.

"Attitudes are caught, not taught." This adage may well express the dilemma of a teacher faced with a desire to give cognitive instruction to the preschoolers in her class. There was an inherent difficulty in trying to plan a curriculum around emotional climate or mental health. Teachers of this persuasion were left with a large hole, almost coterminous with the length of their school day, which had to be filled somehow. *Play* was how they filled it. "In the early days of the nursery school movement, such phrases as good play environment, appropriate play experiences, free play, dramatic play, group play, parallel and solitary play, social play, quiet play, play materials, etc., comprised much of the . . . teacher's professional vocabulary," comments Eveline Omwake. (22:584) Play was the child's work; it was his means for solving problems, setting tasks for himself to complete, and interacting empathetically with his classmates.

There is nothing the matter with play. Indeed, it will always be a vital component of a child's life. It could not alone carry the total burden of a young child's education. For middle-class children who came to school verbal, curious, well-organized by the "hidden" curriculum inherent in their home life, play worked out very well. An environment rich in materials, children with whom to play and a caring teacher, provided the basis for the nursery school experience. Concept development, speech and motor coordination naturally unfolded through the children's play, which was fostered in such a setting. But when lower-class children arrived on the scene, "Just play, dear," was not specific enough for classroom functioning.

Play has been considered the crux of the preschool experience for much of this century. If this belief is held no longer, an important heritage has been left. However, Piaget's emphasis on the relationship between learning and children's play has kindled a renewed respect for, and interest in, play as an important aspect of the curriculum. Omwake speaks sympathetically to this position, ". . . play as a perceptual-motor experience . . . [whose] affective and cognitive elements appear in crude form in the play of the very young child, but gradually are refined to become the problem-solving activities and concepts later associated with more formal learning experiences." (22:578) The art of teaching is accordingly related to an understanding of play, individual differences, play materials, and when and how to intervene. She concludes: "Children's attitudes toward self-initiated, unstructured play are seen to differ from those of adults, in that children view it as a major work and derive their pleasure from the mastery as well as the creativity it represents. Adults may erroneously consider play of this sort as requiring less mental activity than the imposed intellectual task." (22:594)

To suggest that there were no goals in American preschool education for much of the twentieth century beyond mental health or play, is to oversimplify. Of course there were diverse aims. Schools for young children were set up in many different environments as more or less integral parts of many different institutions, in each case, the larger purpose affecting the functioning of the nursery school. In 1932, the United States Office of Education published a comprehensive study of the growth and status of nursery schools which offers a picture of the several forms they had already assumed. Brief sketches though these are, they, nonetheless, indicate how education for young children was adapted to a variety of settings and built into therapeutic, social welfare, and professional training programs as well as those which were concerned only with the education of young children. Mary Dabney Davis, who played an influential role at the Office of Education for the nursery school movement, compiled the program descriptions. The selections below are confined to the nursery school and its role in secondary education.

A Nursery School Laboratory for High-school Students

Ira M. Allen and Alice R. Nallin

The nursery school in the Highland Park schools was organized as a laboratory for high-school classes in child care. While the nursery school has this purpose as its main objective it is of direct benefit to the children enrolled and directly and indirectly acts as a training center for parents. It is also used as an observation center by students from other high schools, by kindergarten and primary-grade teachers within the Highland Park school system, and by students from the Merrill-Palmer School. The school is financed by the board of education, but a fee is charged to cover the cost of the food served.

The school is housed in what was a private residence. It is a three-story building with a wing on one side which is used as an open-air sleeping room. There is adequate floor space, cupboard, and locker space, as well as toilet facilities.

There is a large playground with plenty of open space. The equipment, apparatus, and play material is of the sort that aids in the development

From Mary Dabney Davis and Rowna Hansen, *Nursery Schools: Their Development and Current Practices in the United States* (Washington, D.C.: U.S. Office of Education, 1932).

of large and fine muscles, gives sensori-motor experience and is adapted to the dramatic and constructive play of the child.

Records kept, in addition to nap, feeding, and bowel records, are the general previous history of the child, the physical health history, the psychological record, attendance, and causes for absence. At the end of each year and at the termination of a child's nursery-school experience a report is made to the parents of the personality and habit traits of the child, of changes effected during attendance at nursery school and recommendations for further guidance. The psychological tests, physical records, and personality and habit reports are sent on to the principal of the school which the child enters on leaving the nursery school. Meetings and conferences between kindergarten and nursery-school teachers help to integrate the program for the children.

Sixteen children are enrolled regularly and in addition to this we have three children whom we consider as substitutes to take the places of children absent for any period of time. The children come from homes of varying social and economic backgrounds. This fall the youngest child taken into the nursery school was nineteen months old, while the oldest was four years and four months. We find it best to have some in each age group, but more in the middle group rather than the extremes at the upper or lower level. . . .

A justification of the practical work offered in child care was expressed by junior college girls and their parents in response to an inquiry. This inquiry was made to help determine where best to make certain necessary curtailments in the school budget. Questions addressed to the students inquired whether they would elect an additional course in child care if it were offered either with or without credit and whether they had learned anything through taking the course which they would not have learned otherwise. A third of the forty-four students replying to the inquiry said that they would elect an additional course in child care if it were offered either with or without credit. Approximately three-fourths of the students declared that they had gained information in the high-school course which they would not have learned elsewhere. Explanations of the replies indicate that nearly every girl values the course because she is an only child or because there are no children of nursery-school age in the family. In listing the most valuable features of the course the students emphasized chiefly the opportunities offered for practical experiences with children which vitalized the courses in theory and which threw into relief the need for beginning life with adequate habits and attitudes.

Questions addressed to the parents of the students and a summary of the replies received from fifty-three parents follow:

1) Do you believe the course in child care an essential part of your daughter's education?

Yes, 46. No, 3. Good but not essential, 4.

2) Did your daughter learn anything in the child-care course that she would not have learned at home?

Yes, 49. No, 4.

3) Has the course in child care changed your daughter's attitude toward children?

Yes, 26. No, 24. Uncertain, 3.

4) Check the phrase which to your way of thinking most clearly describes the child-care course.

Most important, 21. Very important, 15. Important, 13. Of little importance, 4. Of no importance, 0.

5) Do you think this course should be compulsory or elective?

Compulsory, 41. Elective, 12.

Explanations for each reply were solicited. For the positive replies of question 1, explanations centered around the essential need of preparation for a parental career. One mother said "I believe every girl is a potential mother and scientific child care should be a part of her education." (2:69, 71-73)

A similar program in the junior high school of the Winnetka public school system was directed by Rose Alschuler:

The nursery school acts as a laboratory for junior high school girls and boys, for teachers in training, and for faculty members of the Winnetka schools. Seventh and eighth grade girls come in and observe the children, work directly with them in some of the more simple situations, and help with luncheon preparations. Seventh and eighth grade boys have built various pieces of equipment for the nursery school, including a tree house, horizontal bars, and small screens to be placed around the beds. Regular discussions are held with the girls in an effort to develop in them better understanding and greater appreciation of family life. It is hoped that this course will soon be given to the boys also. Such subjects as family life in other countries and communities, foods for little children, behavior problems, and such immediate problems in their own lives as attitude toward authority and relationships to brothers and sisters are discussed. This phase of the work of the nursery schools is still in its incipiency. It is being developed in connection with a junior high school course on family life, which supplements and makes practical some phases of the course in biology and human reproduction. In occasional instances on recommendation of the department of education counsel, girls unable to adjust to regular school routine have been sent to the nursery school for special work. Here they have found themselves in this quite different environment which is evidently more suited to them. (2:79)

A richly descriptive monograph by Washburn describes the Yale Guidance Nursery from 1929 to 1936. (27) Founded in 1926 by Dr. Gesell the "school" was used as an adjunct to the Yale Psycho Clinic for children with emotional problems and other handicaps. Forty such children were added periodically to a core group of four normal children over the period of one school year. The major

emphasis of staff work was concerned with making diagnostic evaluation of each child and working with his parents. The operation
of the nursery school, as such, was relegated to listing briefly the
advantages and expectations that such a program could provide for
children.

The mothers were encouraged to observe their children at play
in the nursery school prior to seeing the psychologist, when they
could discuss their feelings relating to their children and child-
rearing practices. They could note what was age appropriate for a
child and how the teacher handled different situations. In brief,
the mothers' workers said: "We cannot tell you just what to do in
any situation. We can show you what we do to help the child eat
his dinner, take his rest, stop sucking his thumb. We can tell you
the reasons we behave as we do and possibly you can learn something that will be useful to you." As the program was perceived,
parent work was clearly the more important aspect. Gesell and his
collaborators give a narrative account of one of the cases.

from **The Guidance Nursery**
of the Yale Psycho-Clinic

Arnold Gesell et al.

Richard L., aged nineteen months, was brought to us by his father on
suggestion of the family physician because of irregularity in eating, slow
progress in talking, and some difficulty in general discipline. The developmental examination made at the time of the first visit indicated that
the boy was of better than average intelligence, yet he showed a very
poor quality of attention even for his age. Speech was a little retarded,
but the conversational quality of his jargon indicated that there was only
a slight delay in this field, and that, once the regular use of words had
begun, conversational ability would be likely to advance rapidly.

On the side of personality Richard appeared a cheerful, attractive
child, responsive, and showing a good quality of interest even though it
was not maintained for any great length of time in a single field. Separation from his father in the Guidance Nursery brought out a little initial
timidity and one or two brief recurrences which were overcome by the
guidance worker without much difficulty. As a result of the first visit it
was decided a) that no special effort need be made to bring on the
development of language since this would probably be aided by the
normal social contacts in the clinic, b) that contact with other children
would be an advantage and that after one or two more visits by himself
he should come into a small group of other children not too much above

From "Preschool and Parental Education," *Twenty-Eighth Yearbook of
the National Society for the Study of Education*, 1929.

his own age, c) that on an early visit he should be served a luncheon with one or more other children and that his attitude towards eating should be observed at that time, d) that the sort of behavior reported was probably the result of unwise home training and of forcing situations, such as feeding at the wrong time, and that this should be the first line of approach in making suggestions to the mother.

On the second visit he was brought by his mother; the initial response indicated a strong dependence upon her presence. He screamed violently when she started to leave after bringing him to the nursery. Her departure was accordingly delayed a few minutes to improve his adjustment. He began to cry when she eventually left him, and although this first crying was soon overcome, there were no further recurrences, and there was no repetition of the incident on later visits. The importance of not permitting too strong a habit of dependency to be formed was pointed out to the mother, who was showing the best possible attitude of cooperation in carrying out our suggestions in the home.

One or two experimental feedings in the guidance nursery with the mother watching from the observation alcove brought out no violent responses of the sort reported in the home. Some things Richard would feed himself, others he would accept when they were fed to him, but there was no negative response to the food itself. A visit to the home during the lunch hour brought out clearly the difference between the response there and at the clinic. As a spoonful of food was presented to him, he shook his head, said "No, No," and put his hands in his mouth. The mother held his head back and forced the food into his mouth, which brought about stiffening and screaming. The food was finally swallowed, but the scene was repeated with each mouthful, so that after even a very small amount of food had been eaten, the child was in a highly tense and excited condition. This attempt of the mother to force the feeding was the result of a misinterpretation of her doctor's instructions. A conference between the guidance worker and the family physician straightened out this point, so that she realized that such forcing to get him to eat was not necessary. It was felt that much of the difficulty was due to the fact that the child became hungry somewhat earlier than his regular lunch hour and that by the time his food was actually ready his hunger had largely disappeared. Lunches given in the clinic at an early hour have seemed to confirm this idea, and it has been recommended that the set hour be changed to correct this situation. Recent visits have shown, as we expected, a very marked improvement in talking, with frequent use of words in combination and even short sentences. The repeated observations have enabled us to make an analysis of the feeding problem and to make suggestions which we are confident will bring about improvement, for the difficulty has already become less marked. The overdependence upon the presence of the mother which the child was beginning to show has been checked and seems unlikely to recur. The repeated conferences with the mother, who has proved to be most intelligently cooperative, have given her a clearer understanding of methods of training and renewed confidence in her ability to apply satisfactory methods. (23:169-171)

World War II and Day Care

The advent of war required women to work outside their homes, which meant arrangements had to be made for the care of their small children. Under the Lanham Act, which provided federal funds until 1946 for child care, many centers were built and staffed by professionals as well as volunteers who considered their long hours as their contribution to the war effort. In some cases, industry also provided care for the children of employees. The needs were immediate and essential: food, rest, shelter, and a substitute mother figure while Mummy packed parachutes or worked a lathe. There were large numbers of children, and group care for long stretches was commonly needed. Occasionally the centers were well equipped, but often the staff made do with minimal play materials, minimal furniture, and minimal skill. Yet, the mother knew her children were safe. Teachers were too harried to focus beyond the pragmatic; concern for the child's emotional adjustment and self-fulfillment did not disappear as goals as much as lose precedence to the crucial reality of every day: "Did all the children get fed? Any contagious diseases today? Are they finally settled down to rest? What on earth has happened to Johnny's left shoe?"

Outstanding among the child care centers run by wartime industry were those in the two Kaiser shipyards, Swan Island and Oregonship, in Portland, Oregon. No need of the shipbuilding families was seen as irrelevant to the centers, making them a model of comprehensiveness. James L. Hymes, Jr. was director of the Child Service Department, Kaiser Company, Inc. He gives an actual account of it in this brief article:

The Kaiser Answer: Child Service Centers

James L. Hymes, Jr.

What happens to young children while mothers work at war jobs? There are many answers, some good, some bad. This is the story of the Kaiser answer — a dramatic, cooperative solution in which a great shipbuilding industry, government, war-working parents and educators have collaborated.

James Hymes, "The Kaiser Answer: Child Service Centers," *Progressive Education.* Copyright 1944, by permission of the author.

The story is laid in Portland, Oregon. Here there are two giant Kaiser shipyards, Swan Island and Oregonship. At the entrance to each yard there is a new building — low-lying, surrounded by lawn and shrubbery, modern in design. This is the Yard's Child Service Center. It is a building planned and designed just for young children.

Part One of the Kaiser answer . . .

. . . is that industry, which needs the labor of women, must shoulder responsibility for the children of these women. The creation of the Child Service Centers was the idea of Edgar F. Kaiser — young son of Henry J. Kaiser — and of his foremen and superintendents from the two yards. The actual construction was financed by the U. S. Maritime Commission. Although parents pay their fair share for tuition, much of the operating cost of the Centers is borne by the two Kaiser Companies.

Part Two of the Kaiser answer . . .

. . . is to put the nursery school plumb on the parents' route — mother, father and Johnny come to "work" together with no detours, no extra stops, no waste of gasoline, steps or energy. If nursery schools are to serve the children of those who work, they must be located where work is.

The Child Service Centers are only five minutes from the ways where Liberty ships, tankers, and now the new Victory Ships are sliding into the Willamette. At shift change time, hundreds of cars and buses pass each Center carrying workers to and from their jobs. For busy parents this location is a convenience; for them it is a straight line from home, to the Center, to the ways.

Part Three of the Kaiser answer . . .

. . . is to provide facilities that have eye-appeal, for this is the threshold to a parent's confidence in a school.

The Centers have been thoughtfully — yes, and tastefully — built. They are wheel-shaped. The hub, protected from all sides, is a grassy play court partitioned so that each age level has its own ample space. The spokes are fifteen play rooms, each with long banks of windows on two exposures. Play rooms, smaller auxiliary rooms and hallways are colorful tints of green, blue, yellow and apricot. In each room and in the out-of-door play space there is excellent nursery school equipment. The total effect is a beautiful building.

Although the Centers are on shipyard property, and although they are intermeshed in many ways with shipyard operations (in finance, publicity, and for many materials and supplies), the operation of the Centers has been fully entrusted to people experienced in nursery education. Because this is an experimental venture, many outstanding teachers and supervisors have been willing to come to Portland. It is in their hands that the working out of the plan rests. And this, too, is a planned part of the Kaiser answer: To recruit the specialists, the best that can be found, and then give them *carte blanche* — freedom to plan and to do as their knowledge of child growth dictates.

But perhaps the concept most basic to the Kaiser answer is indicated by the name. These are good nursery schools, but they are more: They are Child *Service* Centers. The premise is that if a shipyard family needs help involving children, the Centers should provide that help. No peacetime precept, no *a priori* rule must stand in the way of service to children, to families. The flexibility, the trying-out, the adventuring, the adjusting to needs that this means for teachers and for a school can best be seen through examples:

The Child Service Centers must be open twenty-four hours a day, as one illustration. The first children in the morning come at 6:15 A.M.; this is the day shift. But the last children of a day come at 1:00 A.M. the following morning; this is graveyard shift. Mothers and fathers, shipbuilders, need competent help with their children no matter on what shift they labor.

Those children who come at 6:15 in the morning have a hot breakfast. They also have a mid-morning juice, cod liver oil, a hot noon meal, and mid-afternoon food, usually milk, a sandwich and a fruit slice. Not infrequently a parent must work overtime and the child then stays on for supper, too. How much food should a Child Service Center serve? As much as each child needs during his stay at the Center.

Most children stay at the Center during the shift on which their parent works. Suppose, however, that parents who work during the day must attend a union meeting at night, or need one evening to battle Portland's crowds for shopping. Or suppose that tired parents want just one night to go off by themselves — for dinner out or for a movie. Can a child now and again stay through for two shifts, from 6:15 in the morning until midnight? In a Child Service Center the answer is "yes."

Meet Gary Newsom

Most children enroll in the Center on a weekly basis. But think of Gary Newsom, four years old. Gary arrived with his parents one morning at 9:30 A.M. His family had just come to Portland from North Dakota. The car was loaded with bags; Gary was tired, dirty and hungry. Could Gary stay at the Center for a few hours while Mr. Newsom found a job in the shipyard and while Mrs. Newsom found a house for the family to live in?

Gary entered the Center's Special Service Room, a play group set apart always ready to receive children for temporary care whenever a shipyard family faces an emergency. Gary was given breakfast; he had a bath in one of the four specially-designed children's tubs, of which the Center is very proud; he then went to sleep until lunch time. Mid-afternoon, the Newsoms phoned. It was taking longer to clear with the

Union, to find the right job, and most of all to find a home. Could Gary stay longer? Gary stayed until 10:00 in the evening, when his father, now on the payroll, awakened him to take him to the defense home the Newsoms had found. The Special Service Room in each Center sees many such emergencies. The teachers are adept at planning day's programs to meet many individual children's needs, different though these programs may be from what has always been "the nursery school day."

Meet the Taylors

Most children, of course, follow a regular nursery school day and are in one of the age-level groups. But there are many Newsoms...and many Mr. Taylors. Mr. Taylor is a welder and a widower. He has three children and he had a housekeeper. When Mr. Taylor came to the Center his oldest child was well and strong; she could and did go right into a five-year-old group. The younger two, however, were pale, listless and very irritable. The Head Nurse saw them and recommended that they stay in the Center's Infirmary until the doctor could examine them. In the infirmary each had his own hospital crib in a glass-partitioned isolation cubicle. These two children stayed in the Infirmary for three weeks each day on day shift. The nurses gave them simple treatment under doctor's orders to clear up minor ear infections. When they were well, one went into a two-year-old group, one into the fours.

The Infirmary, of course, is used primarily for the care of children who become ill during the day and for the isolation of those who ought not to be with their regular groups. If labor is needed to win this war, the nursery school cannot say to mother or father, "Don't build ships today; take Johnny home because he has a runny nose." It is up to the Center to have facilities and staff to care for even mildly ill children.

The Infirmary recently has taken on a new and important function. With workers coming from every state in the union, living in defense homes, the immunization of children against whooping cough, smallpox and diphtheria is particularly important. But in war-crowded communities, doctors schedule appointments weeks ahead; too many public health clinics are still open nine to five, when parents must be building ships. To meet this situation, the Infirmary staff at each Center, under the doctor's supervision, is administering immunization against these diseases.

New demands

The Child Service Centers were planned for the nursery school age, but parents' needs have pushed the Centers to explore new avenues of service. Both Centers, for example, have groups of 18-month-olds. The teachers of these groups are pioneering in the adapting of what they know about the guidance and education of the "nursery age" to younger children.

Requests have come also for the care of older children. Billy, five, stays at the Center on graveyard shift. May his sister, Mary, stay too? She is eight. Unless the family can leave both children, enrolling Billy alone at the Center does not solve the problem. The answer here is "yes"; both Centers are enrolling older children for the sleeping shifts, if there is a younger one whom the Center was primarily set up to serve.

There are other requests: Many shipyard workers have children in the elementary school. Could a program be arranged for them on Saturdays? The public schools have tried, but some parents feel more secure on a Saturday to bring their school-age children to "work" with them and to leave them at the Center. Many boys and girls, too, feel freer about coming to a building that is club-roomish in atmosphere with no academic taint. The Centers now have flourishing school-age groups on Saturdays, offering a recreational program of arts, crafts, music, dramatics and games that school-agers seem to enjoy thoroughly.

The Centers, of course, cannot care for all ages. There are many requests for the care of infants and of children under 18 months; there are also many situations where twenty-four hour care seems the appropriate answer. The Centers, set up for group living, cannot meet these needs. Parents, however, are not turned away with a flat "no." Each Center has on its staff a Family Consultant, an experienced social worker thoroughly familiar with the resources of the Portland community. It is this staff member's job to help the parent get in touch with the appropriate community family service agency so that he gets the aid he needs.

Obviously, each time the Center extends its services for children, mothers benefit. But war-working women have other roles — as wives and homemakers — to which a Child Service Center can also contribute. The Center's Home Service Food is one example here. Each night any worker in the yard may buy at the Center precooked food for the family's supper. Home Service Food is usually a man-sized meat dish and a dessert, planned by the Center's nutritionist, cooked in the Center's kitchen, attractively packaged and with full directions for reheating and for supplementary salads and vegetables to make a full dinner. The help that this service is to the working mother can easily be imagined. It saves strength that would have to go into shopping, and hours that would be needed for cooking, to say nothing of the advantage of having a specialist plan meals for the family. But think also of how this service aids Mr. Taylor, the widower mentioned above, or Mr. Samson, a foreman who works on day shift but whose wife works on swing. Until Home Service Food began, Mr. Samson had been cooking supper for himself and four children!

Part Five of the Kaiser answer,
then...

...is service, unstinting and ever responsive. Nursery school teachers will see in these examples that it is, moreover, service to parents, service to community, service to war industry that sets the stage. It is the Center which adjusts. It is up to the Center to accept these needs and, within the framework they establish, to work with insight and skill so that children's needs are also met fully.

With this concept of service so firmly a part of the Kaiser answer, nursery school teachers in the Centers have had to make many adjustments. Their own working hours are just one example. Their day is the same as that of the shipyard worker — eight hours long, with a half-hour rest...and six days a week. Still more surprising is the fact that the day begins at no one time but is, in fact, a continuous operation. Some teachers start at 6:15 in the morning, but some start at 11:00 at night, greeting the children of the graveyard shift workers, putting them to bed, staying with them through the waking-up time, toiletry, breakfast, and short play period in the morning.

Perhaps one of the most interesting jobs is that of the teacher on swing shift. She is likely to start with her group in midafternoon, supervising three or four hours of indoor and outdoor play. Supper follows, then a quiet time, and then bed. At the end of swing shift — midnight in one Center, 2:00 A.M. in the other — parents stop at the Center. They wrap up their sleeping children in blankets and carry them, still asleep, to their cars for the homeward trip. Teachers on this shift, in addition to having the full experiences that make up the usual nursery school activities, see what is one of the most tender, affectionate interludes imaginable: parents, mothers and fathers together very often, in rough working clothes, dirty from a night's hard work, stooping low, talking low, gently, lovingly picking up their sleeping child for the homeward trip. This relaxed time of night is a very fruitful one, incidentally, for many conferences between teacher and parent.

Teachers in the Centers, for all adjustments they have had to make, feel several important compensations. Each one believes and rightly, that she is on a real war job — for the prime aim of the Centers is to stabilize the employment of parents and thus to help Swan Island and Oregonship build boats faster. Each one knows, and again rightly, that parents and children are appreciative. Each can see children gaining — physically, socially, in language and in ideas.

Where will this go?

But perhaps most buoying is the hope each teacher has that here in Portland ground is being broken for a vast postwar development in nursery education. There is the vision that perhaps the Kaiser answer to a wartime problem can show the way to a country's answer to similar peacetime needs. This experiment in cooperation may lead other industries, other communities, other government agencies, other parents to provide similar facilities. It may be, these teachers hope, that here is the forerunner of other Centers equally geared to aid families and children. (15)

Hymes's on-the-spot report gives the flavor of the experience as it was happening. Gwen Morgan's condensation of the Centers' final report, pamphlets and articles brings some historical perspective to the "experiment" and discusses why, as soon as the war was over, most of the nursery schools which had flourished for the duration disappeared. (20) America tried to go back to prewar conditions, and the wartime experience with young children was discarded, and, for a while, totally forgotten. (Gwen Morgan's article is reprinted in the Appendix, p. 368.) The number of children in nursery school in the following decade dropped precipitously. Most of the wartime buildings were closed; seldom were they taken over and run by private groups. Yet war experience had contributed to educational thought. A small pamphlet for teachers, *A Social Philosophy from Nursery School Teaching*,(16) compiled from James Hymes's lectures to the staff of the Kaiser Centers (See Appendix, p. 365) can be contrasted with Lawrence Frank's *The Fundamental Needs of the Child*. Although they are similar in philosophy, Hymes's pamphlet is much simpler and more concerned with the practical realities—food, health, everyday tasks—while proclaiming a faith as vigorous as Frank's that experience can make a vital difference in the level of development attained. Hymes's faith has gone beyond the rarefied academic idealism couched in technical terms to a pragmatic approach, an inevitable result of dealing with large numbers of children under harassing, crisis conditions. The fact remained that a great many nursery schools had existed for the benefit of mothers and children who needed their services. As the civil rights struggle of the 1960's began to dramatize the problems of the submerged poor in America, some people remembered the child care in the war years as a partial solution to inexorable generations of poverty. Another brief pamphlet for teachers by James Hymes, written while he was at the Kaiser Centers, is *Who Will Need a Post-War Nursery School?* (17) He predicted the development of new pressures on families, and of new needs pressed on the larger society. It was a portent of the future. Lawrence Frank speaks to a similar concern twenty years later:

When we recall what has taken place in family living, we see what perplexing new problems and family conflicts face men and women, and children and adolescents today. Most of us now live in cities and work indoors, with little contacts with nature, and limited opportunities for outdoor recreation and the releases needed from the constant demands, pressures and deprivations and overloads of city living. Moreover, many women now live in small homes or apartments, with small children, but no helpful grandmothers, aunts and sisters, as in the old, extended family, where she had assistants and comforters, and the child had human buffers when his parents were impatient or angry with him.

Equally, if not more important, are the changes in masculine and feminine roles, as women emerge from their former minority-group status, and increasingly participate in all our social, economic, political and other activities in contemporary society. Especially significant is the rapid increase in the numbers of working wives and mothers, who must bear the dual responsibilities of home life, and outside jobs. We have scarcely begun to recognize or attempt to cope with these many situations and perplexities which these recent changes present. We have been slow to provide young women with the kind of orientation and education they need for meeting these new and often conflicting responsibilities. We must ask what child development research and family life education can do to help women cope with these inescapable life tasks; so that neither the woman nor her children are unnecessarily sacrificed or damaged. We need some new social inventions — such as enlarging day care centers — to provide a variety of assistance and helpful services, as we did during the war; notably at the Kaiser plants in California, under the guidance of James Hymes, Jr. (9:24–25)

Wanted: A National Policy for Young Children

A pervasive concern about the role of children and families in an affluent society began in the late 1950's and early 1960's, and America has been asking itself for a policy statement. The dialogue began with the sudden awareness that environmental factors affected the intelligence of young children. Attention was drawn to the poverty that exists in this country, in particular, the plight of the black man. Educational concern was soon framed in the language of the "war on poverty" and the "civil rights movement." The Head Start Program in 1965 directed federal funds to early childhood education for an impoverished spectrum of the society.

Key words were community control, compensatory education, and parental enrichment. Early childhood programs were advocated for those presumed "deficits" identified among the population of poor youngsters. Frequently the "problem," as variously perceived, led people to an emphasis outside the classroom. CDGM (Child Development Group of Mississippi) was an example of a Head Start group which concentrated on the *process* of building a program for children designed by the expertise of their parents. Although great political turmoil accompanied their efforts, the program directors were determined to help reverse a prevailing sense of racism and powerlessness among the parents. "Many Negro parents here feel that education does not 'belong' to them, that it does not reflect them as it reflects the white middle class for and by whom it was designed, that it is, in fact, alien to them. . . . Rather than starting with an educational program and then trying to work in the child's actual life and draw in his parents, we start with the child's actual life as deeply felt by his parents, and try to offer support services to them as they build an educational program from it . . . ." (14:310,308) The professional acted as catalyst and consultant in this process. Polly Greenberg rephrases the original premise: "We guessed that children living in the midst of adults who valued education enough to build a state-wide Head Start school system out of red dust and cotton fields, would be children much more capable of growing and learning than would be the children of . . . the ambivalent, 'apathetic' poor." (14:311)

No matter what the premise or the design of intervention programs for poor young children, there was no doubt that Americans were more aware of the relationships among education, health, housing, income, recreation, community organization, racism, and child development. These interrelationships raised profound questions about the quality of life in America.

Furthermore, the nation found itself entrenched in a costly war in Vietnam. Defense spending, moon shots, welfare costs, mounting pollution encroached one on the other forcing citizens to challenge priorities. Pressure for decisions has characterized the late 1960's and early 1970's. The federal government tentatively made a commitment of offering early childhood education for poverty families. More recently, the Woman's Liberation movement has emerged demanding that women have the unconditional chance to pursue careers, which presupposes universal day care centers for all children. However, without the impetus of a World War II or national crisis, the old problems inherent in day care became serious obstacles with which to reckon—long hours, staff cohesion, high costs and increasing consumer expectations. While less than adequate work conditions could be tolerated during World War II, a "peace time" mandate for day care could never be maintained without national sanction. This consensus has yet to gather.

References to Part 6

1. Davis, Mary Dabney, "How NANE Began," *Young Children*, November 1964, pp. 106–109.
2. Davis, Mary Dabney, and Hansen, Rowna, *Nursery Schools: Their Development and Current Practices in the United States*, U.S. Department of Interior, Office of Education Bulletin no. 9 (Washington, D.C.: Government Printing Office, 1932).

3. Eliot, Abigail, personal communication, 1970.

4. *Emergency Nursery Schools during the First Year (1933–1934)*, Report of the National Advisory Committee on Emergency Nursery Schools (Washington, D.C.: Government Printing Office).

5. *Emergency Nursery Schools during the Second Year (1934–1935)*, Report of the National Advisory Committee on Emergency Nursery Schools (Washington, D.C.: Government Printing Office).

6. Erikson, Erik to Lawrence Frank, 1965.

7. *57th and Final Report of the Woman's Education Association for the Year Ending January 17, 1929.*

8. "For the Study of Young Children," *Journal of American Association of University Women*, 15 (1922): 147–148.

9. Frank, Lawrence, "The Beginnings of Child Development and Family Life Education in the Twentieth Century," *Merrill-Palmer Quarterly*, 8, no. 4 (1962): 7–28.

10. _____, "The Fundamental Needs of the Child," *Mental Hygiene*, 22 (July 1938): 353–379.

11. _____, personal communication, 1966.

12. Gesell, Arnold, *The Pre-School Child: From the Standpoint of Public Hygiene and Education* (Boston: Houghton-Mifflin Co., 1923).

13. Gesell, Arnold, and Gesell, Beatrice, *The Normal Child and Primary Education* (New York: Ginn and Co., 1912), p. 81.

14. Greenberg, Polly, "CDGM ... An Experiment in Preschool for the Poor — by the Poor," *Young Children*, 22, no. 5 (1967): 307–315. Reproduced with permission from *Young Children*. Copyright © 1967, National Association for the Education of Young Children, 1834 Connecticut Ave., N.W., Washington, D.C. 20009.

15. Hymes, James L., "The Kaiser Answer: Child Service Centers," *Progressive Education*, May 1944, pp. 222–223, 245–246.

16. _____, "A Social Philosophy from Nursery School Teaching," *Kaiser Child Service Center Pamphlets for Teachers*, no. 1, 1944.

17. _____, "Who Will Need a Post-War Nursery School?" *Kaiser Child Service Center Pamphlets for Teachers*, no. 3, 1944.

18. Johnson, Harriet, *Children in the Nursery School* (New York: John Day, 1928), p. v.

19. Meek, Lois, "New Ventures in Education for University Women," *Journal of American Association of University Women*, 20 (1926): 17–19.

20. Morgan, Gwen, "A Proposal to Establish a Work-Related Child Development Center," mimeographed, 1967, pp. 69–74.

21. Nursery Training School of Boston, "Fundamental Principles," mimeographed, 1944.

22. Omwake, Eveline B., "The Child's Estate," in *Modern Perspectives in Child Development*, ed. Albert Solnit and Sally Provence (New York: International Universities Press, 1963).

23. "Preschool and Parental Education," *Twenty-Eighth Yearbook of the National Society for the Study of Education* (Bloomington, Ill.: Public School Publishing Co., 1929).

24. "Report of the Ruggles Street Nursery School and Nursery Train-ing Center of Boston," May 1924.

25. Stolz, Lois Meek, to Abigail Eliot, March 10, 1958.

26. Talbot, Marion, and Rosenberg, Lois, *The History of the American Association of University Women: 1881–1931* (Boston: Houghton Mifflin Co., 1931).

27. Washburn, Ruth W., "Re-education in a Nursery Group: A Study in Clinical Psychology," *Monograph of the Society for Research in Child Development*, vol. 9, no. 2, 1944.

28. White, Edna N., to Lawrence Frank, January 9, 1924.

part 7

The Application of Competence Theory and Crisis Intervention to Education

The principles that have guided teachers have undergone many changes. Until more recent times, teachers have found an underlying purpose in theology or philosophy. Rousseau paid homage to the noble savage; Froebel, to the divine unity in God's universe. Twentieth century attempts to determine teaching-learning principles have been based substantially in psychology. Of the various theories proposed, Robert White's theoretical constructs and notions of competence have particular relevance to the educator.

Dissatisfied with explanations of behavior based soley on drive reduction or stimulus-response theories, White directs attention to exploratory behavior, curiosity, and play. He accumulates a considerable amount of evidence to suggest that much of what is commonly referred to as adaptive behavior or learned behavior cannot be explained on the basis of motivation related to hunger, thirst, sex, aggression, avoidance of pain or anxiety. Similar arguments and evidence are proposed by J. McVicker Hunt in an article which appears on page 233. These contributions are welcome additions to animal psychology as well as to psychoanalytic theory. White makes the case for spontaneous activity and exploration which is unrelated to "instincts":

... Children ... engage in manipulative and exploratory activity which is not unlike that of the animals. They investigate novelties, they try to produce effects on the environment; they tear paper, experiment with locks, and play with light switches. In a book that has become a classic, Karl Groos (1901) spoke of the child's "joy in being a cause," shown in his delight in making a lot of noise, moving everything around, and playing with mud, sand, and puddles where extensive effects could be produced. Intensive observational studies ... continue to be of value with respect to such behavior, but there are also more recent systematic studies of growth such as those of Gesell and his associates (1943, 1946) and the very fine experimental work of Jean Piaget (1946, 1937, 1945). A substantial amount of this work bears ... on behavior that can be classified as play, exploration, or manipulation. (6:25)

White attempts to formulate a theory for explaining exploratory behavior, suggesting that a *feeling of efficacy* is experienced when an individual successfully negotiates with the world of both inanimate and animate objects. White assumes that energy, which he calls *effectance*, is not derived from instincts but, rather, is "biologically basic" to the individual and available for cognitive and social transactions with the outside world. In his view a *sense of competence* develops as one accumulates a number of experiences that are efficacious. (6:38,39)

Where Freud emphasized instincts and the ego's defensive maneuvers, White directs us to the "conflict-free area of the ego" and its coping skills. Sewing threads of continuity between emotions, cognition, and "ego processes," he provides a broad position from which to understand human behavior. His formulations take into account the sequence of child development, acknowledge the existence of an inner life, and also deal with the importance of the external consequences of behavior. He speaks of the learning that takes place when one's activity tries to influence the environment and of the satisfaction inherent in producing effects both on materials and people. That aspect of the human condition that mediates between self and the environment is White's concern. He does not deny an individual's defensive maneuvering but chooses to emphasize the fact that, during times of conflict or crisis, defenses may well lead to *"actions* of an efficacious sort which [work] well upon the particular environment and thus [become] the basis for a continuing growth and confidence." (6:193)

At various times educational programs have embraced one theoretical position to the exclusion of others (e.g., maturation, conditioning, psychoanalytic theory, self-actualization, etc.). The names of Gesell, Skinner, Erikson, Freud, Piaget and others are familiar. Fortunately, White has utilized them all in his synthesis.

Competence and Its
Application to Education

Using terms from White's formulation, Braun and Pollock have attempted to develop four concepts which delineate potential objectives for teachers working with young children. They are:

1) A child can realize his effects on other people and materials.
2) A child has legitimate needs that can be legitimately met.
3) A child can be reflective about his own feelings and behavior.
4) A child can elaborate his ideas and actions when interacting with others or with materials. (2:51)

That increasingly sophisticated skills and an enhanced sense of competence can develop within each area is presumed.

Eli Bower has also drawn from White's foundation. He is an educator who has worked in the child mental health field instigating public school programs which promote the affective and cognitive growth of children. His ideas may not always be easy to implement. Because such phrases as "enhancing mental health" tend to be overworked and lack clear meaning, Bower has devoted considerable energy to conceptualizing the role of mental health in the schools. While he argues in the following selection that teachers and schools are always important mediators of skills, knowledge, and competence, he purposely blurs the distinctions commonly made between a child's emotions and intellect.

What curriculum or what factors in a child's learning experiences will develop his future ability to cope is a question Bower tries to answer in an understandable and relevant way. The ego framework he works with is similar to that of White. To utilize his writings, one should assume that there is such a "thing" as an ego that mediates between environment and self.

from **Personality and**
Individual Social Maladjustment
Eli M. Bower

... The most significant and incomprehensible fact about life in the 1960's and 1970's is the rapid expansion of the "knowledge industry." Whereas, in the past, many of our institutions were concerned with the production and distribution of food and other staples of life, in the present and probably more so in the future, the major occupation of the majority of Americans will be the production and distribution of knowledge. In essence, the basic "commodity" of modern living is knowledge. (a) Therefore, the ability to understand, transact, assimilate, and utilize knowledge has become a mandatory educational, vocational, and social skill. Automation, the arch villain of our future society, is often falsely accused of uprooting and dislocating our economy and way of life. More to the point is the sharp rise in the level of education necessary for vocational and social participation in this society. A society which depends on and fosters communication, development, and creation of knowledge will find it difficult to assimilate the uneducated into its mainstream. Burck (b) suggests that the craving for knowledge, in addition to elevating the productivity and prosperity of a society, feeds on itself—that a rapidly changing society must provide daily opportunities for the exchange of knowledge, most of which is basically neither economically nor productively relevant. We read, listen, phone, and watch TV. We go to night school and to concerts, lectures, meetings, and movies. We scan the paper, talk with our colleagues, wife, and children, and vote. The crux of the problem of today's society is that the uneducated have been disenfranchised and exiled. Economists have calculated that the average worker in 1960 has spent twice as many days in school as a worker in 1930. While there will be some increase in the length and comprehensiveness of education, it is estimated that such growth will level off and that the growth acceleration and lift will come in the improvement of the quality and process of education. (c)

As our society has increased the level of education required to participate in it, it has at the same time reduced the number of institutional alternatives available for the education of children. In the past, children could learn at home, in church, in trade or craft unions, or by correspondence. Few, if any, of these alternatives remain. The public, parochial, or private school must take on and be successful with all children. In addition, many of the socializing and humanizing tasks formerly shouldered by other institutions have been gradually transferred to the school. The school has a role to play in the health of children, in their discipline, in their social development, and in their physical fitness. As a result of these and other societal changes, the school has become a primary institution in the sense that all children are required to pass through it successfully and to learn the significant skills taught therein in order to function as adults. Individual adjustment or maladjustment, therefore, is a function of a child's ability to manage this experience effectively and productively.

The two basic changes in our society—the raising of the educational level necessary to function in it and the shifting to the school of major socializing and humanizing tasks for large groups of children—have produced stormy debates between those espousing emphasis on "intellectual excellence" and those hoping to extend the scope of learning to environmentally deprived lower-class children. Education, however, whether it is dispensed in Harvard or Harlem, has as its primary goal helping the individual take in, digest, and use knowledge. As a consequence of the expansion of knowledge, education, more than ever, needs to focus on those skills which enable students to process and mediate information rather than on "covering-a-subject" or "comprehensive-textbook" kind of learning. One needs to consider the problem of what happens to intellectual digestive processes in attempting to ingest our present banquet of knowledge. On the other hand, for those children with limited environmental experience with books, language, and school tasks, the problem is one of developing processes and experiences which can begin to bridge the gap between things, ideas, events, and feelings and their representation. Both these convergences in our society suggest that educational and social competence will depend on the individual's ability to learn how to process and use symbols as the representations of the real and the imagined.

Maladjustment and individual effectiveness.   Unlike pregnancy, maladjustment cannot be considered an either-or condition. One can vary from being a little maladjusted to being very much maladjusted with respect to a variety of social tasks and endeavors. In this paper, maladjustment will be considered a result of a variety of ego processes which lead to or are part of learning-failure in school. One can also argue that for some children the school is maladjusted and that the processes which lead to failure lie in the institution. Schools, as institutions, can be competent with many children but ineffective with others. In large part, the competence of both, individual and institutions, is a product of the interaction between the degrees of freedom of the mediating processes of the individual and the degrees of freedom or constriction of the mediating agent, in this case the school.

Ego Processes*

The adjustment of an individual in the school (and later in society) can be conceptualized as a function of his competence to use referents or representations of objects and events. Such referents or representations are systematized in words, language, mathematics, and other symbol systems. Symbols are learned by individuals as a function of "experiencing" objects, events, and relationships. To convert an event or a happening into an experience (something learned), its essence must be ingested, processed, and assimilated via symbolic vehicles, such as words or mathematical formula. In the following sections, maladjustment will be discussed as a function of specific but interrelated deficiencies and skills in the processing and utilization of symbols. Before getting into specifics it might be helpful to delineate the general characteristics of ego processes.

The nature of ego processes. The space between the environment and an individual's responses to it has been conceptualized as a dark box or unlit tunnel called ego or ego processes. (Although ego and ego processes will be used interchangeably, the latter term is preferred since it reminds the reader and the writer that what is being discussed is a kind of activity and not a thing.) Since the terrain in this black tunnel cannot be explored at first hand, behavioral scientists have had to map its dimensions and topography by what it seems to do to objects, events, or feelings.

Basically, ego processes are data processes, i.e., they pick out of the environment those objects, ideas, and feelings which have survival value, "process" them, and respond to the processed data. At a higher level of abstraction, ego processes can be regarded as ways in which each individual has learned to manage himself and his environment to produce the highest survival benefit to himself. Or one can conceptualize ego processes as the organization of the personality of an individual related mainly to the perceptual system which acts as a mediator and interpreter of the external world and as a mediator of the individual himself.

One of the major tasks of the ego is to guide the individual in the path of reality and to its mastery. Ego processes move or push the individual toward experiences which can improve his skill and ability to deal with the environment. Conversely, ego processes seek ways of keeping the individual away from what may appear to be painful or discomforting encounters with the environment. As such, the ego acts as a watchman scanning both the outer and the inner world for possible danger. In time, the ego helps the individual learn to evaluate the reality of a brick wall (if you walk into it you'll bruise your head), signals and signs from a teacher (how far can I go before she blows

---

*For a more detailed discussion of the materials of this section and of specific ego processes, see W. G. Hollister and E. M. Bower, *Behavioral Science Frontiers in Education* (New York: John Wiley & Sons, 1966).

up?), and feelings inside one's self which are about to burst to the surface (how far can I go before I blow up?). Moreover, such learnings cut a groove in which future experiences with the environment are perceived and channeled.

In their beginning stages, ego processes help define "me," which is then incorporated into the further development and growth of ego processes. In the early life of "me," ego processes scan the evironment on the pleasure principle (I want what I want when I want it). As an individual matures, ego processes become more closely allied to reason and logic. In the mature adult, ego processes are able to perceive, evaluate, and act on the consequences of present action, i.e., to conceptualize the future. This skill was aptly stated by G. B. Shaw as "being able to choose the line of greatest advantage instead of yielding in the direction of least resistance." Ego processes which are able to learn to use this "reality principle" must, of necessity, be able to conceptualize the notion of "tomorrow and tomorrow and tomorrow." Such conceptualization is, of course, difficult for some children whose survival is a daily or hourly question and whose experience with symbols has been limited. To process the concept of time, children need experience with abstractions. Children with little language or mediational skills find the future an elusive concept to pin down.

To take in, digest, and utilize the meaning of time, the ego processes need to bind or tie symbols to the concept or idea of time. When one can conceptualize the future in a meaningful and realistic way, one has learned to use symbols to enlarge one's self and one's environment. American education by its very nature requires the ability to develop and hold onto time concepts. This, as has been mentioned, may be difficult for some lower-class children where the future is bound by the next meal or in a Mexican-American family where the values and orientation of time are related to ancestral heritages and tradition.

In essence, ego processes can only bind time and space concepts in the form of symbols such as words, pictures, numbers, gestures, smells, designs, sounds, textures, and tastes. The nature and the strength of binding determine the effectiveness and flexibility of ego processes. If, for example, there are insufficient objects and events available in the environment, the organism may have little opportunity to mediate a variety of words, pictures, sounds, textures, and tastes. As a consequence, the ego processes may be insufficiently developed or differentiated to insure proper growth and development. Or, in some cases, the environment may be so stressful and so difficult to mediate in a pleasurable, nonpainful manner that the resulting inputs are significantly modified or distorted. There are also times when environmental stimuli overflow ego processes and are discharged in erratic or inappropriate behavior. In addition, one can develop a hardening or constriction of perceptual categories so that ego processes constrict or channelize environmental inputs which are allowed to enter. Finally, one can compartmentalize one aspect of an experience in one water-tight unit and

other aspects in other parts of the personality; or one can separate knowing from doing and doing from knowing so that there are, in reality,
two selves.

To some extent, all civilized human beings have given hostages to
fortune, i.e., lost several degrees of freedom in becoming a member of a
group which insists on all playing the game according to the rules. This
does not necessarily mean that society and the individual are inherent
enemies. On the contrary, society, by establishing rules, traditions, and
guidelines to behavior, can encourage individual autonomy and self-
realization. But, in each case in each society, the game must be played
according to the rules. Where, however, the interaction of the individual with his group produces ego processes of diffusion, distortion,
overloading, constriction, or fragmentation in the personality, there is a
loss or reduction of the individual's degrees of freedom to act, discover,
and change.

In addition, sensory deprivations may produce ego handicaps. A person
born deaf may learn signs, but without language such signs have limited
social utility. Most importantly, without an adequate array of symbols for
representing events and objects, little, if anything, of human experience
can be stored and used. Consider an intelligent human being cut off
from vision and auditory input very early in life and lacking any way
of storing or communicating meaning. "The few signs I used became
less and less adequate and failures to make myself understood were
invariably followed by outbursts of passion. I felt as if invisible hands
were holding me and I made frantic efforts to free myself . . . after
awhile the need of some means of communication became so urgent that
these outbursts occurred daily, sometimes hourly." (d)

Ego processes and language. The sparking between an event or object and its eventual incorporation within self through ego processes is
a function of the symbolic posts to which the event or object can be tied.
An event which cannot be tied securely to a symbol has limited educational utility. An object which has no representational correlate cannot
be conceptualized or held in the mind. Our basic tool for this sparking
between objects and symbol has been the written and spoken word.
Indeed, language is our royal road to defining not only what surrounds
us in the environment but what we are as an organism. It seems important, however, to re-emphasize that the meaning of language as representative of objects or events cannot be separated from the action or
behavioral setting in which the symbol action or symbol object were
tied together. Conceptually this has been understood as the process of
association, contiguity, or integration of symbol with action or event.
It seems probable, as Werner and Kaplan (e) conclude, that the presence of organismic or ego activity is the central and overriding factor in
the development of an adequate symbol system. The structure and function of symbols are built out of ego processes which not only link symbols to contexts and meanings but fuse them into the basic perceptual
processes of the personality. Symbols, therefore, are not just signs; nor

can human beings be conceived as Pavlovian dogs reacting to signals which set off salivation or hunger. When a connection between a symbol and its meaning is lost, the facts suggest that it is not the result of a breaking of the "conditioning" bond but, rather, a loss of the dynamic organization in the ego processes of personality. This is evident in emotional disturbance, where symbols are utilized in highly idiosyncratic and dissociated ways.

Symbols cannot be bound into ego processes without some degrees of feelings finding their way into the knot. High degrees of emotion may, as suggested before, overload the symbol. Insufficient degrees of affect may produce a kind of blandness or coldness. Or in some instances, the nature of the human relationship in which the symbolic transactions take place induce ego processes to constrict intake, i.e., polarize or modify the meaning of what is perceived.

In summary, effective ego processes result in educational competence and effective interaction with the school. Ineffective ego processes produce nonadaptive behavior in managing school tasks and make learning increasingly difficult.

Dimensions of ego processes. In dealing with skills and deficiencies in the processing and use of symbols, it may be helpful to think of ego processes as involving five specific dimensions:

1. Differentiation *vs.* diffusion—the processes by which objects, events, and feelings are separated out and perceived clearly.
2. Fidelity *vs.* distortion—the processes by which objects, events, and feelings are seen and reproduced faithfully as they are experienced.
3. Pacing *vs.* over- or underloading—the processes by which objects, events, and feelings are attached to appropriate emotional loads and stresses.
4. Expansion *vs.* constriction—the processes by which new symbols, or new meanings for old symbols, are assimilated and used.
5. Integration *vs.* fragmentation—the processes by which symbols are processed within the individual as a whole rather than in one or another separated compartment.

1. *Differentiation vs. diffusion.* Processes of ego differentiation must be learned early in the child's life. With the help of such processes, the child begins to master the nature of things and people, the difference between the real and the imagined, and the boundaries between "me" and "not me." As a child's ability to differentiate grows, he learns to separate, compare, and identify objects, experiences, and people in a clear and focused way.

Children who have developed ego-diffusion processes perceive and conceptualize in misty and impressionistic images. One could, for purposes of differentiation, illustrate ego-diffusion processes by the mythical work of an *avant garde* impressionistic painter, such as a 1970 Monet or Renoir. (f) In impressionism, Monet, Renoir, and others were primarily interested in communicating patches of color or feeling, out of which one might, if one wished, discern form and shading. Impressionists painted in rough brush strokes—concerned as they were in impressions of things rather than their form, shape, or texture. A child who has learned to process data through ego-diffusion processes takes in such data as vague, overlapping, and highly general impressions. As a result, the child may find attaching crisp and meaningful symbols to objects and events a difficult task. This is, of course, most critical in the child's attempt to resolve a picture of himself out of the cloudy impressions and misty symbols he has to work with. It should be noted that . . . ego differentiation and diffusion represent the ends of a continuum and are not discrete and separated processes.

These and the other specific notions are highlighted to entice the more creative planners and developers of curriculum to spell out more clearly how children can be helped to learn and use effective ego processes and to unlearn ineffective ego processes. For example, school programs which widen a child's experience with objects, events, and people in such a way that these objects, events, and people can be assimilated (symbolized) would, in all probability, enhance ego-differentiating processes and erode ego-diffusion processes. Although it may not be too clear to the reader (and the writer) how each of the characteristics of effective ego processes . . . can be taught, the concepts may have possibilities for curriculum-planning and development. It seems certain, however, that individual and social adjustment in the latter half of the twentieth century will require that effective ego processes be acquired by children and that humanizing institutions such as the school become increasingly concerned with children as effective data processors rather than data sponges.

In order for a child to learn processes of ego differentiation, a number of interrelated ingredients are required. Among these are: *a*) language, *b*) an opportunity to contact, sense, and experience a wide variety of things and people, and *c*), most important, bridges or mediational agents to help the child fit symbols and experiences together comfortably and functionally. A number of researchers such as Bowlby, (g) Skodak and Skeels (h) point out the consequences of lacks in each of these ingredients for the development of children. The processes of ego differentiation are, however, the major whetstones upon which other ego processes are sharpened and welded. It is probable that a productive and creative relationship between a child and a school environment cannot be managed without moderate degrees of ego differentiation.

At present, experimental curriculum programs—especially with kindergarten and preschool children—are attempting to find ways of reversing ego-diffusion processes in lower-class children. In one such preschool program the teacher, when speaking to a child, will face the child at eye level and enunciate with full mouth and lip movement so that the words are clearly and distinctly differentiated from others. Such programs (i) also include games in which symbols and objects are linked in various contexts or in which unfamiliar and familiar objects are placed in a box, identified and differentiated by touch, sight, or description.

Ego-differentiation processes are difficult processes for lower-class children to acquire because of their lacks in three prerequisites mentioned above.

Games are extremely helpful in encouraging language usage and the differentiation of objects and words. For example, a child may verbalize more spontaneously via a toy telephone in a toy booth than in a face-to-face situation. The results can be taped and fed back as part of the game. In addition, preschool and school programs seeking to enhance ego-differentiation processes may utilize exercises in figure-ground discrimination, training in the differentiation and identification of sounds and manipulation of new objects, pictures, and words. Some teachers use photographs, pictures, or silhouettes to assist the child in differentiating himself. Others help children differentiate the concept of time through ordered and predictable experiences which move methodically from one time period to another. One of the pioneer attempts in this field, the Higher Horizon's Program of New York, began in 1956 and is still exploring new possibilities in this field. These and other projects have demonstrated that the ego horizons of disadvantaged children could be raised and broadened by expanded and differentiated school and community programs.

In addition to school-centered programs, some investigators have approached the problem of differentiation from another direction—that of making the mother a more effective mediational agent of symbols and experiences. In his preliminary research on how mothers represent and mediate ideas to their children, Hess (j) asked mothers to teach their children three different tasks. These were: a) simple sorting of objects by color and function, b) complex sorting, using blocks with varied shapes and markings, and c) copying designs on an "Etch-a-Sketch" toy. This is a device on which lines can be drawn which are controlled by two knobs, one for horizontal movement, one for vertical movement.

Following is an example given by Hess of one mother responding to a sorting task:

> "All right, Susan, this board is the place where we put the little toys; first of all you are supposed to learn how to place them according to color. Can you do that? The things that are all the same color you put in one section, in the second section you put another group of colors, and in the third section you put the last group of colors. Can you do that? Or would you like to see me do it first?"
> Child: "I want to do it." She does.

Here is another mother who introduces the same task thus:

> "Now I'll take them all off the board; now you put them all back on the board. What are these?"
> Child: "A truck."
> "All right, just put them right here; put the other one right here; put the other one right here; all right put the other one there."

Here is an example of a third mother:

> "I've got some chairs and cars; do you want to play the game?"
> No response.
> "OK what's this?"
> Child: "A wagon."
> Mother: "Hm?"
> Child: "A wagon."
> Mother: "This is no wagon — what's this?"

There is nothing in the relationship of the latter two mothers which mediates or differentiates the essential nature of the task or learning to the child. There is also very little differentiation of objects processed in this relationship, since their use and meaning is unclear and unfocused for the child. As Hess points out, the latter two mothers lack tags for conceptualizing the task, and, consequently, the child lacks experience in relating concepts to objects and actions. As a result, ego processes remain diffused and are unable to process the particular objects as they relate to one another and to the assigned task.

The lack of sufficient ego-differentiating experiences in lower-class, deprived children makes this personality defect a major source of individual and social maladjustment. This is especially critical for children in the school since this institution demands skill and competency in differentiating words, ideas, and concepts. Processes of differentiation cannot go far forward without a repertoire of representational tags by which things, events, and feelings can be delineated. In essence, the processes of differentiation require both symbols in the form of language and a mediational relationship with an adult to help encode and place together things, ideas, and words.

Lastly, it is important to note that differentiation processes require biological and physiological capacities able to differentiate objects and to use symbols. Severely retarded or neurologically impaired children often find ego-differentiation processes hard to come by. Some of the earliest and best work in creating instructional exercises in differentiation was developed by professional persons concerned with the education of environmentally or biologically retarded children. Such contributions varied from Itard's creative and partially successful attempts to educate Victor, the Wild Boy of Aveyron, by "preparing the senses to receive keener impressions" to the contributions of Seguin, Froebel, Pestalozzi, and Montessori. There have been many new ideas and revisions of older ones proposed for increasing human capabilities for differentiation. Montessori's idea of encouraging discovery and work in a prepared environment and Froebel's use of play as a learning mode have found new utility in devising new and imaginative experiences for lower-class and environmentally deprived children.

2. *Fidelity vs. distortion.* ... Ego processes having high fidelity process data accurately. Sullivan proposed the term "consensual validation" as one of the major attributes of this ego process—the ability to see objects and people, including one's self, as others do. All ego processes distort objects, events, people, or feelings *to some extent*, since the external world exists in the experiences and symbols of each of us on the basis of slightly or markedly different experiences. In essence, our perceptions are always, as someone noted, deviations from our approximations of the external world.

To differentiate ego-distorting processes from ego-diffusing processes, one might compare a cubistic painting, such as Picasso's "The Three Musicians," (k) with an impressionistic landscape. The latter painting would be made up of a few rough, apparently misty smudges of paints.

The image is unclear and undelineated. In "The Three Musicians," the figures are clearly delineated except that eyes, mouths, instruments, and appendages seem out of joint, or disproportionate to each other. A wide-angle lens can produce a sharp but *distorted* image. A poorly focused lens will produce an unclear, uncertain *diffused* image.

For some children with moderate or marked tendencies to distort objects and events, it may be necessary to unmediate the major distorting symbols before effective processing of data can take place. For the others, one of the basic tasks of the school is to help them use symbols as accurately as possible *but* with sufficient degrees of freedom to permit changes in meaning as a result of new learnings. Learning to attach one meaning to a symbol must not prohibit a child from learning other attachments. Symbols, such as language, must be learned with flexibility and with awareness of all the denotative and connotative baggage which each symbol carries. People can only change as their symbolic equipment changes.

It is also important for schools to provide real events, objects, and relationships to which symbols can be tied. "Democracy" or "freedom," as words, are meaningless and their use dangerous unless a child learns them in a context of doing and thinking. This is especially true of symbols with high-level abstract meaning. Such symbols, unless tied down by first-hand experiences, are like boats in a storm, to be tossed this way or that, depending on the wind or current.

Further, ego-fidelity processes require an awareness of symbols as representatives of objects, events, and feelings and not objects, events, and feelings in themselves. Yet, these unreal, squiggly lines formed into words, sentences, paragraphs, and books can cut like a sword, initiate a religious movement, make suicide the only alternative to life, and give life a scope and depth which Shakespeare, Van Gogh, and Beethoven communicated via their symbolic modes. Such men create or combine symbols for our pleasure and enjoyment; others have used such skills for destructive and pernicious ends. Since much of the child's environment from ages two to sixteen and beyond will be a highly verbal and symbolic one, the child must be helped to recognize how easily words often become their own realities rather than representatives. Much of what goes on in our social and educational relationships, *vis a vis* the use of symbols, is blatantly illustrated by the master semanticist of Titi Pu–Koko, the Lord High Executioner. Koko is asked to explain to his majesty the Mikado why an order to execute someone (1) has not been carried out. "It's like this," says Koko, "when your Majesty says, let a thing be done, it's as good as done—practically, it is done—because your Majesty's will is law. Your Majesty says, 'Kill a gentleman' and a gentleman is told off to be killed. Consequently that gentleman is as good as dead—practically, he *is* dead—and if he is dead, why not say so?" To which the Mikado replies as any educated person would "Nothing could possibly be more satisfactory!" (m)

A more up-to-date fable stressing the need for ego processes which tie symbols to real experiences is given by Rovere. (n) He points out that a late senator knew something "arcane and delicate" about the American people: "That we will take the symbols of the established fact for the fact itself. I discovered this weakness in myself," says Rovere.

> ... Examining his photostats and his onion-skin carbons of official correspondence, I had taken their relevance for granted; relevance had seemed somehow a condition of their existence and the "fact" that they were "facts," i.e., they existed, they could be seen with the naked eye, they could be held in the hand had induced me to follow him quite a distance down his garden path. But of course they were not "facts," relevant or otherwise, but only symbols of factuality and he knew it was characteristic of most Americans to make the mistake I had made. The characteristic is encouraged if it is not developed by our education and its emphasis on the approach to data.(o)

3. *Pacing vs. under- or overloading.* ... Essentially, this dimension has to do with learning ways of pacing and controlling one's relationship to floods or droughts of inputs and of pacing and controlling the release of inner storms. Children who blow up under minor frustrations or moderate pressures may be already emotionally overloaded and unable to process experiences without risking further emotional burdens. On the other hand, there are children whose past experiences may have led to a blandness or coolness toward others, born of a fear of possible hurt and pain in assuming any emotional burden. Overloading may also take place in processing cognitive data where a flood of data cannot be processed because there are relatively few conceptual dams behind which the data can be stored.

Pacing processes entail learning how to release energies spontaneously when appropriate, the ability to show joy as well as to shed tears when the slings and arrows of outrageous fortune strike. All must learn to bear stress, personal losses, and unrealized symbolic goals. Many of Georges Rouault's paintings, particularly "Tragic Clowns," (p) symbolize graphically the notion of emotional heaviness and overburdening. On the other hand, much of what is called "noninvolvement" or detachment in today's society probably stems from ego processes frightened of any emotional loading.

Ego-pacing processes are learned in a context of healthy emotional exchanges and school permission to become involved both cognitively and affectively. If educational experiences cannot provide students with processes for release and control, learning has limited utility. For example, Weisberg and Springer (q) studied the home environment of children with similar IQ's but with differing amounts of creative ability. Children with high creativity lived in families in which there was open and not always calm expression of strong feelings. Further, such feelings were not used to bind the child to the parent or vice versa. Issues and conflicts were confronted in the open—seldom was a problem run away from or hidden. Neither suppression nor withdrawal was used as primary means of dealing with problems or people.

Other types of learning experiences can be helpful in building balanced and paced ego processes. One is the conscious introduction of humor into the content of school subjects. Humor supplies a healthy vehicle for the conveyance of small loads of emotional energy. Humor indicates an ability to understand incongruities. Moreover, a child's delight in play can be extended to words and to that producer of mass groans, the pun. A pun is an excellent device upon which to raise a child's consciousness and understanding of the arbitrary nature of symbols. If a word can be played with, it must have properties of its own. When we shift the context and meaning of a word as we do in a pun we have been tricked but enlightened. As Boswell put it, "A good pun may be admitted among the smaller excellencies of lively conversation." Learning to use and appreciate humor entails learning a flexibility with words and a cognitive lightness which enables one to take good and bad fortune in stride.

Another resource in helping children learn ego-pacing processes is the establishment of an ego-rehearsal or play area in a classroom. In one fourth-grade classroom such an area, which included a puppet stage and a box of puppets, had been set up on a raised platform. This was used by students at appropriate times to play out vignettes in English, social studies, and related subjects. At other times, the area was available for anyone or any group that wished to use it. A boy in one of the classes often arrived early so he could replay an apparently hectic and distressing breakfast scene that he had just left. This was done as a *sotto voce* solo while the teacher straightened the room and other children were readying themselves for reading groups.

Problem stories as foci for discussion or for role-playing have been used by some teachers. (r) Such stories make interesting reading and stop at a point which permits a choice of several possible endings. Such possibilities can be discussed or role-played. In some classrooms, children make up their own stories for discussion or role-playing. The T-group learning programs of the National Training Laboratory have been tried with adolescents in a few schools. These and other similar experiences provide children with learnings which permit the expression of normal feelings in a socially acceptable manner. Such experiences do not need to await special occasions or courses. Any class in English poetry, literature, social studies, history, or humanities can provide unloading platforms. With the help of the teacher, feelings and ideas touched by writers, poets, and historians can be identified, expressed, and discussed. Perhaps these and other human vents need encouragement and development. As Huxley says so well,

> Moral equivalents must be found not only for war but also for delinquency, family squabbles, bullying, puritanical censoriousness, and all the assorted beastliness of daily life. ... It is obvious that we must take a hint from the Greeks and provide ourselves with physical safety valves for reducing the pressure of negative emotions. No ethical system which fails to provide such physical safety valves and which fails to teach children and their elders how to use them is likely to be effective. (s)

Huxley has other suggestions for educational programs in the nonverbal humanities. Among such suggestions are programs for the development of wise passiveness — lessons in watching and perceiving, in harnessing imagination and its suggestive power in the service of the individual, and in the art of controlling physical pain "an art which, as every good dentist knows, can be learned by most children with the greatest of ease." (t)

One final note on the pacing-loading dimension. Overloading can and often does occur as a a result of physiological or sensory deficits, such as sight and hearing deprivation or injury to the central nervous system. Periodic grand-mal seizures pose major mediation problems for ego processes and undoubtedly make children with such problems highly vulnerable to overloading and other ego defects. The need for release mechanisms by children with sensory or motor handicaps is illustrated by Helen Keller's recounting of her life when she had no language but a few signs with which to communicate. (u)

4. *Expansion vs. constriction.* Graphically, constriction is illustrated by some of the works of Modigliani. (v) Ego processes — like other aspects of the person — need to grow, to take on new adaptive skills, to move to new levels in the use of symbols, and to seek new experiences by which this growth and enrichment can be nourished. Education by its very nature is in the business of expanding ego processes.

Expansion is a process of increasing the conceptual, imaginative, and symbolic degrees of freedom of an individual. One cannot consider such growth analogous to an increase in girth or plumpness after a hearty meal of facts and information. Processes of expansion result from temptations by tasty tidbits of knowledge, succulent ideas, and provoking mysteries which are examined and undergone.

Very little ego expansion can result from processes which perceive knowledge as additive or cumulative. It is important, therefore, for children to be comfortable in relationships which transpose and transport a "set" of facts from one conceptual schema to another. One possibility for this development would be for teachers to place emphases on metaphors as a unifying glue in the content of instruction. The concept of "growth," for example, has metaphorical relationships across subjects such as biology, geology, political science, economics, embryology, psychology, mathematics, and philosophy. To enhance this process one could expand on parlor games played by many families (w) in which a well-known person is to be identified through a series of wild but appropriate metaphors. For example, the guesser would ask the knower, "If the unknown person were an automobile, which one would he be; if he were an animal which one would he be," and so on through painter, a dish, a musical composition, a book, a tree, an idea, a dance, a color, a form, or an object. Symbols are only meaningful within their own conceptual framework; their transposition within another framework can open new doors and new avenues of thought.

Processes of constriction reduce the degrees of freedom of an individual to perceive and to act. Constricted ego processes limit the indi-

vidual's access to new information and data. In addition, such processes
reduce the individual's behavioral or exploration alternatives to a limited number and type of responses. In severe constriction, the individual may perceive and act as if he has only one choice available where,
in fact, many exist. In ego constriction, symbols are used rigidly and
inflexibly, spontaneity and zest are rare, and the channels to change
have hardened and frozen the individual, as it were, in place.

To some extent, all education and socialization processes constrict—
having learned to think or act in one way, other possibilities are reduced.
Nevertheless, education can be freeing if constriction processes are not
too deeply embedded in unconscious factors. Collinson, (x) for example,
suggests a strong linkage between any learned concept in history, science, mathematics, English, or home economics and ego expansion. He
points out that both ego processes and concept formation are the end
result of processes of selection which occur at the boundary of the individual and his environment. What is permeable or even semipermeable
for ego growth are learnings which modify or induce concept formation.
Conversely, learning new concepts expands ego processes.

Perhaps the greatest single skill and tool in ego expansion is reading.
Without it, an individual's bridge between thinking processes and the
internal and external world is dangerously narrowed and rickety. Reading, however, exists only feebly as skill unless it is accompanied by
enjoyment or pleasure. It is the *pleasure* of reading which makes a sentence or a story real. To one who enjoys reading, life's possibilities are
expanded. As Richard Wright said so well:

> It had been only through books — at best no more than vicarious cul-
> tural transfusions — that I had managed to keep myself alive in a nega-
> tively vital way. Whenever my environment had failed to support or
> nourish me I had clutched at books. Consequently my belief in books had
> risen more out of a sense of desperation than from any abiding convic-
> tion of their ultimate value. . . .
> It had been my accidental reading of fiction and literary criticism that
> had evoked in me vague glimpses of life's possibilities. . . . And it was out
> of these novels, stories, and articles, out of the emotional impact of imagi-
> native constructions of heroic or tragic deeds, that I felt touching my face
> a tinge of warmth from an unseen light. . . . (y)

It may be more important in teaching reading to consider interest,
excitement, and the "imaginative constructions of heroic or tragic deeds"
than to worry about vocabulary, word meaning, phonics, or phonetic
competences. To be taught to read as a stolid, mechanical process is to
learn to use it in a stolid, mechanical way.

The relationship between reading disability and social maladjustment
has become increasingly significant. Fabian (z) studied reading disability in children in a public school, a child guidance clinic serving deprived,
delinquent children, a clinic serving mixed groups, a children's observation unit of a psychiatric hospital, and a child placement agency. The
reading disability rates for children in school were ten percent; in a
regular child guidance clinic, thirteen percent; in the placement agency,
sixty-three percent; in a children's psychiatric hospital, seventy-three

percent; and a clinic serving deprived, delinquent children, eighty-three percent. It is not surprising to find reading failure and delinquency interwoven comrades. A child who cannot conceptualize and utilize other possibilities of adventure, hope, and a future life must play out his circumscribed alternatives in a limited environment. His constrictions are twofold; his ego processes and his environmental resources conspire to straitjacket his perceptions and his thinking, leaving only senseless rebellion or withdrawal. As a young man, it was always puzzling to me, when I worked with delinquent boys and girls, how desperately they wanted to have fun but how difficult it was for them to do so. Often they confused fun and fight. They wanted to do things well but seldom could. They sought to create but had no vision. They wanted to learn but were frightened of the consequences. After having been burned repeatedly in school, another singe was seldom attractive. To help them learn is the task of a modern miracle-worker.

5. *Integration vs. fragmentation.* Chagall's painting "The Poet or Half Past Three" illustrates components of the process of fragmentation. (aa) In brief, an individual using ego-fragmentation processes is much like a submarine with many compartments all watertight, sound proofed, and lacking communication with any other compartment on the ship. Ego-fragmentation processes pinch and take in data in a disassociated or walled-off manner.

Ego-incentive processes orchestrate the old emotions, skills, cognitive content, thoughts, and imagination with the new. Such processes need to relate the more formal aspects of learnings with the more meaningful aspects of living. School learning can, in some instances, be placed in a special compartment in the personality so that what one knows and what one does are separate and discrete entities. Two significant aspects of integration should be emphasized here. One is that a child's world is activity-centered. Objects and things are perceived in the context of what can be done with them. As the child acts, discovers, and changes, it is this experience which gets bound, via symbols, into the object-action. It is not at all uncommon for adults who revisit neighborhoods where they had lived as small children to be surprised by the difference in distance and in the size of such physical objects as roads, lakes, houses, which were experienced when the self was small.

If objects are not bound into symbols by action, they tend to remain unintegrated and fragmented. Bergson suggested that, in some men, perceiving and acting are separate entities. When such persons look at a thing "they see it for itself not for themselves. These are people who are born with or have developed a detachment from life. This is a reminder of the Swiss gentleman who, when given a choice between going to paradise or going to a lecture about paradise, chose the latter."

In addition to the integration of action and knowledge, ego-integrative processes need to contend with feelings and intellect. Ego processes have not only to help the organism to adapt but to synthesize its interactions with the environment. Without such integrating processes, differentiation, fidelity, pacing, and expansion are difficult to execute. Teachers must look for opportunities to cement knowing and feeling or at least must avoid the notion that feelings have no place alongside the mighty intellect. Emotion is senseless without intellectual guidance; conversely, intellect without emotion produces a robot lacking the "tinge of warmth" necessary for love and work.

Lastly, as in every phase of living, the process of integration varies as do individuals. Each individual has a unique way of synthesizing experiences and symbols. This individual style has repetitive, recognizable aspects which Rosen (bb) suggests may be studied through the individual's characteristic responses to ambiguity or in responses to situations where definitive answers are not available. They may be observed in his artistic creations, his use of fantasy, the nature of his differentiation processes, his work, and his interpersonal relationships. Styles in personality change as they do in clothes. One needs to keep in mind that a variety of integrative styles are within the normal deviations of personality and development in a free society.

Conclusion

Individual and social maladjustment is herein defined, described, and discussed as a function of how individuals take in, ingest, assimilate, and use data. An individual's style in processing information and his response to these mediational activities produce ego dimensions which broaden or narrow his interaction with his environment.

Ego processes of differentiation, fidelity, pacing, expansion, and integration enhance an individual's ability to use symbols, thereby increasing his degrees of behavioral freedom. Ego processes of diffusion, distortion, over- or underloading, constriction, and fragmentation limit and reduce an individual's ability to use symbols, thereby decreasing his degrees of behavioral freedom. Reduction of behavioral freedom tends to freeze an individual's growth potential. Such reduction is reinforced by and, in turn, reinforces the narrowing of the individual's own ego processes. Such styles of development leave individuals with few, if any, personal resources in a world made up of rapid and continuous transactions of knowledge, of interaction with others, and technological and social change. Personal and perceptual rigidity in a world in motion can only produce heat, wear, and noxious stress. Effective individual and social functioning with limited or inadequate ego processes becomes difficult, if not impossible. . . .

The world of tomorrow will place heavier burdens on ego processes than does the world of today. Those children who cannot develop effective ego-processing styles will become adolescents and adults with high vulnerability to individual and social maladjustment. With our society rapidly becoming a nation in which our basic commodity is knowledge and our basic vehicle a system of symbols, such as language and numbers, effective ego processes will increasingly become the *sine qua non* of adaptive and creative individual and social functioning.

Selected Readings

Levitt, Morton, *Freud and Dewey on the Nature of Man* (New York: Philosophical Library, 1960).

Machlup, Fritz, *The Production and Distribution of Knowledge in the United States* (Princeton: Princeton University Press, 1962).

The Protection and Promotion of Mental Health in Schools (Mental Health Monograph 5 (Washington: U.S. Public Health Service, 1964).

Werner, Heinz, and Kaplan, Bernard, *Symbol Formation* (New York: John Wiley & Sons, 1963).

White, Robert W., *Ego and Reality in Psychoanalytic Theory* (New York: International Universities Press, 1963). (1)

Notes

a. See Fritz Machlup, *The Production and Distribution of Knowledge in the United States* (Princeton, N.J.: Princeton University Press, 1962).

b. Gilbert Burck, "Knowledge — the Biggest Growth Industry of Them All, *Fortune Magazine* 70 (November 1964): 128–31.

c. E. F. Denison, *The Sources of Economic Growth in the U. S.* (New York: Committee for Economic Development, 1960).

d. Helen Keller, *The Story of My Life* (New York: Grosset & Dunlap, 1902), p. 17.

e. Heinz Werner and Bernard Kaplan, *Symbol Formation* (New York: John Wiley & Sons, 1963).

f. See, for example, Monet's "Water Lilies," p. 189, and Turner's "Steamer in a Snowstorm," p. 273, in Walter Canaday's *Mainstreams of Modern Art, David to Picasso* (New York: Holt, Rinehart & Winston, 1959).

g. John Bowlby, *Maternal Care and Mental Health,* World Health Organization Monograph Series, no. 2, 1952 (Paris: United Nations Educational, Scientific, and Cultural Organization, 1952).

h. Marie Skodak and Harold Skeels, "A Final Follow-up Study of One Hundred Adopted Children," *Journal of Genetic Psychology* 75 (September 1949): 85–125.

i. M. P. Deutsch, "The Disadvantaged Child and the Learning Process," in *Education in Depressed Areas,* ed. A. Harry Passow (New York: Bureau of Publications, Teachers College, Columbia University, 1963).

j. Robert D. Hess, "Educability and Rehabilitation: The Future of the Welfare Class," mimeographed (Chicago: University of Chicago, Committee on Human Development).

k. See Canaday, *Mainstreams of Modern Art, David to Picasso,* p. 482.

l. The Mikado's son, no less.

m. *The Complete Plays of Gilbert and Sullivan* (Garden City, N. Y.: Garden City Publishing Co., 1938), p. 399.

n. Richard H. Rovere, *Senator Joe McCarthy* (New York: Harcourt, Brace Jovanovich, Inc., 1960), p. 28.

o. Ibid., p. 167.

p. Canaday, *Mainstreams of Modern Art, David to Picasso,* p. 411.

q. P. S. Weisberg and K. J. Springer, "Environmental Factors in Creative Function," *Archives of General Psychiatry* 5 (1961): 554-64.

r. George and Fannie Shaftel, *Role Playing the Problem Story* (New York: National Conference of Christians and Jews, 381 41st Street, 1952.

s. Aldous Huxley, "Education on the Nonverbal Level," *Daedalus* 91 (Spring 1962): 292.

t. Ibid., p. 293.

u. Keller, *The Story of My Life*, p. 17.

v. See "Female Portrait," in Canaday, *Mainstreams of Modern Art, David to Picasso*, p. 5.

w. Suggested by E. H. Gombrich, "The Use of Art for the Study of Symbols," *American Psychologist* 20 (January 1965): 34-50.

x. J. B. Collinson, "The Concept," *Archives of General Psychiatry* 6 (February 1962): 168-81.

y. Richard Wright, *Black Boy* (Yonkers, N. Y.: World Book Co., 1950), p. 282.

z. Abraham A. Fabian, "Reading Disability: An Index of Pathology," *American Journal of Orthopsychiatry* 25 (April 25, 1955): 319–29.

aa. Canaday, *Mainstreams of Modern Art, David to Picasso*, p. 533.

bb. V. H. Rosen, "The Relevance of Style to Certain Aspects of Defence and the Synthetic Function of the Ego," *International Journal of Psychoanalysis* 42 (1961): 447-57.

School Entry as a Time of Crisis

Bower has looked at the possibilities of teaching competence in the school and family. He emphasized the role the ego plays in mediating affective and cognitive information about events and objects in *everyday life*. Other investigators have been more interested in examining situations which have the potential for *crisis*, e.g., loss of a loved one, birth of a sibling, graduation from school and so on. Kindergarten entry presents such a time of probable crisis for children and their families. Attention has been directed toward helping school and family to more fully understand and to more effectively cope with school entry as a crisis.

The concept of crisis intervention was evolved by two psychiatrists, Gerald Caplan and Erich Lindemann, the latter while studying loss and the mourning process in a hospital setting. Out of these experiences evolved the notion that crisis often accompanies role change, at which time an individual finds himself in a state of disequilibrium, disorganization, or turmoil, usually limited to about four to six weeks. Painfully preoccupied with past failures and successes, he longs for some resolution.(3) In such a state of mind, people are often more amenable to help. In addition greater personality growth and integration are possible and desirable outcomes. For these reasons Lindemann and Caplan felt that a crisis was an ideal time in which to offer help. They assumed that a more favorable resolution would occur when the helping person encouraged his "client" to ventilate his feelings, clarified the dilemma, and kept the issues focused—whether it be grief work or worry work. This thesis was tested on kindergarten entry at the Human Relations Center in Wellesley, Massachusetts, under the assumption that both child and family were undergoing role change.

**Kindergarten Entry:
Its Effects on
Children and Their Families**

Donald C. Klein

To those interested in preventing or reducing the incidence of children's emotional difficulties, school entry is an important event. It marks a significant change in the relationship between child and family, between child and the outside world and, indeed, between the family and a major social system external to it, namely, the school. It is a time of new social, emotional, and intellectual demands upon the child; it also is a time when parents are often more than usually willing to review a child's development in these three spheres, just as they are prepared to inquire into the possible existence of physical deficiencies which may warrant attention as part of preparation for school.

The Nature of Emotional Hazards

Experiences during World War II gave special impetus to investigations into the impact of stressful circumstances upon individuals and groups, and into the consequences of the availability or lack of supports at such times. Young children suffered less psychological damage from undergoing the London blitz when they remained with their mothers than when separated from them. Psychiatric casualties among combat troops were found to be related to intensity of combat and its prolongation, to whether units were advancing or retreating, and to such other factors as general morale and group cohesiveness.

A line of inquiry on the effects of bereavement on physical and emotional well being was carried out by Lindemann (Lindemann, 1944.) Since then a rapidly growing number of studies have been made of situations involving rapid shifts in interpersonal relationships and in the roles people are expected to play within emotionally relevant human groups. The preponderance of evidence indicates that each type of

Donald C. Klein, "Kindergarten Entry: Its Effects on Children and Their Families," in *Going to School.* Copyright 1963, by permission of American Academy of Pediatrics, Massachusetts Chapter, and the author.

shift poses unique emotional challenges, has unique patterns and sequence of events, and extends over a typical period of time. Among the presumed emotional hazards which have been studied is entry into school (Gruber, 1954; Lindemann and Ross, 1955, pp. 79-93; McGinnis, 1954, 1960; Klein and Ross, 1958, pp. 60-69).

Predicting School Adjustment

One line of inquiry has been concerned with the development of procedures for identifying children prior to school entry who, without help, may develop school adjustment problems. Procedures were devised which tapped into three aspects of the adaptation faced by the child:
1) the child's ability to separate from the mother and enter a strange environment, which, of course, also involves the mother's ability to separate from the child;
2) the child's ability to enter into a relationship, however tenuous in its initial phases, with a stranger;
3) the child's ability to deal realistically and in an appropriately organized fashion with a simple task (i.e., handling a semi-structured doll play situation) which the strange adult has assigned to him.

The procedures involved observation of the child in the semi-structured playroom setting and a brief interview with one or both parents covering aspects of the child's social and emotional development. They were highly successful in identifying children on the extremes, those judged to be almost certainly facing school adjustment difficulties and those to be almost certain to make the transition without disturbance. In the middle, however, were the greatest number about whom certain predictions could not be made, and their adjustments, as rated by teachers in follow-up studies through the primary grades, tended to fluctuate. Insofar as could be determined, the fluctuations seemed to depend upon a variety of factors within both home and school.

School Entry as an Emotional Hazard

As the studies progressed, the focus was broadened to consider the adaptation of the family network as a whole. It seemed clear that school entry was a time of rapid transition and increased tension for the family unit as well as for the child. It was hypothesized that the family's way of handling the event would have a significant effect upon how well the child fared. So attention was turned to a study of families during the period just before and during the first weeks of school. Mothers and fathers met with the research discussion leader and an observer-recorder at weekly intervals, starting the week before school began and extending for five or six weeks into the term. Parents were asked to observe their children and themselves; their job in group meetings was to discuss with one another the behavior they had observed.

Certain consistent observations appeared from one group drawn from schools in two different communities. First, parents were confronted by an increase of developmentally opposed reactions of their children during the initial weeks. Many of the children manifested regression to babyish patterns (e.g., clinging, thumb sucking, bed wetting) while at the same time making surprising (to the parents) new leaps towards maturity (e.g., independence in dressing, conscientiousness in chores, insistence upon freedom to wander farther from the house). Second, parental reactions of anxiety, depression, and hostility exceed the expectations of the research team. Moreover, they followed a typical sequential pattern, which can be described in four stages:

1) Anticipatory anxiety. During this period, which peaks in the week before school begins, parents view the child as an extension of self and family. Entry into school is defined as a debut. Questions are raised about the child's ability to handle the new situation. Parents wonder whether they have done what is necessary to prepare the child for the step towards independence. School entry becomes a test of parenthood.

2) Postentry relief coupled with depression. The child is felt to be lost to the family, as indeed he is. The old relationship can never be fully recaptured, and there is an entirely appropriate though highly attenuated grief reaction. Parents were suprised at their reactions. A mother said, "I should be happy, and I am I guess, but I miss him." Many reported one or more periods of crying during the first week of school. These reactions were apparently as prevalent among parents of later children as among parents of older children experiencing the separation for the first time.

3) Period of exclusion and resentment. The child has formed a relationship with someone outside the family circle. Moreover, the new adult, the teacher, usually has been able to influence the child in ways the parents have tried to without success. Feelings towards both child and teacher are ambivalent. Teacher is remarkably effective, but remains a mysterious and apparently most powerful figure. Parents try to form a link to the schoolroom through the reports of the children but this avenue is not usually successful. Children either cannot put their experiences into words, often seeming secretive; or they deluge the parents with unwanted details about the classroom, classmates, and teacher which lack meaning for the parents because of their ignorance of the new world in which the child now lives. Increased irritability appears among the parents during the few weeks in which the sense of exclusion prevails. Some become critical of some aspect of the school routine, such as the teacher's approach to discipline, the curriculum, and the like. At the same time, however, there is a reluctance to approach the school to talk with teacher or visit the classroom.

4) Resolution of the transition. By the end of four to six weeks the parents not only reported that the children were settling into an ap-

parently stable pattern; they also noted that the parents, too, were experiencing less distress and more satisfaction with the immediate situation. Parents now felt able to visit the school, and in one community responded eagerly to the teacher's customary invitation to attend a kindergarten mother's tea. Group discussions typically turned to the future, ranging from new demands to be faced in first grade all the way to college choice and the children's vocational training decisions.

Though the group meetings were intended solely to be a vehicle for the research, participants reported that they had helped them in at least two respects. First, the fact that other parents were experiencing similar reactions helped allay undue anxieties. Second, the opportunitiy to discuss reactions and experiences in a supportive setting led to certain new and more satisfactory ways of understanding intrafamilial relationships.

The Challenge for Pediatrics

There are now in existence in Wellesley and a few other communities in the United States collaborative programs involving mental health centers and school systems wherein attempts are made to identify children who may need preventive intervention if they are to meet the social and psychic challenges of school (Lindemann and Klein, 1964). In some of them attempts are being made to involve family physicians and pediatricians in the check-up process, preventive intervention or both. It seems clear that responsibility for pre-school mental health screening should be shared by those professional groups most directly in touch with child and family at the time the latter are experiencing the emotional hazard. Any one group alone probably could carry out the procedures necessary for identifying endangered or emotionally handicapped children. Planning for the supports necessary to forestall or treat difficulties, however, should involve the knowledge and skills of the educator, physician, and mental health worker.

The pediatrician already is in contact with many children and their families in the months just prior to school. The study of school entry as an emotional hazard suggests several ways in which the pediatrician is able, within his present professional role and setting, to play a significant part in the life of the family as an agent for mental health. First, of course, he is the one to assess the physical status of the child and, on the basis of his assessment, to help family and school modify the environment where indicated or institute physical remediation when possible. Second, he can devote time to discussion of the child's social and emotional development as school looms on the horizon. In so doing, he may help the parents express and sort out their concern about their efforts to prepare the child for his debut. Third, he can help the parents anticipate and sometimes even rehearse the steps which they will be taking to prepare the child for school, and to introduce themselves and their offspring to principal and teacher. Fourth, and most important, he can provide the sympathy and understanding of the informed medical man upon whom the parents can depend for support. Such a physician will be able to convey his recognition and understanding of the emotions engendered by the experience of loss and the reshaping of the family network that occurs when the child takes a major step out into the world.

References

Gruber, S. The concept of task-orientation in the analysis of play behavior of children entering kindergarten. *American Journal of Orthopsychiatry*, 1954, 24, 326-335.

Klein, D. Early school adjustment. In H. Steward and D. Prugh (eds.), *The healthy child*. Cambridge: Harvard University Press, 1960.

Klein, D., and Ross, A. Kindergarten entry: a study of role transition. In M. Krugman (ed.), *Orthopsychiatry and the school*. New York: American Orthopsychiatric Association, 1958.

Lindemann, E., and Klein, D. Approaches to preschool screening, summary of workshop. American Orthopsychiatric Association, March, 1962. Mimeographed.

Lindemann, E., and Ross, A. A follow-up study of a predictive test of social adaptation in preschool children. In G. Caplan (ed.), *Emotional problems of early childhood*. New York: Basic Books, Inc., 1955.

Lindemann, E. Symptomatology and management of acute grief. *American Journal of Orthopsychiatry*, 1944, 101, 141-148. (4)

Summary

White's concept of competence was utilized by Bower to suggest curriculum strategies that might strengthen the ego's ability to cope. Klein demonstrated how families and children responded to the potential crisis of kindergarten entry. Further practical and theoretical considerations for elementary school guidance programs can be found in *Guiding Human Development: The Counselor and the Teacher in the Elementary School.* (5)

During the last two decades complementary efforts to increase the emotional and cognitive competence of children have been made by affecting changes in both the school and the family—the two socializing institutions with which the child has intimate contact. Three major groups of professionals have advocated change: those concerned with the primary prevention of mental disorders in children, those concerned with curriculum changes in science and math instigated by the Russian space satellite program in the 1950's, those concerned with compensatory education of the disadvantaged during the 1960's. Optimistic phrases accompanied their overtures: "Prepare for the future." "Increase your child's ability to learn." "Learn to cope with change."

While these attempts to change the school or the family continue, the country has been jolted in the 1960's by the sudden realization of the profound complexity of our technological society and the demands it makes on the individual, and by the enormous discrepancies of experience between minority groups and a more affluent majority. To alleviate both problems, social institutions have been pressured to make reforms. A few have advocated more *fundamental* changes which go quite beyond what has been described here. For some, communes or the free school movement soften the impact of the demands made by a technological society. The concept of competence is relevant whatever the educational goals.

References to Part 7

1. Bower, Eli M., "Personality and Individual Social Maladjustment," in *Sixty-fifth Yearbook of the National Society for the Study of Education: Social Deviancy among Youth* (Chicago, Ill.: National Society for the Study of Education, 1966), pp. 106–34.

2. Braun, Samuel J., and Pollock, Sylvia Woodaman, "Teaching Disturbed Preschoolers: Making Observations Operational," in *Curriculum Is What Happens: Planning Is the Key* (Washington, D.C.: National Association for the Education of Young Children, 1970), pp. 51–61.

3. Caplan, Gerald, *An Approach to Community Mental Health* (London: Tavistock Publications, 1961).

4. Klein, Donald, "Kindergarten Entry: Its Effect on Children and Their Families," in *Symposium on Going to School* (Boston: Committee on Mental Health of the Massachusetts Chapter of American Academy of Pediatrics, April 1963), pp. 22–27.

5. Shane, June; Shane, Harold; Gibson, Robert; and Munger, Paul. *Guiding Human Development: The Counselor and the Teacher in the Elementary School* (Worthington, Ohio: Charles A. Jones Publishing Co., 1971).

6. White, Robert W., "A Way of Conceiving of Independent Ego Energies: Efficacy and Competence," *Ego and Reality in Psychoanalytic Theory: Psychological Issues*, monograph 11, vol. 3, no. 3 (New York: International Universities Press, 1963).

part 8

Stimulation in
Early Childhood

The past quarter of a century has been marked by a shift in viewpoint concerning the function and importance of stimulation in infancy and early childhood. The child's first years have consequently taken on new significance.

A generally accepted belief of the 1920's and the 1930's held that an infant unfolded according to an innate maturational blueprint. As the nervous and muscular systems developed, he gradually and predictably did tasks he was incapable of at birth. Attempts to train him to sit or to talk before he was "ready" would not only be fruitless but might well prove harmful. Development was considered fundamentally a physical process. If his major physical needs were met (sufficient food, warmth, and rest) and those conditions necessary to foster trust, autonomy, and initiative were present, then he would progress at his own inherent pace. Gesell was an influential advocate of a bland, placid environment for the infant.

These ideas were a tenet of faith: an individual's level of intelligence was a lifelong constant, deriving from his hereditary makeup and developing according to a genetically predetermined pattern. Level of intelligence could not decline, except in the case of major physical trauma (for example, head injury or high fever) or severe emotional disturbance. Only under extraordinary circumstances might test results improve, (e.g., illiterate mountain children learning to read). IQ scores of children under six years of age, obtained on the Stanford-Binet scale or other comparable test might vary markedly when they were retested at some later date, but this finding was attributed to the difficulties of testing very small children and the instrument's imperfections. For many years American educators and psychometrists clung to the immutability of the IQ; the real inner level of intelligence behind performance scores could not be altered by instruction or stimulation.

An Early Experiment
in Cognitive Enrichment

A series of cooperative studies between the Iowa Child Welfare Research Station and the Iowa Board of Control of State Institutions, under the leadership of Harold Skeels, produced some truly startling findings during the 1930's. They not only challenged the concept of the fixed IQ but were also one of the earliest research projects to demonstrate the effects of environment on young children's cognitive growth. J. McVicker Hunt comments:

...Their work...was picked to pieces by critics and in the process lost much of the suggestive value it was justified in having. Many of you will recall the ridicule that was heaped upon the "wandering IQ" and the way in which such people as Florence Goodenough (1939) derided in print the idea of a group of 13 "feeble-minded" infants being brought within the range of normal mentality through training by moron nursemaids in an institution for the feebleminded. (10:209)

In Skeel's most dramatic study, thirteen mentally retarded children were transferred at an early age from a nonstimulating institution to one where greater opportunity existed for an individualized relationship with adults who became emotionally invested in them and provided ample stimulation. Eleven of these thirteen were subsequently placed in adoptive homes, where they grew up. Twelve children in the contrast group, though brighter initially, remained in the nonstimulating institution. The initial results were published in 1939:

from **A Study of the Effects
of Differential Stimulation
on Mentally Retarded Children**
*Harold M. Skeels
and Harold B. Dye*

The study of the nature of intelligence challenges the interest of psychologists and educators not only because of the theoretical concepts involved but also because of the implications relating to child care and education. If, on the one hand, intelligence is static, a fixed entity, and relatively unmodifiable by changes in environmental impact, then changes in living conditions and amount and kind of education can be expected to have little influence on the mental level of individuals.

On the other hand, if intelligence shows change in relation to shifts in the environmental influence, then our concept must include modifiability, and the implications for child welfare become more challenging.

This latter concept was postulated by Alfred Binet. In his significant book entitled, *Les Idees Modernes Sur Les Enfants* (a), published in 1909, Binet devotes an enlightening chapter to the topic, "Intelligence: Its Measurement and Education." He is surprised and concerned at the prejudice against the concept of modifiability of intelligence.

To quote: "Some recent philosophers appear to have given their moral support to the deplorable verdict that the intelligence of an individual is a fixed quantity which cannot be augmented. We must protest and act against this brutal pessimism. We shall endeavor to show that it has no foundation whatsoever." (pp. 54–55)

Binet goes on to cite observations and situations relating to the teaching of subnormal children, summarizing as follows: "A child's mind is like a field for which an expert farmer has advised a change in the method of cultivating, with the result that in place of desert land, we now have a harvest. It is in this particular sense, the only one which is significant, that we say that the intelligence of children may be increased. One increases that which constitutes the intelligence of a school child; namely, the capacity to learn, to improve with instruction." (p. 55)

Statement of the Problem

The purpose of this study was to determine the effects on mental growth of a radical shift in institutional environment to one providing superior stimulation, introduced into the lives of mentally retarded children of early preschool ages. These children were placed singly or in some cases by twos on wards of brighter girls in an institution for feeble-minded children. Preliminary observation had given some indication that such an environment was mentally stimulating for children

Reprinted from Proceedings and Addresses of the American Association on Mental Deficiency, 1939, vol. 54, no. 1.

two to three years of age. As a correlary aim, it seemed pertinent to study a contrast group of dull-normal and normal children of somewhat similar ages residing over a period of time in a relatively nonstimulating orphanage environment.

Origin of the Study

This research project was the outgrowth of a clinical surprise. Two children under a year and a half, in residence at the state orphanage, gave unmistakable evidence of marked mental retardation. Kulhmann-Binet intelligence tests were given both children. C. D., thirteen months of age at time of examination, obtained an IQ of 46, and B. D., at sixteen months, scored an IQ of 35. Qualitative observations of the examiner substantiated a classification of imbecile level of mental retardation. In the case of B. D., the examiner felt that the child's actual level was perhaps slightly higher, but not to exceed ten points or an IQ level of 45. As check tests for further corroboration, the Iowa Tests for Young Children were used, Mental ages of approximately six and seven months respectively were obtained.

Obviously a classification of feeble-mindedness would not be justified if based on results of intelligence tests alone, particularly at these young ages. However, behavioral reactions in conjunction with the examinations of the pediatrician, and observations by the superintendent of nurses relative to activity or lack of activity of these children in the nursery in contrast with other children gave ample substantiation for a classification of marked mental retardation. C. D., at thirteen months, was making no attempts to stand, even with assistance. She could not pull herself to an upright position with the aid of crib or chair, nor did she display much manipulative activity with blocks or play materials. Spontaneous vocalization also was lacking. B. D., at sixteen months, was not vocalizing, was unable to walk with help, and made relatively no responses to play materials in the nursery.

There were no indications of physiological or organic defects. Birth histories were negative, both children being full term normal delivery with no indications of birth injury or glandular dysfunction. Social histories were not flattering. Both children were illegitimate. In the case of C. D., the mother had been adjudged feeble-minded and a legal guardian was appointed. Although the mother claimed to have finished the eighth grade at sixteen years, the social workers felt that she was very retarded and probably had had a difficult time in school. A Stanford-Binet (1916 revision) intelligence test given at the University Hospital showed a mental age of nine years and an IQ of 56. She had always been healthy. Her father was a miner, had been unable to learn in school, and had deserted his family. Little is known of the father of the child, although it was reported that he had gone to high school.

B. D.'s mother was an inmate in a state hospital, diagnosed as psychosis with mental deficiency. She was slow to sit up, walk, and talk, and went only to the second grade in school. The maternal grandfather drank to excess and his brother died in a state hospital of general paralysis of the insane. One maternal great aunt died of epilepsy. B. D.'s father is unknown; the mother named an inebriate formerly released from the state hospital.

Accordingly, these two children were recommended for transfer to the school for feeble-minded. We quote from the recommendations for transfer as follows: C. D.: "Diagnosis of mental ability: Mental deficiency of imbecile level, which will probably continue with an increase in age. Prognosis: Poor. With this deficiency in mental development, C. D. will be unable to make her way outside the care and protection offered by an institution for feeble-minded children. Her relatives are not in a position to give her the continuous care she will need." Diagnosis and prognosis on B. D. were similar to the one just quoted.

Following this recommendation, the children were committed to the school for feeble-minded. They were placed on a ward of older girls, ranging in age from eighteen to fifty years and in mental age from five to nine years.

Six months after transfer, the psychologist visiting the wards of the institution was surprised to notice the apparently remarkable development of these children. Accordingly they were re-examined on the Kuhlmann-Binet, C. D. obtaining an IQ of 77 and B. D. an IQ of 87. Twelve months later they were tested again with IQ's of 100 and 88, respectively. Tests were again given when the children were forty months of age respectively, with IQ's of 95 and 93.

In the meantime, inquiries were made as to reasons for this unusual development. Their "home" or ward environment was studied. It was observed that the attendants on the ward had taken a great fancy to the "babies." They were essentially the only preschool children on the ward, other than a few hopeless bed patients with physiological defects. The attendants would take these two children with them on their days off, giving them car rides and taking them down town to the store. Toys, picture books, and play materials were purchased by these admiring adults. The older, brighter girls on the wards were also very much attached to the children and would play with them during most of the waking hours. Thus it can be seen that this environment turned out to be stimulating to these preschool children of low initial mental level.

Following these last examinations, it was felt that the stimulation value of this particular kind of an environment had been pretty well exhausted. If the resulting level of intelligence were to be maintained, a shift to a more normal environment seemed essential. Furthermore, since the children were then well within the range of normal intelligence, there ceased to be any justification for keeping them in an institution for the feeble-minded. Accordingly, they were transferred back to the orphanage and from there placed in rather average adoptive homes, their ages then being three years, six months, and three years, eight months. After approximately fifteen months in the foster homes, the children were again examined, this time using the Stanford-Binet. IQ's of 94 and

93 were obtained. From the evidence obtained, there is every indication that they will continue to classify as normal individuals as they increase in age. Accordingly, legal adoption has been completed in both cases.

From these startling preliminary findings, several questions were presented. Observations of similarly retarded children comparable in ages, remaining in an orphanage nursery, showed continued lack of mental development. In such a situation, the retarded child with numbers of other children of higher intelligence but of the same age seemed to make no gain in rate of mental growth. Also, since there was a ratio of only one or two adults to twelve or eighteen children, adult contacts were at a minimum and limited largely to physical care. Obviously, the retarded child could not be placed directly in an adoptive home as there could be no marked assurance that later development would be normal. Boarding home care to permit further evaluation and observation of development would, of course, be a logical solution of such a problem. However, the code of Iowa provides only for institutional care or placement in free or adoptive homes. Consequently, there seemed to be only one alternative, and that a rather fantastic one; namely, to transfer mentally retarded children in the orphanage nursery, one to two years of age, to an institution for feeble-minded in order to make them normal. . . .

Subjects

Experimental Group

Accordingly, from time to time, retarded children from the Iowa Soldiers' Orphans' Home at Davenport were sent to the Iowa Instituition for Feeble-Minded Children at Glenwood. The experimental group includes all children so transferred who were under three years of age at time of transfer, a total of thirteen. The following tabulation shows sex, chronological age at time of examination before transfer, Kuhlmann-Binet mental age, and IQ; and chronological age at time of transfer.

Examination Prior to Transfer

Case	Sex	Chronological Age, Months	Mental Age, Months	IQ	Chronological Age, Months at Transfer
1	M	7.0	6.0	89	7.1
2	F	12.7	7.2	57	13.1
3	F	12.7	10.8	85	13.3
4	F	14.7	10.8	73	15.0
5	F	13.4	6.0	46	15.2
6	F	15.5	12.0	77	15.6
7	F	16.6	10.8	65	17.1
8	F	16.6	6.0	35	18.4
9	F	21.8	13.2	61	22.0
10	M	23.3	16.8	72	23.4
11	M	25.7	19.2	75	27.4
12	F	27.9	18.0	65	28.4
13	F	30.0	10.8	36	35.9

The mean chronological age at time of transfer was 19.4 months, median 17.1 months, with a range from 7.1 to 35.9 months. Range of IQ's was from 35 to 89 with a mean of 64.3 and a median of 65.0. In eleven of the thirteen cases, additional tests had been given shortly before or in conjunction with the tests reported above. These were either repeated Kuhlmann-Binet examinations or Iowa Tests for Young Children. Such tests gave further corroboration of classifications of marked mental retardation. . . .

Contrast Group

This group did not exist as a designated group until the close of the experimental period. These children were simply examined as individuals from time to time along with the other children in the orphanage as routine procedure. It was only after the data on the experimental group had been analyzed that the decision was made to study a group of children remaining in the orphanage for contrast purposes. Children were included who 1) had had initial intelligence tests under two years of age, 2) were still in residence in the orphanage at approximately four years of age, and 3) were in the control group of the orphanage preschool study (e), or 4) had not attended preschool. The study of the orphanage preschool referred to included two groups of children matched in choronological age, mental age, IQ, and length of residence in the institution. The one group had the advantages of the more stimulating environment of preschool attendance while the control group experienced the less stimulating environment of cottage life. Since the purpose of the contrast group for the present study was to include children in a relatively nonstimulating environment, children who had attended preschool could not be included. Such limitations, however, did not constitute a selective factor as far as the make-up of the children was concerned. A total of twelve children met these requirements and have been designated as the contrast group in the present study.

The following tabulation shows sex, chronological age at time of first examination, Kuhlmann-Binet mental age, and IQ:

Case	Sex	Chronolog-ical Age, Months	Mental Age, Months	IQ
14	F	11.9	11.0	91
15	F	13.0	12.0	92
16	F	13.6	9.6	71
17	M	13.8	13.2	96
18	M	14.5	14.4	99
19	M	15.2	13.2	87
20	M	17.3	14.0	81
21	M	17.5	18.0	103
22	M	18.3	18.0	98
23	F	20.2	18.0	89
24	M	21.5	10.6	50
25	M	21.8	18.0	83

The mean chronological age at time of first examination was 16.6 months with a median at 16.3 months. The range was from 11.9 months to 21.8 months. The mean IQ for the group was 86.7 (median 90.0). With the exception of two cases (16 and 24) the children had IQ's ranging from 81 to 103.

Reasons for earlier nonplacement in adoptive homes were in general for those other than mental retardation. In fact, nine were, or had been considered normal as far as mental development was concerned. Five children were withheld from placement simply because of a poor family history. Two were held because of improper commitment, two because of luetic condition, and one because of mental retardation. . . .

Medical Histories

In the evaluation of the medical histories of both the experimental and contrast groups, little of significance was found in the relationship between illnesses and the rate of mental growth. In the experimental group, one child, Case 9, had congenital syphilis, but immediate anti-luetic treatment following birth was adequate and serology was negative during the experimental period. In the contrast group, two children, Cases 14 and 16, were luetic, but Case 16 responded to early antiluetic treatment and all serology has been negative during the period of the study. However, in Case 14, a question may be raised as to the contributing effects of persistent syphilis. Blood Wasserman and Kahn were negative at nine months of age, but examination at thirty months revealed 4 plus Wasserman and Kahn. Treatment was again instituted, and at forty-six months both blood and spinal fluid serology were negative. Case 16, on admission to the orphanage, had enlarged spleen and liver, a tentative diagnosis of Gaucher's disease being made. This did not seriously affect the activity of the child during the course of study.

Considering all children of both groups, they have had various upper respiratory infections, occasional contagious diseases, mild eczemas, but nothing more severe that the ordinary child of preschool age would have in the average home.

Family Backgrounds

Social histories revealed that the children of both experimental and contrast groups came from homes of low social, economic, occupational, and intellectual levels. The family background is comparable to that reported by Skeels and Fillmore (d) in their study of the mental development of children from underpriviliged homes and Skodak's study (f) of children in foster homes placed at ages two to five. The backgrounds of the children in the two groups were comparable.

Mothers. Information relating to education was available for eleven of the thirteen mothers in the experimental group and ten of the twelve mothers in the contrast group. The mean grade completed by mothers of children in the experimental group was 7.8 with a median at grade eight. Only two had any high school work, one having completed the eleventh grade and one the tenth grade (Cases 3 and 6). In one case, it was doubtful if the second grade had been completed (Case 8). Two

(Cases 1 and 5) had dropped out of the eighth grade at the age of sixteen.

In the contrast group, the mean grade completed was 7.3 with a median at 7.5. One mother (Case 19) had completed high school and one had an equivalent of ninth grade education.

Occupational history of mothers, available on seven of the mothers of the experimental group and nine of the contrast group, included mainly housework, either in the homes of parents or working out as domestics. In only one instance was there a higher level indicated (Case 24 of the contrast group) in which the mother had been a telephone operator and had done general office work.

Intelligence tests* had been obtained on five of the mothers in the experimental group and nine of the mothers in the contrast group. The mean IQ for mothers of the experimental group was 70.4, with a median at 66. One additional mother, although not tested, was considered feeble-minded and had gone only as far as the second grade. Four mothers had IQ's below 70, and one classified as normal with an IQ of 100.

Of the nine mothers in the contrast group, only two had IQ's above 70, one being 79 and the other 84. The others ranged from 36 to 66. The mean IQ was 63, with a median at 62.

Fathers. Little information was available on the fathers; in fact, in many cases paternity was doubtful.

A qualitative analysis of social histories seems to justify the conclusion that within these educational and occupational classifications of true parents, the individuals represent the lower levels in such groups. Most of these fathers and mothers dropped out of school because of having reached their limits of achievement, and in no sense of the word represent the averages of their grade placements. The same may be said with reference to occupational status.

Description of the Environments

Experimental Group

Children in this group were transferred from the orphanage nursery to the school for feeble-minded, and placed on the wards with older, brighter girls. Wards in the girls' division were used. This included a large cottage of eight wards with a matron and an assistant matron in charge and one attendant for each ward. There are approximately thirty patients on each ward, including girls ranging in ages from eighteen to fifty years. On two wards, (wards 2 and 3) are girls of the higher levels, mental ages from nine to twelve years. On two other wards (wards 4 and 5) the mental levels are from seven to ten years, and on another ward (ward 7) the mental ages are from five to eight.

---

*Stanford-Binet (1916) intelligence tests. Most of these were given by psychologists either at the Psychopathic Hospital or the University Hospital of the University of Iowa. Maximum chronological age used was sixteen years.

With the exception of ward 7, there were few, if any, younger children on the wards aside from the experimental children. In some cases, there were one or two other young children on the ward, usually a mongol or a spastic paralysis case. In general, one, or at the most two, children in the experimental group were placed on a given ward.

The attendants and the older girls became very fond of the child placed on the ward and took great pride in its achievement. In fact, there was considerable competition between wards to see which one would have their "baby" walking or talking first. The girls would spend a great deal of time with the children, teaching them to walk, talk, play with toys and play materials, and in the training of habits.

Most of the clothing for these children was made by the older girls. The girls were so fond of the children that they would actually spend their small earnings and allowances to buy them special foods, toys, picture books, and materials for clothing. Similarly attendants gave of their time, money and affection, and during their free hours frequently took the children on excursions, car rides, and trips. In addition, it was the policy of the matron in charge of the girls' school division to single out certain of these children whom she felt were in need of special individiualization, and permit these children to spend a portion of time each day visiting her office. This furnished new experiences including being singled out and given special attention and affection, new play materials, additional language stimulation, and contacts with other office callers.

An indication of the interest in these children was shown by the fact that a baby show was held for one of the Fourth of July celebrations. Each ward made a float upon which its "baby" rode, dressed in costume. Prizes were awarded for the winning baby, most attractive costume, and best float.

The spacious living rooms of the wards furnished ample room for indoor play and activity. Whenever weather permitted, the children spent some time each day on the playground, supervised by one or more of the older girls. In this situation, they had contacts with other children of similar ages. Outdoor play equipment included tricycles, swings, slides, sand box, etc.

In addition to the opportunities afforded on the wards, the children attended the school kindergarten. They were sent to school as soon as they could walk. Toddlers remained for only half of the morning, whereas those of four or five years of age were in kindergarten the entire morning. Activities carried on in the kindergarten were more in the nature of a preschool than the more formal type of kindergarten.

As a part of the school program, the children each morning attended fifteen minute chapel exercises, including group singing and music by the orchestra. The children also attended the dances, school programs, moving pictures, and Sunday chapel services.

In considering this enriched environment from a dynamic point of view, it must be pointed out that in the case of almost every child, some one adult, (older girl or attendant) would become particularly attached to a given child and would figuratively "adopt" him. As a consequence there would develop a rather intense adult-child relationship with the other adult contacts being somewhat more marginal. This meant that such a child had some one person with whom he was identified and who was particularly interested in him and his achievement. It was felt that this constituted an important aspect of the environmental impact on the child.

Contrast Group

The environment of the children in the contrast group is considered to be rather representative of the average orphanage. The outstanding feature is the profound lack of mental stimulation or experiences usually associated with the life of a younger child in the ordinary home.

Up to the age of two years, the children were in the nursery of the hospital. This was limited to a rather small play room with additional dormitory rooms of two to five beds each. The children were cared for by two nurses with some additional assistance by one or two girls of ten to fifteen years of age. The children had good physical and medical care, but little can be said beyond this. Contacts with adults were largely limited to feeding, bathing, dressing, and toilet details. It can readily be seen that with the large number of children per adult, little time was available for anything aside from the routines of physical care. The girls who assisted the nurses accepted the work as a necessary evil and, in general, took little personal interest in the children as individuals. Few play materials were available and little attention was given to the teaching of play techniques. The children were seldom out of the nursery room except for short walks or short periods of time out of doors for fresh air.

At two years of age these children were graduated to the cottages. A rather complete description of "cottage" life is reported in the study by Skeels, Updegraff, Wellman, and Williams on *A Study of Environmental Stimulation: An Orphanage Preschool Project*, from which the following excerpts are taken:

> Overcrowding of living facilities was characteristic. Too many children had to be accommodated in the available space and there were too few adults to guide them.... Thirty to thirty-five children of the same sex under six years of age lived in a "cottage" in charge of one matron and three or four entirely untrained and often reluctant girls of thirteen to fifteen years of age. The waking and sleeping hours of these children were spent (except during meal times and a little time on a grass plot) in an average sized room (approximately fifteen feet square), a sun porch of similar size, a cloak room,... and a single dormitory. The meals for all children in the orphanage were served in a central building in a single large dining room....
>
> The duties falling to the lot of a matron were not only those involved in the care of the children but those related to clothing and cottage maintenance, in other words, cleaning, mending, and so forth.... With so much responsibility centered on one adult, the result was a necessary regimentation. The children sat down, stood up, and did many things in rows and in unison. They spent considerable time sitting on chairs, for in addition to the number of children and the matron's limited time, there was the misfourtune of inadequate equipment....

*This inadequacy was true of permanent fixtures, supplies, and play equipment. The lavatories in the wash room, for example, were too high for the children to reach. Individual towels, washcloths, and combs were not the rule.... The hooks in the cloakroom were placed well above the heads of all of the children; in the sense that it is quicker for the adult to handle clothing than for her to teach the children to do it, this arrangement may have been considered helpful. In short, there was little in the cottage to indicate that small children lived there excepting for rows of small chairs in one room. As for play equipment, it was all but nonexistent.... It is small wonder that these children frequently occupied themselves by fastening and unfastening their own and others' clothing and shoes; it was difficult to keep shoes on the children in the cottages.

No child had any property which belonged exclusively to him except, perhaps, his toothbrush. Even his clothing, including shoes, was selected and put on him according to size. Small wonder that the children were backward in developing responsibility or pride in property. Why should Johnny worry about the hole he tears in his suit? Next week Tommy will probably wear it, and if the hole gets big enough someone will have to mend it or see about providing a new suit....

In addition to their isolation from life outside the institution they had no contact with the activities of the institution other than those which actually affected their daily routines. For example, it is difficult to convey the idea of far distances to children whose idea of the end of the world is "down town." Moreover, the nature of "down town" is equally ephemeral. For most of these children, for example, the words *store, bank* or *restaurant* were nothing but a succession of sounds calling up no remembered images. It is difficult to discuss everyday, ordinary happenings with children who have, for instance, never experienced an ordinary home dwelling, who know food in no state except that in which it appears on their plates in the dining hall. Their experiences were limited to their own immediate needs. Their background of information was not only sadly lacking, but their learning through question was curtailed; the asking of questions was discouraged, for the answering of questions consumes time. Too frequently the children were expected to accept things as they were.... (e:10–13)

From this it may be seen what a remarkable contrast there was between the environment of the experimental transfer group and the contrast group. Such a radical shift in environment as was experienced by each of the children in the experimental group would scarcely occur in an unselected sampling of children in their own homes more than two or three times in a thousand cases.

Following the completion of these research studies on preschool childrent, the orphanage has made radical changes in the program for the preschool child. Number of children per cottage has been reduced, thus alleviating to a great extent the overcrowded conditions. Each cottage now has two matrons with additional domestic service. The preschool has been made an integral part of the school system with all children of preschool age in attendance. With the assistance of the state emergency nursery school program a pre-preschool program has been set up for the children in the nursery under two years of age. A trained teacher, in addition to the regular nursing staff, spends full time with the infants providing a more enriched play and educational program.

---

*Further description of the environment has been included from the same source (14) and did not appear in the original article.

Mental Development of
Children in Experimental
and Contrast Groups

The mental development of individual children in the experimental group is presented in Table 1. As the standard measure of intelligence the 1922 Kuhlmann Revision of the Binet was used, excepting in the cases of two or three tests on children who were four years of age or more where the Stanford-Binet (1916) was used. All examinations were made by trained and experienced psychologists. Test one was the measure of intelligence just prior to transfer. Tests two, three, and last test, were given at subsequent intervals of time following transfer. "Last test" is the test at the end of the experimental period, and represents the second, third, or fourth test, depending on the number of tests available at representative time intervals on a given child.

Similar data showing the mental growth of the individual children in the contrast group are presented in Table 2. In the column marked "last test" is given the test on each child at the end of the period of study. This was either the third or fourth test, depending upon the number of available tests at representative time intervals on each child.

Mean, median, and standard deviation comparisons of mental growth from "first" to "last test" for experimental and contrast groups are presented in Table 3. Mean IQ at time of transfer was 64.3 with a median at 65. The average gain in intelligence quotient for the experimental group during the course of the experiment was 27.5 points with a median of 23. The mean IQ on "last" test was 91.8 with a median at 93. The difference between "first" and "last" tests yielded a critical ratio (Fisher's t) of 6.3 or practical certainty of a true difference. Every child showed a gain, the range being from 7 to 58 points. Three children made gains of 45 points or more, and all but two children gained more than 15 points (Table 1).

The average chronological age at time of transfer was 19.4 months with a range from 7.1 months to 35.9 months, the median being 17.1 months. Length of the experimental period was from 5.7 months to 52.1 months with a mean of 18.9 months and a median of 14.5 months. The length of the experimental period was not a constant for all children, but depended upon the rate of development of the individual child. As soon as a child showed normal mental development as measured by intelligence tests and substantiated by qualitative observations, the experimental period was considered completed; the child's visit at the school for feeble-minded was terminated; and he was placed in an adoptive home or returned to the orphanage.

The mental growth pattern for children of the contrast group is quite the opposite from that of the experimental group. The mean IQ on "first" examination was 86.7, whereas on the "last" test it was 60.5, showing an average loss of 26.2 points. The critical ratio (Fisher's t) was

TABLE 1

MENTAL DEVELOPMENT OF INDIVIDUAL CHILDREN IN EXPERIMENTAL GROUP AS MEASURED BY KUHLMANN-BINET INTELLIGENCE TESTS BEFORE AND AFTER TRANSFER

| Case Number* | Before Transfer Test 1 | | Chronological Age, Months, at Transfer | After Transfer | | | | | | | | Length of Experimental Period, Months | Change in IQ, First to Last Test |
| | Chronological Age, Months | IQ | | Test 2 | | Test 8 | | Last | | | | | |
				Chronological Age, Months	IQ	Chronological Age, Months	IQ	Chronological Age, Months	IQ				
1	7.0	89	7.1	12.8	113			12.8	113			5.7	+24
2	12.7	57	13.1	20.5	94	29.4	83	36.8	77			23.7	+20
3	12.7	85	13.3	25.2	107			25.2	107			11.9	+22
4	14.7	73	15.0	23.1	100			23.1	100**			8.1	+27
5	13.4	46	15.2	21.7	77	32.9	100	40.0	95**			24.8	+49
6	15.5	77	15.6	21.3	96	30.1	100	30.1	100			14.5	+23
7	16.6	65	17.1	27.5	104			27.5	104			10.4	+39
8	16.6	35	18.4	24.8	87	36.0	88	43.0	93			24.6	+58
9	21.8	61	22.0	34.3	80			34.3	80			12.3	+19
10	23.3	72	23.4	29.1	88	37.9	71	45.4	79			22.0	+7
11	25.7	75	27.4	42.5	78	51.0	82**	51.0	82**			23.6	+7
12	27.9	65	28.4	40.4	82			40.4	82			12.0	+17
13	30.0	36	35.9	51.7	70	81.0	74**	89.0	81**			52.1	+45

*Arranged according to age at time of transfer from youngest to oldest
**Stanford-Binet IQ

TABLE 2

MENTAL DEVELOPMENT OF INDIVIDUAL CHILDREN IN CONTRAST GROUP AS MEASURED BY REPEATED KUHLMANN-BINET INTELLIGENCE TESTS OVER A PERIOD OF TWO AND ONE-HALF YEARS

Case Number*	Test								Length of Experimental Period, Months	Change in IQ, First to Last Test
	1		2		8		Last			
	Chronological Age, Months	IQ	Chronological Age, Months	IQ	Chronological Age, Months	IQ	Chronological Age, Months	IQ		
14	11.9	91	24.8	73	37.5	65	55.0	62	43.1	−29
15	13.0	92	20.1	54	38.3	56	38.3	56	25.3	−36
16	13.6	71	20.6	76	40.9	56	40.9	56	27.3	−15
17	13.8	96	37.2	58	53.2	54	53.2	54	39.4	−42
18	14.5	99	21.6	67	41.9	54	41.9	54	27.4	−45
19	15.2	87	22.5	80	35.5	74	44.5	67	29.3	−20
20	17.3	81	43.0	77	52.9	83**	52.9	83**	35.6	+ 2
21	17.5	103	26.8	72	38.0	63	50.3	60	32.8	−43
22	18.3	98	24.8	93	30.7	80	39.7	61	21.4	−37
23	20.2	89	27.0	71	39.4	66	48.4	71	28.2	−18
24	21.5	50	34.9	57	51.6	42	51.6	42	30.1	− 8
25	21.8	83	28.7	75	37.8	63	50.1	60	28.3	−23

*Arranged according to age at time of transfer from youngest to oldest
**Stanford-Binet IQ

6.1. The median IQ on "first" test was 90 and on "last test" 60, with a median of individual losses of 32.5 points. . . .

With the exception of one child who gained two points in IQ from first to last test, all children showed losses, the range being from −8 points to −45 points. Ten of the twelve children lost 15 or more points in IQ (Table 2).

. . . the greatest gain for children in the experimental group was made during the first ten months of the experimental period. Similarly, in Table 2, the greatest loss for children in the contrast group was during the first year with a somewhat lower rate of loss during the second and third years.

In the following tabulation children in the experimental group have been arranged in the order of gains from the greatest to the least; children in the control group have been arranged in order of losses from the greatest to the least.

Case	Changes in IQ First to Last Test	Chronological Age, Months First Test	IQ First Test
	Experimental Group		
8	+58	16.6	35
5	+49	13.4	46
13	+45	30.0	36
7	+39	16.6	65
4	+27	14.7	73
1	+24	7.0	89
6	+23	15.5	77
3	+22	12.7	85
2	+20	12.7	57
9	+19	21.8	61
12	+17	27.9	65
10	+ 7	23.3	72
11	+ 7	25.7	75
	Contrast Group		
18	−45	14.5	99
21	−43	17.5	103
17	−42	13.8	96
22	−37	18.3	98
15	−36	13.0	92
14	−29	11.9	91
25	−23	21.8	83
19	−20	15.2	87
23	−18	20.2	89
16	−15	13.6	71
24	− 8	21.5	50
20	+ 2	17.3	81

There is a tendency for children in the experimental group initially at the lower levels to make the greater gains. The three children classifying at the imbecile level on first examination made gains of 58, 49, and 45 points IQ. Also greatest losses in the contrast group were associated with the highest initial levels. Six children with original IQ's above 90 lost from 29 to 45 points in IQ. While this shift may be partially due to regression, there must be other factors operating to bring about such a large and consistent change.

These results, although more marked, are comparable to the findings reported in the orphanage preschool study by Skeels, Updegraff, Wellman, and Williams (e). In that study, children of the preschool group initially at the lower levels made the greatest gains following a period of preschool attendance, and children in the control group originally at the higher levels showed the greatest losses.

There appears to be a marked lack of relationship between mental growth patterns and factors pertaining to the family histories of the children. Numbers of cases are too small to permit statistical treatment of the data. Comparisons are therefore on a more general inspectional basis. In the experimental group, children whose mothers were classified as feeble-minded showed as marked gains as children whose mothers were at a higher mental level. The greatest gain in intelligence (58 points IQ) was made by Case 8 whose mother was known to be feeble-minded and had only gone as far as the second grade in school.

In the contrast group, the only child who failed to show loss in rate of mental growth (Case 20) from "first" to "last" test was the son of a mother with an IQ of 36. Case 24, the most retarded child in the group on first examination with an IQ of 50, had a rather flattering family history. His father had graduated from high school and was talented in music. His mother was an eighth grade graduate and had gone to an evening business school. She had been a telephone operator and had done general office work.

That the gains in intelligence evidenced by the children of the experimental group were true gains and not due to an artifice in testing seems validated. Practice effects could not have been a contributing factor to these gains as the children in the contrast group, who showed continual losses in IQ, actually had more tests than children in the experimental group. Improvement was noted independently by members of the medical staff, attendants and matrons and school teachers.

Teachers are required to submit written reports to the principal at the end of each semester on all children enrolled in classes. Repeated reference is made in these reports to the marked improvement of these children in the experimental group. The following excerpts are taken from such reports: Case 12 after one year preschool or kindergarten: "Well behaved, interested. Joins group for simple games and rhythms. From my observations she apparently possesses about average intelligence for a child her age." Later report: "Very great improvement. Has good vocabulary and muscular coordination. Takes directions readily and can be depended upon. A good leader in games. Does fair handwork." Case 3, after one year: "Very quiet. Has shown a very great improvement this year. Has a fair vocabulary and will take part in games when asked." (This child, two years of age, was one of the youngest in the group.) Case 9, after one year: "Has improved a good deal. Enjoys games and rhythms. Is speaking quite a little. Very attentive."

A close bond of love and affection between a given child and one or two adults assuming a very personal parental role appears to be a dynamic factor of great importance. In evaluating these relationships, nine of the thirteen children in the experimental group were favored with such a relationship. The four other children tended to be less individualized and their adult relationships were more of a general nature involving more adults, the bonds of relationship being less intense with a given individual adult. It seems significant to note that the children favored with the more intense personal contacts made greater gains than those considered as being limited to the more general contacts. The nine children in the "personal" group made gains in IQ ranging from 17 to 58 points with an average of 33.8 points gain. The four children in the more general contact group made average gains of 14 points. Two children made gains of only 7 points, one 19 points, and one 20 points.

Two children (Cases 10 and 11), showed little progress on ward 7 over a period of a year and a half. This ward differed materially from the other wards in that there were from eight to twelve children of younger ages (3 to 8 years), and the older grils were of a lower mental level. The attendant on the ward was especially fine with young children, but, of course, was unable to give as much individual attention as was possible on other wards because of the large number of young children. At the time it was feared that these two children would continue to be hopelessly retarded. However, they were subsequently placed as singletons on wards with brighter girls, and after a period of six months with more individualization they showed marked gains in intelligence.

The possibility of "coaching" on test items may be ruled out as a factor. Adults and other older girls working with the children were not in any way familiar with the tests used or when they would be administered. Results in terms of IQ's were never given out; the only reports made were qualitative ones indicating the general improvement of the child.

As has been indicated, all thirteen children in the experimental group were considered unsuitable for adoption because of mental deficiency. Following the experimental period, seven of these children have been placed in adoptive homes. Of the remaining six, five are considered well within the range of normality and were returned to the orphanage. Only one child (IQ 77) will continue in residence at the school for feeble-minded for further observation as to subsequent mental development.

Of the children in adoptive homes, four have been examined following one year's residence in the foster home. These are Cases 1, 5, 7, and 8. Final IQ's are respectively as follows: 117, 94, 97, and 93. Three of the five children returned to the orphanage have been given an additional test following "last test" reported in Table 2. These are Cases 3, 10, and 11 with subsequent IQ's of 115, 84, and 85.

Accordingly, on a basis of last test reported, of the thirteen children two now classify as above average intelligence with IQ's of 117 and 115; five have IQ's between 90 and 100.; five at the 80 to 90 level and only one child with an IQ below 80. No child is now considered to be feeble-minded.

In an evaluation of the contrasting mental growth patterns of children in the two groups, one is impressed by the marked relationship between rate of mental growth and the nature of the environmental impact. In the case of the contrast group, the psychological prescription was apparently inadequate as to kinds of ingredients, amounts, and relative proportions. Accordingly, the children became increasingly emaciated in mental growth as time went on.

Conversely, when the psychological prescription was radically changed, the children in the experimental group already retarded at the time of transfer showed marked improvement and either achieved or approached normal mental development after a period of time. The environment of the experimental group apparently included a more adequate prescription as relating to the kinds and proportions of ingredients needed by children of these young ages for normal mental development. It must not be inferred that the environment of the experimental group represented an optimum prescription. Perhaps even greater improvement would have resulted had there been greater facilities and more adequate knowledge of proportioning the ingredients operative in producing optimal mental growth. No instructions were given as to what should or should not be done with the children when they were placed on the wards. This was largely a matter of chance. The general prescription, however, did include certain unmeasured quantitative and qualitative ingredients such as love and affection by one or more interested adults; a wealth of play materials and ample space and opportunity for play with supervision and direction; varied experiences such as preschool or kindergarten attendance and opportunity to be in group gatherings; and a number of other diversified experiences associated with the opportunities afforded a child in a rather adequate home situation. This rather general prescription proved to be conducive to increase in rate of mental development.

With more adequate knowledge as to the correct proportioning of such ingredients in relation to the specific inadequacies or gaps in the developmental pattern of a given child, possibly even more marked mental improvement could have been brought about.

That such increase in rate of mental development may be brought about at older ages through provision of a more adequate psychological prescription is suggested in the studies of Kephart (c) at the Wayne County Training School. He found that boys of fifteen to eighteen years of age showed increase in rate of mental growth following environmental changes pointed toward alleviation of the developmental gaps or inadequacies.

It therefore appears that there is an added challenge in the education of the so-called "functional" feeble-minded, that is those not evidencing physiological deficiencies or organic diseases. Not only should the educational program of a school for feeble-minded include the teaching of skills at the individual's mental level, but it should be so individualized as to provide for the specific developmental needs of a given child with the strong possibility that the level of mental capacity can be materially augmented.

Summary

This study attempts to determine the effect on mental growth of a radical shift from one institutional environment to another which provided superior stimulation. The experimental group included thirteen mentally retarded orphanage children from one to two years of age, placed singly or by twos on wards with brighter, older girls. This environment was stimulating and had many adult contacts. The mean IQ of the group at time of transfer was 64.3. As a contrast group twelve average and dull normal children (mean IQ 86.7) in an orphanage nursery were studied. Few adult contacts were afforded with limited opportunities for play and development.

Results and conclusions are as follows:

1) Over a period of two years the mean level of intelligence of the experimental group increased markedly while that of the contrast group showed an equivalent decrease. The experimental group made an average gain of 27.5 points while the contrast group showed a mean loss of 26.2 points.

2) Critical ratios (t's) based on differences between first and last tests for experimental and contrast groups were 6.3 and 6.1 respectively.

3) A change from mental retardation to normal intelligence in children of preschool age is possible in the absence of organic disease or physiological deficiency by providing a more adequate psychological prescription.

4) Conversely, children of normal inelligence may become mentally retarded to such a degree as to be classifiable as feeble-minded under the continued adverse influence of a relatively nonstimulating environment.

5) An intimate and close relationship between the child and an interested adult seems to be a factor of importance in the mental development of young children.

6) In a child placing program if children are to be withheld from placement in adoptive homes pending further observation of mental development, it is imperative that careful consideration be given to the type of environment in which they are to be held.

7) The possibility of increasing the mental capacity of "functionally" feeble-minded children should be considered as an essential objective in setting up an individualized treatment and educational program in a school for feeble-minded.

References

a. Binet, Alfred, *Les idees modernes sur les enfants* (Paris: Ernest Flamarion, 1909), pp. 346. Cited from Stoddard, George D., "The IQ: Its Ups and Downs," *Educ. Rec.*, 20 (1939): 44–57. (Supplement for January)

b. Fillmore, Eva A., "Iowa Tests for Young Children," *University of Iowa Studies in Child Welfare,* 11, no. 4 (1936): 58.

c. Kephart, Newell C., "The Effect of a Highly Specialized Institutional Program upon the IQ in High Grade Mentally Deficient Boys," Wayne County Training School, Northville, Mich.

d. Skeels, Harold M., and Fillmore, Eva A., "The Mental Development of Children from Underprivileged Homes," *Ped. Sem. & J. Genet. Psychol.,* 50 (1937): 427–439.

e. Skeels, Harold M.; Updegraff, Ruth; Wellman, Beth L.; and Williams, Harold M., "A Study of Environmental Stimulation: An Orphanage Preschool Project," *University of Iowa Studies in Child Welfare,* 15, no. 4 (1938): 190.

f. Skodak, Marie, "Children in Foster Homes: A Study of Mental Development," *University of Iowa Studies in Child Welfare,* 16, no. 1 (1939): 155   (12)

Later Skeels and Skodak located the twenty-five children in the original sample after a lapse of twenty-one years as part of a larger effort to follow up 125 children studied earlier. Persistence and ingenuity made it possible for them to talk to 100 percent of the cases, a feat rarely duplicated. The accounts of the tracing of these individuals make remarkable reading.

The following vignette exemplifies some of the difficulties the investigators encountered:

On October 20, 1961, I stopped at Bradshaw, population 355, to try to find the Ted Mitchell family. Their daughter, Ruth, was one of the 13 experimental children, and the last contact with this home had been in 1941. I went to the Post Office but the postmistress said she did not know them at all. I asked her if there was some old-timer who might know them, and she suggested that I see Dr. Gifford, a dentist who had been the previous postmaster. I went to his office and waited until he had finished with the patient in the chair. I then stated my case and he indicated he had known the Mitchells, but did not know what had happened to them.

He suggested seeing John Richmond and Albert Johnson, farmers in the area where the Mitchells used to live. At the John Richmond farm no one was home. The man at the next farm did not know about the Mitchells, as he had lived there only 11 years. He pointed out the third house up the road as that of the Albert Johnsons, so I went there, but they were also away from home.

I then stopped at one or two farms on the way back, and an elderly gentleman told me that the Mitchells were members of one of the less common religious faiths, the one family of that denomination in the area, and that they had not had much truck with the people in the village, which probably accounted for the fact that it was so difficult to find out about them. He stated that Mr. and Mrs. Mitchell had separated, and Mrs. Mitchell had married again. He said that one person who had been in rather close contact with their daughter, Ruth, was a Mrs. Wilbur Marshall who lived out beyond the Albert Johnsons.

I went back out to see Mrs. Marshall, but no one was at home. I then stopped at a filling station on my way back to get the telephone numbers of some of these people, and the operator of the filling station told me that the Marshalls were building a house in town, and might be working over there. He showed me where it was and I went over, but apparently they had quit work and, I thought, perhaps gone home. I therefore went out again to the Marshall residence, but still no one was there. On the way back I stopped at the Albert Johnsons and was able to talk with him, but he did not know where the Mitchells had gone. Finding that John Richmond and his wife were now at home, I also stopped there, but they, too, did not know the present whereabouts of the Mitchells.

For the next three days I tried periodically to call the Wilbur Marshalls and had no success. Finally, the rural operator said that apparently they could not be reached because they had moved in to town and had no phone as yet in their new house. Therefore, I may have to go back to this town at a later time and see if I can possibly find Mrs. Mitchell.

From a later report:

October 25, 1961, I again drove out to Bradshaw, going directly to the Marshalls' new house. This time I found both Mr. and Mrs. Marshall there. Mrs. Marshall said that her daughter had been a friend of Elizabeth, a daughter by birth of the Mitchells; that Elizabeth was married to a Ralph Strand, and was living in Des Moines. She thought that Elizabeth could tell me where Ruth was and where Mrs. Mitchell, the adoptive mother, could be located. She mentioned that Mrs. Mitchell had remarried. She couldn't remember the specific address, but thought Ralph Strand would be listed in the Des Moines telephone directory. (I had visions of there being several Strands listed.) On further question, she said they lived somewhere on Fourth Street Place.

I felt very fortunate to have secured this information. I drove back to Des Moines and immediately looked up the Ralph Strands in the telephone directory. As expected, there were two of them, but fortunately one lived on Fourth Street Place. I went there that same afternoon, only to find no one at home. The next morning I went out there, and again no answer to my knock on the door. I then went to the house of a neighbor to ask if the Strands were on vacation.

From the neighbor I learned a great deal without divulging the purpose of my inquiry. She informed me that the Strands had separated, and that Ralph came home in the evenings. I indicated that in earlier years I had been acquainted with Mrs. Strand's mother, and that I was interested in locating either Elizabeth or her mother. She did not know where Elizabeth was, but the mother, formerly Mrs. Ted Mitchell, worked at the Green Lantern Restaurant; that she was now Mrs. Donald White, and lived at 4078 Grand Avenue.

The next morning I went to the indicated residence and had a very satisfactory interview with Mrs. White, the adoptive mother of Ruth, one of the 13 children in the experimental group. Early in the interview she asked, "How did you find me?" and I gave the obvious reply, "Well, it wasn't easy!" (13:253)

As the data were amassed, Skeels and Skodak found that eleven of the thirteen in the experimental group were married. Nine had children of their own. All were self-supporting. The median educational grade completed was twelve. Four had gone on to college; one received a B.A. degree.

One girl in the experimental group who initially had an IQ of 35 has subsequently graduated from high school and taken one semester of work at college. She is married and has two boys. These boys have been given intelligence tests and have achieved IQ scores of 128 and 107. (11:34)

In the contrast group of twelve, five remained wards of state institutions. Of those living on their own, two were married, one divorced. This group's median level of educational achievement was the third grade. Of the fifty percent employed, all but one were unskilled laborers.

New Concepts of the
Relationship Between
Environment and Intelligence

In the 1950's major shifts in opinion came from the work of the cognitive psychologist. J. McVicker Hunt at the University of Illinois, Benjamin Bloom at the University of Chicago, Jerome Bruner at Harvard, and Kenneth Wann at Columbia accumulated evidence and argued for the responsiveness of intelligence to experience. Greater familiarity in America with the interactionist viewpoint of Jean Piaget was an important root influence for this change.

In his book, *Stability and Change in Human Characteristics*, Bloom examined longitudinal studies of the various characteristics of human development. Of intelligence he writes:

from **Stability and Change
in Human Characteristics**

Benjamin Bloom

The stability of intelligence test scores has been a concern of many investigators. General intelligence is regarded as a very basic and useful

From Benjamin Bloom, *Stability and Change in Human Characteristics* (New York: John Wiley & Sons, 1964). By permission of John Wiley & Sons, Inc.

measurement of the individual. However, the educator, clinician, guidance worker, social worker, etc., cannot make long-term decisions about the individual or give help based on observed intelligence test scores unless he can assume some degree of stability of general intelligence. Many longitudinal studies have been done with measures of general intelligence and scholastic aptitude. These studies all demonstrate that stability is greater for shorter time periods than for longer time periods. In addition, the studies reveal increased stability with increased age. When a number of longitudinal studies are compared with each other and allowances are made for the reliability of the instruments and the variability of the samples, a single pattern clearly emerges.

This general pattern of relationships approximates the absolute scales of intelligence development formulated by Thorndike (1927), Thurstone (1928), and Heinis (1924). The Thorndike absolute scale fits the longitudinal data most closely during ages one to seventeen. Both the correlational data and the absolute scale of intelligence development make it clear that intelligence is a developing function and that the stability of measured intelligence increases with age. Both types of data suggest that in terms of intelligence measured at age seventeen, about 50 percent of the development takes place between conception and age four, about 30 percent between ages four and eight, and about 20 percent between ages eight and seventeen.

These results make it clear that a single early measure of general intelligence cannot be the basis for a long-term decision about an individual. These results also reveal the changing rate at which intelligence develops, since as much of the development takes place in the first four years of life as in the next thirteen years.

There is little doubt that intelligence development is in part a function of the environment in which the individual lives. The evidence from studies of identical twins reared separately and reared together as well as from longitudinal studies in which the characteristics of the environments are studied in relation to changes in intelligence test scores indicate that the level of measured general intelligence is partially determined by the nature of the environment. The evidence so far available suggests that extreme environments may be described as *abundant* or *deprived* for the development of intelligence in terms of the opportunities for learning verbal and language behavior, opportunities for direct as well as vicarious experience with a complex world, encouragement of problem solving and independent thinking, and the types of expectations and motivations for intellectual growth.

The effects of the environments, especially of the extreme environments, appear to be greatest in the early (and more rapid) periods of intelligence development and at least in the later (and less rapid) periods of development. Although there is relatively little evidence of the effects of changing the environment on the changes in intelligence, the evidence so far available suggests that marked changes in the environment in the early years can produce greater changes in intelligence than will equally marked changes in the environment at later periods of development.

Much more research is needed to develop precise descriptions and quantitative measurements of environments as they relate to the development of intelligence. More research is also needed, especially of a longitudinal nature, on the amount of change in intelligence which can be produced by shifting a person from one environment to another. However, a conservative estimate of the effect of extreme environments on intelligence is about twenty IQ points. This could mean the difference between a life in an institution for the feeble-minded or a productive life in society. It could mean the difference between a professional career and an occupation which is at the semi-skilled or unskilled level. A society which places great emphasis on verbal learning and rational problem solving and which greatly needs highly skilled and well-trained individuals to carry on political-social-economic functions in an increasingly complex world cannot ignore the enormous consequences of deprivation as it affects the development of general intelligence. Increased research is needed to determine the precise consequences of the environment for general intelligence. However, even with the relatively crude data already available, the implications for public education and social policy are fairly clear. Where significantly lower intellience can be clearly attributed to the effects of environmental deprivations, steps must be taken to ameliorate these conditions as early in the individual's development as education and other social forces can be utilized. . . .

Our attempts to describe the development of intelligence have been really attempts to describe stability and change in measurements of intelligence. Such measurements are based on particular tests and test problems, and these measurements are undoubtedly affected by the experiences individuals have had both in school and out of school. It seems likely that performance on these tests is responsive to the experiences individuals have had and that the change in the general picture of stability and change could be produced by new developments in education and by different child-rearing practices. All this is merely an attempt to alert the reader to the view that our picture of stability and change in measured intelligence is one based on things as they now are, and this includes the particular tests to measure intelligence, the child-rearing practices of families in Western cultures and educational practices in the schools. It is conceivable that changes in any or all of these could produce a very different picture than the one we have been able to draw. . . .

References

Heinis, H., "La loi du developpement mental," *Archives de Psychologie*, 74 (1924): 97–128.

Thorndike, E.L., *The Measurement of Intelligence* (New York: Teachers College, Columbia University, 1927).

Thurstone, L.L., "The Absolute Zero in Intelligence Measurement, *Psychological Review*, 35, (1928): 175-197   (1:87-91)

Bloom's conclusions about the effects of environment on intelligence lead us to the inevitable dilemmas posed earlier in this book. How does society provide equality of opportunity so that each individual's development can be maximized?

... Differences in general intelligence are likely to be related to:
1) Stimulation provided in the environment for verbal development.
2) Extent to which affection and reward are related to verbal-reasoning accomplishments.
3) Encouragement of active interaction with problems, exploration of the environment, and the learning of new skills. (1:190)

Such differences in environments in the periods of most rapid growth may make substantial differences in the career and history of individuals. We are not able to state glibly what is good or bad for the individual or for society. However, we are able to state emphatically that the conditions under which individuals live during the period of most rapid development for a particular characteristic will have far reaching consequences for the qualitative and quantitative development of *that* characteristic and that this development, in turn, will have far reaching consequences for each individual's conditions of life, career, and sources of fulfillment and happiness.

The nature of the individual's pursuit of life, liberty and happiness may be largely determined by the nature of the environmental conditions under which he has lived in his formative years. Futhermore, although individuals in a democracy may not be equal at birth, much of their inequality at maturity may be ascribed to the lack of *equality of opportunity* if we see opportunity and environmental conditions as partial reflections of each other. (1:193)

J. McVicker Hunt is a strong advocate of preschool enrichment programs for the poor so that equality of opportunity can be assured. Edmond Gordon assesses him as a man who "has devoted a considerable portion of his time for the last few years to the development of a theoretical rationale for early intervention in the development of young children as an antidote to the ravages of poverty. In response to an earlier work, *Intelligence and Experience* (New York: Ronald Press, 1961), some critics argued that he made too generous a leap from animal research to inferences concerning human behavior. Other critics argued that he went beyond his data in making a case for the maleability of human intellect. Despite these criticisms, Hunt, along with others, has succeeded in focusing attention on the fact that intellectual development is a highly complex process that simple concepts of fixed genetic endowment seem inadequate to explain." (6:39)

Hunt's thesis is here presented as it appeared in an article in 1964, a condensed version of an earlier paper prepared for the

Arden House Conference on Preschool Enrichment of Socially Disadvantaged Children in December 1962: (10)

The Implications of Changing Ideas on How Children Develop Intellectually
J. McVicker Hunt

The task of maximizing the intellectual potential of our children has acquired new urgency. Two of the top challenges of our day lie behind this urgency. First, the rapidly expanding role of technology, now taking the form of automation, decreases opportunity for persons of limited competence and skills while it increases opportunity for those competent in the use of written language, in mathematics, and in problem solving. Second, the challenge of eliminating racial discrimination requires not only equality of employment opportunity and social recognition for persons of equal competence, but also an equalization of the opportunity to develop that intellectual capacity and skill upon which competence is based.

During most of the past century anyone who entertained the idea of increasing the intellectual capacity of human beings was regarded as an unrealistic "do-gooder." Individuals, classes, and races were considered to be what they were because either God or their inheritance had made them that way; any attempt to raise the intelligence quotient (IQ) through experience met with contempt. Man's nature has not changed since World War II, but some of our conceptions of his nature have been changing rapidly. These changes make sensible the hope that, with improved understanding of early experience, we might counteract some of the worst effects of cultural deprivation and raise substantially the average level of intellectual capacity. This paper will attempt to show how and why these conceptions are changing, and will indicate the implications of these changes for experiments designed to provide corrective early experiences to children and to feed back information on ways of counteracting cultural deprivation.

Changing Beliefs

Fixed Intelligence.

The notion of fixed intelligence has roots in Darwin's theory that evolution takes place through the variations in strains and species which enable them to survive to reproduce themselves. Finding in this the implicit assumption that adult characteristics are determined by hered-

---

J. McVicker Hunt, "The Implications of Changing Ideas on How Children Develop Intellectually," *Children* (Washington, D.C.: Department of Health, Education and Welfare, 1964).

ity, Francis Galton, Darwin's younger cousin, reasoned that the improvement of man lies not in education, or euthenics, but in the selection of superior parents for the next generation — in other words, through eugenics. To this end, he founded an anthropometric laboratory to give simple sensory and motor tests (which failed, incidentally, to correlate with the qualities in which he was interested), established a eugenics society, and imparted his beliefs to his student, J. McKeen Cattell, who brought the tests to America.

About the same time G. Stanley Hall, an American who without knowing Darwin became an ardent evolutionist, imparted a similar faith in fixed intelligence to his students, among them such future leaders of the intelligence testing movement as H. H. Goddard, F. Kuhlmann, and Lewis Terman. (a) This faith included a belief in the constant intelligence quotient. The IQ originally conceived by the German psychologist Wilhelm Stern, assumes that the rate of intellectual development can be specified by dividing the average age value of the tests passed (mental age) by the chronological age of the child.

The considerable debate over the constancy of the IQ might have been avoided if the work of the Danish geneticist Johannsen had been as well known in America as that of Gregor Mendel, who discovered the laws of hereditary transmission. Johannsen distinguished the genotype, which can be known only from the ancestry or progeny of an individual, from the phenotype, which can be directly observed and measured. Although the IQ was commonly treated as if it were a genotype (innate capacity), it is in fact a phenotype and, like all phenotypes (height, weight, language spoken), is a product of the genotype and the circumstances with which it has interacted. (a)

Johannsen's distinction makes possible the understanding of evidence dissonant with the notion of fixed intelligence. For instance, identical twins (with the same genotype) have been found to show differences in IQ of as much as 24 points when reared apart, and the degree of difference appears to be related to the degree of dissimilarity of the circumstances in which they were reared. Also, several investigators have reported finding substantial improvement in IQ after enrichment of experience, but their critics have attributed this to defects in experimental control.

When results of various longitudinal studies available after World War II showed very low correlation between the preschool IQ and IQ at age 18, the critics responded by questioning the validity of the infant tests, even though Nancy Bayley (b) had actually found high correlations among tests given close together in time. Blaming the tests tended to hide the distinction that should have been made between cross-sectional validity and predictive validity. What a child does in the testing situation correlates substantially with what he will do in other situations, but attempting to predict what an IQ will be at age 18 from tests given at ages from birth to 4 years, before the schools have provided at least some standardization of circumstances, is like trying to predict how fast a feather will fall in a hurricane.

Predetermined Development.

Three views of embryological and psychological development have held sway in the history of thought: preformationism, predeterminism, and interactionism. (a) As men gave up preformationism, the view that the organs and features of adulthood are preformed in the seed, they turned to predeterminism, the view that the organs and features of adulthood are hereditarily determined. G. Stanley Hall in emphasizing the concept of recapitulation — that the development of the individual summarizes the evolution of his species — drew the predeterministic moral that each behavior pattern manifested in a child is a natural stage with which no one should interfere. The lifework of Arnold Gesell exemplifies the resulting concern with the typical or average that has shaped child psychology during the past half century.

The theory of predetermined development got support from Coghill's finding that frogs and salamanders develop behaviorally as they mature anatomically, from head-end tailward and from inside out, and from Carmichael's finding that the swimming patterns of frogs and salamanders develop equally well whether inhibited by chloretone in the water or stimulated by vibration. Such findings appeared to generalize to children. The acquisition of such skills as walking, stair climbing, and buttoning cannot be speeded by training or exercise; Hopi children reared on cradleboards learn to walk at the same age as Hopi children reared with arms and legs free . (c)

Again, however, there was dissonant evidence. Although Cruze found that chicks kept in the dark decreased their pecking errors during the first five days after hatching — a result consonant with predeterminism — he also found that chicks kept in the dark for twenty days failed to improve their pecking. Moreover, studies of rats and dogs, based on the theorizing of Donald Hebb, suggest that the importance of infantile experience increases up the phylogenetic scale. (d)

Evidence that such findings may apply to human beings comes from studies by Goldfarb (e) which indicate that institutional rearing (where the environment is relatively restricted and unresponsive) results in lower intelligence, less ability to sustain a task, and more problems in interpersonal relations than foster-home rearing (where the environment provides more varied experiences and responsiveness). Wayne Dennis (f) has found that in a Teheran orphanage, where changes in ongoing stimulation were minimal, sixty percent of the two-year-olds could not sit alone and eighty-five percent of the four-year-olds could not walk alone. Such a finding dramatizes the great effect preverbal experience can have on even the rate of locomotor development. Presumably the effect on intellectual functions would be even greater.

Static Brain Function.

In 1900, when C. Lloyd Morgan and E. L. Thorndike were attempting to explain learning in terms of stimulus-response bonds, they used the newly invented telephone as a mechanical model of the brain's operation. Thus they envisioned the brain as a static switchboard through which each stimulus could be connected with a variety of responses, which in turn could become the stimuli for still other responses.

Soon objective stimulus-response methodology produced evidence dissonant with this switchboard model theory, implying some kind of active processes going on between the ears. But it took the programming of electronic computers to clarify the general nature of the requirements for solving logical problems. Newell, Shaw, and Simon (g) describe three major components of these requirements: 1) memories, or information, coded and stored; 2) operations of a logical sort which can act upon the memories; and 3) hierarchically arranged programs of these operations for various purposes. Pribram (h) found a likely place for the brain's equivalents of such components within the intrinsic portions of the cerebrum which have no direct connections with either incoming fibers from the receptors of experience or outgoing fibers to the muscles and glands.

So, the electronic computer supplies a more nearly adequate mechanical model for brain functioning. Thus, experience may be regarded as programing the intrinsic portions of the cerebrum for learning and problem solving, and intellectual capacity at any given time may be conceived as a function of the nature and quality of this programing. (a, i)

As Hebb (d) has pointed out, the portion of the brain directly connected with neither incoming nor outgoing fibers is very small in animals such as frogs and salamanders, whence came most of the evidence supporting the belief in predetermined development. The increasing proportion of the intrinsic portion of the brain in higher animals suggests an anatomic basis for the increasing role of infantile experience in development, as evidenced by the greater effect of rearing on problem solving ability in dogs than in rats. (i) Frogs and salamanders have a relatively higher capacity for regeneration than do mammals. This suggests that the chemical factors in the genes may have more complete control in these lower forms than they have further up the phylogenic scale.

Motivation by Need, Pain,
and Sex.

Our conception of motivation is also undergoing change. Although it has long been said that man does not live by bread alone, most behavioral scientists and physiologists have based their theorizing on the assumption that he does. Freud popularized the statement that "all behavior is motivated." He meant motivated by painful stimulation, homeostatic need, and sexual appetite or by acquired motives based on these; and this concept has generally been shared by physiologists and academic behavioral theorists.

Undoubtedly, painful stimulation and homeostatic need motivate all organisms, as sex motivates all mammalian organisms, but the assertion that all behavior is so motivated implies that organisms become quiescent in the absence of painful stimulation, homeostatic need, and sexual stimulation. Observation stubbornly indicates that they do not: Young animals and children are most likely to play in the absence of such motivation; young rats, cats, dogs, monkeys, chimpanzees, and humans work for nothing more substantial than the opportunity to perceive, manipulate, or explore novel circumstances. This evidence implies that there must be some additional basis for motivation.

Reflex vs. Feedback.

A change in our conception of the functional unit of the nervous system from the reflex arc to the feedback loop helps to suggest the nature of this other motivating mechanism. The conception of the reflex arc has its anatomical foundations in the Bell-Magendie law, based on Bell's discovery of separate ventral and dorsal roots of the spinal nerves and on Magendie's discovery that the dorsal roots have sensory or "input" functions while the ventral roots have motor or "output" functions. But the Bell-Magendie law was an overgeneralization, for motor fibers have been discovered within the presumably sensory dorsal roots, and sensory fibers have been discovered within the presumably motor ventral roots.

The most important argument against the reflex as the functional unit of the nervous system comes from the direct evidence of feedback in both sensory input and motor output. The neural activity that results when cats are exposed to a tone is markedly reduced when they are exposed to the sight of mice or the smell of fish, thus dramatizing feedback in sensory input. Feedback in motor output is dramatized by evidence that sensory input from the muscle spindles modulates the rate of motor firing to the muscles, thereby controlling the strength of contraction. (i)

Incongruity as Motivation.

The feedback loop which constitutes a new conceptual unit of neural function supplies the basis for a new mechanism of motivation. Miller, Galanter, and Pribram (j) have called the feedback loop the Test-Operate-Test-Exit (TOTE) unit. Such a TOTE unit is, in principle, not unlike the room thermostat. The temperature at which the thermostat is set supplies a standard against which the temperature of the room is continually being tested. If the room temperature falls below this standard, the test yields an *incongruity* which starts the furnace to "operate," and it continues to operate until the room temperature has reached this standard. When the test yields *congruity*, the furnace stops operating and the system makes its exit. Similarly, a living organism is free to be otherwise motivated once such a system has made its exit.

Several classes of similarly operating standards can be identified for human beings. One might be described as the "comfort standard" in which incongruity is equivalent to pain. Another consists of those homeostatic standards for hunger (a low of glycogen in the bloodstream) and for thirst (a high level of hydrogen ion concentration within the blood and interstitial fluids). A third class, which stretches the concept of incongruity somewhat, is related to sex.

Other standards derive from the organism's informational interaction with the environment. Thus, a fourth class appears to consist of ongoing inputs, and, just as "one never hears the clock until it has stopped," any change in these ongoing inputs brings attention and excitement. Repeated encounters with such changes of input lead to expectations, which constitute a fifth class of standards. A sixth class consists of plans quite independent of painful stimulation, homeostatic need, or sex. Ideals constitute a seventh class.

There is evidence that incongruity with such standards will instigate action and produce excitement. (i) There is also evidence that an optimum of such incongruity exists. Too little produces boredom as it did among McGill students who would remain lying quietly in a room no more than three days, although they were paid $20 a day to do so. (i) Too much produces fearful emotional stress, as when a baby chimpanzee sees his keeper in a Halloween mask, (k) a human infant encounters strangers, or primitive men see an eclipse.

While this optimum of incongruity is still not well understood, it seems to involve the matching of incoming information with standards based on information already coded and stored within the cerebrum. (i) Probably only the individual himself can choose a source of input which provides him with an optimum of incongruity. His search for this optimum, however, explains that "growth motivation" which Froebel, the founder of the kindergarten movement, postulated and which John Dewey borrowed; and it may be the basic motivation underlying intellectual growth and the search for knowledge. Such motivation may be characterized as "intrinsic" because it inheres in the organism's informational interaction with the environment.

Emotional vs. *Cognitive*
Experience.

Another fundamental change is in the importance attributed to early — and especially very early — preverbal experience. Traditionally, very little significance had been attached to preverbal experience. When consciousness was believed to control conduct, infantile experience, typically not remembered, was regarded as having hardly an effect on adult behavior. Moreover, when development was conceived to be predetermined, infantile experience could have little importance. While Freud (1) believed that preverbal experiences were important, he argued that their importance derived from the instinctive impulses arising from painful stimulation, homeostatic need, and especially pleasure striving, which he saw as sexual in nature.

Freud's work spread the belief that early emotional experiences are important while early cognitive experiences are not. It now appears that the opposite may possibly be more nearly true. Objective studies furnish little evidence that the factors important according to Freud's theory of psychosexual development are significant. (m, n) Even the belief that infants are sensitive organisms readily traumatized by painful stimulation or intense homeostatic need have been questioned as the result of studies involving the shocking of nursling rats.

Rats shocked before weaning are found to be less likely than rats left unmolested in the maternal nest to urinate and defecate in, or to hesitate entering, unfamiliar territory, and more likely to be active there. Moreover, as adults, rats shocked before weaning often require stronger shocks to instigate escape activity than do rats left unmolested; they also show less fixative effect from being shocked at the choice point in a T-maze. (o) Evidence that children from low socioeconomic and educational classes, who have frequently known painful stimulation, are less likely to be fearful than middle-class children, who have seldom known painful stimulation, suggests that the findings of these rat studies may apply to human beings. (p)

While such observations have contradicted the common conception of the importance of early emotional experience, the experiments stemming from Hebb's theorizing (d) have repeatedly demonstrated the importance of early perceptual and cognitive experience. At earlier phases of development, the variety of circumstances encountered appears to be most important; somewhat later, the responsiveness of the environment to the infant's activities appears to be central; and at a still later phase, the opportunity to understand the causation of mechanical and social relationships seems most significant.

In this connection, a study by Baldwin, Kalhorn, and Breese (q) found that the IQ's of four- to seven-year-old children tend to increase with time if parental discipline consists of responsive and realistic explanations, but tend to fall if parental discipline consists of nonchalant unresponsiveness or of demands for obedience for its own sake, with painful stimulation as the alternative.

*Motor Response and
Receptor Input.*

One more important traditional belief about psychological development which may have to be changed concerns the relative importance of motor response and receptor input for the development of the autonomous central processes which mediate intellectual capacity. A century ago, the "apperceptive mass" conceived by Herbart, a German educational psychologist, was regarded as the product of previous perceptual input; and Froebel and Montessori both stressed sensory training. However, after World War I, the focus of laboratory learning-studies on response, coupled with the notion of brain function as a static switchboard, gradually shifted the emphasis from the perceptual input to the response output. It is hard to make the great importance attributed to the response side jibe with the following findings:

1. Hopi infants reared on cradleboards, where the movements of
arms and legs are inhibited during waking hours, learn to walk at the
same age as Hopi infants reared with arms and legs free. (c)

2. Eighty-five percent of the four-year-olds in a Teheran orphanage,
where variations in auditory and visual input were extremely limited,
did not walk alone. (f)

Such observations and those of Piaget (r, s) suggest that the repeated correction of expectations deriving from perceptual impressions
and from cognitive accommodations gradually create the central processes mediating the logical operations of thought. Wohlwill (t) and
Flavel (u) have assembled evidence which relates the inferential processes of thought to experience and have given this evidence some
formal theoretical organization.

Counteracting Cultural
Deprivation

The intellectual inferiority apparent among so many children of parents of low educational and socioeconomic status, regardless of race, is
already evident by the time they begin kindergarten or first grade at
age five or six. (v) Such children are apt to have various linguistic
liabilities: limited vocabularies, poor articulation, and syntactical deficiencies that are revealed in the tendency to rely on unusually short
sentences with faulty grammar. (w) They also show perceptual deficiencies in the sense that they recognize fewer objects and situations
than do most middle-class children. And perhaps more important, they
usually have fewer interests than do the middle-class children who are
the pace setters in the schools. Moreover, the objects recognized by
and the interests of children typical of the lower class differ from those
of children of the middle class. These deficiencies give such children
the poor start which so commonly handicaps them ever after in scholastic competition.

So long as it was assumed that intelligence is fixed and development
is predetermined, the intellectual inferiority of children from families
of low educational and socioeconomic status had to be considered an
unalterable consequence of their genes. With the changes in our conception of man's intellectual development, outlined in the foregoing
pages, there emerges a hope of combating such inferiority by altering,
for part of their waking hours, the conditions under which such children
develop. The question is "how?"

Clues From Intrinsic Motivation.

A tentative answer, worthy at least of investigative demonstration,
is suggested by the existence of a change during the preschool years
in the nature of what I have called "intrinsic motivation." An approximation of the character of this change has been supplied by the
observations which Piaget made on the development of his three chil-

dren. (r, s, x) At least three stages in the development of intrinsic motivation appear. These may be characteristic of an organism's progressive relationship with any new set of circumstances and seem to be stages in infant development only because the child is encountering so many new sets of circumstances during his first two or three years.

In the first stage the infant is essentially responsive. He is motivated, of course, by painful stimulation, homeostatic need, and, in Freud's sense, by sex. Russian investigators have shown that the orienting response is ready-made at birth in all mammals, including human beings. (y) Thus, any changes in the ongoing perceptual input will attract attention and excite the infant. During this phase each of the ready-made sensorimotor organizations — sucking, looking, listening, vocalizing, grasping, and wiggling — changes, by something like Pavlov's conditioning process, to become coordinated with the others. Thus, something heard becomes something to look at, something to look at becomes something to grasp, and something to grasp becomes something to suck. This phase ends with a "landmark of transition" in which the infant, having repeatedly encountered certain patterns of stimulus change, tries actively to retain or regain them. (x)

During the second stage the infant manifests interest in, and efforts to retain, something newly recognized as familiar — a repeatedly encountered pattern of change in perceptual input. The infant's intentional effort is familiar to anyone who has jounced a child on his knee and then stopped his jouncing only to find the child making a comparable motion, as if to invite the jouncing adult to continue. Regaining the newly recognized activity commonly brings forth such signs of delight as the smile and the laugh, and continued loss brings signs of distress. The effort to retain the newly recognized may well account for the long hours of hand watching and babbling commonly observed during the child's third, fourth, and fifth months. This second stage ends when, with these repeated encounters, the child becomes bored with the familiar and turns his interest to whatever is novel in familiar situations. (x)

The third stage begins with this interest in the novel within a familiar context, which typically becomes noticeable during the last few months of the first year of life. Piaget (r) describes its beginnings with the appearance of throwing, but it probably can be found earlier. While he throws the child intentionally shifts his attention from the act of throwing to the trajectory of the object that he has thrown.

Interest in the novel is also revealed in the infant's increasing development of new plans through an active, creative process of groping, characterized by C. Lloyd Morgan as "trial-and-error." It also shows in the child's increasing attempts to imitate new vocal patterns and gestures. (s, x)

Interest in the new is the infant's basis for "growth motivation." It has also been found in animals, particularly in an experiment in which rats in a figure-eight maze regularly changed their preference to the more complex loop.

Thus Piaget's (r) aphorism, "the more a child has seen and heard, the more he wants to see and hear," may be explained. The more different visual and auditory changes the child encounters during the first stage, the more of these will he recognize with interest during the second stage. The more he recognizes during the second stage, the more of these will provide novel features to attract him during the third stage.

Effects of Social Environment.

Such development prepares the child to go on developing. But continuing development appears to demand a relationship with adults who enable the infant to pursue his locomotor and manipulative intentions and who answer his endless questions of "what's that?", "is it a 'this' or a 'that'?", and "why is it a 'this' or a 'that'?". Without these supports during the second, third, and fourth years of life, a child cannot continue to profit no matter how favorable his circumstances during his first year.

Although we still know far too little about intellectual development to say anything with great confidence, it is unlikely that most infants in families of low socioeconomic status suffer great deprivation during their first year. Since one distinguishing feature of poverty is crowding, it is conceivable that an infant may actually encounter a wider variety of visual and auditory inputs in conditions of poverty than in most middle- or upper-class homes. This should facilitate the intellectual development of the infant during his first year.

During the second year, however, crowded living conditions would probably hamper development. As an infant begins to move under his own power, to manipulate things, and to throw things, he is likely to get in the way of adults who are apt already to be ill-tempered from their own discomforts and frustrations. Such situations are dramatized in Lewis's "The Children of Sanchez," an anthropological study of life in poverty. (z) In such an atmosphere, a child's opportunity to carry out the activities required for his locomotor and manipulative development must almost inevitably be sharply curbed.

Moreover, late in his second or early in his third year, after he has developed a number of pseudo-words and achieved the "learning set" that "things have names," the child in a crowded, poverty-stricken family probably meets another obstacle: His questions too seldom bring suitable answers, and too often bring punishment that inhibits further questioning. Moreover, the conditions that originally provided a rich variety of input for the very young infant now supply a paucity of suitable playthings and models for imitation.

The effects of a lower-class environment on a child's development may become even more serious during his fourth and fifth years. Furthermore, the longer these conditions continue, the more likely the effects are to be lasting. Evidence from animal studies supports this: Tadpoles immobilized with chloretone for eight days are not greatly hampered in the development of their swimming patterns, but immobilization for thirteen days leaves their swimming patterns permanently impaired; chicks kept in darkness for as many as five days show no apparent defects in their pecking responses, but keeping them in darkness for eight or more days results in chicks which never learn to peck at all. (a)

Possible Counteracting Measures.

Such observations suggest that if nursery schools or day-care centers were arranged for culturally deprived children from age four — or preferably from age three — until time for school at five or six some of the worst effects of their rearing might be substantially reduced.

Counteracting cultural deprivation at this stage of development might best be accomplished by giving the child the opportunity to encounter a wide variety of objects, pictures, and appropriate behavioral models, and by giving him social approval for appropriate behavior. The setting should encourage him to indulge his inclinations to scrutinize and manipulate the new objects as long as he is interested and should provide him with appropriate answers to his questions. Such varied experiences would foster the development of representative imagery which could then be the referents for spoken words and later for written language.

Children aged three and four should have the opportunity to hear people speak who provide syntactical models of standard grammar. The behavioral models would lead gradually to interest in pictures, written words, and books. The objects provided and appropriate answers to the "why" questions would lead to interest in understanding the workings of things and the consequences of social conduct. Thus, the child might gradually overcome most of the typical handicaps of his lower-class rearing by the time he enters grade school.

There is a danger, however, in attempting to prescribe a remedy for cultural deprivation at this stage of knowledge. Any specific prescription of objects, pictures, behavioral models, and forms of social reinforcement may fail to provide that attractive degree of incongruity with the impressions which the toddler of the lower class has already coded and stored in the course of his experience. Moreover, what seem to be appropriate behavioral models may merely produce conflict.

At this stage of history and knowledge, no one can blueprint a program of preschool enrichment that will with certainty be an effective antidote for the cultural deprivation of children. On the other hand, the revolutionary changes taking place in the traditional beliefs about the development of human capacity and motivation make it sensible to hope that a program of preschool enrichment may ultimately be made effective. The task calls for creative innovations and careful evaluative studies of their effectiveness.

Discoveries of effective innovations will contribute also to the general theory of intellectual development and become signficant for the rearing and education of all children. Effective innovations will also help to minimize those racial differences in school achievement which derive from cultural deprivation and so help to remove one stubborn obstacle in the way of racial integration.

Although it is likely that no society has ever made the most of the intellectual potential of its members, the increasing role of technology in our culture demands that we do better than others ever have. To do so we must become more concerned with intellectual development during the preschool years and especially with the effects of cultural deprivation.

Notes

a. Hunt, J. McV., *Intelligence and Experience* (New York: Ronald Press Co., 1961).

b. Bayley, Nancy, "Mental Growth in Young Children," in *Thirty-Ninth Yearbook of the National Society for the Study of Education, Part II* (Bloomington, Ill.: Public School Pub. Co., 1940).

c. Dennis, W.; and Dennis, Marsena G., "The Effect of Cradling Practice upon the Onset of Walking in Hopi Children," *Journal of Genetic Psychology*, vol. 56, 1940.

d. Hebb, D. O., *The Organization of Behavior* (New York: John Wiley & Sons, 1949).

e. Goldfarb, W., "The Effects of Early Institutional Care on Adolescent Personality," *Journal of Experimental Education*, vol. 12, 1953.

f. Dennis, W., "Causes of Retardation among Institutional Children: Iran," *Journal of Genetic Psychology*, vol. 96, 1960.

g. Newell, A.; Shaw, J.C.; and Simon, H. A., "Elements of a Theory of Human Problem-Solving," *Psychological Review*, vol. 65, 1958.

h. Pribram, K. H., "A Review of Theory in Physiological Psychology," *Annual Review of Psychology*, vol. 11, 1960.

i. Hunt, J. McV., "Motivation Inherent in Information Processing and Action," in *Motivation and Social Interaction: Cognitive Determinants*, ed. O. J. Harvey (New York: Ronald Press Co., 1963).

j. Miller, G. A.; Galanter, E.; and Pribram, K. H., *Plans and the Structure of Behavior* (New York: Henry Holt & Co., 1960).

k. Hebb, D. O., "On the Nature of Fear," *Psychological Review*, vol. 53, 1946.

l. Freud, S., "Three Contributions to the Theory of Sex," in *The Basic Writings of Sigmund Freud*, ed. A. A. Brill (New York: Modern Library, 1938).

m. Hunt, J. McV., "Experimental Psychoanalysis," in *The Encyclopedia of Psychology*, ed. P. L. Harriman (New York: Philosophical Library, 1946).

n. Orlansky, H., "Infant Care and Personality," *Psychological Bulletin*, vol. 46, 1949.

o. Salama, A. A., and Hunt, J. McV., " 'Fixation' in the Rat as a Function of Infantile Shocking, Handling, and Gentling," *Journal of Genetic Psychology*, vol. 100, 1964.

p. Holmes, F. B., "An Experimental Study of the Fears of Young Children," in *Children's Fears*, A. T. Jersild and F. B. Holmes, Child Development Monographs, no. 20 (New York: Teachers College, Columbia University, 1935).

q. Baldwin, A. L.; Kalhorn, J.; and Breese, F. H., "Patterns of Parent Behavior," *Psychological Monographs*, vol. 58, 1945.

r. Piaget, J., *The Origins of Intelligence in Children* (1936), trans. Margaret Cook (New York: International Universities Press, 1952).

s. _____, *Play, Dreams, and Imitation in Childhood* (1945), trans. C. Gattegno and F. M. Hodgson (New York: W. W. Norton & Co., 1951).

t. Wohlwill, J. F., "Developmental Studies of Perception," *Psychological Bulletin*, vol. 57, 1960.

u. Flavel, J. H., *The Developmental Psychology of Jean Piaget* (New York: D. Van Nostrand Co., 1963).

v. Kennedy, W. A., et al., "A Normative Sample of Intelligence and Achievement of Negro Elementary School Children in the Southeastern United States," *Monographs of the Society for Research in Child Development*, Serial no. 90, vol. 28, 1963.

w. John, Vera P., "The Intellectual Development of Slum Children," *Merrill-Palmer Quarterly*, vol. 10, 1964.

x. Hunt, J. McV., "Piaget's Observations as a Source of Hypotheses Concerning Motivation," *Merrill-Palmer Quarterly*, vol. 9, 1963.

y. Razran, G., "The Observable Unconscious and the Inferable Conscious in Current Soviet Psychophysiology: Interoceptive Conditioning, Semantic Conditioning, and the Orienting Reflex," *Psychological Review*, vol. 68, 1961.

z. Lewis, O., *The Children of Sanchez* (New York: Random House, 1961). (8)

By the late 1950's and early 1960's an avalanche of research and intervention efforts were begun which explored the relationships of early experience, poverty, and compensatory education. Quite like the mental health, nursery school, and child study movement that began in this country during the teens and twenties, the time had come to embrace the idea of intellectual stimulation. Of the many studies and reports, a unique one by Hess and Shipman (7) contrasts ways in which cognitive functioning, linguistic codes, and expectations of school behavior are transmitted to four-year-olds by Negro mothers from four different social classes. Bower makes reference to it in his article on page 190.

Compensatory Education

Compensatory education projects that existed in the early 1960's probably numbered no more than twenty. One of the earliest was Martin Deutsch's group at the Institute for Developmental Studies at New York University which supervised prekindergarten classes in Harlem and attempted to develop a curriculum with special emphasis on making up cognitive skill deficits. Deutsch comments on the problems in designing a remedial focus on language:

...Would it be more effective to place the greatest emphasis on the training of auditory discrimination, or on attentional mechanisms, or on anticipatory receptive language functions in order to achieve the primary goal of enabling the child to understand his teacher? (4:51)

... It is thus not surprising to find that a major focus of deficit in the children's language development is syntactical organization and subject continuity. In preliminary analysis of expressive and receptive language data on samples of middle- and lower-class children at the first- and fifth-grade levels, there are indications that the lower-class child has more expressive language ability than is generally recognized or than emerges in the classroom. The main differences between the social classes seem to lie in the level of syntactical organization... [This suggests] training in the use of word sequences to relate and unify cognitions.... (4:52)

In 1965 federal programs were designed to provide compensatory education for young children in disadvantaged areas throughout the country. Head Start has been ambitious and comprehensive: education, medical care, psychological services, social services, nutrition, parent participation, career development; its impact can not yet be assessed. No sooner had it been hatched when the original group of investigators began to express doubts since gains made by "graduates" were "washing-out" in the public schools. In order to continue the thrust of Head Start, the Follow-Through program was designed to bring the comprehensive approach into the public schools.

Others suggested that age three was already too late to effect lasting change, and this led to consideration of programs for infants, toddlers, and their parents. America's first advertised pilot demonstration day care center for infants and toddlers was begun cautiously at Syracuse by Bettye Caldwell and Julius Richmond (the first national director of Head Start). One gets an indication of how pioneers feel in the statement: "... Announcing that one *intends* to enrich and creating an atmosphere and a congeries of experiences which in truth *do* enrich the child are not necessarily the same things." (3:357) Such endeavors have proved expensive but feasible. The original doubts about group care for very young children were raised primarily by those who questioned the effect such experiences might have on the child's emotional well-being. Maternal deprivation and the sterility of traditional institutional upbringing were being confused with the young child's need for an individualized, consistent, stimulating relationship with a constant adult. Even with some of these doubts answered, there is still no proliferation of such group-care centers around the country. A willingness to spend the money for adequate staffing and more experience are unquestionably needed.* Bettye Caldwell's article

---

*For a more comprehensive review of new early childhood programs in the U.S., consult Evelyn Weber's *Early Childhood Education: Perspectives on Change.* (15)

on page 372 of the appendix describes a new undertaking at the Kramer school in the Little Rock School System in Arkansas. In addition to training and research components, the school in conjunction with the University of Arkansas offers a comprehensive program for a wide age range, from infants to elementary-aged youngsters and their parents. The scope of the project is a broad one indeed; many of the features in other programs are combined into one.

Parental Enrichment
of Young Children

Considerable thought and effort has been given to "develop a way to intervene in the lives of families of poverty to enable *parents* [italics added] to help their children acquire the cognitive and linguistic skills, the motivational systems and the standards of conduct required." (9:29) The younger the child, the more critical are his parents to his future development. Hunt reviews some programs which emphasize parental enrichment of young children.

from **Parent**
and Child Centers
J. McVicker Hunt

... Susan Gray, (a) Rupert Klaus (b) and their colleagues associated with the "Early Training Project" at the George Peabody College for Teachers in Nashville ... first developed a special summer nursery school for disadvantaged children of poverty. The curriculum aimed at teaching children the language skills, attitudes, and motives required for coping with elementary school. Moreover, the teachers using this curriculum served as models that the mothers of these children could imitate. During the summer, home visitors brought each mother to the nursery school. There she could see for herself not only what the teachers were doing with her child, but also the results in the behavior of her own child and of other neighborhood children familiar to her. The home visitors were certified teachers with a background that made them well-acquainted with the views and attitudes of these mothers of low socioeconomic status. They interpreted what the teachers were doing and why, while the mothers observed them. The home visitors also attempted to relate the teacher's efforts to what each mother did with her own child at home. During the periods between the summer sessions (September to May), moreover, a home visitor saw each mother every

From J. McVicker Hunt, "Parent and Child Centers: Their Basis in the Behavioral and Educational Sciences," *American Journal of Orthopsychiatry.* Copyright © 1971, the American Orthopsychiatric Association, Inc. Reproduced by permission.

week. There she undertook to demonstrate for each mother such matters as how to read a story with enthusiasm to a two-year-old, how to reinforce very young children for acquiring such new skills as the ability to get dressed, how to talk with them about such homely matters as the source of potatoes while in the process of peeling them. The home visitors also let the mothers discuss their own problems and helped them to find new ways of coping.

Examiners tested the nineteen children in each of these two groups and also those in two other contrast groups. One of the former attended nursery-school for three consecutive summers (1962, 1963, 1964) and got weekly visits during the course of three successive periods of fall-winter-spring. The other group attended nursery school for two summers (1963, 1964) and got weekly visits during two winters. The two contrast groups each consisted of twenty children of families of socio-economic status comparable to the families of children in the nursery school. One of these groups lived in the same neighborhood as the families in the nursery school. The other group lived in a comparable neighborhood some sixty miles distant. The examiners tested all groups at approximately the same time. The pretests were made with the 1960 edition of the Stanford-Binet, and later testing employed the Wechsler Intelligence Scale for Children, the Peabody Picture Vocabulary Tests (c,d) and the Illinois Test of Psycholinguistic Abilties. (e) Once the children got into the public school, they received the regular tests of readiness and achievement.

As has been typical in such studies, the performances of the children in the nursery school showed spurts of improvement between the testings made before and after the summer sessions. These improvements clearly separate the children who got the nursery school and the home visits from those who did not. The superiority of their test performances continued through the first grade. The test results also showed two other phenomena of highly significant promise. First, the younger siblings of the children in the two nursery school groups showed test performances significantly superior to those of the younger siblings of children in either of the two contrast groups. This finding implies that what the mothers had learned about child-rearing improved their management of their younger children as well as of those attending the nursery school. This Klaus and Gray call "vertical diffusion." Second, the children of the contrast group who lived in the same ghetto neighborhood as those attending the nursery school earned test scores significantly superior to those of the children living some sixty miles distant. This finding, termed "horizontal diffusion," suggests that these mothers who had learned new child-rearing practices were somehow communicating them to their neighbors. Other innovators, like Ira Gordon (f) and Ronald Lally of the University of Florida, also appear to be finding evidences of both "vertical diffusion" and "horizontal diffusion." Moreover, the Demonstration and Research Center for Early Education at the Peabody College has underway another project, building upon the "Early Training Project" of Klaus and Gray, in which such evidences of improved test performance and of both kinds of diffusion are even more substantial. (g)

Another innovative program of intervention, under the direction of Merle Karnes and her associates at the University of Illinois, has demonstrated that mothers of poverty on Aid to Dependent Children can be taught to be effective teachers of their own preschool children. In one of these studies, Karnes et al. (h) selected as subjects thirty children between the ages of three-years-three-months and four-years-three-months from families known to the school authorities to be among the most economically and educationally deprived in their neighborhoods. These thirty children were divided equally into two groups, but none of those in either group were enrolled in a preschool. From the mothers of the control group, the investigators merely got permission to test and retest the children. The mothers of the experimental children were invited to attend a training program where they made instructional materials and learned to use them to teach their children at home. These mothers attended eleven weekly two-hour sessions in the neighborhood elementary school. They were paid $3 a session, an hourly rate of $1.50 selected to approximate the usual wage of such mothers so that attendance would cost them nothing. These sessions were led by three preschool teachers, each of whom was responsible for a group of five mothers. The teachers encouraged the mothers to believe that their assistance was highly important for the development of the educational competence of their preschool children. During the first portion of each session, the mothers made such inexpensive educational materials as a sock puppet; a homemade flannel board; lotto and matching games made with gum seals, geometric shapes and color chips; counting books made from magazine pictures; sorting and matching activities utilizing miscellaneous household items and an egg carton for a sorting tray; and classifying activities based on pictures cut from furniture and clothing catalogs. The teachers also taught the mothers appropriate songs, and books were made available for the mothers to take home for use with their children during the following weeks.

Following that hour of each meeting in which these educational materials were made, the mothers discussed appropriate ways to use them at home during the following week. The teachers emphasized repeatedly the importance of combining language with all of the activities planned. They also involved *these* mothers in role playing to demonstrate for each other various, sometimes original, ways of using the materials. Finally, a teacher visited each of the mothers in her home at two-week intervals to acquaint herself with the child, to offer the mother teaching suggestions, and to help herself evaluate the appropriateness of the activities for these children.

Pretests and posttests with the 1960 Stanford-Binet scale and the Illinois Test of Psycholinguistic Abilities (ITPA) were given by trained examiners who knew nothing about the study or about the circumstances of given children. The results show that these mothers, as teachers, obtained gains in the Binet IQ over the relatively short period of twelve weeks averaging 7.46 points. This mean gain of 7.46 points is significantly greater than that of .07 points made by the control group (p<.05). The children of the teaching mothers also made statistically significant gains on three of the subtests of the ITPA (visual decoding, auditory verbal association, and auditory-vocal sequential).

In another demonstration study of the feasibility of teaching mothers of poverty to become effective teachers of their children, Karnes (i) has compared the test gains of four-year-olds taught by their mothers who got such training as that already described with the test gains made by children matched for age, intelligence, sex, and socioeconomic status and taught by professional preschool teachers who implemented the Karnes structured-preschool program. The children taught by their mothers gained in mean Binet IQ from 93.4 to 105.9 (12.5 points); those taught by professional teachers gained from 96.0 to 110.3 (14.3 points). The difference between these two mean gains is both negligible and nonsignificant. This second study also employed the ITPA, the Frostig (k) Developmental Test of Visual Perception, and the Metropolitan Test of School Readiness. Although the gains in the scores on each of these tests obtained by the mothers was slightly less than that obtained by professional teachers, none of the differences even approached significance.

In yet another innovative demonstration in the Karnes program at the University of Illinois, Earla Badger (l) has developed what has been called the "Mothers' Training Program." This program employed a group process combined with an opportunity for imitation and direct tutelage to stimulate mothers' awareness of the educational needs of their infants, and to provide them with educational procedures and materials with which to become effective teachers of their infants. Like those in the former studies, the twenty mothers—eighteen black and two white who were nearly all on ADC—were paid $1.50 for coming to weekly meetings of two hours. These weekly meetings were divided between child-centered activities and mother-centered needs. During the child-centered portion of these meetings, the staff provided strong leadership. The mother-centered portion was far less directive, and the program depended heavily upon the interests and direction supplied by the mothers. The staff based their effort on the faith that mothers of poverty can change their lives, that they want to, and that they can become effective teachers if they are convinced of the educational importance of their mother role and are provided with "know-how."

This demonstrative effort was sustained for two years. At the end of the first year, during which the mean attendance of the two groups of ten mothers was eighty-one percent, the members in each group were asked to vote on whether they wished to participate for a second year. Fifteen of the twenty mothers voted to continue. During the second year, class times for these fifteen were again divided equally between child-centered activities and mother-centered activities that aimed especially to demonstrate the abilities for indigenous leadership within the group. During the first year, home visits had been a function of the staff only. The staff had supplied eleven educational toys, shown the mothers how to use them in the weekly meetings, had the mothers take turns at role playing their use, and then had made home visits to reinforce further the teaching principles introduced at the meetings and to help individual mothers establish positive working relationships with their infants. The staff also made a follow-up contact whenever a mother missed a meeting. During the second year, the mothers themselves were asked to plan the mother-centered portion of the meeting programs, to rotate the leadership among themselves, and to participate in the home visiting. During the second year the mean attendance, now of fifteen mothers, was again eighty percent. A contrast group of mothers, matched as nearly as possible for racial mixture, sex of child, and educational level of mother, had been arranged from the start of the first year and was continued. The children in both the treated group and the control group were tested with the Cattell Infant Scale before the project started, again after the first year with the Stanford-Binet and the ITPA, and yet again at the end of the second year with a different form of the Stanford-Binet and with the ITPA. At the beginning of the two-year experiment, the infants ranged in age between 14 months and 26 months. The mean age was 19 months. Their Cattell IQs ranged from 79 to 120 with a mean of 97.6. While some of the infants whose mothers were treated showed gains, others did not, and at the end of the first year the infants of the mothers trained failed to differ significantly from the infants of the mothers in the contrast group. A drop in IQ is typical of infants during their third and fourth years, but these infants of the mothers trained to be teachers gained. At the end of the second year, the infants of the trained mothers had attained a mean IQ on the Binet scale of 106.3 while those of the contrast mothers averaged 90.6, and this difference of 15.7 points is highly significant ($p<.005$). At the end of this second year, moreover, the infants of the trained mothers also showed significantly superior language performances to those of the infants of the untrained mothers in the contrast group — as language performances are assessed by the ITPA. Thus, although it took two years to bring out the difference, the test performances of their children indicate that these mothers from a very low level of poverty were able to become through such training sufficiently effective teachers to bring their children, by their fourth year of age, to a mean IQ of about one-third of a standard deviation above the average of our population as a whole (for these data see Karnes et al.) (j)

This study contains other evidence that is perhaps even more impressive. In six of these families, there were older siblings who had been tested at the same age as their younger siblings, but who at the time had not had the advantage of their mothers' two-year training as a teacher. The six older siblings had developed to about age four before their mothers received this training, and their mean IQ had been 89 (S.D.=10.28). For the six matched younger siblings, who had profited from their mothers' training as teachers, the mean IQ was 116.7 (S.D.=12.43). This difference of 27.7 points of IQ between these two means is highly significant (p<.01) despite the fact that the number of sibling pairs is but six. Such a comparison has the advantage of showing that, at least in these six families, the effect of the training on the mother as a teacher appears even more effective than it does from comparing the scores of the children of the trained mothers with the scores of the children of untrained mothers in the contrast group (see again Karnes et al.) (j)

In yet another of these innovative demonstrations, this one in Freeport, New York, reported by Phyllis Levenstein, (m) substantial gains in the IQs of children have been obtained over a two-year period by providing a set of educational toys and a model for the mothers by interacting verbally with the child while playing with the toys in the homes. The children were two years of age at the beginning of the study. The obtained changes in the IQs of children ranged from a maximum of 32-point gain in Stanford-Binet IQ for one of the thirty-three children to an actual loss of 7 points for one other. The mean gain for the group was 17 points of either Stanford-Binet or Cattell IQ and was highly significant. During the first year, those who demonstrated the toys and the verbal interaction were professional social workers, but during the second year they were either volunteers or mother-participants with demonstrated aptitude who were paid to serve as paraprofessional interveners. A drop in IQ occurred where the children were merely repeatedly tested, and an absence of gain occurred in a group where the social workers provided no special educational toys and merely entered the home to illustrate for mothers how to talk with their children. Levenstein (m) also divided the children of the treated group into high gainers and low gainers and found associated with low gains a relatively unhappy flavor to their lives, and such characteristics of interaction during the demonstrations as a relative absence of asking questions and initiating conversation, an absence of associating verbally to the stories read aloud, a tendency to play less with the toys provided, and a reluctance to initiate activities or even to comply with suggestions.

Finally, gains have also been obtained in programs of work with parents led by Ira Gordon (f) at the University of Florida, and by Weikart and Lambie (n) of the Ypsilanti Public Schools.

References

a.   Gray, S., and Klaus, R. Early training for culturally deprived children. Research project. George Peabody College and Murfreesboro, Tenn. city schools, 1963.

b.   Klaus, R. and Gray, S. The early training project for disadvantaged children: a report after five years. *Monographs Soc. Res. Child Develpm.*, 1968, 33 (4: no. 120), 1–66.

c.   Dunn, L. Peabody Picture Vocabulary Test. American Guidance Service, Minneapolis, 1959.

d.   _____. *Expanded manual for the Peabody Picture Vocabulary Test.* American Guidance Service, Minneapolis, 1965.

e. Kirk, S., and McCarthy, J. Illinois Test of Psycholinguistic Abilities. University of Illinois Press, Urbana, 1961.

f. Gordon, I. (Ed.) *Reaching the child through parent education: the Florida Approach.* Gainesville: University of Florida, 1969.

g. Miller, J. Diffusion of intervention effects in disadvantaged families. Occasional paper, National Laboratory of Early Childhood Education, University of Illinois, Urbana, 1968.

h. Karnes, M. et al. An approach for working with mothers of disadvantaged preschool children. *Merrill-Palmer Quart.*, 1968, 14, 173–184.

i. Karnes, M. *A new role for teachers: involving the entire family in the education of preschool disadvantaged children.* Urbana: University of Illinois, 1969.

j. Karnes, M. et al. Educational intervention at home by mothers of disadvantaged infants, *Child Develpm.*, 1970.

k. Frostig, M. *The Frostig program for the development of visual perception.* Chicago: Follett, 1964.

l. Badger, E. Mother's training program: the group process. ERIC Clearinghouse for Early Childhood Education (Order no. ED032926), Urbana, Ill., 1970.

m. Levenstein, P. Individual variation among preschoolers in a cognitive intervention program in low-income families. Presented at Conference on Early Childhood Education, Council for Exceptional Children, Freeport, N.Y., Dec. 1969.

n. Weikart, D., and Lambie, D. Preschool intervention through a home teaching program. In *The disadvantaged child*, vol. 2, J. Hellmuth (Ed.). Seattle: Special Child Publications, 1967.   (9:29–34)

By the 1970's the country had begun to polarize the issues raised by compensatory education — the younger the child involved the more heated the argument. Would not the money be better spent on more adequate income, medical care, and living conditions for families? Why prepare children to enter the mainstream of the American society which some consider racist? Why not change the society? If an intervention is to be made who shall make the decisions? How does one reach an alienated and separatist Black, Chicano, Indian, and Puerto Rican minority? Gordon suggests: "If we can combine the scholarships of the Professor Hunts with the political sensitivity and commitment of some members of Third World movements, we just may evolve a strategy for enabling poor people and minority group members to participate from a position of parity in a pluralistic society." (6:42)

In 1960 Bruner challenged educators by proposing that the "foundations of any subject may be taught to anybody at any age in some form." (2:12) The curriculum development movement began with the National Defense Education Act, passed in the aftermath of the launching of Sputnik, had intermingled with the interest in compensatory education. Both were caught up in the larger issues of the society: racism, separatism, and community control.

Techniques developed at the Learning Centre at Montreal Children's Hospital with children who have learning disabilities and suggestions made to parents can be read for their application to learning and young children without raising the political arguments mentioned previously:

from **Strictly for
Parents—A Parents'
Guide to Learning Problems**
Margaret Golick

... Out of ... [our] observations grows conviction that the real remedial work for a child with a learning disability must go on at home. The twice-a-week tutoring sessions at a clinic, or the half hour a day *adjustment* periods at school, can only make a small dent in the problem. The only way of ensuring the repetition, the frequency, the variety, the activity and real emotional impact is to incorporate remedial teaching principles into daily life. This does not mean helping with homework, or even the homework assignments from the remedial teacher. I have given parents home-training exercises, or paper and pencil assignments, and though they have started out enthusiastically, more often than not they complain that the children balk. Who can blame them? The training exercises which may go over well in the Learning Centre are boring and artificial at home!

On the other hand there is an enormous, often neglected, opportunity to engage them in the life of the household, to teach them real skills, and at the same time to work on their deficits.

1. *The Kitchen.* The kitchen is a good place to start. Mothers, whether they like it or not, find themselves spending much of their time there. (Fathers do not have to skip these subsequent paragraphs, because the principles discussed will apply to the workshop, or the garden or the golf course—wherever they might be apt to spend time with the children). The kitchen, with its association of food and fellowship, has natural attractions for children. Many who have their own rooms, with well-equipped, well-lit desks, still prefer to do their homework at the kitchen table. Although every mother knows it is much easier to get the work done without the kids around, there are tremendous dividends to be had in letting them pitch in and help.

For example, the kitchen is an ideal place to help a child develop the skills needed in writing, that is, flexible finger movements, a range of hand movements, and the ability to distinguish between the right and left side of the body by learning to use each differently.

There are innumerable exercises that can be built into the kitchen routine.

Using a rolling pin is a good two-handed activity. If the lady of the house cannot make a decent pie crust she can let the children use the rolling pin to crush graham wafers in a paper bag, and make a graham cracker crust. If she does roll dough, so much the better. This leads to cookie cutters. Cutting out circles, squares, and triangles is an excellent lesson in form perceptions; and when they can be eaten later, the impact is tremendous.

Think of the variety of movements in hulling strawberries, snapping beans, peeling potatoes and carrots (with a potato peeler), apples with a paring knife; in beating eggs with an egg beater; in stirring and beating with a spoon; in slicing and chopping, in turning the handles of a meatgrinder; in grating cheese; in pouring liquids.

Many clumsy children never get a chance to do these things. In trying to judge the independence of a child, we often ask his parents if he can go to the refrigerator and get himself a glass of milk. "No, we don't let him, because he always spills it," is a common reply. Some of these skills have to be taught systematically. If pouring milk is a chronic problem, work on the pouring motion itself. Let the child pour split peas or rice from one container to another; or to make it more interesting, chocolate chips or miniature marshmallows. (The incentive can be that they may eat the ones that aren't spilled). Then he can progress to viscous liquids—those that pour slowly—molasses, honey, ketchup, corn syrup.

The kitchen setting is a fine place for language training. If new experiences are introduced, children should be taught the words for them. The value in this does not lie in learning the technical vocabulary of the kitchen, but in the chance to see how language is differentiated. This helps him sharpen his perception. In some ways it is like learning a foreign language. Some people believe that to learn alternate ways of saying things, and to be able to recognize which situations call for which ways of saying them, increase a child's intelligence. Words like "hulling," "dicing," "chopping," "slicing," "stirring," "beating," are good ones to teach in conjunction with an activity. First teach the action, then the word.

The kitchen is the logical place for experiencing and learning "hard," "soft," "greasy," "sticky," "clean," "dirty," "liquid," "powder," "hot," "cold," "lukewarm," "cool." There is an opportunity to heighten both visual and auditory perception by teaching simmering and boiling. Help them *hear* the difference between a full rolling boil of the kettle (when it is ready for tea), and a slow simmer (for soft-boiled eggs). Let them *see* the big bubbles in one, and the tiny, pin point bubbles in the other. The kitchen is the ideal place to stimulate the senses of taste and smell, and to teach the appropriate words:—sweet, sour, salty, bitter. To develop perception of smells, bring out the whole spice cabinet. Have the child close his eyes and guess, through smelling, or tasting what you have. Assign smelling jobs. See who can be the first to tell when the coffee is perking; who can guess what is in the oven.

Developing awareness of sequence, order, and system can be done in the kitchen through cooking. Teach a recipe. Start with a simple one. Divide it into steps. Make sure that each of the individual steps is understood. Then introduce them in order—step 1, step 2, step 3... Demonstrate the importance of doing them in that order. Then encourage your child to do them independently.

One of the staff members at the Learning Centre was working with a kindergarten boy, described by his teacher as hyperactive and disorganized. He certainly could not sit still for more than a few minutes to do any of the paper and pencil work sheets she had assembled to improve his eye-hand coordination. He flatly refused to do a puzzle or play games with her. But when she took him into the little kitchen in the Centre and announced that she would teach him to make fudge, she had him involved and attentive for an hour. What is more, he learned many things in the process.

1) First he assembled his ingredients, canned milk, butter, sugar, chocolate chips, and marshmallows.

2) Then he assembled his utensils — a hook opener, a pot, a baking pan, a pyrex measuring cup, a wooden spoon and a spatula.

3) Then he opened the can with the hook opener and poured the milk into the pot (two new activities for him).

4) Next he greased the pan, and learned how to get the butter right into the corners of the square.

5) Then he measured 1½ cups of chocolate chips, 1½ cups of sugar, and 1½ cups of marshmallows. Matching the level each time with the right mark on the measuring cup was good visual training and he learned about measuring and about fractions in the process.

6) He poured the sugar into the pot with the milk, and put it on low heat. (The difference between high and low was shown and discussed).

7) He stirred for five minutes. (He was taught how to tell on the clock when five minutes was passed; and was shown how to make nice round arm movements for effective stirring...).

8) He added the chocolate chips and marshmallows (stirring against more resistance, thus varying the gross motor exercises).

9) He poured his mixture into the greased pan. (This was only part of the operation he could not manage alone).

10) He smoothed the fudge with a spatula, then sliced it — (a dandy pre-writing exercise) dividing it into rectangles and squares (enhancing his form perception).

11) He counted the pieces — (more mathematics).

12) He passed them around to all of the children and staff in the Centre. This was one of his first ventures into socialization.

The most exciting part of all this is that the lesson was retained without the endless repetition that is often necessary. The whole activity made such an impression on this youngster that he remembered the ingredients, the amounts, the steps and how to do them.

If a project like fudge seems too complicated, a child can start more simply. Canned soups, gelatin desserts, instant puddings, cake mixes, slice-and-bake cookies all have some of the operations done, but the cook finishes with a whole thing that can be admired, shared and eaten.

One of the most useful things ever taught one little boy was how to make a peanut butter sandwich. We had been working on finger dexterity, handedness and form perception. I had given him many paper and pencil exercises which bored him and which he rarely completed. One day when he was hungry, I showed him how to make himself a snack. We took a square slice of white bread, spread the peanut butter over it, (and learning how to do it carefully right to the crusts is a good precursor to learning how to color within the lines) we put another square on top, cut it from corner to corner getting two triangles. The next one we cut down the middle, producing two rectangles. After that there was no need to assign homework. He made himself a peanut butter sandwich every day.

If motor activities, form perception, language building and sequencing can be taught in the kitchen, so can elementary chemistry and physics, especially if there is a parent around to make timely comments which focus attention on what is happening. We have discovered that many bright school age children cannot answer correctly the question "What must we do to make water boil?" "Put it in a pot" is a common answer from children who have never grasped what is the crucial part of the process, because no one has ever made it explicit. There is so much we assume our children understand. As a result we do not grab the opportunity to demonstrate and discuss some of the magical things that happen all around us. Just by putting a couple of ice cubes in a pot on the stove yon can demonstrate how matter can change its state — as heat is applied — from solid to liquid to gas.

Condensation of moisture, facts about solubility, mixtures, compounds, chemical combinations are all relevant in cooking. Even if mother does not have the vocabulary of physics and chemistry, the opportunity to experience these things lays the groundwork for understanding these subjects.

Other Aids in the Home. To approach home training from another angle, let us consider it from the point of view of the *skill* we are trying to develop or the deficit we are trying to repair. Here are some suggestions for each category:

To Improve Visual Skills.

1) Tidying a room — learning to spot things out of place.

2) Dusting.

3) Hobbies — flower, leaf, rock, sea shell collections; bird-watching — activities where the child is directed to differences in shape, size and color, and learns to spot them quickly.

4) At the supermarket — give him a list of items to find. If he cannot read yet, bring along a few labels of items he is to locate by matching; or cut out the trademarks, or print the letters of items to be found like FAB or DUZ or JELLO.

To improve motor skills (where the aim is to ensure that the child can manage his body skillfully in large muscle movements and use his hands in many different precise movements).

1) Carrying parcels.

2) Hanging out the laundry.

3) Mopping, waxing floors.

4) Moving furniture.

5) Mowing lawns.

6) Raking leaves.

7) For hands and fingers, all of the kitchen activities mentioned above are ideal.

To give practice in left-right discrimination.

1) Table setting.

2) Organizing the boots and shoes in the cupboards, with mates together. (An outline of a left and right shoe drawn on a cardboard can provide a guide to correct alignment)

3) Sorting out all mittens and gloves and arranging them in pairs.

4) If a child consistently puts his shoes on the wrong feet, an outline on a cardboard mat beside his bed can show him how to place them. A small mark with a felt marker on the inner edge of the sole of each shoe will go unnoticed by other children, but will give him the clue he needs to tell which shoe goes where.

To help visual-motor skills. Where precision in combining eye and hand are needed.

1) Folding napkins.

2) Icing cakes.

3) Blue-berrying.

4) Picking up paper and cigarette butts from the lawn.

5) Going for a walk can become a visual-motor exercise if you play: "Step-on-a-crack,

You'll break your mother's back."

6) Sorting out father's nails, screws, nuts and bolts into jars.

7) If child has trouble catching a ball the skill can be taught at a simpler level by tossing something that moves more slowly and is easier to catch. One father made his son into a ball player with a daily workout in the bedroom by tossing his shirt, pajamas and socks across the room to the boy whose job it was to put the dirty clothes in the clothes hamper.

To strengthen Auditory Skills.

1) Listening for something specific — use the stove timer or the alarm clock to signal important events.

2) Answering the telephone — learning to discriminate voices (for example, get friends and relatives to call to test the child's skills).

3) Listening to some of the recorded announcements on the telephone that repeat themselves indefinitely. In this way no adult's goodwill is taxed, and the message can be heard over and over again until it is assimilated. (In Montreal, for example, there is the service that gives all the movie listings, 273-9121, or Dial-a-Prayer, 769-9641).

4) Listening to the radio. Children brought up on television have little practice in listening for information without a visual image to help. If the whole program seems too demanding, encourage *directed* listening — tuning in to find out specific things — the weather report, the ski conditions, or who won last night's hockey game.

5) Learning to recognize bird calls.

6) Interesting conversation, slowed up and fed in short units without too many distractions, will help the child who assimilates speech poorly. (One mother tells how her four-year-old who was very late in learning to talk seemed to catch on finally in the car on a long trip across Canada one summer. The family was in close quarters for a long period of time, and there was constant conversation, singing and word games).

7) Regular reading aloud — short stories or stories with chapters, so that there is something to look forward to and to think about; and poetry, especially poems with refrains that tempt the child to join in.

To Help Concept Development

A. Practice Categorizing

1) Sorting laundry — into light and dark colors, children's and adults, cottons and woolens.

2) Putting away groceries — dividing them into refrigerator goods and pantry products, fruits and vegetables, fresh foods and canned goods.

B. Learning about numbers

Sorting, matching, ordering (arranging things in order of size) are all necessary precursors to counting.

1) Table setting.

2) Putting out milk bottles.

3) Helping to decide how many pieces of cake are needed for supper.

4) Using the measuring cup.

5) Helping with shopping.

6) Playing games — especially board games like Snakes and Ladders, where a dot pattern on the dice is matched to the number of squares the player moves. Any games that require keeping score.

C. Getting a clearer picture of the world around them through real experiences

1) Take them to the grocery store, the post office, the bank and see that they understand their functions.

2) Give them some skills which will help them develop independence. Teach them how to buy a paper, or a loaf of bread. (You may have to start with borrowing sugar from a neighbor).

3) Help them learn the neighborhood, not just one specific route. Let them see that you can arrive at the same place by two different routes; try going around the block to get to the next-door neighbor.

4) Teach them important addresses and phone numbers.

5) Teach days of the week by tying them to specific activities or television programs that occur on each day.

6) Where necessary, help compensate for poor memories or poor perception by making crutches available to them, e.g., a calendar, where the days can be torn off or marked off, helps keep track of the week. Circle or color in important dates as reminders. A cuckoo clock in the house is a marvellous way to heighten awareness of the passage of time. The gift of the first alarm clock or watch often creates a fascination with time that accomplishes what much instruction in time-telling failed to do.

D. Becoming familiar with the short-cuts and conventions of our society.
   1) The measuring device that records
      a) time (clock, calendar)
      b) distance (the ruler, yard stick, mileage gauge on the car)
      c) speed (speedometer)
      d) temperature (the one that helps decide what clothes to wear). A small thermometer in his room or outside his window intrigues a youngster.
      e) weight — the bathroom scale, the grocer's scale.
   2) Our way of translating three dimensional space into two dimensions — maps. (A first step might be a map of the neighborhood, or a treasure hunt, with a map of the house as a guide).
   3) Translating time into two-dimensions — as we do in comic strips and some diagrams and charts, where we illustrate successive steps. Sometimes this way of representing events in time makes them intelligible to children who have trouble organizing temporal material. For one child a family tree helped him understand the family relationships he could never get straight. Another child got organized through picture-charts which indicated the steps to take in dressing and tidying his room.
   4) Learning to make use of the device we have invented to compensate for short memories — telephone books, dictionaries, encyclopaedias, cook books, even the slide rule. This is essential in the age of the computer and the storage of massive quantities of information.
   5) Learning to use the tools that extend our capacities.
      a) telephones
      b) binoculars
      c) cameras
      d) machines of all kinds

Do not overlook the importance of games. When there is an element of excitement or fun, learning takes place faster. This is one of the reasons for great reliance on games for teaching. Play is the natural medium of childhood. It is the way children discover and practice many important things. In early childhood it is through spontaneous play, in later childhood through more formal play with another child. A youngster with a "short attention span" for his classroom activities or his homework assignments may play endless rounds of Monopoly, or skip rope nonstop for an afternoon. The crucial ingredients here seem to be the presence of other children, the play element, or perhaps even the competitive possibilities. Since games are fun, children want to play them and therefore practice is automatic. Furthermore, children have much to learn from the association with other children that are created by games. They learn social relations, they pick up rules of games, skipping rhymes, and conventions of childhood that grown-ups have forgotten. They take criticism that would be resented from an adult. One child can scream at another, "You stupid nut — that's not the way you play," and it becomes an effective teaching technique.

One of the saddest problems for many children with learning disabilities is that they miss the chance to become one of the gang. In the preschool years they may be erratic in their development, overactive, exciteable. Because they need protection longer, they are not turned loose on the street. Those who are late in learning to talk may find this an obstacle to joining other children. When they reach school age they may not have some of the necessary play skills, for example, ability to catch, or skip rope, or connect with a hockey puck. As a result they avoid, or are avoided, by the group. Even those athletic ones are often so bogged down with extra homework or tutoring sessions to help their school difficulties that they rarely get outside to play. These children are all losing out. They miss the skills that come from the games themselves, and the opportunity to learn about the world from other children.

Good advice to parents would be to make a point of teaching your child games. Give him the skills that his peers have. If possible help him, in slow motion, to learn to catch and throw a ball. Even if he is clumsy and you know he will never become a ball player, teach him the point of the game, its rules, its vocabulary — so that he will make an intelligent observer or scorekeeper. Teach him games in which he can participate and even excel. There are games that cut across all ages and provide many fringe benefits for the child with a learning problem. Involvement in card games leads to improved finger dexterity, (one eight-year-old worked for an hour to teach himself to shuffle the deck), number recognition, number concepts, form perception, notions of sequence and grouping. It is much less boring for a parent to sit down and have a game of Black Jack with a child than to help him with a page of arithmetic. Yet while they are playing, much arithmetic is getting practiced. The same is true for Snakes and Ladders, checkers, Scrabble, and the fad games that pop up every season. Besides games, parents of a child with a learning problem can try to help him achieve other nonacademic interests and skills of children his age so that he can hold his own with the gang. In the case of the teenager this may include teaching the words to the pop tunes. One fifteen-year-old, with a severe reading disability, partly due to his great difficulty in learning by rote, had seen the Beatles' film "A Hard Days Night" five times without being able to learn the words to any of the songs. His reading teacher endeared herself to him by typing out the words to several songs, and using them as his introductory reading test. Another reading teacher devoted part of every session with a twelve-year-old girl to teaching her to dance. She knew that the poor sense of rhythm and poor appreciation of left and right which were part of this girl's learning problem would be a big handicap on the dance floor. She thought that the girl had enough problems in school without having to face life as a wall-flower.

Parents of children with a reading disability may have to read the geography and history texts to their children to help them keep abreast of the classroom work. They should not stop there, but take the trouble to read aloud from Nancy Drew or the Hardy Boys or *Mad Magazine* — or whatever the current preoccupation of the age group. This will allow the child with the handicap to be a part of that world.

Fun is an essential ingredient in the life of every human being. But it sometimes gets lost in the shuffle when everyone is worried about schoolwork. Children and parents alike get overwhelmed and depressed. The life of many of the children we encounter seems empty and dis- couraging — filled with school (where they are a failure), after school teaching sessions, homework that is too hard, rigid routines and parents who continually nag about the school work. We find they never get to go anywhere or do anything interesting. Many of them express them- selves poorly, but we have the feeling that they have little to talk about. We urge parents to exploit their community and occasionally give the children outings that will stimulate their imagination — an art ex- hibit, the zoo, the Botanical Gardens, a dog show, a cat show, a fabric shop, a factory, a farm. Just an unexpected change in routine sometimes brightens a day.

Summary

The job of the parents of children with learning disabilities is a big one. They must see to it that the children have:
1) Opportunities to experience the world in a meaningful, exciting way.
2) Chances to assume responsibilities.
3) Opportunity to learn to use the common devices of our society.
4) Opportunity to learn games so that practicing a skill is fun.
5) An opportunity to participate with other children, because this is where the most important lessons of childhood are learned.

(5:371–377)

References to Part 8

1. Bloom, Benjamin S., *Stability and Change in Human Character- istics* (New York: John Wiley & Sons, 1964). By permission.
2. Bruner, Jerome, *The Process of Education* (New York: Vintage Books, 1960).
3. Caldwell, Bettye M., and Richmond, Julius, "The Children's Cen- ter in Syracuse, New York," in *Early Child Care: The New Per- spectives*, ed. Laura Dittman (New York: Atherton Press, 1968).
4. Deutsch, Martin, *The Disadvantaged Child: Selected Papers of Martin Deutsch and Associates* (New York: Basic Books, Inc., 1967).

5. Golick, Margaret, "A Parent's Guide to Learning Problems," *Journal of Learning Disabilities,* 1, no. 6 (June 1968): 366–377.

6. Gordon, Edmund W., " 'Parent and Child Centers: Their Basis in the Behavioral and Educational Sciences', an Invited Critique," *American Journal of Orthopsychiatry,* 41, no. 1 (January 1971): 39–42.

7. Hess, Robert D., and Shipman, Virginia C., "Early Experience and the Socialization of Cognitive Modes in Children," *Child Development,* 36, no. 4 (December 1965): 869–886.

8. Hunt, J. McVicker, "The Implications of Changing Ideas on How Children Develop Intellectually," *Children,* 11, no. 3 (May–June 1964): 83–91.

9. ———, "Parent and Child Centers: Their Basis in the Behavioral and Educational Sciences," *American Journal of Orthopsychiatry,* 41, no. 1(January 1971): 13–38. Copyright © 1971, the American Orthopsychiatric Association, Inc. Reproduced by permission.

10. ———, "The Psychological Basis for Using Preschool Enrichment as an Antidote for Cultural Deprivation," *Merrill-Palmer Quarterly,* 10 (July 1964): 209–248.

11. Skeels, Harold M., "Effects of Adoption on Children from Institutions," *Children,* 12, no. 1 (January–February 1965): 33–34.

12. Skeels, Harold M., and Dye, Harold B., "A Study of the Effects of Differential Stimulation on Mentally Retarded Children," *Proceedings and Addresses of the American Association on Mental Deficiency,* 44, no. 1 (1939): 114–136.

13. Skeels, Harold M., and Skodak, Marie, "Techniques for a High-Yield Followup Study in the Field," *Public Health Reports,* 80, no. 3 (March 1965): 249–257.

14. Skeels, Harold M.; Updegraff, Ruth; Welman, Beth; and Williams, Harold, "Study of Environmental Stimulation: An Orphanage Pre-School Project," *University of Iowa Studies in Child Welfare,* 15, no. 4 (1938): 11–13.

15. Weber, Evelyn, *Early Childhood Education: Perspectives on Change* (Worthington, Ohio: Charles A. Jones Publishing Co., 1970).

part 9

Approaches
to Learning

A teaching style is influenced by many forces: the children a teacher works with, the setting he teaches in, how he conceives of learning itself, and which human values resonate within him. For most of us there is no closure in the search for what we consider ideal. Some of us painfully discover that what we think and what we do are not congruent.

There are two extremes along the learning continuum: rote learning and insight learning. Reinforcement or operant conditioning techniques are often associated with rote learning. In this chapter their use is exemplified by two types of educational programs: one, in dealing with children's problem behavior; the other, in teaching the three R's. Insight learning is more frequently the underlying premise of those who embrace a developmental point of view. Piaget

264

and Erikson are used to provide the theoretical background for the intellectual and emotional aspects of early childhood educational programs of this kind. The *open education movement,* begun in England and now capturing the imagination of Americans, relates to a developmental point of view. It is concerned with bringing definition to how a total school or a portion of the school can deal with individual differences. It is also a vehicle through which continuity in early education can be achieved for children, teachers, and their parents.

Review of Learning

The behaviorists, such as Thorndike, believed learning to be a matter of trial and error, the accidental discovery of a correct solution, which became incorporated into a living system through the creation of many small associative bonds, one after the other. *Rote learning, habit formation,* and *practice-makes-perfect* were the tenets to consequently come from such a theory. Cognitive psychologists, on the other hand, believe that there is a rational element in learning which cannot be fully explained by the rather mindless creation of associative bonds. According to their viewpoint, *insight* and *understanding* are manifested with increasing regularity as the human being garners experience and gains concepts.

These two points of view had been irreconcilable since the turn of the century until Donald O. Hebb of McGill University presented a rationale that incorporates both; i.e. one forms the basis for the other. He theorizes in *Organization of Behavior* that an infant's earliest learning depends on his forming a multitude of connections between groups of neurons in the cortex of the brain. (7:107–126) Through repetition of similar stimuli coming into his orb again and again, the child learns to "read" meaning in the cues his sense organs are continually feeding his nervous system so long as he is awake to any degree. Thus, early learning is a matter of forming bonds, though more complex bonds than those postulated by the early behaviorists. Hebb calls these patterned sequences of cells, "cell assemblies," and hypothesizes that the ability to perceive the environment is developed by the organism as the cell assemblies are formed.

Every normal infant moves on to the creation of higher order relationships on the basis of an adequate number of cell assemblies, which then combine. These new groupings form what Hebb calls "phase sequences." (7:126–134) He suggests that what a physiologist calls the phase sequence is synonymous to what a psychologist defines as a concept. In other words, concepts are made possible in human beings by the formation of intricate, multilevel groupings of neurons in the cortex of the brain. When an individual arrives at the level of development in which he possesses perhaps millions of phase sequences, he need no longer learn chiefly by making associations through repetition, but can learn by combining and recombining concepts (phase sequences) already existing in his head. Symbolic thinking involves one or many phase sequences. A mental image, such as a memory of a vase of flowers or a person's face, is a concept dependent on phase sequences. A word can only have meaning if it, too, depends on phase sequences.

Imagine a fire engine. Say the word out loud or silently and notice all that it evokes: images of color (probably red), noise, a tearing hurry, men in waterproof coats clinging to the hook and ladder, danger, a clanging bell, a wailing siren. These images are attended by sets of sensory signals: the body tenses, muscles prepare to leap out of the way. This multiple imagery is accompanied by rush words: speed, fire. Imagining is like a pebble flung into a pond creating concentric circles of images and concepts. The structures that made this reaction possible are there, established during one's entire life before this moment. Perhaps a new connection between two of them or among several can be seen. If so, this is an example of conceptual learning, or adult learning, as Hebb explains it.

This kind of learning is based on the existence of conceptual frameworks, and it cannot begin until a child reaches a degree of maturity in which he can function symbolically. By two years, even by eighteen months, young children remember things, search for objects which have vanished, and begin to use words, all of which clearly indicate that some phase sequences have already been established and that symbolic functioning has begun.

The most advanced sort of learning which can be explained by this theory is that of insight. Archimedes leaping from his bath yelling "Eureka" because he suddenly understands why ships float is a paradigm of the insight experience. Typically, insight comes only after one has wrestled long and deeply with a problem, after all the relevant facts have been gathered (i.e., after one has built as many related phase sequences as possible). Struggling for an elusive solution causes bafflement and frustration. A breakthrough feels possible, but fails to materialize. Then with a flash of instant revelation, the answer springs to mind. Further checking may follow, but the answer is certain. This is insight. Hebb explains it as a true breakthrough, a physical connection between organized groups of cells, phase sequences (primed and focused) which have never previously functioned together and which forever after will be conceptually connected for the individual. This kind of learning is utterly different from the slow building of connections through repetition or habit formation. (7:158–165)

Human beings do, in fact, learn by both rote and insight or from one end of the continuum to the other. To say that the slow building of neurological connections through repetitive sensory experience must come first in the infant, that very soon conceptual learning appears, and that they thereafter coexist is probably true. Middle childhood conceptual learning clearly becomes the more important and continues to dominate from that time on.

The preschool child actively learns both ways. When he plays at the water table, examines textures, identifies new sounds, forms, or colors, anything which basically involves him in sensory learning — he is forming associative bonds. When he uses words, looks at picture books, he is already engaged in conceptual learning. A rich nursery school experience provides opportunities for both.

One may ask what motivates learning. Perception, we are told, is inherently self-motivating. (14:29–30) To see, to hear, and to feel are satisfying in themselves; they need no external reward. Learning follows as a by-product. The experience of discovery is as self-motivating, in turn, as perception.

Conditioners have chosen to study that aspect of learning which is responsive to external reward and punishment (a pigeon's ability to peck at a door behind which will appear a kernel of grain, the human being's learning of nonsense syllables). These behavioral habits are themselves only meaningful to the extent that the reward makes them so.

Habit Learning

From experiments with animals in behavioral laboratories, the concepts of operant conditioning began to be applied to humans. At first, reinforcement principles were widely used in the education of retarded children; more recently, they have been successfully applied to disadvantaged children and children with behavioral problems. The rewards may be physical (instead of food pellets, perhaps candy) or symbolic (words of praise or a token which is itself valueless but may be exchanged for something desired). These rewards are given in what is called a "schedule of reinforcement" which refers to the conditions which are necessary prior to introducing the reward, and the frequency with which that reward is given. In all cases the conditioner has in mind the target behavior he wishes to encourage. Behavior does have consequences; both the behavior and the consequences, using the knowledge of reinforcement principles, can be made explicit.

Use of Reinforcement to
Modify Behavior Problems.

The use of social reinforcement can be seen in a laboratory pre-school directed by Florence Harris at the University of Washington. The children mentioned in this study felt rewarded by adult social attention, so there was no need for food reinforcers or tokens. In general, an approximation of the desired behavior brought an immediate response, while undesirable behavior was ignored.

Field Studies of Social
Reinforcement in a Preschool

Florence Harris

Over the past five years our staff has been studying the use of adult social reinforcement to modify problem behaviors of individual children in the Laboratory Preschool. By "problem" I mean behaviors that are of concern to both teachers and parents because they seem to impede the child's development. As a result of these studies, we are convinced that among the most useful tools a teacher can acquire are skills in using reinforcement principles. Such skills require knowledge of operant learning theory, familiarity with objective observation and recording of behavior, practice in defining goals and planning (programming) successive steps toward those goals, and control of one's own responses.

Reinforcement principles, as you know, are based on the premise that most behavior is controlled by its immediate consequences. Any consequence which consistently leads to increase in the rate of the immediately preceding behavior is called a positive reinforcer. Now an almost inevitable consequence of a child's behavior, and particularly of his "problem behavior," is adult attention. "Attention" is defined as going to the child and smiling at, talking to, or touching him, or any combination of these behaviors. This consequence, moreover, unlike most other consequences, is completely under the control of the adult. Also unlike most other consequences, it is continuously and readily available to teachers. Giving or withholding attention requires only that the teacher

---

Florence Harris, "Field Studies of Social Reinforcement in a Preschool," originally appeared as a Seminar Paper for Consultant Series, Education Improvement Program (sponsored by the Ford Foundation), Duke University, Durham, North Carolina. Copyright 1967, by permission of the author.

be present. It seemed, therefore, both necessary and convenient that we study the effects on child behavior of teacher attention, to determine whether it functioned as a reinforcer, in accordance with reinforcement principles. If it did, then by controlling their own attending behaviors teachers might help children who showed problems. Teachers would simply need to 1) give attention to behaviors considered desirable and 2) withhold or withdraw attention from behaviors considered undesirable.

Although the process proved to be far from simple, we have systematically studied effects of adult attention on many kinds of problems, from behavior deficits such as extreme passivity, excessive isolate behavior, regressed crawling, and lack of speech, to behavior excesses such as hyperactivity, excessive aggression, and excessive crying. Brief descriptions of some of these studies will familiarize you with our procedures and the nature of our findings.

Operant Cryer Studied

Bill was a sturdy, handsome, capable four-year-old who morning after morning did far more crying than any other child in the group. The first few weeks of school passed with no diminution in Bill's screams and tears, though most children adjusted easily. If anything, the tears increased. After several weeks of dashing to "save" Bill, teachers noted that 1) the crying was usually set off by some very minor bump or frustration, 2) that rarely did he get really hurt, *never* seriously, 3) that he often cast a quick glance around before emitting his piercing cries, increasing the volume if no one came at once, and 4) that at least one teacher, sometimes all three, usually hurried to rescue him from the current disaster and stayed to wipe his tears and to comfort him. In other words, crying was getting a great deal of adult attention. It was decided to study systematic application of adult social reinforcement to help Bill acquire more constructive ways of dealing with minor hurts and rebuffs.

Before starting any procedures, teachers used pocket counters to determine the rate, or operant level, of the crying behavior. Over a period of ten days they found that Bill averaged about eight all-out crying episodes per morning.

Teachers then planned and instituted reinforcement procedures; that is, they ignored Bill completely whenever he burst out crying, remaining busy elsewhere until his crying had completely ceased. Concurrently, whenever he made the slightest effort to resolve his problems verbally or physically, they went to him immediately and gave appreciative attention. Had he genuinely hurt himself at any time, of course, a teacher would have gone to him at once and given help.

Figure 1 shows a cumulative graph of Bill's crying episodes. The black circles indicate the average rate of eight episodes for each of the ten days of baseline. The open circles show what happened under social reinforcement procedures: within five days the number of crying episodes

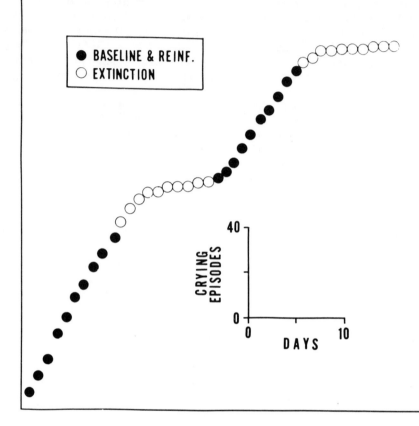

Figure 1:   "Bill"

per day had dwindled to one. During all of the next five days there was only one crying episode.

Reinforcement Pattern Reversed

At this point a test procedure was necessary to ascertain whether the changes had actually been brought about by the social reinforcement procedures used, and not by some other variable, such as the weather. The test procedure consisted of reversing the first pattern of differential reinforcement. Teachers ignored all of Bill's constructive responses to problems which arose, but gave immediate and continuous attention (re-inforcement) for any crying behavior. Since at this time there was prac-tically no crying to attend to, teachers had to develop it from minimal signs of distress. They watched for times when Bill frowned or screwed up his face over some bump. At once a teacher was there commiserating, patting, and delivering solicitude in any appropriate fashion. As you can see by the second series of black circles, teachers succeeded in shaping up crying again, but not quite in the strength obtained during baseline (about six episodes per day, on the average). Presumably, Bill had begun to find more constructive behaviors reinforcing in themselves.

As soon as the data showed that the behavior change was indeed a function of contingent adult attention, the teachers returned to the original pattern of differential reinforcement. The crying dropped out almost immediately and did not recur as a problem during the rest of the school year.

This study of "an operant cryer," done by Betty Hart, Eileen Allen, Joan Buell, Montrose Wolf, and myself, clearly illustrates our basic procedures which follow observing and defining the behavior problem, discussing it with the child's parents and reaching agreement that a study should be made. Our first procedure, then, was to secure precise data on the prevailing, or operant, rate of the behavior. Second came differential reinforcement of the behavior, with appreciative attention given to all desirable responses and no attention to the defined problem behavior. Third, if the child's behavior altered significantly in the desired direction, teachers tested whether their attention was actually the significant factor producing change. They reversed procedures, giving no attention to the desirable responses, but continuous attention to the problem behavior. Teachers had to develop the problem behavior again by attending first to very faint approximations to it, then to stronger signs and finally to "cries audible more than three feet away," the criterion for the problem behavior. (It seems likely that a similar procedure produced the problem in the first place.) Recurrence of the problem behavior under these conditions indicated a high probability that the attending behavior of adults was the causative factor in both eliminating and in building the behavior.

When a test of the significant variable had given reasonably conclusive information, the fourth step was instituted: teachers again attended continuously to the desired behavior and ignored the undesirable behavior. A fifth step involved slowly reducing the amount of attention given immediately consequent upon desirable behavior, until the child was getting the daily amount usual in our school situation. Presumably desirable behavior, or successful behavior, draws reinforcement from many other sources, both social (peers and other adults) and intrinsic (accomplishment and success).

Parents were, of course, kept informed of the progress of any study. Usually they were delightedly aware of changes that occurred and inaugurated the more helpful attending behaviors at home.

Mark's Passivity
Hampered Development

The technique of building a new behavior out of the closest approximation to it that the child happens to emit was demonstrated in another early study, this one done by Margaret Johnston, Susan Kelley, Montrose Wolf, and myself. The subject was a three-year-old boy, Mark, whose extreme passivity seemed to hamper his development of skills in every area of growth, social and intellectual as well as motor. Despite traditional teacher efforts to stimulate and encourage him into activity, records taken toward the end of winter quarter showed that his letharigc and aimless behavior was not diminishing. Indeed, it was increasing. The records also showed that his behavior, while repelling or failing to hold playmates. was drawing a good deal of teacher attention. It was decided, therefore, to study whether Mark could be helped to become more vigorous, and thus better able to participate in the group activities, by giving teacher attention systematically in accordance with reinforcement principles.

Now, vigorous activity is very difficult to define precisely in behavioral terms. The staff agreed, however, that use of a piece of yard equipment called a "climbing frame" required vigorous activity and could be readily and reliably observed and recorded. Therefore, use of the climbing frame by Mark was designated the goal behavior. The criterion for recording its occurrence was that he be touching the apparatus.

Before teachers made any change in their guidance procedures, an observer was assigned to record the operant level of Mark's climbing frame behavior. She also noted his use of other climbing equipment and the occasions on which he received teacher attention. Using a clipboard, a stopwatch, a code and a special form, the observer recorded these behaviors in 10-second intervals for eight days. In Figure 2, baseline, it can be seen that Mark's climbing frame behavior was practically zero. Moreover, he used other climbing equipment less than five percent of the outdoor play time. The data also indicated that Mark spent about seventy-five percent of the time in sedentary pursuits and about twenty-five percent in wandering about or simply standing. Furthermore, for almost forty percent of the time, teachers were giving him attention such as suggesting activities, talking about what children were doing, and in any way encouraging him to play. Since reliability measures were taken on climbing behaviors only, the other behaviors, while considered by the staff to be reasonably accurately recorded, were not graphed as data.

Having secured a clear picture of Mark's ongoing behaviors, teachers inaugurated reinforcement procedures. Teachers attention was to be given to Mark as soon as and for as long as he touched the climbing frame. Immediately upon cessation of climbing frame behavior, the teacher was to withdraw her attention and occupy herself with other duties. One of the two teachers was designated the "reinforcer teacher." She carried primary responsibility for seeing that contingencies for reinforcement were immediately and precisely met.

Since there was practically no climbing frame behavior to attend to, the teacher had to develop it out of the behavior Mark already emitted: an occasional lackadaisical wandering down a nearby cement walk. Stationing herself beside the climbing frame, she busied herself until Mark

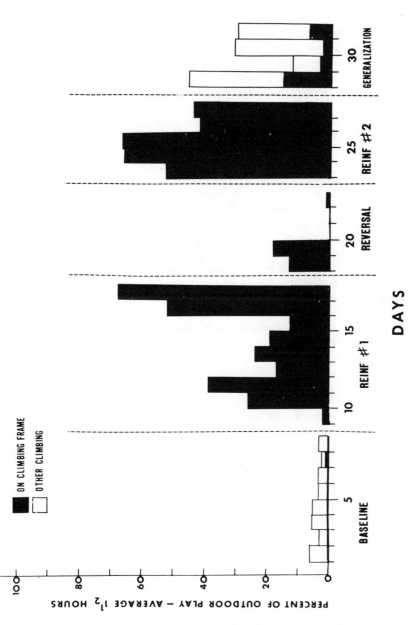

Figure 2: "Mark"

wandered down the walk to a point closest to the frame. Then she turned to him, spoke, and remained smilingly attentive so long as he paused in that spot or came closer. When he moved on, she immediately turned back to her work with other things. The next time Mark came closer and paused longer. Soon he was not reinforced until he touched the frame. He got on the frame and began climbing on the first day. By the third day of reinforcement, climbing frame behavior had markedly increased. On the ninth day (Day 18), Mark spent more than sixty percent of the play period using the climbing frame. Although the data do not show the vigor of his play, teachers reported that he was in almost constant motion on Days 17 and 18, having seemingly overcome the stiffness that his mother reported had developed over Days 11 and 12. The reinforcer teacher was, of course, giving continuous social reinforecement so long as he remained on the climbing frame.

In order to determine whether the new behavior was indeed a result of the social reinforcement, contingencies for reinforcement were reversed on Day 19. Teacher attention was withheld or withdrawn the moment Mark touched the climbing frame. But he was given attention as soon as he engaged in any other activity. For two days he spent frequent brief periods on the climbing frame. Then that behavior dropped to zero and remained very low for the rest of the reversal period. Mark engaged actively in many other forms of outdoor play, however, including use of other climbers, easel painting and block building. During these activities, of course, he received continuous adult reinforcement. The data were considered sufficient proof that changes in his behavior were indeed due to the adult attention he received.

On Day 24, therefore, reinforcement of climbing behavior was again instituted. The behavior reconditioned very rapidly, rising at once to over fifty percent of the play time. Since it remained in strength from day to day, the staff decided that their objectives for Mark had been achieved and an attempt was made to generalize the behavior through gradually reducing the amount of reinforcement given to climbing frame behavior. Both teachers also began to reinforce other kinds of play behavior, particularly climbing activities. They made an effort not to attend to the old, passive behavior if it occurred. They reported, too, that Mark's social play had increased.

Post checks made the following year showed that Mark maintained his vigorous play behavior, spending about half of his outdoor play time in spontaneous and skilled use of the varied pieces of climbing apparatus. Presumably, vigorous activity had come under the control of other reinforcers than teacher attention alone.

Teachers hearing accounts of our studies often question whether the reversal procedure, however necessary experimentally, is not detrimental in some way to the child. We had the same concern about it in the earliest studies we did, watching particularly for any signs in the child's behavior that the procedure was damaging. Not one such sign have we found. Indeed, the climber study, as well as the many others in which we have used reversals, has led us to think that the procedure may actually be beneficial to a child. For example, we have noted that, following a reversal, desirable behaviors returned in even greater strength than previously. We also have evidence that a reversal may help the child to generalize the desirable behaviors. In the climbing frame study, for example, Mark began during reversal to use actively and purposefully for the first time such materials as easel paint, finger paint, and blocks.

In the course of the climbing frame study and others it was noted that, while teacher efforts concentrated on modification of one behavior, other behaviors also changed. For example, as Mark climbed, he played and talked with children who came to join in the fun. Social and verbal behaviors increased along with the motor behavior, suggesting that classes of behaviors might be functionally related. This matter was investigated two years later in a second study of the modification of passive behavior. This study was conducted by Joan Buell, Patricia Stoddard, Donald Baer, and myself.

Gross Motor Skills Improved

The subject, three-year-old Polly, was exceedingly passive and silent, interacting with no one. Traditional teacher efforts to get her to participate in play had no success. Since it was considered that primarily she needed to become more active, teachers decided to study use of reinforcement principles to help her gain gross motor skills.

As the baseline data show (Figure 3,A), Polly scarcely touched any of the active outdoor equipment, even after several weeks of school. Section B, 1 and 2, shows the initial reinforcement period.

In this study, instead of slowly getting the child to a piece of climbing equipment through reinforcement of her successively coming closer to it (through successive approximations), the reinforcing teacher tried speeding the process by lifting Polly onto a piece of equipment and then staying close and enthusiastically reinforcing her so long as she stayed on it. The moment she climbed off the teacher turned to other duties. Each morning for nine successive mornings (see B, 1) the teacher placed Polly on a different piece of climbing equipment. She did this only once for each piece. Thereafter, whenever Polly touched that piece of equipment the teacher at once came to reinforce her with verbal and tactual appreciation and any necessary help. After the ninth day, all such cuing was terminated, but reinforcement continued as before. As you see in B, 2, climbing dropped slightly when cuing ceased but soon recovered its previous rate. Section C shows an inadvertent reversal occasioned, presumably, by two events: a long holiday season between B and C and the absence during C of the reinforcer teacher through illness. Reinforcement during this first week after vacation was imprecise and lean. When the reinforcer teacher returned (D) and reinstituted precise contingencies, climbing behavior at once rose and remained stable. Section E shows the results of the intentional reversal of reinforcement contingencies and Section F the return to reinforcement of desired behavior.

While these data were being secured, the observer was also recording information on the several other parameters of Polly's behavior: her

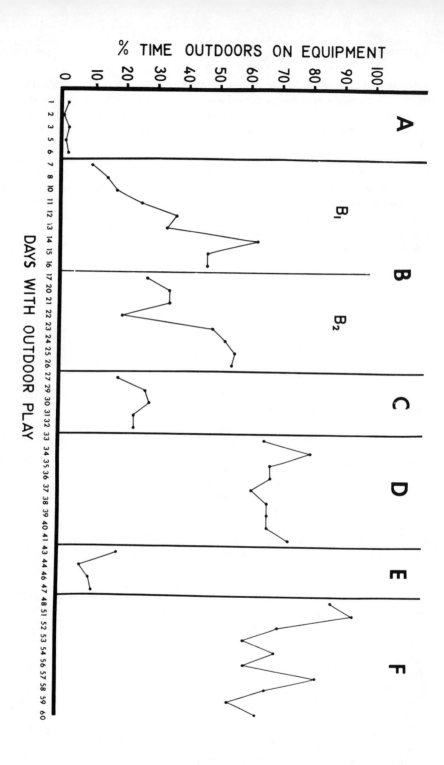

Figure 3: "Polly"

touching of others, speaking to others, the types of play she engaged in and some regressed behaviors defined and designated "baby behaviors." As you can see in Figure 4, all of these behaviors rose irregularly throughout the course of the study, except for baby behavior, which diminished. In no case, however, did a reversal observably alter the rate of any one of these behaviors. Moreover, the evidence strongly suggests that no conclusion can be drawn regarding relations between the several kinds of behavior recorded. All we can say is that in the work we have done to date, although concurrent changes in several behaviors have been noted, we have found no evidence of a functional relation between one class of behavior and another.

Systematic Attention
Modified Behavior

In reporting early studies we often heard this remark: "Of course the child's behavior changed. Look at all the attention he was getting!" The idea that the amount of adult attention makes significant differences in child behavior also underlies advice often given to parents: "You just need to give him more time and attention." An occasion arose for us to examine this assumption in a study done by Betty Hart, Nancy Reynolds, Eleanor Brawley, Donald Baer, and myself.

The subject, Mary, was a five-year-old child who day after day engaged almost exclusively in solitary pursuits. She spent much time playing with small toy animals, telling them long stories and carressing them. Whenever children approached her, however, she quickly alienated them with such "snide" remarks as, "You don't know how to do it ... Yours is no good ... Mine is better ... Go Away!" Teachers tried by all the usual methods to help Mary become more friendly. But they, too, frequently met with such things as "accidental" spills of materials, reckless behavior in high places, dawdling, or being greeted with "bathroom" talk or an order to go away. It was finally decided to study whether application of reinforcement principles could improve Mary's social behaviors.

Perusal of the baseline records of Mary's behavior (see Figure 5) showed that, while she usually played close to children (proximity was defined as within 3 feet) she engaged in almost no cooperative play. The records also showed that she was getting very little attention from adults. Presumably she had become as aversive to them as to the children.

The staff decided, therefore, to begin this study by simply increasing the amount of teacher attention, without making it contingent on any specific behavior. Although adult attention was defined as verbalization and touching, and only these were recorded, a teacher actually remained physically near Mary through most of the afternoons. Days 11 through 17 show the period of high "noncontingent" social reinforcement. As you can see, cooperative play remained very low, although proximity to children increased slightly. Obviously, a greater amount of teacher attention did not bring about any significant behavior change.

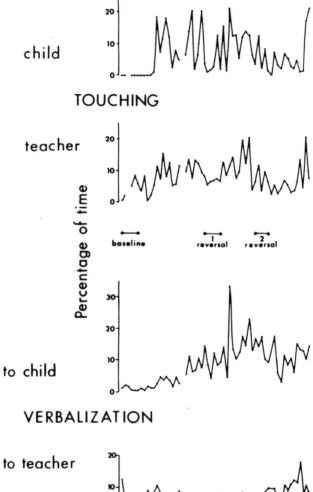

child

TOUCHING

teacher

baseline   reversal   reversal

to child

VERBALIZATION

to teacher

Percentage of time

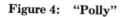

5 10 15 20 25 30 35 40 45 50 55 60

DAYS

Figure 4: "Polly"

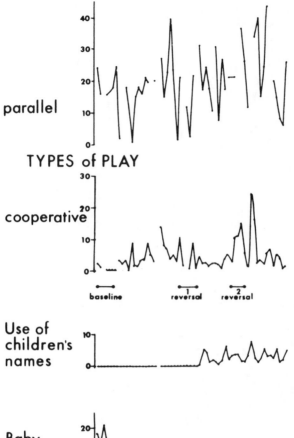

parallel

TYPES of PLAY

cooperative

baseline   reversal 1   reversal 2

Use of
children's
names

Baby
behavior

5 10 15 20 25 30 35 40 45 50 55 60

DAYS

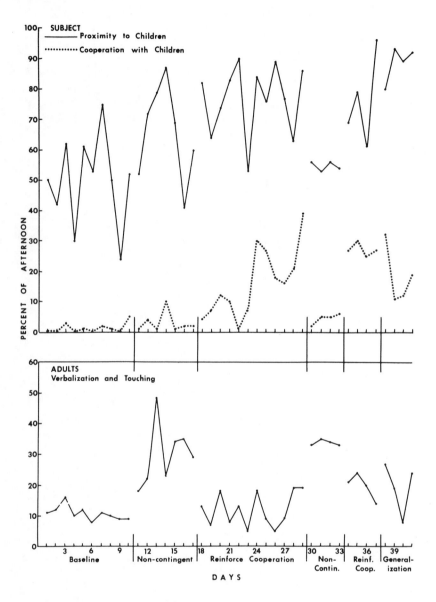

Figure 5: "Mary"

Contingencies for receiving attention were then instituted. A teacher went to Mary and verbalized to her or touched her, only when she engaged in cooperative play with children. Since cooperative play was at first practically nonexistent, teachers cued such behavior for seven days. Cuing consisted of giving another child something to take or to tell to Mary that might start some activity together (e.g., cups for a doll tea party or a request to come in for a snack). The teacher accompanied the child and reinforced the two children as long as interaction continued. Adult reinforcement during this period dropped to no more than that given during baseline. Nevertheless, cooperative play increased markedly.

The reversal procedure in this study was a return, not to baseline conditions, but to the heavy, noncontingent adult attending maintained during the previous noncontingent period. The data show that Mary's cooperative play behavior immediately fell to a very low rate, in spite of increased adult attention.

When adult attention was again made contingent upon cooperative play, interaction with children again rose. The higher rate was maintained surprisingly well, even when teachers attempted what they considered to be too rapid a generalization, because of the close of school. Teachers also reported that during the course of the study, Mary's behavior changed qualitatively in desirable directions: the negative verbalizations to children and teachers became very rare. Caressing of toys and talking to herself dropped out completely, and her play became less sedentary. All in all, the noxious aspects of her play diminished considerably. Mary became a much more rewarding child in many relationships. This study strongly suggests that it is not the *amount* of adult attention but the precision with which contingencies for attention are maintained that brings about behavior change.

Cuing Maintained
Precise Contingencies

The maintenance of precise contingencies is not an easy matter. If the problem and the staffing are such that we can do so, we assign one teacher to carry major responsibility for seeing that reinforcement is given or withdrawn immediately, in accordance with the specified procedure. The other teachers, of course, know the contingencies in force and behave accordingly if occasion arises. If there is not a designated "reinforcer teacher," then each teacher carries full responsibility when the subject is near her. In the cryer study, for example, each teacher had to be responsible, but no difficulties arose since everyone at once knew when a cry occurred.

In a study of hitting behaviors, all three teachers again were responsible. The research design involved extinguishing (ignoring) hard hits, while maintaining (attending to) soft hits and disruptive behaviors. Teachers had difficulties at once. First, they found it difficult at times to discriminate between hard and soft hits. Second, the subject child had a way of running off just as soon as he hit someone. Frequently, he ran right around a corner to a second teacher who greeted him warmly, not knowing that she was reinforcing a "hard hit."

Each day the supervising psychologist brought the morning's data to the teacher's noon staff meeting. He showed the evidence that, far from extinguishing hard hits, the teachers were actually putting them on an excellent schedule for maintaining them indefinitely: that is, they ignored them most of the time, but occasionally and on an irregular schedule they reinforced them. I do not recall any learning experience that was more powerful or more painful for everyone involved.

To help all the teachers maintain precise contingencies, the observer was asked to provide a cue. She was given a red flashlight. As soon as the subject child emitted a "hard hit," the observer placed the flashlight on top of her clipboard clamp for two minutes. While the flashlight remained there, no one was to attend to the subject child. The observer then replaced the flashlight underneath her clipboard and the subject was again "reinforceable." This cuing resolved the problem. Teachers could glance at the observer before approaching the subject, and thus maintain the necessary reinforcing behavior. However, time had unfortunately run out. For the few remaining days of school, all classes of aggressive behavior were put on extinction. Under this contingency they rapidly diminished to a very satisfactory low rate. Teachers and parents were delighted over the child's improved behaviors. Teachers were disappointed, however, over having "lost" a study, since there was no time to conduct a reversal for the necessary testing procedure. Various kinds of cuing devices—lights, electronic equipment—have since been effectively used in studies in which adults could not readily discriminate when to attend to the subject child.

Social Reinforcement
Extinguished Aggression

A later study of aggressive behavior (by Allen, Reynolds, Brawley, Harris, and Baer) involved two children, both bright, capable four-year-old boys. These two were wonderful boys, gratifyingly creative and constructive—so long as they were apart. Together, they were dynamite! And the school year was scarcely well started before they were together through every minute of the morning, tearing about the yard, stepping on other people's play materials, knocking over paints and blocks, punching, pushing, disrupting (ostensibly, of course, by "accident"), using bathroom language, calling names, and generally defying both children and adults. Using every traditional teaching method from suggest to scold, teachers could get them to participate in constructive learning activity, or to separate, only briefly, if at all.

Although prospects for success in using social reinforcement to separate the two boys looked dim, we decided to try. First, two observers were assigned, one to each child, to get baseline data on the operant level of the time each spent with the other and the time each spent with other children. Since the two graphs turned out to be practically identical, Figure 6 illustrates what occurred in both cases. As you can

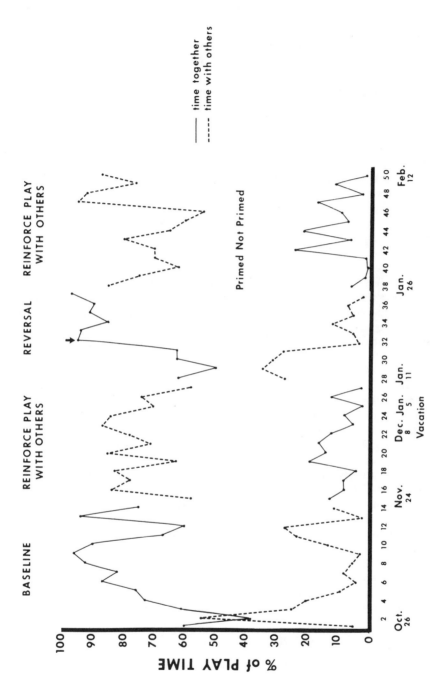

Figure 6: "Child B"

see, Child B spent an average of about seventy-five percent of each morning with Child A. Concurrently, he spent about ten percent of the morning with some other child. Note the unusual data for the second day of baseline. On this day occurred one of the rare instances of a quarrel between the two boys and they stayed apart practically the whole morning. By the next day the rupture had healed, however, and the two continued their demolition and defiance as usual.

Beginning on the fifteenth day, a teacher was assigned to each boy. Each teacher greeted her child the moment he arrived and, moving with him, took appreciative interest in any activity he selected, attempting to include nearby children in the activity, if possible. Each teacher continued such social reinforcement so long as the two boys remained apart. If they came together, the teachers left and all adults ignored them until they again separated. Although initially teachers were dubious about being able to keep the boys separated, the data show how highly successful they were. Each boy's play with other children at once increased to about seventy-five percent of each morning, while play together decreased to about ten percent of the morning. And since play with other children, you will recall, was usually gratifyingly creative and constructive, desirable play patterns were getting continuous and appreciative teacher attention.

After thirteen days of reinforcing play with others, the teachers tested the strength of the social variable by reversing their procedures. So long as the two boys were together, the teachers now gave full attention. As soon as they separated to play alone or with others, the teachers turned to other duties. Within three days the play pattern of the two boys was completely reversed and they played together most of the time. It was evident that the social behavior of both was strongly influenced by adult reinforcement.

When the teachers once again attended only to play with others, that behavior at once recurred. Presumably, the constructive and productive aspects of play with other children was itself reinforcing. Shortly, indeed, if the two boys joined each other briefly their play together showed none of the earlier distressing destructive-aggressive characteristics. Teachers gradually diminished their attending, to the amount usual in the situation, and from then on for the rest of the year each boy played with a variety of playmates, enjoying many friends in addition to each other, and developing social and preacademic skills in highly desirable and obviously satisfying fashion.

"Attending Behaviors" Increased

In the area of preacademic behaviors, a skill that seems basic to all learning is the ability to attend to a stimulus or a set of stimuli long enough to develop appropriate responses. Occasionally, however, a child enters our preschool with very limited "attending behaviors." We usually refer to such a child as a "flitter," for he seldom settles to any one activity long enough to develop constructive and creative skills. With the passage of time, such behavior becomes an increasing handicap to the child's learning.

Such a "flitter" was enrolled in the four-year-old group. Since some children show rather flightly behavior when they are first exposed to an environment rich in attractive materials and activities, it was almost mid-winter before the staff agreed that James needed special help to increase the span of his attending behavior, even though in all other respects he seemed adequately skilled. This study was done by Allen, Brawley, Reynolds, Harris, and Baer.

An observer was assigned to record his behavior, noting his activities and the time he spent in each. Over five school mornings, these records showed that although occasionally James spent one, two, or three minutes with an activity, the average duration of each activity was less than one minute, and he was busy all the time.

The procedure for increasing the duration of time James spent in any activity was to make adult attention contingent solely on his spending one minute emitting "attending behavior." Attending was defined as play activity 1) with a single material such as blocks or paint, 2) in a single area such as in the sand box or at a table, or 3) in a single dramatic role such as fireman, or telephone repair man. One teacher was assigned responsibility for maintaining reinforcement contingencies.

It seemed unlikely that the teacher would be able to accurately time duration of the child's activities so she could reinforce him when—and *only* when—he had attended for precisely one minute. The observer, who timed all observations with a stopwatch, was therefore asked to provide a cue as soon as James reached criterion and was "reinforcible." She used a red flashlight, as in the uncompleted aggression study.

Figure 7 shows the progress of the study. Data were graphed in terms of the number of activity changes that occurred within successive 50-minute time units. In most instances, but not invariably, two 50-minute periods indicated one day of recording of free-play time. The more teacher-controlled activities such as group times were not recorded.

The baseline record (Stage 1) shows that James was changing activity on an average of 56 times every 50 minutes. He averaged 53 seconds per activity. Concurrently, teachers were giving him noncontingent attention about seventeen percent of the time.

During Stage 2, the teachers gave him attention as soon as he had spent one minute in one activity, continuing to attend steadily so long as he remained in the activity. As you can see, James at once began making fewer shifts in activity, and spending longer periods with each one. The average duration of each activity rose to almost 2 minutes.

Teachers then instituted a brief reversal with reinforcement again on a noncontingent basis to check on whether adult attention was indeed causing the change. Obviously it was, as Stage 3 indicates. After four 50-minute checks, teachers returned to the reinforcement contingencies of Stage 2. During Stage 4 A, reinforcement was given immediately and continuously after James had engaged in one minute of play, and discontinued as soon as he left the activity. The average duration of each activity rose to two-and-one-half minutes.

Contingencies were then changed (Stage 4 B). The criterion for receiving teacher attention was raised to two minutes of continuous attention to the same activity. As you can see, although James' attending

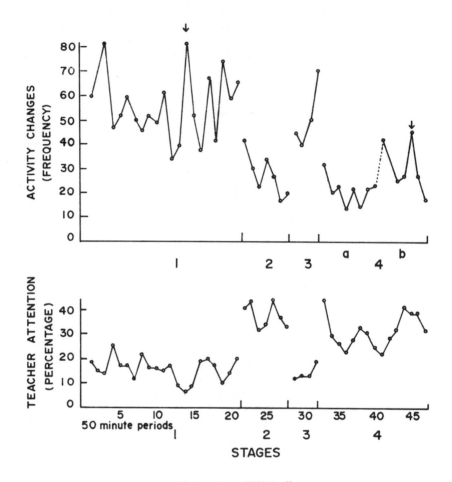

Figure 7: "Flitter"

behavior was slightly disrupted, it soon was meeting the new criterion
very acceptably. Actually, teachers noted that he often spent 15, 20, or
25 minutes in one activity. But since this sometimes involved his going
to join him in his work, each departure was recorded and treated as a
change of activity although he returned to the same activity at once.
For this reason, data at the close of the study did not fully reflect the
improvement teachers considered James to have made in his attending
behaviors.

Note the arrows at two periods showing the highest number of activity changes within their respective stages of the study. The arrows mark
days on which James' mother came for her regularly scheduled visit. No
restrictions were placed on her interactions with James, since visits tend
to be exciting for both parents and child. In her usual fashion she interacted steadily with him, making many suggestions that he bring her
this or show her that or "settle down" to the other. She was, of course,

reinforcing behavior incompatible with the attending behavior (less frequent activity changes) that teachers were trying to shape. In a way, the data on those days seem to increase the evidence that James' short attention span was due to adult social reinforcement.

Child's Silence
Hindered Relationships

We have conducted studies in another area of behavior that might be considered preacademic: that of verbal behavior. The study I shall describe focused on a four-year-old girl who had a perfect command of language but who failed to use it. The study was done by Eileen Allen, Betty Hart, Joan Buell, Montrose Wolf, and myself.

Sally's excessive silence seemed to be seriously hindering her relationships with both children and adults: children eventually left her entirely alone.

Baseline data in Figure 8 showed that Sally talked very little to anyone, children or adults. They also revealed that a fair percentage of the little talking she did took place when she was off by herself. With three aspects of language behavior to work with — speech to adults, speech to children, speech in isolation or "to herself" — the staff decided to use a research design in which one speech variable at a time was reinforced. Teachers planned first to reinforce (attend to) Sally's speech to adults. Should significant increase in this one variable occur, teachers would then reinforce speech with children, while maintaining speech with adults. This design, in which one dependent variable after another was modified, made unnecessary a reversal type of test of the independent or significant variable.

As you can see, warm and intensive adult responsiveness (reinforcement) to all verbalizations to teachers rapidly increased the rate of this behavior. Talking to other children and to herself, which were not reinforced, remained at a low level. On days 20 through 28 teachers extended reinforcement to include similar attention to all of Sally's verbalizations to children. There followed a marked rise in verbal behavior with peers, while verbal behavior with adults maintained a high rate. Verbal behavior when by herself remained at a low, constant rate.

Teacher Attention
Stimulated Verbalizations

This study, although not completed to the full satisfaction of the staff due to the close of the school year, was repeated in its major aspects two years later, with the addition of a reversal period following reinforcement of verbalizations to adults and a consequent increase in that behavior. Again, the subject was a capable four-year-old girl who simply did not use the language she had. Initial data secured (Figure 9, Baseline) showed that Jennifer spoke very little to either adults or children, but there was no talking when she was apart from people. Procedures were instituted that paralleled those used with Sally (the

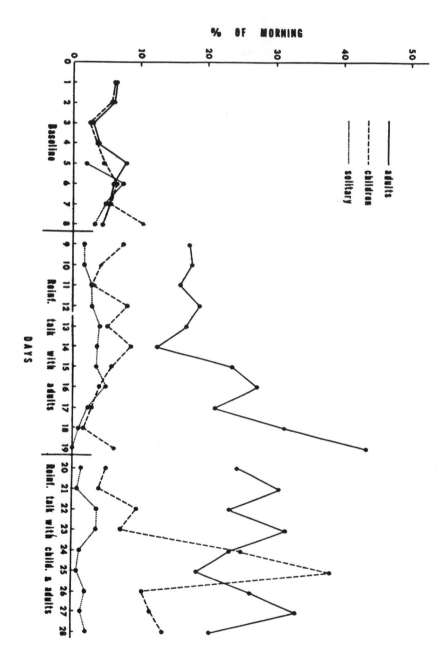

Figure 8:   "Sally"

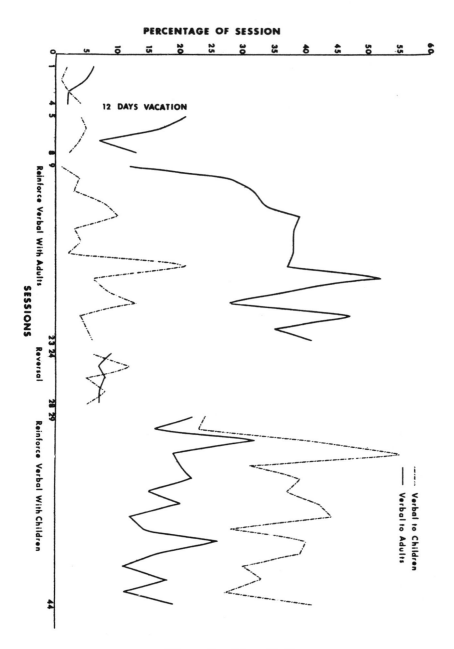

Figure 9: "Jennifer"

previous nonspeaking child) ; teachers gave immediate interested attention whenever she spoke to them, continuing until she stopped responding verbally. Then they at once turned to other things or children. As Figure 9 shows, while these contingencies were in effect (Day 5 through Day 23), there was a marked rise in her verbalizations to teachers. A slight increase also was evident in her verbalizations to children; possibly this indicated a generalization effect of the increased talking. More probably, the teachers thought, it was due to the fact that a teacher and child in animated conversation tended at times to draw other children.

On Days 24 to 28 a reversal procedure clearly indicated that adult attention was the significant factor affecting Jennifer's verbal behavior. Starting with Day 29, therefore, teachers gave immediate and continuous attention to all of her verbal behavior to children. For the first seven or eight days, they also gave cues as to how she might initiate, or even respond to, verbal approaches of children. (e.g., You can tell her, "I'd like some blue paint.") Such cues were then gradually dropped, and Jennifer was reinforced only for self-initiated responses. Throughout this period, teachers held to a minimum their reinforcement of verbalizations to an adult alone, since this was now somewhat incompatible with the primary objective of verbalization to children.

The contingencies applied were obviously effective, since by the close of the study Jennifer was freely verbalizing to both children and adults, the rate to children being about twice that to adults. Both teachers and parents were highly pleased with the outcome.

As the above review of studies has indicated, reinforcement principles have proved to be effective tools for helping children modify behaviors that handicap them. Acquisition of skills in using these tools, consequently, becomes highly reinforcing to teachers and parents alike. After all, the modification of behavior is a primary function we have in common. It is stimulating to consider that by simply using systematically a behavior we already employ we may help children learn faster and with less apparent strain.

References

Allen, K. Eileen; Henke, Lydia; Reynolds, Nancy; Harris, Florence R., and Baer, D. M. The control of hyperactivity in social reinforcement of attending behavior in a preschool child. *J. Educ. Psychol.*, August, 1967.

Allen, K. Eileen, and Harris, Florence R. Elimination of a child's excessive scratching by training the mother in reinforcement procedures. *Behav. Res. Ther.*, 1966.

Ayllon, T., and Haughton, E. Control of the behavior of schizophrenic patients by food. *J. Exper. Anal. Behav.*, 1962, 5, 343–352.

Baer, D. M. Effect of withdrawal of positive reinforcement on an extinguishing response in young children. *Child Develpm.*, 1961, 32, 67–74.

Bijou, S. W. Application of operant principles to the teaching of reading, writing, and arithmetic to retarded children. Paper presented at the 43rd Annual Council for Exceptional Children Convention, April, 1965.

Birnbrauer, J. S., and Lawler, Julia. Token reinforcement for learning. *J. Ment. Retard.*, 1964, 2, 275–279.

Brady, J. P., and Lind, D. L. Experimental analysis of hysterical blindness. *Arch. Gen. Psychiat.*, 1961, 4, 331–339.

Brawley, Eleanor R.; Harris, Florence R.; Peterson, R. F.; Allen, K. Eileen; and Fleming, R. E. Behavior modification of an autistic child. Unpublished manuscript, University of Washington, 1966.

Ferster, C. B.; Nurnberger, J. I.; and Levitt, E. B. The control of eating. *J. Mathetics*, 1962, 1, 87–109.

Goldiamond, I. The maintenance of ongoing fluent verbal behavior and stuttering. *J. Mathetics*, 1962, 7, 57–95.

Harris, Florence R.; Johnston, Margaret K.; Kelley, C. Susan; and Wolf, M. M. Effects of positive social reinforcement on regressed crawling in a preschool child. *J. Educ. Psychol.*, 1964, 55, 35–41.

Harris, Florence R.; Wolf, M. M.; and Baer, D. M. Effects of adult social reinforcement on child behavior. *Young Children*, 1964, 20, 8–17.

Hart, Betty M.; Allen, K. Eileen; Buell, Joan S.; Harris, Florence R.; and Wolf, M. M. Effects of social reinforcement on operant crying. *J. Exp. Child Psychol.*, 1964, 1, 145–153.

Johnston, Margaret K.; Kelley, C. Susan; Harris, Florence R.; and Wolf, M. M. An application of reinforcement principles to development of motor skills of a young child. *Child Develpm.*, 1966, 37, 379–387.

Risley, T. R., and Wolf, M. M. Establishing functional speech in echolalic children. *Behav. Res. and Therapy*, 1967, 5, 73–88.

Wolf, M. M.; Risley, T. R.; and Mees, M. L. Application of operant conditioning procedures to the behavior problems of an autistic child. *Behav. Res. and Therapy*, 1964, 1, 305–312.

Wolf, M. M.; Risley, T. R.; Johnston, Margaret K.; Harris, Florence R.; and Allen, K. Eileen. Application of operant conditioning procedures to the behavior problems of an autistic child: a follow-up and extension. *Behav. Res. and Therapy*, 1967, 5, 103–111.   (6:2–16)

Use of Reinforcement to Teach the Three R's.

Carl Bereiter and Siegfried Engelmann have become controversial figures through their method of direct teaching of spoken language, reading, and mathematics to deprived prekindergarten and kindergarten children. Maya Pines gives a vivid description of their teaching technique in *Revolution in Learning*, calling it the "pressure-cooker approach." (12:50–72) In their own book, *Teaching Disadvantaged Children in the Preschool*, Bereiter and Engelmann describe the rationale behind their approach:

1) By the age of three or four, disadvantaged children are already seriously behind other children in the development of aptitudes necessary for success in school.

2) Disadvantaged children must somehow "catch up" in the development of these abilities, or they will enter elementary school with handicaps that will spell failure for a large percentage of them and a limited future for all of them.

3) If they are to catch up, they must progress at a faster-than-normal rate.

4) A preschool program that provides the usual opportunities for learning cannot be expected to produce learning at above normal rates.

5) A short-term preschool program cannot be expected to produce above normal gains in all areas of development at once; a "well-rounded" program is therefore incompatible with the goal of catching up: selectivity is necessary.

Taken together, these points indicate that radical departures from established practices of early childhood education are needed. It was shown that preschools for disadvantaged children that are patterned after the familiar upper-middle-class nursery school have not succeeded in meeting the challenge of providing a faster than normal rate of learning in areas significant for school success. An examination of the structure of the upper-middle-class nursery school suggested an important reason for its inadequacy as a model of preschool education for disadvantaged children: the nursery school complements the influences of the privileged home instead of duplicating them, and thus exerts many of the influences of a lower-class social environment while minimizing many of the influences that have been responsible for the superior intellectual development of the upper-middle-class children. It is therefore incompatible with the requirements for a compensatory educational program for disadvantaged children. (1:19)

In addition to an hour of less structured activities, the children attend three twenty-minute classes each day (language, math, and reading), where in small groups of five they are intensively taught by direct instruction and reinforced for appropriately answering the "test" questions posed by the teacher. Instruction is rapid, lively, and economical. The teachers "teach" as if their students' lives depended on it! The approach is analogous to emergency aid given to an accident victim; in this case, the child's language deficits need intensive treatment rather than experiences which a more conventional nursery school might give. Pressure clearly is applied. The adults foster an air that the children are undertaking a tremendous challenge which they *can* meet. The children respond with a sense of excitement and of mastery. Movies taken of these sessions show this attitude. They are not timid or defeated. To get them involved and to allow them to get rid of tensions, the children are encouraged to yell out their answers; and in time they do, though when they first arrive in school they are almost inarticulate.

A number of searching questions may be asked about this approach. What happens to relationships within their families when the children undergo this intensive learning process which, when successful, results in the alteration of their speech and their very manner of thinking, setting them apart? What happens to their sense of self? Does a dichotomy occur between the learning situation and the rest of life which eventually creates a personality conflict for the individual? Are such gains retained as the children progress through school? Do they become technicians? It is too early to know most of the answers, but this method will be followed with interest even though it is applicable to only a discrete population. Clearly, not everyone needs such emergency treatment.

This form of learning is one that involves practice and rote learning of concepts which at first are not meaningful. During the early period, tangible rewards, such as cookies, as well as punishments are used. Later, to know the answer and to be able to say it aloud acquires great meaning for the children.

Developmental Points of View

An Emphasis on Developing a Cognitive Curriculum.

Sonquist and Kamii have attempted to apply Piaget's concepts in the classroom. Although there are some similarities to the Bereiter and Englemann approach, there are significant differences. Kamii's summary of Piaget's theory suggests the point of departure: "... *We interact with the environment through our cognitive structures which transform the sensory information that we receive from our environment.* The transformation is very deforming [distorting] in infancy, and comes to correspond more and more closely to reality as the cognitive structures become richer and more elaborate. The child goes through many stages of constructing these structures, and the sequence of this development is the same for all children." (8:7) If one accepts these propositions, Kamii suggests that it must then follow that "we must a) let the child go from one stage after another of being "wrong" rather than expecting him to reason logically like an adult and b) allow for a certain slowness in the developmental process." (8:9)

A review of Piaget's propositions with regard to intelligence and adaptation has relevance here. (11) Man begins his life with a set of reflexes, a more flexible version than lower animals' instinctual mechanisms. Even in the first hours these are being altered and supplemented, soon to be overridden by learned behaviors which, within the second year, shift from physical to mental or symbolic bases. The nature of intelligence itself does not shift, but from creature to creature, and in man from one stage of his development to the next, the structures through which intelligence can be expressed alter, allowing for a more and more abstract form of cognitive functioning.

The newborn baby possesses only a few innate capabilities with which he adapts immediately to the world: he breathes, cries, sucks and swallows food, moves, grasps, and is sensitive to light, sound, odor, and pressure, and so on. These capabilities are sufficient for survival until he develops habits, which come first, and then the ability to carry out intentional physical acts and to solve problems. This last stage Piaget defines as the dawning of true intelligence;

unless the organism is aware in a totally physical kind of cause-effect, ends-means, and spatial-temporal relationship, he cannot *purposely* hit a dangling doll with his hand to make it move. The first two years of life are largely focused on the growth of this sensori-motor intelligence. The child then moves on to the development of symbolic processes: *mental images*, which allow him to remember objects, situations, people, and *words*, the essential medium for abstract thought.

At maturity, the human being is fully capable of abstract thought which is logical, consistent, and possibly original and creative. He operates by means of laws governing perceptual reality, so that he no longer necessarily accepts as true the raw data given him by his senses (though his senses ordinarily give him accurate information). An example might be helpful: if a four-year-old and a forty-year-old were to come upon the proverbial leprechaun under a toad-stool hammering away at an inch-long shoe, the child would have no problem. Little green men are no stranger than many other things in his world. He sees it; he believes it to be reality. But the adult would have a more demanding problem. He *knows* there are no little green men. In spite of the fact that he "sees" it, he would have no conviction of its factual reality. So depending on his previous experience, the forty-year-old would construct any one of several hypotheses: he needs new glasses; it is an optical illusion; he is drunk; he is losing his mind; someone is playing a trick on him. What he would not do, unless he had exhausted every other possibility, is simply accept the evidence of his senses unexamined. What he has learned about physical reality and the laws of nature, tells him that, in fact, no matter what he seems to hear or see, little green men just do not sit under toad stools tapping shoes.

Piaget's theory of the growth of human intelligence is a *stage* theory. That is, he believes that at each developmental level people express their intelligence (their ability to assimilate from and accommodate to the environment) in consistently differing ways because at each of these stages there is a significant difference in the inner structures (schemata) which make intelligent behavior possible. Each age is successively able to handle mental problems that the preceding one could not have handled. Each retains all previously developed capabilities, but then uses them in differing proportions. Thus, the adult still uses sensori-motor intelligence (try driving a car without it!) but carries on far more of his conscious life at symbolic, abstract levels.

Kamii explains clearly to the reader who is unfamiliar with Piagetian theory just what its implications are in the teaching of young children at the preschool level. In Piaget's approach, which differs radically in this regard from that of Bereiter and Engelmann, learning is not initially presented to the child as a technique that exists completely outside of his own life to be mastered through building rote associations; instead, the various tasks are fitted to the child's level. He is never asked to do anything which is incomprehensibly beyond him. This crucial distinction means that learning from the start is the child's own. In Piagetian terms, *he* is doing the assimilating of experiences planned to match his capabilities, and *he* is actively accommodating his understanding to take them in, altering himself in the process. Whether such an approach is more effective, or success comes more quickly than with Bereiter and Englemann's method, is still not known. Perhaps each reader's final assessment will basically depend more on his own philosophy or understanding of what makes for sound growth and learning.

A Sketch of the Piaget-Derived Preschool Curriculum Developed by the Ypsilanti Early Education Program (a)

Constance Kamii (b)

When an early childhood educator reads Piaget's theory, he is sooner or later likely to become convinced that in view of these insights we must change the way we teach young children. While this need for change is obvious to most people who study the theory, how to go about applying it to preschool education is not at all obvious.

When we try to apply Piaget's theory to preschool education, our first tendency is to simplify certain Piagetian tasks and try to help children to go from one stage to the next as quickly as possible. This tendency can be seen in my earlier papers written on the Perry Preschool Project (Kamii and Radin, 1967; Sonquist and Kamii, 1967) and the Ypsilanti Early Education Program (Kamii and Radin, 1970; Sonquist, Kamii, and Derman, 1970).

As I continued to study the pedagogical implications of Piaget's theory, it became increasingly clear that our aim should be not to move the child from one stage to the next in concepts studied by Piaget, but, rather, to enable him to develop his total cognitive framework so that he will be able to apply it to any task including classification, seriation, conservation, arithmetic, and reading. If, in contrast, we teach classification, seriation, number, etc., as separate skills, we end up in effect fertilizing only a few soil samples when our real aim is to fertilize the entire field.

One of the most intriguing and fundamental aspects of Piaget's theory is the fact that when the child has attained a certain level of cognitive development, he becomes able to solve a host of problems that

Constance Kamii, "A Sketch of the Piaget-Derived Preschool Curriculum Developed by the Ypsilanti Early Education Program," Ypsilanti Public Schools, Ypsilanti, Michigan. August, 1971. Copyright © 1972 by the Charles A. Jones Publishing Company, Worthington, Ohio 43085.

he has never encountered before. Cross-cultural replications of Piaget's research (Bovet, 1971; Dasen, 1970; Elkind, 1961; Greenfield, 1966; Lovell and Ogilvie, 1960) have shown consistently that children all over the world become able to conserve without having been taught to conserve, and become able to seriate without having been taught to seriate.

A difference consistently observed in cross-cultural replications is in rate of development. Generally, children in a more developed culture develop faster than those living in a less developed culture. Within the same culture, children living in the city and more advantaged groups develop faster than those living in the country and in a less advantaged socioeconomic group. Piaget says that the causes of these differences are not known in a precise manner, but the following five factors are necessary for cognitive development (Piaget, 1970a):

1) Biological factors (particularly maturation)
2) Experiences with physical objects
3) Social factors and interindividual coordination
4) Cultural and educational transmission
5) Equilibration.

Piaget's theory thus puts the emphasis on the child's development outside school and laboratory situations. It may be useful to base a curriculum on this theory precisely because it examines the mechanisms of cognitive development in a context broader than traditional schools and laboratories.

For psychologists and educators who are used to viewing teaching as a series of specific skills to be taught, and broken down into smaller skills when children show difficulties, the idea of a general cognitive framework is hard to accept. However, if we study the research done in Geneva, it becomes equally hard to view cognitive development in any other way except as the development of a total structure. Piaget and his collaborators invent perhaps thirty to fifty new tasks every year, and with any one of these tasks, we almost invariably find a higher level of solution at ages seven to eight than at four to five. Since care is taken to create tasks that children have not been taught to solve before, it is not possible to attribute the correct solution to specific teaching.

The idea of a child's cognitive framework becomes clearer when we try to teach a four-year-old what we mean by "inflation," "the capital of the U. S.," or "the atmosphere of a place." With older children, verbal explanations quickly produce comprehension. With four-year-olds, however, not all the language in the world will lead to any degree of understanding. The ability to understand these ideas requires a well structured, rich cognitive framework that takes many years to develop. The word "inflation," for example, can be understood only if the child has a cognitive framework which integrates notions of number, seriation, time, and a system of exchange in which there is a common unit. The "capital of the U. S." can likewise be understood only if the child has a cognitive framework capable of integrating class inclusion, the organization of space, and the political organization of people. Not all the attempts in the world at teaching specific skills (such as how to say by heart the verbal definition of "capital" and "the United States," how to read "t-h-e c-a-p-i-t-a-l o-f t-h-e U-n-i-t-e-d S-t-a-t-e-s," and how to say the names of other capitals such as France-Paris and England-London) will result in the development of the cognitive framework, or "readiness," that enables the child to learn what a capital is.

The causal relationships explaining precisely what environmental factors enhance the development of the child's cognitive framework are unfortunately not yet known. However, the five factors mentioned earlier, plus other ideas which will be elaborated later in this paper (e.g., the distinction Piaget makes between physical and logico-mathematical knowledge, his constructivism, and insistence on the increasing mobility and structure of thought processes) do serve to build a preschool curriculum that attempts to develop children's general cognitive framework, or "readiness" for a wide range of school subjects (e.g., reading, writing, arithmetic, science, social studies, and music).

Whether or not it is possible for a school program to help the child develop his cognitive framework remains to be tested experimentally. One thing that must be remembered about our approach is that the Piagetian perspective is a long-range view. The teaching of specific skills on a short-term basis, such as how to read "c-a-t" and how to do $7 + 2$, is relatively easy. How to develop the cognitive framework of "disadvantaged" children to enable them to go beyond these mechanistic skills is a different problem.

I have gone to some length to insist on the development of the child's cognitive framework as a whole because the following objectives of the curriculum give the impression of being separate areas to work on separately. Although the objectives are listed in outline form, the teacher needs to remember at all times that intelligence functions as an integrated whole and develops as an integrated whole. This point will be elaborated further in the second part of the paper on teaching methods.

I. Objectives

A. Socioemotional objectives

According to Piaget (1954), there are no cognitive mechanisms that are without affective elements, and there is no affective state that has no cognitive element. The relationship between cognition and affectivity for him is that the latter provides the energy that makes intelligence function (like gasoline which makes a car engine run).

The more intelligence is used, the more it develops. Therefore, according to Piaget, affectivity can accelerate, retard, or block cognitive development as can be seen in the student who gets excited or discouraged in class. The following socioemotional objectives are thus important not only in themselves but also as essential elements for the child's cognitive development.

    1. In relation to peers
        a. Ability to respect the feelings and rights of other children (decentering and moral development).
        b. Ability to listen to others and exchange opinions (decentering, which leads to the coordination of different points of view).

2. In relation to adults
   a. Ability to listen to adults, cooperate with them, and use them as a source of friendship, guidance, and information.
   b. Ability to control one's own behavior rather than being controlled by adults. By learning to make plans and decisions, carrying them out, and evaluating their own activities, children learn to control their own behavior.
   c. Ability to cope with situations as they come up. By learning to assess situations and making appropriate decisions on their own, children develop independence rather than the passivity of waiting to be told what to do. For example, if someone spills juice, the appropriate action is to bring a wet sponge.
3. In relation to learning
   a. Being active. Intelligence develops by being used. As long as children have the initiative to keep on doing *something*, each activity is likely to lead to a new challenge. Therefore, we want children to be busily doing things with initiative, enthusiasm, and excitement. (The important thing in being active is that the child be mentally active. Physical activities may, or may not, accompany these activities.)
   b. Being curious. Curiosity is more focused than the above objective. Examples are 1) exploring things to figure out how they are made and how they work, 2) experimenting with cause-effect and means-end relationships, and 3) asking questions.
   c. Being confident. We want children to have the self-confidence that they *can* figure things out on their own (rather than depending on the teacher to provide the answer). Even when their answer is "wrong" from the standpoint of adult logic, we want children to speak their mind with confidence and conviction, rather than scrutinizing the teacher's face for feedback as to whether or not one is saying "the" right thing.
   d. Having the habit of divergent thinking. We want children not to look for the one "correct" answer the adult wants, but to come up with many different ways of doing the same thing. Even in simple activities like make believe, which is described later, and physical activities like going down the slide, we want children to do the same thing in many different ways (e.g., coming down with one hand on the head, on the stomach, or lying down).

If children are excited, curious, resourceful, confident about their ability to figure things out and eager to exchange opinions with other children and adults, they are bound to go on learning, particularly when they are out of the classroom and throughout the rest of their lives. Therefore, socioemotional development may well give more educational mileage in the long run than the learning of specific skills and behaviors or even intellectual operations. Within the context of the above socioemotional objectives, we conceptualize the following cognitive objectives.

B. Cognitive objectives

Generally speaking, we stay within the preoperational period and would like to see behaviors which Piaget describes as characterizing stage II. (See Kamii, 1971, for further details.) Our goals, however, are not to produce stage-II *behavior* as such but to develop the cognitive *processes* which might manifest themselves in stage-II behavior and eventually lead to concrete and formal operations.

Although cognitive processes develop as part of a total framework, it is useful to conceptualize our educational objectives in terms of the different areas Piaget delineated as having different modes of structuring. He delineated two major areas of knowledge, i.e., physical knowledge and logico-mathematical knowledge. Sinclair adds a third area, social knowledge. The fourth area, spatio-temporal notions, lies halfway between physical and logico-mathematical knowledge (because time and space are observable like physical knowledge, but are also like logico-mathematical knowledge in that they have to be constructed by the child and introduced into external reality). Finally, the child needs to become able to represent all four types of knowledge both to think about things that are absent and to exchange ideas with other people. These five objectives are elaborated below.

1. Physical knowledge

   Physical knowledge in this context refers to observable properties of objects and physical phenomena such as what happens when we let go of a marble on an incline. The way the child finds out about these properties and phenomena is by acting on objects and observing and systematizing the objects' reactions. Dropping, folding, stretching, squeezing, and tapping are examples of actions the child can attempt on almost any object in his environment to find out how it reacts. Physical knowledge is thus structured from feedback from objects. We see the following two objectives in this area.

   a. Developing the child's repertoire of actions he can perform on objects to find out how they react. For example, the child finds out about the properties of a large ballbearing by picking it up, rolling it, bringing it close to his face and looking at the reflection of his face, etc. If this repertoire is well developed, the child will know the properties of the objects around him and how to go about finding out the physical nature of new, unfamiliar objects.

   b. Developing an attitude of curiosity and anticipation of what will happen, and the habit of figuring out means to achieve desired ends. For example, four-year-old children make an exciting game out of predicting that a ballbearing will sink in water, as they enjoy the suspense before empirically verifying this prediction. They also enjoy being asked how they could make the ballbearing stay on top of the water.

   Two remarks are in order. First, preschool children can observe simple mechanical changes that result from their own direct actions (e.g., breaking objects, bouncing them, and rolling them). However, a complicated change such as the transformation of water into steam is too difficult. Second, it is wise with preschool children to stay within the realm of predictions and not insist on explanations. The better question for the teacher to ask is "What will happen if . . . ?" and not "Why did . . . happen?" For example, four-year-olds can learn to predict what will happen if they drop a ping-pong ball on water, but unless they ask, an explanation of why it will float is pointless.

2. Logico-mathematical knowledge

While physical knowledge is structured from feedback from objects, logico-mathematical knowledge is structured from the child's own coordinated actions and the results of these actions. By "coordinated actions" Piaget means coordination in a logical sense and not in a motoric sense. By "the results of these actions" he means results in a logical sense and not in a physical sense (i.e., feedback from objects). For example, when the child brings two, three, or four objects together, the result is a group of objects. When he makes two groups of objects by one-to-one correspondence between the action of the two hands, the result is two groups that are numerically equivalent.

In physical knowledge, the specific properties of each object are all-important, since the child finds out about and systematizes the reactions of each object. In logico-mathematical knowledge, on the other hand, what is important is not the properties of each object but the *relationship* between and among objects. The properties of objects exist *in* objects, but the relationship among them does not. They are constructed by the child and introduced by *him*, and not by external reality.

Piaget delineates three areas of logico-mathematical knowledge: classification, seriation, and number. In classification, the relationships the child introduces are those of similarities and differences (leading to the logic of classes). In seriation, the relationship is that of relative differences. In number, the child makes groups of objects and compares the number of objects in two or more groups. The objectives we conceptualize for the preschool curriculum are listed below.

a. In classification

(1) Developing the child's ability to find similarities and differences among objects, and to *group* them according to their similarity and *separate* them according to their differences.

(2) Developing the child's mobility of thought, so that he will become able to see many different relationships among the same group of objects. For example, we would like the child to regroup the following objects in different ways as shown below.

> Grouping 1: 3 red pens
> 3 blue pens
> 3 red caps (for the pens)
> 3 blue caps
> 3 yellow pencils
>
> Grouping 2: All the pens
> All the caps
> All the pencils

        Grouping 3: All the pens and caps
                     All the pencils
        Grouping 4: Everything that is blue
                     Everything that is red
                     Everything that is yellow

b. In seriation

Developing the child's ability to compare differences among objects along some dimension and to order them according to their relative differences. (In classification, the child only separates objects that are different. In seriation, he orders them according to their relative differences.) For example, we would like children to group a dog, a horse, a mouse, and a deer together because of their similarity (preclassification), and to arrange them according to their relative sizes (preseriation).

c. In number

(1) Developing the child's logical structure that is necessary to make judgements of equivalence, "more," and "less."

(2) Developing the child's mobility of thought so that conservation will become possible as a byproduct. (Conservation should come as a result of the child's mobility of thought and not as a result of direct teaching.)

3. The structuring of space and time

As stated earlier, space and time lie halfway between physical and logico-mathematical knowledge. Space and time are like physical knowledge in that they are observable in external reality. However, they are like logico-mathematical knowledge in that the space and time that are involved in spatio-temporal *reasoning* have to be constructed and structured by the child himself. (See Piaget, 1970b, and Piaget and Inhelder, 1967, for an elaboration of this statement). The objectives of the preschool curriculum are listed below.

a. Space

(1) Developing topological structures toward Euclidean structures on the representational level. For example, most of the disadvantaged children in the Ypsilanti Early Education Program copied a square like the following more or less round, closed configuration at the beginning of the year: ⬭ We try to develop this topological structure into a Euclidean one through a variety of indirect approaches. (See Piaget and Inhelder, 1967, ch. 2, for an explanation of topological and Euclidean space.)

(2) Increasing the child's mobility of thought on the representational level (e.g., linear ordering, arranging and rearranging blocks to copy a model, and predicting an object's trajectory)

b. Time

Enabling the child to structure time into sequences (intervals come later).

4. Social knowledge
   Social knowledge refers to social conventions which are structured from feedback from people. (c) Examples are that tables are not to stand on, that water is not to be spilled all over the floor even in waterplay at school, and that we engage in certain rituals on birthdays and traditional holidays.
5. Representation
   a. On the level of symbols (d)
      Developing children's ability to represent things and ideas in imitation and sociodramatic play, onomatopoeia (e.g., making the sound of a horn while pretending to drive a car), make believe (making an object stand for something else, such as making a block stand for a car), and making other symbolic representations with a pencil, paint, clay, blocks, pipecleaners, sticks, etc.
   b. On the level of signs
      Developing the child's ability to represent things and communicate ideas through arbitrary signs (e.g., traffic signs) and language. We try to develop language as a tool for precise communication and exchange of opinions. While we believe that language is an important tool and stimulator of cognitive development, we do not believe that language is the source or cause of logico-mathematical operations.

II. Teaching methods

The preceding objectives give to the teacher a framework for conceptualizing and diagnosing different aspects of cognitive development as part of an organized whole. Our general procedure is for the teacher to set up a situation, sometimes proposing an activity, and see how the children react. With the above objectives in mind, she tries to use almost any situation that seems particularly suited to activate certain aspects of intelligence. Three activities will be described below as examples that focus on particular aspects of cognitive development (i.e., predicting what will sink and what will float, the pendulum, and make believe). Two activities will then be discussed as examples of traditional nursery school situations that can be used within a Piagetian framework (i.e., block building and sociodramatic play). Finally, juice time will be discussed to show that every situation in daily living can be used for educational purposes. Some principles of teaching will be given at the end of the paper.

A. Situations

1. Predicting what will sink and what will float
   This activity focuses on *classification* and *physical knowledge*. For each group of two or three children, the teacher prepares a pail of water and an array of objects (e.g., a sponge, blocks of various sizes, a fork, a stone, a rubber band, paper clips of various sizes, an old sock, a crayon, a cup, and a small glass bottle). The game

is to divide the objects into the two groups of "things that will float" and "things that will sink." After making this dichotomy, the children verify their predictions by putting the objects in the water, discussing all along what they think will happen and what they found out.

2. The pendulum

The teacher makes a large pendulum by putting a weight at the end of a long string suspended from the ceiling and almost touching the floor. After allowing a sufficient amount of time for the children to play freely to find out how the pendulum works, she introduces a game of knocking down a rubber doll which is placed standing on the floor. The rule of the game is to hold the weight at a particular spot and let go of it, rather than giving it a push. The children take turns to place the doll at different spots.

This is primarily a *physical knowledge* activity because the doll responds to the child's action by falling to the ground or not falling. However, the activity cannot take place without *spatial reasoning* and the comparison of distances and angles *(preseriation)*. When the child lets go of the weight, the weight follows a predictable trajectory in space. As shown below, if he holds the weight at a wide angle from its original position at rest, it will travel farther.

Serial correspondence of angles must also be made on a horizontal plane. If the weight travels as shown below, the child has to cor-

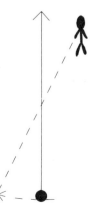

rect his prediction. To the extent that he can systematize all the ways in which he missed the target, the child is more successful on subsequent trials.

3. Make believe

The teacher gives a cylindrical block to each one of the five or six children sitting around the table. She asks them to think of all the things they can make the block be, and asks them to raise their hand when they have an idea they want to show to the group. The ideas that came out in one of our sessions were "a whistle," "corn on the cob," "pop," "a hotdog," "a comb," "a cigar," "lipstick," "a rolling pin," and "a pirate" (meaning "a telescope").

This activity can be varied by using other blocks of different shapes and sizes, paper cutouts, and clay.

The activity focuses on *representation,* and the child has to decenter from one point of view to another as he tries to see something different in the same object. The most noteworthy characteristic of this activity is *divergent thinking.* Within the limits imposed by the task, the children have to come up with many different ideas.

When a child comes up with an idea that has already come up, *time* and *classification* both come into play. *New information* can come in when a child has ideas such as "pirates (meaning "a telescope")." A great deal of social interaction takes place as children imitate each other's actions and evaluate whether or not they can see what others claim to be symbolizing.

4. Block building

The first level of play in block building seems to involve *physical knowledge* and *spatial reasoning.* Typically, the child tries to make a taller and taller tower until it topples. He then repeats the same action over and over, sooner or later with variations.

Block building develops into *representation.* Rather than simply experimenting with the spatial arrangement of blocks, the child begins to represent objects and ideas, such as a road, a gas station, and a house. These representations of individual objects can be elaborated into the spatial organization of several objects (the beginning of map making) or the organization of a sequence of activities (going to buy gas, having an accident at the intersection, and ending up going to the hospital).

As they use many short blocks or a few long ones to build a road (or the wall of a house), children compare different sizes (the beginning of *seriation*). At clean-up time, they put away the long blocks on one shelf, the cylindrical ones, curved ones, and hollow ones on other shelves, each with subgroups (the beginning of *classification*).

The pride and excitement children show in their creation are well known. Divergent thinking is enhanced as they represent many different things with the same blocks. For many children, block building is a comfortable situation in which social relationships develop both with peers and with adults.

5. Sociodramatic play

We see sociodramatic play mainly as a reading-readiness activity that strengthens the *symbolic process*. The mechanistic skills of reading (e.g., perceptual discrimination) enable the child to know what sounds the letters stand for. What enables him to derive meaning from written and spoken language is the symbolic process.

In other symbolic activities, the child has to express his ideas indirectly with paint, clay, and blocks. In sociodramatic play, on the other hand, he externalizes his ideas directly with his body. (The child is thus both the symbol and the symbolizer.) Paint and blocks do not permit the representation of a sequence of events (e.g., "going shopping" and "having a birthday party"), but sociodramatic play allows symbolization to go beyond static representation. It also has the advantage of involving the use of language.

In a simple situation like pretending to have coffee with friends, children represent their knowledge of reality in all areas of the cognitive framework. For example, they represent their *physical knowledge* by heating the coffee, pouring it, spilling it, stirring it, and burning oneself with it. They represent the idea of pouring more coffee than cream, or giving a lot of cream and sugar to some people, and less or none to other people (*preseriation*). They construct elementary *number concepts* as they get just enough cups, saucers, napkins, and spoons for everybody. They represent the *temporal sequence* of making coffee, getting the cups and saucers out, pouring coffee, drinking it, and then cleaning up. They learn to serve the guests first (*social knowledge*). Sometimes, they invite people by phoning them beforehand. When they pretend to call a friend, some children dial first and then pick up the receiver! Some accept the invitation before being invited!

Children constantly decenter in sociodramatic play to play the part of somebody else in interaction with other roles. As they decenter and externalize their knowledge, they relive, digest, and integrate their previous observations.

6. Juice time

Juice time is first of all for drinking juice and for having conversations. When a child says, "I had a tummy ache last night. I ate too much," for example, the teacher can expand the remark into a discussion of stomach aches, illness, health, etc. She can also use the juice time in the following ways to activate certain aspects of the cognitive framework:

a. The construction of elementary number concepts

   (1) The teacher can ask a child to take out just enough cups, placemats, or cookies for everybody who is at a particular table (or in school today).
   (2) She can give three counting blocks to each child to "buy" what he wants. Since each item costs a block, each child can buy two cookies and one cup of juice, or one cookie and two cups of juice, or any other combination of three items.

b. The comparison of quantities (leading to seriation)
  (1) A helper can go around asking each child if he wants the same amount of juice as another child, or more or less juice.
  (2) Another helper can ask each child how much peanut butter he wants on his cracker (a lot, a little bit, or none at all).
c. Classification
  (1) When everybody has finished, the teacher can ask one helper to collect "all the cups and empty cans" and another helper to collect "everything that we don't throw out."
  (2) The teacher can ask, "What do you see on the table that rolls (can be eaten, broken, poured, folded, torn, etc.)?"
d. Physical knowledge
  (1) The teacher can ask whether or not the juice can on the table is empty, and how we can find out (and how else we can find out).
  (2) She can ask where the juice will go "if I spill this much juice right here on the table."
e. The structuring of space
  (1) When juice is spilled by accident, after cleaning up the mess, the teacher can ask where the juice ran, and where it is likely to run if we spilled some again.
  (2) The teacher can ask the children to break their cookie and see whether or not the pieces can be reassembled into the original shape.
f. The structuring of time
  Juice time lends itself to reviewing what the children did earlier in the day and exchange opinions about what happened (e.g., "Would you like to tell us what you built with the blocks today?"). It is also a good time to plan the activities for the rest of the day (e.g., "What do we do next?" "What would you like to do then?" "What do we have to get ready to make play-dough?").

B. Principles of teaching

As stated earlier, in our general approach, the teacher sets up a situation, sometimes proposing a specific activity, and watches how children react before deciding what to pick up on to extend their thinking. This diagnostic interpretation of children's reaction is one of the most crucial points in the teaching process, where Piaget's exploratory method must be applied skillfully. (e) The teacher's ability to figure out what goes on in a child's head at each moment makes the difference between elaborating *his* way of thinking and disrupting it. Piaget's theoretical framework enables her to make this diagnostic interpretation of how the child is thinking.

In the classification of "things that will sink" and "things that will float," for example, the teacher needs to give to the children enough time to explore each object before suggesting that they make a dichotomy. Children need to examine each object by assimilating it to their previous knowledge (i.e., schemes) and accommodating to its particular aspects before they can think in terms of whether it will sink or float. When the object contradicts his anticipation, the child often does many things to make it conform to his anticipation (e.g., holding a block down at the bottom of the pail for a while, and repeating this action several times when the object returns to the surface). The teacher in this situation can pick up on the child's line of reasoning by saying, "Can you think of another way to make it stay down?" She can also turn to other children and ask if *they* can think of a way to make the block stay down.

In block building, if the child has been experimenting with the stability of a tower by rebuilding it each time it topples, the teacher might suggest that he build another tower next to it and lead him to compare the two towers in various ways. She might also suggest trying to build a small tower that will topple, or she might try to involve other children in the activity. When the child is concentrating on physical and spatial reasoning, one thing she might do well to avoid is the sudden imposition of a totally different line of reasoning. For example, suddenly shifting into representation by saying "Let's pretend it's the church tower across the street" is probably the wrong thing to do.

In sociodramatic play, the teacher needs to know the events in the child's real life before trying to elaborate his play. For example, she can try to elaborate the play by saying "Let's plan a birthday party" or "Can you call a taxi for me?" only if she knows these activities to be familiar to the child. Since the child cannot represent knowledge that he does not have, any imposition of foreign ideas is likely to interfere with his thinking.

The role of the teacher thus grows out of Piaget's interactionism. The teacher does not shape a response, nor transmit or program the input of knowledge (the empiricist approach). She does not go to the other extreme either of passively watching children play while waiting for "readiness" to unfold (a maturationist approach). (f) She structures the environment for children to activate and apply their schemes (i.e., the cognitive structures through which external stimuli are understood). She then intervenes unobtrusively by applying Piaget's exploratory method so that the children will test out their ideas against objects and other people, and build new schemes by differentiation and integration of previously constructed schemes. A curriculum based on this interactionism can, therefore, never be presented in a cookbook fashion. It goes without saying that the six situations described above can easily turn into teaching that is completely contrary to Piaget's theory.

As stated in the introductory part of this paper, the aim of a Piagetian preschool is to develop the child's total cognitive framework, so that operations will become eventually possible in many different areas, and the child's "readiness" for a variety of school subjects will increase. The precise mechanisms of development of this cognitive framework are unfortunately not known, particularly at the four-year-old level, but the hypothesis which seems closest to the truth states that the cognitive framework is a by-product of the child's use of his intelligence. In other words, the more he uses his preoperational intelligence in *his* own way, the more his cognitive framework is likely to develop. This philosophy of encouraging preoperational children to think in their own way is in sharp contrast with our traditional view of "teaching" which puts the accent on the correct answer.

One of the most effective ways we found of encouraging preoperational children to think in their own way is through the use of activities that emphasize physical knowledge. Objects always react in the same way no matter what the child wants them to do. The four-year-old's natural curiosity makes him repeat the same action over and over with intrinsic motivation as was seen in the situation where he tried to make a block stay at the bottom of the pail. Whether a block sinks or floats, and whether or not the child succeeds in knocking down a doll with the pendulum are in themselves unimportant. What is important is the fact that these activities stimulate the child's curiosity to anticipate the result of his actions and to systematize the outcome observed.

Compared to negative feedback from people (i.e., being told, "Your answer is not quite right"), negative feedback from objects is easy for young children to accept. When a block does not react in the way he anticipated, the child repeats his action and studies the object's reaction under *his* control. Activities involving physical knowledge thus stimulate the child's initiative and confidence to figure things out by himself. (Confidence and curiosity are among the qualities "disadvantaged" children seem to lack conspicuously.)

Negative feedback from people, especially in logico-mathematical knowledge, is something quite different. For example, the child who thinks that there are more cups than saucers in the conservation of number task is using *his* logic and telling the truth as he honestly sees it. When we tell him he is wrong, or try to mask his opinion by teaching an overlay of correct answers, we in effect make him unsure of his own judgment. He will then stop thinking in his own honest way and learn to read the teacher's face for signs of social approval. If we try to teach logical thinking through social conformity, we may succeed in producing the correct answer for a while, but we also prevent the child from developing *his* way of reasoning and his initiative to think. Inadvertently, we may hold the child back from building the cognitive framework that will make later development possible.

. When we remember how logico-mathematical knowledge is structured and recall that children become able to conserve, seriate, and classify without ever being taught to do so, we come to the conclusion that the best strategy to develop the logico-mathematical framework of four-year-old children is an indirect one. The use of physical knowledge activities was already discussed above as having a motivating and structuring effect. Another method of "teaching" in the logico-mathematical realm is the use of "interindividual coordination," the third of the five factors listed at the beginning of this paper as being essential to development according to Piaget.

Interindividual coordination refers to the bilateral exchange and coordination of opinions among equals. By exchanging opinions with his peers, the child begins to decenter from his egocentric point of view and to coordinate his opinion with that of other children. This exchange among equals is very different from the unilateral imposition of viewpoints involved in cultural and educational transmission (the fourth factor). To encourage the exchange of opinions among peers, the teacher says, "What do *you* think?" to a child and then goes around the group asking everybody else what *he* thinks. As the children disagree, argue, and agree with each other, they can think in their own preoperational way without having to yield to adult pressure and ready-made answers.

For the construction of elementary number concepts, for example, the teacher can make small groups of three, four, or five children and ask one of them to bring "just enough" scissors, paper, pencils, cups, or cookies when things have to be distributed to the group. When the child returns to the group supposedly with "just enough cups for everybody," the teacher encourages one or two other children to check the number of cups and children. If the children later wash the cups to grow plants in them, the teacher can ask, "Do you think there will be a cup for everybody (including Mark and Johnny who are absent)?" Needless to say, the important thing here is that children engage in the process of thinking, agreeing, and disagreeing. The correctness of the answer itself is secondary in importance.

The above example illustrates another principle of teaching, i.e., the idea that it is best for children to have a personal reason for reflection, rather than the mere fact that when the teacher asks a question, *she* wants an answer. The distribution of cups to a real group in a real-life situation gives to the child a meaningful reason for thinking about number. Artificial exercises tend not to motivate the child to the same extent.

Time, too, can become structured through the use of real-life situations. At free activities time, (g) we ask children to decide what they want to do, and they indicate their choice by picking out one of the pictures the teacher selected for the day as a possible activity. For example, a child can select the picture of a paint brush when he decides to paint, or the picture of a book when he decides to look at books. When children have to make a decision and live with it for a while rather than simply obeying orders all day, they have to anticipate the future in terms of past experiences. Mobility of thought (thinking about the future and the past at the same time) is provoked, and the child structures time as part of everyday living.

At the end of free activities time, the teacher sits down with the group to ask each child to report what he did and to encourage the group to evaluate each other's activity. If a child says to another child at this point, "You left your baby all by itself, and you went out to play!" evaluation serves not only to recapitulate a sequence of past events but also to plan how to do things better in the future.

Equilibration, the last of the five factors, is the vaguest and hardest one to understand. According to Piaget, intelligence develops by a process of differentiation and integration of schemes through equilibration.

The teacher cannot influence equilibration directly in the same way that she can control the second, third, and fourth factors (experiences with physical objects, social factors of interindividual coordination, and cultural and educational transmission). Therefore, the only important thing for her to keep in mind is that equilibration takes place optimally when she follows the principles of teaching already discussed above.

Many important aspects of the curriculum have been left out of this paper, such as how we approach language development, how we try to achieve our socioemotional objectives, and how we adapt some Piagetian tasks from time to time in the classroom. We believe these tasks are very useful, provided they do not become the central part of a Piagetian curriculum, and the focus is on the process of reasoning rather than on the answer the child gives. In the limited space available in this article, I overemphasized the use of rather common activities to insist that the way to develop the preoperational child's general cognitive framework is not by having him go through all the stages on Piagetian tasks.

How to help "disadvantaged" children develop this cognitive framework is not obvious, and I do not claim to know how to accomplish this task. Nevertheless, I tried above to sketch some recent ideas based on the implications of Piaget's theory as I understand it today. We are, after all, still far from being able to isolate the environmental variables that make a difference to the long-term cognitive development of preschool children.

Notes

a. The Ypsilanti Early Education Program was in operation in 1967–70 with funds under Title III, ESEA, No. 67-042490. One of the objectives of this program was to develop a preschool curriculum based on Piaget's theory for socioeconomically disadvantaged four-year-old children. I am grateful to M. Denis-Prinzhorn of the University of Geneva for critically reading this paper and contributing many ideas.

b. On leave in 1970–71 at the University of Geneva and the International Center of Genetic Epistemology on a fellowship from the National Institute of Mental Health (1 FO3 MH32554-01).

c. The distinction among physical, logico-mathematical, and social knowledge is based on different modes of structuring knowledge, rather than different sources of knowledge. Social knowledge is not to be confused with moral development.

d. Symbols, in Piaget's terminology, are individual in nature and bear a resemblance to the object being represented. Signs, on the other hand, do not resemble the object and make up a system which serves social communication (e.g., language, the Morse code, and algebraic signs).

e. In a standardized test situation, the examiner asks one question after another by following precisely and literally the directions given in a manual. In contrast, in a Piagetian interview, the examiner has a theory behind what he wants to find out, and formulates one question after another depending on what the child said before. In the conservation of liquid task, for example, if the child says that the tall, thin container has more water than the original wide container because the level of water is higher in the former, the examiner can pose a variety of questions, e.g., "But this one is narrow. Doesn't that make a difference?" or "Do you remember how we poured the Kool-Aid out of the bottle?" This flexible way of interviewing children is called the "exploratory method." (Piaget used to call it the "clinical method.")

f. See Kohlberg (1968) for a clarification of the empiricist, maturationist, and interactionist views of "learning."

g. We feel that free activities time is the major part of a Piagetian preschool curriculum, but that group activities are also desirable, such as rhythmics, singing, outdoor play, and games.

References

Bovet, M. Etude interculturelle des processus de raisonnement — notions de quantités physiques et relations spatio-temporelles chez des enfants et des adultes non-scolarisés. Unpublished doctoral dissertation, University of Geneva, 1971.

Dasen, P. Cognitive development in aborigines of central Australia. Unpublished doctoral dissertation, Australian National University, Canberra, 1970.

Elkind, D. Children's discovery of the conservation of mass, weight, and volume: Piaget replication study II. *Journal of Genetic Psychology*, 1961, 98, 219–227.

Greenfield, P. On culture and conservation. In J. Bruner et al. *Studies in cognitive growth*. New York: John Wiley & Sons, 1966.

Inhelder, B., & Piaget, J. *The early growth of logic in the child*. New York: Harper & Row, 1964.

Kamii, C. Evaluation of learning in preschool education: Socio-emotional, perceptual-motor, and cognitive development. In B. S. Bloom, J. T. Hastings, & G. Madaus (Eds.), *Handbook on formative and summative evaluation of student learning*. New York: McGraw-Hill, 1971.

Kamii, C., & Radin, N. A framework for a preschool curriculum based on some Piagetian concepts. *Journal of Creative Behavior*, 1967, 1, 314–324.

Kamii, C., & Radin, N. A framework for a preschool curriculum based on some Piagetian concepts. In I. J. Athey & D. O. Rubadeau (Eds.), *Educational implications of Piaget's theory*. Waltham, Mass.: Ginn-Blaisdell, 1970.

Kohlberg, L. Early education: a cognitive-developmental view. *Child Development*, 1968, 39, 1013–1062.

Lovell, K., & Ogilvie, E. A study of the concept of conservation of substance in the junior school child. *British Journal of Educational Psychology*, 1960, 30, 109–118.

Piaget, J. Les relations entre l'intelligence et l'affectivité dans le développement de l'enfant. *Bulletin de Psychologie*, 1954, 7, 143–150.

Piaget, J. *Play, dreams, and imitation in childhood*. New York: Norton, 1962.

Piaget, J. *The child's conception of number*. New York: Norton, 1965.

Piaget, J. *Psychologie et Epistémologie*. Paris: Denoël, 1970a.

Piaget, J. *The child's conception of time*. London: Routledge & Kegan Paul, 1970b.

Piaget, J., & Inhelder, B. *The child's conception of space*. New York: Norton, 1967.

Sonquist, H., & Kamii, C. Applying some Piagetian concepts in the classroom for the disadvantaged. *Young Children*. 1967, 22, 231–245.

Sonquist, H., & Kamii, C., & Derman, L. A Piaget-derived preschool curriculum. In I. J. Athey & D. O. Rubadeau (Eds.), *Educational implications of Piaget's theory*. Waltham, Mass.: Ginn-Blaisdell, 1970.   (9)

An Emphasis on
Fostering Affective Growth.

The specification of the sequence of intellectual development is more recent and is gradually being assimilated by the field of early childhood education. In articulating affective growth during different stages of the life cycle, the work of Erik Erikson is well known. (4) His formulations of the socioemotional development of young children have been widely applied.

The struggles around developing a sense of trust, autonomy, and initiative are experienced daily by children in a nursery school setting. But so are the remnants of these issues also alive in the teacher. To fully appreciate the children's plight, she must tune into herself. It is this *process* of awareness, however, that is elusive to describe and difficult to inculcate.

Adults deal with problems of trust when they yearn to be cared for or when they experience the frustration of relying totally on another person for their creature needs. Many people who have been hospitalized, have felt the uncertainty of not knowing when they would be taken care of or by whom. The teacher is responding to issues of trust when she strives to build a reliable, predictable environment in the classroom. Time, space, routines, and her own nurturing relationship vis a viz children are her medium for this accomplishment.

On a grim day when all looks bleak and we feel helpless, it would not be uncommon for someone to sieze the least likely person and begin to boss him around. Indeed the toddler is not the only person who likes to boss others! The teacher takes into account a child's sense of autonomy when she offers choices within certain limits and depersonalizes or presents the rules as outside her control. "What *can* we do? It's eleven o'clock and time to pick up!" "Shall I help you with the soap or can you do it for yourself?" Her appreciation of his need for controls is balanced by equal attention to his need to exercise his will. A game of traffic cop is a way of practicing putting on brakes. However it may not help at all when the brakes give out and a child needs to be held.

We all have day dreams. In the din of city life we imagine ourselves in romantic far off places, perhaps deep in the quiet of the countryside by a waterfall. At other times we have successfully led a school board to take new and unprecedented action. Whatever we do to actually take the necessary first steps, the initiatives, even our fantasies are trial runs at making come true what we imagine our potential could be. Our later efforts to make them come true are put to test. The boy who wishes to build a life-sized airplane in the nursery school can experience great disappointment when it does not fly. He will have to wait until he possesses the necessary skills to realize his potential; i.e., he will probably have to have more schooling. These initiatives in the nursery school appear in other ways; a sensitive teacher resonates with a child's emerging sense of discovery, curiosity, and imagination. She encourages him to explore new roles, new materials, new problems — aware of the anxieties and sadness that attend some of his initiatives. While a young child is "learning how to learn," he is becoming acquainted with the role of the "student." He is painfully learning that wishing will not make it so.

In light of these issues Lois Murphy's concept of coping ability and vulnerability helps to make us alert and compassionate to the individual needs of children. (10) Her longitudinal study of preschoolers identifies those factors in a child's temperament which she feels make him vulnerable: imbalance among motor, cognitive, and affective drives; improper controls in relation to his own impulsivity; low energy reserves or easy fatigability; low sensory threshold; unstable bodily functions, or autonomic reactivity. The successful "copers" were best characterized as showing flexibility and resilience. She has written eloquently about the consuming interest a child will take as he struggles for mastery over meaningful life issues.

To many early childhood educators, attention to socioemotional development takes top priority. Barbara Biber has tried to achieve a balance. Cognitive-affective learning is, for her, interactive and conducive to building a healthy personality. Her formulations are:

Learning Experience in
School and Personality:
Assumptions and Application
Barbara Biber

The recognition of the role of the school in the last few decades has passed through several phases. There was the "educated" man (in the European tradition) who knew a great deal, was well read, spoke many

Barbara Biber, "Learning Experience in School and Personality: Assumptions and Application," excerpt from Chapter XV, "Integration of Mental Health Principles in the School Setting," of *Prevention of Mental Disorders in Children,* edited by Gerald Caplan. Copyright © 1961 by Basic Books, Inc., Publishers, New York.

The material in this section has been condensed and excerpted from previous presentations (a, b)

languages, a member of the informed *élite*. Not only scholars but ordinary people recognized the gap that often existed between the amassing of information and wisdom in the transactions of living. At a later phase, when information per se was being disparaged, great emphasis was put upon knowing *how to find out* what one needed to know. This shift had value insofar as it led to increased independence of thinking and more security in approaching problems; its weakness lay in the tendency to carry it to an extreme degree: failure to recognize that little progress in knowing *how to find out* can be made, without substantive strength in the *what* aspects of the search. A third phase is the one that concerns us now: how to make knowledge and the experience of learning available to growth processes; how not merely to keep children interested in their lessons but to make the process of learning functional at deeper levels of the total process of integration; in other words, how to make the experience of learning 1) yield ego strength and 2) contribute to positive feelings and attitudes toward self and others.

This involves rethinking and reordering the content, procedures, and settings of education so as to make maximal use on a planned basis of psychological interdependencies, as we have come to understand them. Significant theoretical approaches have been made in this direction, for example, Kubie's (c) position concerning the importance of taking greater account of the interaction of preconscious and conscious factors in educational planning and practice. In this presentation, the interdependency between cognitive and affective modes of responding to and assimilating experience is the common thread underlying both assumptions and practices.

Operationally, this means that education must take responsibility for providing and developing integrating mechanisms and relationships. Integration can be expected to take place only to the extent that dynamic processes of identification, adaptation, objectification, self-awareness, and self-discovery are facilitated through the general quality of the educational milieu, through the specific content of mastery and expressive experience and interaction with teachers, who can mediate balanced roles of stimulation, support, and control.

First Assumption. It is assumed that schooling will contribute to ego strength to the extent that learning can be made viable, that learning power can be enhanced by basing curriculum content and method on knowledge of capacity, interests, drives, and motivations of children at successive stages of development.

Psychodynamic theory in general, Erikson's work (d) in particular, has transformed a general idea about changing drives, associated with shifting life challenges and crises, into a tool for educational thinking and planning. For example, any curriculum for the middle years of childhood can and should be testable against the basic trends of that period: the child's drive toward independence by loosening himself from the bonds of parental attachment, authority, and omniscience, the drive toward becoming competent in the world of ideas and functions that is not family-encompassed, the need to objectify, structure, have rules to go by as the media for feeling control and mastery, to replace phantasy with reality resolutions of cognitive problems, to be admitted to the world of "real" work.

It needs also to be tested against the conflicts implicit during this span of growth; the ambivalence of independence-dependence needs and wishes, the oedipal shift from conflict-with to identification-with the parent of the same sex, the sacrifice as against the gratification involved in yielding subjective meaning and impulse to the requirements of socialized functioning and communication. It must also be remembered that scope of mastery and achievement alone do not constitute ego strength; for competence to be felt as adequacy it is essential that the course of becoming competent is such that it preserves for the learning child a sense of autonomy and active participation, that it takes account of the learning "idioms" characteristic of individuals, as well as of successive stages of development.

The elements of an educational technology intended to contribute to ego strength can only briefly be indicated and illustrated here:

Increasing the Range and Depth of Children's Sensitivity to the World Around Them. Richness of sense experience is the beginning point: color on the walls, on the easel, in the pictures in the readers, the light of afternoon in the wintertime; the bong of the drums and the whisper of the triangles; the way the wind blows through one's hair at the top of the jungle gym and the special dark quiet inside the packing case, the stance of a robin and the swush of a ferry boat. These are materials for accent by the teacher; they are also resonators for the children's feelings.

Stimulating the children to more differentiated observation, to perception of contrasts, to articulation of what is perplexing and wonderful to wonder about, is the task to which the teacher brings newly developed techniques. One of these is a highly developed method for firsthand study of the environment* that appears in increasing numbers of instances in the curriculum for the primary grades. The children you see standing with their teacher, watching the hoisting of the steel girders, are learning about how work gets done and who does it, at the same time that they are feeling that there are safe ways for a great heavy thing to ride in the air and not fall on one's head. There is another educational rationale for extending the direct exposure of young children to the sights, sounds, and processes of the world around them, namely, that this differential awareness, directly experienced, is an important foundation for the mastery of the symbol system.

Supporting the Elaboration and Integration of Cognitive Experience. Exposure alone cannot be assumed to lead to more ordered and disciplined thinking. As long as the use of symbols as tools of reference to experience is still in a relatively early stage, it is necessary for children to have concrete objects and active relations to the object world

---

*One of the imaginative contributions of Lucy Sprague Mitchell to the field of education (e).

as foundation for ideation. It is not enough for classrooms to be places with books on the desk and spelling words on the board; they become workrooms: busy places for doing things and talking about them, as well as reading about them, housing a great variety of things, puzzles, picture books, as well as reading books, a terrarium, a few easels, a bench for woodworking, a sink, a collection of stones found in the neighborhood, a child-made model of a housing project.

The things, from the viewpoint of learning, are just so much clutter unless through them the teacher is leading the children to increasingly clearer understanding of connectives: similarities and differences, the movement of experience through time, cause and effect relationships, and, as they mature in their intellectual capacities, the relation between evidence and proof, between behavior and motivation, between fact and opinion. By helping the child penetrate experience, concrete and abstract, to the level of relationships, the school is preparing the child to order and deal with his world in terms of his society's logic and perception of reality (f).

The discussion period, replacing the traditional recitation session, is a potent technique in this connection. The teacher does not ask a question in the hope of eliciting a ready-made answer, known in a priori finished form; instead she encourages the children to sustain a question, to turn it about, to explore its ramifications, to bring it back to its core after tossing it back and forth to each other and absorbing their spontaneous associations. She guides the partly formed but freely expressed ideas of young minds through an intellectual course enriched with personal meanings, toward increasing clarity and depth of understanding (g).

There is another way to look at the question of integrating cognitive experience in the interest of ego strength. It is reflected in the work of imaginative teachers who select those themes for the content of a program of studies that come closest to dominant psychological processes. For example, with preschool children, *origin* is a theme that has basic meaning on a psychodynamic level in terms of the child's highly motivated interest in his own origin. To study "Where did the carrots come from?" is not a cold intellectual inquiry; it interacts with the deeper question: "Where did I come from?" At another stage, the study of the struggle of the American colonies for independence from the mother country may have similarly intermingled cognitive-affective overtones for the adolescent.

Providing Opportunity for Discovery and for the Synthesis of Subjective and Objective Meaning. It is not difficult to create a school setting in which children will take a stance of exploration and discovery. Natural curiosity and energy for the search are easily tapped. The necessary accompanying stance of the teacher is not easily sustained, however. Whether the content is first contact with an art material or preparation of a report on a social studies topic in the school library, the children are free to explore and discover for themselves only to the extent that the teacher consciously values exploration as a preparatory stage for arriving at insights, and is not herself a compulsively right-wrong organized personality.

There are, however, technical questions to weigh and consider. Some of the subject matter to be mastered is internally right-wrong structured, such as spelling or arithmetic. An extended exploratory phase in these areas may be more disrupting than insight-producing. So there is the choice to be made as to the content most suitable for independent exploration and discovery. Even where content is suitable, there is a point of judgment as to when children have learned all they can from free exploration and are ready for cues, leads, guidance, and direction. This is one of the many instances when teaching becomes a matter of skillful footwork within a network of balances. One of these is how to achieve optimal balance between the need for and the satisfactions from learning through directed, structured presentations on the one hand and exploratory, independent discovery on the other. Looked at in terms of what the child internalizes, this becomes a matter of experiencing one's independent powers of pursuit and initiative at the same time that one accepts and uses established fact and method without feeling intellectual dependence to the synonymous with submission. Achieving such equilibrium represents a portion of the life task for working through autonomous processes.

Exploration, discovery, insight advance comprehension. To comprehension must be added absorption of experience and the techniques for providing opportunity for expression, if we are to approach the level of integration of subjective and objective experience. Expression in the child's own idiom, through whatever medium is naturally his: words, paint, sound, rhythm, dramatic play, serves the need of clarifying and reordering new experience in terms of his already existing system of ideas and feeling, and in so doing, making it more deeply part of himself.

Learning is not a matter of ingesting from outside the self. Each child develops a pattern for maintaining coherence between subjective phantasy and perception of objective reality that makes it possible for him to deal with the vast complexity of impressions, feelings, insights, and demands. Nobody can give him or teach him the pattern for his coherence, but the school carries responsibility to feed this process with enriched experiences and full opportunity for reexpression and thus keep it active.

This is most openly observable in school situations* where the technique of how to provide for and guide undirected dramatic play has been highly developed. Reality is reproduced, fragmented, transformed, misunderstood, and corrected through the same fabric and interplay of characters onto which inner feelings of love and pain and joy and sorrow and phantasies of one's lowliest and most magnificent self are projected. The child creates and recreates the world around him, building a pattern of coherence for his impressions, concepts, roles, and relations, and integrating knowledge and feeling; at the same time,

---

*At nursery school, kindergarten or, occasionally, primary levels.

through selective identification he creates and recreates his sense of himself.

Nurturing Communication. When communication is used to refer to verbal discourse, it is called "language arts" among teachers and educators. It takes account of children's strong drive to make themselves understood to others and to be in touch with other people's meanings. The newer techniques in the area of "language arts" accent the importance of protecting the transmission of individual meaning, rational or projected, and accepting and valuing original forms of expression as the way to preserve and strengthen creative processes. Here again, teaching becomes a balancing act. Overzealous correcting of spelling and grammatical errors may smother creativity and produce stereotypy and formalism; but language is a system of order with powerful social purposes and potential. Mastery requires accuracy of form and control of the meaning to be transmitted. The school needs to proceed from a consciously balanced design, taking these diverging needs and purposes into account.

There is another dimension of communication, in terms of contributing to ego strength, which one might call empathy with the child's thinking processes, using that term here as we are accustomed to using it with respect to emotional aspects of experience. The child's perception of and attitude toward his own intellectual powers is influenced by whether the teacher can penetrate the course and process of his thinking or is content to act as judge of rightness or wrongness, considering only the end products of his mental activity. Children pull the threads of similarities and differences, use analogy and metaphor in ways that often lead to wrong conclusions and circumstantial irrelevance. The intellectually resilient teacher, the one who can enjoy the intriguing course that the young mind takes in ordering the world of ideas, can perceive and accept the importance of the underlying thought processes while she supplies information and experience relevant to the correction of errors of fact and inference. On this level, teacher and child are interacting cognitively: communicating.

The drift of argument concerning the first assumption stated above can be briefly summarized. The learning functions having to do with intellectual power, acquisition of knowledge, competence, and communication can be mediated through experiences that simultaneously support the strengthening of personality processes: the equilibria to be attained between dependence and independence, originality and communication, exploration and regulation.

Teachers can be involved in the processes of child thinking and learning in ways that lead children to see and enjoy themselves as thinkers and discoverers. Pleasure in the self as a learner represents gain in the maturing of self-feeling which, in turn, strengthens motivation for further learning. Knowledge of the self as a learner is significant with respect to the relative congruence between self-image, aspirations, and ego ideals.

Learning is contrapuntal in character: as the child masters the outer world, he also discovers himself; in his feeling about himself there is the cumulative residue of the affect that pervaded the total learning experience. The fundamental maturing process of objectification can take place without violating the subjective continuity between personal and impersonal experiences, in itself an essential ingredient of ego-identity.

Second Assumption. It is assumed that the teacher-child relationship, through which learning in school is mediated, can contribute toward the maturing of positive feelings toward self and others, deepen the potential for interpersonal relatedness, and increase the flexibility of the adaptive process.

This assumption is based on the premise that self-feeling in childhood is, to a large degree, an introjection of the opinions and attitudes of important adult figures. It is necessary to penetrate the mechanisms by which this process becomes a factor of school life, beyond the level of simple advocacy of an accepting climate and a warm teacher. Apart from these general, pervasive qualities, there are specific relationship systems between teacher and child that have bearing on the nature of self-feeling. What these are will be briefly described and illustrated below.

Establishing Mutuality between Teachers and Children. There is a quality of "knowing" that can exist between teacher and children, a kind of interrelationship that is akin to Kurt Goldstein's concept of "immediacy" (h). It happens where children are perceived and responded to as individuals, not as part of a conglomerate mass, the "class"; where the teachers themselves feel buoyed up by the freshness and ebullience of children, their capacity for naïve wonder and intense involvement, the quick, turning tides of their feelings. It depends on how free the teacher feels about being known to the children as a fallible, feeling human being. It is manifested in communication that takes place in nonverbal ways as well as in the adaptation of language usage to child levels and modes of comprehension.

We cannot here consider the intricate question of how much this kind of connectedness with children is a function of teacher personality, how much it might become a universally accepted style of teacher-child relationship if social mores and traditional role-concepts did not inhibit it, and how much it could be facilitated by preparing teachers in newer ways. In any event, knowledge of childhood processes, in psychodynamic terms, is a reinforcing factor for being able to sustain meaningful contact with children. For example, the teacher who has learned not to equate maturity wholly with reasonableness, who has insight into the creative potential inherent in phantasy, is more likely to keep contact with the nonlogical, subjective side of the growing personality at the same time that she maintains what is fundamentally the teacher position, namely, to be on the side of objectification of life for the child and carry responsibility for leading children toward competence in the reference systems of reality.

Through this kind of mutuality with teachers one assumes the child will feel there is an expanding orbit of people he can "trust" and feel akin to, though with a quality of intimacy different from that appropriate to family life; that this will be partial protection against feelings of alienation and will facilitate his identification with the teacher's goals for his learning and growth. In a more general sense, the extent to which he constructs a more positive image of the human universe saves him from expending himself in illusory defense against projected hostility.

Sustaining a Supporting Role. The extent to which the life of feeling has a genuine, accepted place in the school world is a major determinant of how supported children can feel in school. It conditions ease and richness, lack of embarrassment in offering support and sympathy in case of trouble, rejoicing in response to pleasure. Another important element is sensitivity about what constitutes acceptable modes of expression of support, which differ with respect to age level, ethnic group mores, as well as individual personality; they need to be thought through in terms of sex differences between teacher and children and other, general features of psychosexual changes during childhood.

For the teacher to be able to sustain a supporting role requires knowledge and understanding of childhood, as well as the mature capacity to be a giving person. She needs to act on the basic expectation that growth will be gradual, wavering, regressive, uneven, and to understand, therefore, why it is unreal to expect face consistency of behavior. Recognizing conflict as inevitable in the growth process, she is not surprised by children's fears, weaknesses, guilt, anxiety. She is able to help children feel comfortable in having their troubles, doubts, shame, known to her with the confidence that they will not thus be downgraded in her eyes. She becomes a source of emotional support even when she can only listen to and understand problems that are outside the scope of solution within the school.

On the preventive side, there is the important matter of how constructively and objectively the functions of criticism and evaluation are handled, how free they are of the destructive elements of sarcasm and other forms of ad hominem humiliation. There is a difficult, technical problem involved: how to evaluate children's work in terms of concrete assessments, using individual capacity as the reference point, and yet satisfy the child's need for evaluation in peer-comparative terms. This is an area of active experimentation, of trying to find methods that will support children's realistic self-perception and evaluation and avoid fixed self-typing.

Building Functional Controls. The change in the authority role of the teacher from an arbitrary, role-invested to a rational, relation-dependent function represents a central alteration in teacher-child interaction. It has proved to be one of the most difficult to enact. A system of controls, limits, rules, regulations is essential protection against the potential damage (in the form of what is acted out and what is felt as guilt or anxiety) of excessive impulse release; it is also an essential protection of the learning atmosphere: the work, the play, the discourse intrinsic to constructive group life in school.

Means of control that breed hostility (threat, fear humiliation, harsh punishment), retaliatory or repressed, that undercut the child's image of himself and diminish his courage to test his powers, are rejected as psychologically corrosive. Potent motivating forces must be substituted, strong enough to check and channel behavior impulses originating in the basic energies, drives, and conflicts of young, growing children. Not only potent but positive motivating forces are available when the teacher communicates in depth with the children, acts sensitively and responsibly in supporting them as individuals, and introduces them to the life of learning in ways that augment their ego strength and regenerate the drive to pursue and fulfill curiosity.

Positive motivation, dependent as it is on the building of relationship rather than submission to power, is the foundation for the acceptance of control and the regulations of group functioning. The measures that constitute the actual system of control are attuned to the requirements of social necessity, not to the fulfillment of arbitrary status requirements. Since her goal is a rational, not arbitrary control system, the teacher gears rules and regulations to the children's capacity for control, admits flexibility in their application, defines them clearly, helps children to understand their basic reasonableness and function in sustaining the learning atmosphere. For the children, experiencing control and support from the same authority figure should reinforce internalization of a rational, nonpunitive authority mode as part of the growing conscience.

Incomplete as it is, perhaps this roster is adequate in illustrating the relevance of all aspects of the learning experience to the question of primary prevention. A more comprehensive account would certainly include such additional topics as the significance of how the teacher guides the child-group process in connection with dependence-independence and dominance-submission conflicts, and the place of teachers as ego-ideal figures. In this brief formulation, an effort has been made to trace the interconnectedness of learning functions and personality factors by showing how teaching methods, designed to build ego strength, contribute to positive elements of personality growth, and how relationships between teacher and child, designed to support positive self-feeling and prevent defensive alienation, constitute an important, determining condition for the degree to which the child will have the energy and flexibility available for transforming information, knowledge, skill, and competence into ego strength.

It is necessary to repeat, at this point, that these techniques and relationships are *assumed* to have these positive effects on ego strength and feelings and attitudes toward self and others; in other words, to be defensible ways of making schooling an influence for healthy personality. No matter how reasonable this assumption may appear, how strengthened by congruence with sound concepts of personality formation and certain aspects of learning theory (i), only systematic research can validate it or, more realistically, advance our understanding of the problems and mechanisms, by objective processes of analysis and differentiation.

Notes

a. Barbara Biber, "Schooling as an Influence in Developing Healthy Personality," in *Community Programs for Mental Health*, eds., R. Kotinsky and H. Witmer (Cambridge: Harvard University Press, 1955).

b. Biber, B., Gilkeson, E., and Winsor, C., "Basic Approaches to Mental Health: Teacher Education at Bank Street College," *Pers. and Guid. J.*, April 1959, p. 558.

c. Kubie, L.S., "Education and Maturity," *5th Annual Bank Street College Conference* (New York: 69 Bank Street Publications, 1957).

d. Erikson, E.H., *Childhood and Society* (New York: W. W. Norton, 1950).

e. Mitchell, L.S., *Our Children and Our Schools* (New York: Simon & Schuster, 1950).

f. Bruner, J.S., "Learning and Thinking," *Harvard Educ. Rev.*, 29 (1959): 3.

g. Biber, B., "Premature Structuring as a Deterrent to Creativity," *American Journal of Orthopsychiatry*, 29, no. 2 (1959): 280.

h. Goldstein, K., "Individuality — the Psychological Process," *7th Annual Bank Street College Conference* (New York: 69 Bank Street Publications, 1959).

i. Biber, B., "The Implications of Research in Learning for Public Education," *New Directions in Learning* (Summary of Proceedings of the California Association of School Psychologists and Psychometrists, Asilomar, California: March, 1959). (2:330–341)

Open Education

"The open classroom," "family grouping," "the integrated day" are some phrases used to characterize an approach to learning in England and Wales, often called "the Leicestershire method" in America. Although in England one might hear that it is every bit as characteristic of West Riding or Yorkshire, open classrooms and freedom of choice for children have been carried on for fully forty years in some London schools and particularly the schools in or near Bristol.

Joseph Featherstone informatively describes and analyzes this approach in a series of three brief articles published in *The New Republic*. (5)

Within the framework of the open classroom, there seem to be as many variations as there are teachers. Despite a generally high level of flexibility, some teachers must work in a more structured fashion than others. Some allow children complete freedom of choice within the range of possible activities, limited only by the bounds of the school building or its grounds. Others suggest certain undertakings to the class as a whole, or to certain children: "Come along, Henry, Sheila, Tim, you've not done any reading all week and it's time you did. Let's sit here together and we'll take turns." Some schools offer particular classes; for example, in Sea Mills School in Bristol, the seven-year-olds combine a rhythmic physical education, bodily movement activity, with math. (5) This is a planned part of the curriculum which the children do all together (with evident enjoyment) and no one has questioned the right of the school to ask for this much conformity.

But there are certain broad general characteristics which the schools share. Among these are a structuring of the experience through the use of physical space and the objects in it, rather than through temporal schedules, as American schools tend to do. A classroom is arranged with several different areas: a science table with an aquarium, a terrarium, a microscope with slides, collections of insects, shells, leaves; a reading corner; easels; a carpentry bench; a puppet theatre; tables laden with all sorts of tangible devices for working out mathematic relationships, from Cuisenaire rods to Dienes blocks. Some of the materials are professionally produced; however, collections of homemade devices abound: bundles of matches; containers of acorns, nuts and bolts, pebbles, a balance to weigh things on, cards with problems to be solved written on them. The profusion of material — store-bought, teacher-made, child-made — is remarkable and much of it is in active use. However, it is placed in a rational order enabling children to find it and use it freely.

The five-year-old who first steps into one of these rooms sees a wealth of things he can examine, handle, manipulate, learn from — there they are, inviting him to pick them up. These objects are not threatening: no one is saying, "Write properly with this pen, or you will show yourself a fool." "Solve these problems, or everyone will think you dumb." The child makes choices, when to do what. He may stand on the sidelines and watch. He may use clay, paint at the easel, draw with crayons, cut and paste, build with blocks — all "safe" activities which do not strain his capabilities — until he feels ready to tackle something more advanced. Or if he feels ready right away, nothing is holding him back. The choice is up to him.

The room is full of models for him to copy. Six- and seven-year-olds are there, at home with all the materials and activities. The siblings are usually placed together, the *older child* with a *special responsibility* to *start* the *younger* one off happily. The five-year-old watches his big brother or sister reading, writing in his notebook, solving desparate problems with abacus or number line. When he is ready to ask, someone will always be available to answer. The children learn from each other. The elder children pass on the skills and information they have mastered to the younger ones. In the process of teaching, the older children come to understand more fully what they know.

The classroom is structured through the use of space and choice of materials. The utilization of the children's own insights, feelings, knowledge and skills to teach and to learn from each other, leaves the teacher free to use her energy working with an individual, a small group or the whole group. She teaches children who are at that moment ready to learn, rather than wasting her energies in a day-long struggle to get everyone focused on a lesson many are not ready to learn. Most children are not and never will be able to tackle the same task in unison — fully alert and motivated, simply because a bell has rung or someone clapped his hands.

Therein is the crucial advantage of the new British schools. They set boundaries, but these boundaries are generous. Within them, each child is free to decide for himself what he will do. He has the option, the joy, and the misery of this freedom. He makes his choices based on his own level of understanding and his own set of interests in an environment designed to foster both.

E. Marianne Parry, a supervisor of Infant and Nursery Schools in Bristol, suggests that an important impetus of open education came from World War II:

In air raid shelters we couldn't structure our groups so that we had the four-year-olds in this end, six-year-olds in that, and the seven-year-olds somewhere else. So, by sheer force of circumstances, we were confronted with a mixed bag which rejected chronological age grouping. We were frequently left with large groups of children in our care for long periods of time and were thrown willy-nilly, whether we liked it or not, onto our own resources. We often found ourselves with nothing to aid in teaching except the raw materials around us.

The experiences in improvising material were, for me, the real beginning. Rethinking, I learned that children get much more from a real situation, handling the real thing, than from artificial so-called structural material. I acquired raw materials from all sorts of places. (3:21)

The transition to such an open education model in America is occurring slowly in various places. Jane Prescott describes this process in a private school in Cambridge, Mass. Preparations, triumphs, and pitfalls are emphasized in a particularly personal fashion in her article.

Live and Learn
Jane Prescott

Those of you who came to visit a classroom at Shady Hill several years ago could have expected to find the familiar set of desks and chairs facing the blackboard, the teacher in front of the room speaking to the whole class, and children of the same age working or listening with varying degrees of attention and involvement. Since that time a new movement in education has been launched in America which stems from some exceptional work being carried out in many British schools. The changes being undertaken in our school and by our teachers over the past three years are directly traceable to this movement and our growing interest in it. Today when entering some of our lower school classrooms you may be surprised at the change in atmosphere as well as in classroom set-up. You may not find the teacher right away as she could be out of sight, sitting on the rug in the reading corner playing "Consonant Lotto" with a small group of children. Some desks you may find, but they will be pushed together at angles to form tables or large places to exhibit work or to hold projects. You may wonder which is the front of the class and, as you stand musing on this, a group of children in aprons will sweep by you bearing paints and brushes to the hall to work on their mural. If you look carefully you will see all the children involved in some purposeful activity. The variety of activity and options may astonish you. It might seem overwhelming, but if you stay long enough, you will discover that these children, though using personal initiative and choice, are making wise decisions for themselves. What you won't see is that the background for this kind of self-discipline and responsibility has been carefully built by the teacher through discussions with the children and the preparation of a stimulating, responsive environment. The creation and nurture of this kind of environment is what I would like to discuss in this article.

Today one can pick up many books and magazine articles in America which attempt to explain the "new approach" to teaching. It is called by different names which all mean an emphasis on individualized teaching, self-directed work, real experiences in a constantly shifting environment rich in materials which promote learning, and the freedom and time to choose and explore for oneself.

At Shady Hill our recent changes in approach to teaching have come in response to some serious questioning on the part of our teachers about the optimum conditions for learning. There have always been teachers in our school with gifts to inspire and enthusiasms to excite. These teachers have held to ideals in education which combined the best in whatever was innovative or traditional with academic excellence. One of these teachers, Kathleen Raoul, says "I had read of the schools of Leicestershire (England). I had seen pictures of them but, until I walked almost straight from the plane into my first Infant School, I didn't quite believe that little children could make big decisions about their own education; that teachers could help them learn without teaching them." Kathleen goes on to describe her visit in glowing terms. (a) She returned to Shady Hill after that summer visit in 1967 and went right to work to build into her curriculum with first graders some of the freedom of movement and activity, some of the individualized teaching she had seen working so successfully in English schools. It was from this beginning that the ripple effect in our school began. The time for this idea was ripe and is now gaining force as can be seen by its spread among schools, both private and public, around our country. But to return to our story. Kathleen's job was not easy. She was trying to implement what was best of what she had seen plus continue her fine teaching of central subject and reading to twenty six-year-olds. Consent and blessings from the school had been given and explanations to parents were most cooperatively received. The difficulties of working this way with one age group, of feeling "alone" in one's struggles, and the insecurity brought on by not always feeling successful and rewarded would be hard on the best of us. Yet, as with all powerful ideas, this one gained interest and strength as the year progressed. Those of us who had long been wanting to break the bounds of homogeneous age grouping and rigid scheduling, and find ways to be more free and creative in our teaching, listened to Kathleen, read Joseph Featherstone (b) and the Plowden Report, (c) saw slides of English schools taken by Edward Yeomans, (NAIS Consultant), and talked and thought and planned.

We were convinced that to bring this reform, or change, to our school needed slow, careful, responsible work. Our director, Mr. Segar, was willing to plan with us, so as 1968 began we sat down to add to the beginning which Kathleen had made. There was no magic formula, no package plan. It became obvious that small moves would be apt to be most successful. Other schools might make grand sweeping changes, but we would be better off with much study and time spent on finding direction, gathering equipment, and reorganizing our instructional program. We focused on two main ideas we wanted to try: one; the "integrated day" with its emphasis on a "synthesis of learning experiences" (d) for each child with the least scheduling possible, and two; "family grouping," which means combining two or more age groups into classes. We saw in our vision all the glorious possibilities of these two ideas — activity centered classrooms, freedom to initiate one's own projects, older children helping younger ones, children less dependent on teachers, and rooms divided into special areas where small groups could meet to work, communicate, and learn. The wholeness of the day looked at this way had especial appeal for us, as did the idea of a natural flow of activity and talk, uninterrupted by artificial breaks. Learning becomes integrated for no limits are set as to subject or time. Exploration of all kinds would be a natural outgrowth of children's choices.

As we read, talked, and studied our ideas began to take shape. We agreed that the ideal way to try this at Shady Hill would be with five-, six- and seven year-old children. The choice of ages having been made, the next step was to decide which teachers and which classrooms would initiate the project. This was not easy. Many were interested but not all ready. The decision, of course, became an administrative one. Once "the team" was announced they met together and the compiling of lists began. I always look back on this time as the paper and pencil stage and I have reams of notes, lists, charts, and so on, to prove it. Briefly the plan was this: there were to be three classrooms of twenty-one children each: seven five-, seven six-, and seven seven-year-olds.

We were to use a building containing three large classrooms, already inhabited by two of the team teachers. We would remove all doors from these rooms, cut a section through one wall and thereby join and open the three rooms. We counted on much movement and lots of sharing of equipment.

We had many other decisions to make such as:

-What should we call ourselves or our groups?

-How could we best budget our needs?

-What about the use of special teachers?

-How and when should we communicate with
  parents?

-How uniform should we be in our use of
  teaching materials?

-What about report forms and record keeping?

The list is long. It took much time to iron out the details of our beginnings and to communicate about it to parents, teachers, and interested visitors.

As our group planning time came to an end with the school year of 1968, we knew that individually we would be thinking about our new venture on through the summer. Happily for us, we were to attend a workshop which was to be held at Shady Hill during July, and "organized to acquaint teachers from public and independent schools with the basic philosophy of the British movement and with some of the techniques that have been developed for implementing it." (e) There were to be thirty of us with an excellent staff headed by Roy Illsley, headmaster of Battling Brook School in Leicestershire County, England.

At the beginning of that summer I remember writing: (we were all asked to write autobiographical notes beforehand) . . . "I desperately need to become involved in materials and ideas on my own level, so I will be more ready to help and believe in children as they come into my class next fall. I hope to become more relaxed and to drop constraints and fears I may have gathered through the years" . . .

The plan was to give us, as adults, time to feel, think, gather impressions, and do. The course was not to be a series of "tips for tired teachers but a time to explore and think about our own learning, and to question the basic assumptions and premises of the educative process." (f) Well, we did do just that. We worked and played happily, on our own level, not thinking about children (outloud anyway) or September, knowing at last the wonderful feeling of children, that *now* is the only reality. I became happy sorting stones collected on a beach, painting pictures of seaweed and watery places, creating a sculpture of driftwood and stone, writing poems again, making a wooden doll's bed for my room, and solving a tricky math puzzle. We went on trips together, ate daily sandwiches together, danced together, met together to share our important thoughts, but mostly we worked apart yet together, which is the way life is and the way school should be.

I learned about freedom of choice at this workshop. In retrospect I know that I left a lot out of my own planning and that one is just as responsible for what one does not do as for what one does do. This has helped me enormously in working with the children on their plans. So that they won't feel guilty about what they lack and leave out, we plan together to get in all the things they need as well as all the things they want. I began to feel the rhythm and flow of work-play, hard-easy, active-quiet times during a day and a week, and to realize the frustration a child must feel when interrupted as well as the hopelessness of needing help and not getting it. I also watched expert teachers deal with my problems and learned how often one should step back and let the child struggle. "Centering" a clay pot became a real challenge to me and one I wanted to master but could not. However, I was led to understand that it was not easy and something I would want to return to again when the need to renew personal creativity should arise in me.

As those short four weeks drew to a close we parted knowing we needed time for reflection and renewal, but eager to move forward toward September and the creation of our new classroom environment.

We knew that in the physical arrangement of furniture would lie much of the success or failure of the room, and that by providing the right materials and equipment we could condition situations for specific leads into learning. We had spent hours pouring over supply lists; we had asked Mr. Illsley's advice about room arrangement; we had requested donations of vital pieces of equipment and furniture and received much more than we had asked for. We felt rich and ready. We spent August thinking, making private lists, collecting things like year old wall-paper sample books, egg cartons, costumes, extra cooking utensils, old tires, scrap materials, and making pillows and "discovery boxes." We had each assigned ourselves the task of preparing one "discovery box" which could be used and shared among us. Mine was to be on rocks. (The others were electricity, pulleys, and magnets.) Each box was to contain equipment as well as suggestions on cards as to possible projects to undertake or experiments children could make and record by themselves.

A week before other teachers convened at Shady Hill we came back to continue our planning together and to prepare our rooms. No one could imagine the amount of "things" to be sorted! Each room was to contain all of the basic learning materials for the three ages plus our own individual choices for the centers of interest into which we would divide our rooms. All of the large third grade desks had been removed from my room. The blackboard had been given to another teacher and I had five tables, six desks, two screens, and thousands of chairs.

Before I even unloaded my car I arranged everything in the room into "corners" and eliminated all but twelve school chairs. The "corners" I created first were Reading, Science and Math, Blocks, House, Teaching, Paper and Paste (so named later by the children). Construction and Art work were to be in my back room with the sink, Woodworking went into the hall. Then came the big job of creating the atmosphere with the materials in each corner. I can only say though we were tired beyond belief, when the time before the opening of school was over, we each thought our creations beautiful, and I can't remember ever feeling so happy, anxious, and empty all in one. But it felt good. The room looked like a workshop waiting only for the children who would bring it to life and fill my emptiness. With their arrival would begin the testing of our beliefs. Our basic tenets of trust and respect for the child, his needs, his individuality, desire to learn, plus our newly gained flexibility with which to work were about to go on display. I was plainly scared. I believed in the children, but I wasn't so sure about myself.

The role of the teacher changes in this kind of classroom setup; it has to be redefined and it feels very different. Those of us who have long been successful teachers in traditional classrooms can not deny that there is security in knowing you can "teach" something well. I had become very dependent in my teaching on sure-fire material to capture children's interest and upon certain routines and traditions which made life easy for all of us living together. It had been a long time since I had felt the insecurities I was about to feel.

Teaching in the integrated day situation is very demanding. "The teacher does not play an authoritarian role, but is rather a participant in the living and learning situation in the classroom. She has the final responsibility for making decisions and setting the boundaries between what is acceptable and what is unacceptable in the room; but the discipline of the group is based on mutual respect between the teacher and the child, and between child and child and is gradually assumed as a group responsibility." (g) This does not sound very different, but its implementation is. Now the teacher is in the role of observer, guide, and partner to each individual child. She can be in immediate communication with him where he is working by a look, word, or gesture or just by being nearby. Her participation with the children is of enormous importance. The harmony she can create by her presence, mood, or tone can make or break the day. The teacher must keep track of what the children are doing, talk with them about their work, extend it for them in proper directions. She must move, change, add to, or subtract from the environment constantly. There are times when small groups need to be called to her for specific teaching, just as there are times when she must play her teaching role by ear, picking up cues as she goes along. At the same time that she is steering and expanding thinking, feeding ideas, and asking questions, she must be prepared to stop, observe, and listen to the child's explanation of what he has done. So much of learning for small children centers around communication. But it is tricky knowing when to interfere.

So, in the teacher's management of her room and in her response to children's needs and interests lie the key differences of this new role. "The emphasis is on children learning rather than the teacher teaching." (h) She must still be an enthusiastic, warm, sensible, alert diagnostician, but now, a ringmaster too! There is little preparation for this new role which would make a difference in a short time. The best supports I had were: the conviction within myself that what we were doing was right; the experience behind me of the summer's workshop;

the backing of parents and school; and the good rapport we as a team felt in working together. Even now, as I look back on that first year, I know we could not have come through without each other to lean upon. You need a lot of sympathy and trust in beginning new ventures plus a lot of talk between the people doing it.

I suppose, that to our colleagues not directly involved with us, we seemed selfish, one track, frazzled and too busy for them. I know my friends felt that way. It seemed as though I could never do anything but think, talk, and work on school projects that year. I was a tired old bore to them. Sometimes to myself, too, which brings up an important point for those headed in this direction. It is essential that the teacher not devote all of her time to making the classroom work. This kind of obsession is not devotion but stupidity. It is impossible to bring humor, freshness, and ease into the classroom when one has not been refreshed by things other than worry and work. I know I will not let it happen to me again. Even now I have to force myself sometimes to remember that all work and no play doesn't make Jack dull, it makes him dead. No one wants dead wood in the classroom. In order to keep the balance of a happy, relaxed yet busy and motivated atmosphere in school one must practice the balancing on oneself out of school. That and patience with self. Too often we expect too much too soon.

We are often asked at meetings or by visitors what three things we think were the most important to us in beginning this work with our classes. Our answer is always the same and was from early on. We all agree we could not do without a long-arm stapler, our Nuffield Books, (i) and each other. I have discussed how and why we needed each other. Let me explain the other two in connection with some of our work.

While visiting schools in England, Kathleen looked carefully at the kinds of work being done by the children and at the way the work was recorded. She discovered that all of the children had "blank books" of different sizes into which went their writing, pictures, answers to questions, practice lessons and assignments. Books of this kind used in England were not available from American school supplies so she made her own. The best size for many of these books is bigger (approx. 9″ x 13″) than ordinary staplers could reach into, hence the need for a long-armed one. It has since become an indispensable tool of trade with us. Often vinyl wallpaper is used for book covers. It is less destructible than tag board. We find many children enjoy making their own books on special topics, but we always have a supply of ours on hand in varying sizes for the recording of daily work. Often we go through the children's "blank books" after school and add questions or ideas of our own as extensions to a child's work, but a strict rule with us is to go over the work itself only with the child present. Yesterday's errors can only be tomorrow's learnings if the communication about them is individual and fully understood by the child. This is one way we use to pick a child up on reversals, spelling, handwriting, English usage, and correct use of information. Better than a workbook, these books allow for thought, creativity, and personal style.

All of the writing of the Nuffield Mathematics guides is directed towards the teacher. They are in three categories; "Computation and Structure," "Graphs Leading to Algebra," and "Shape and Size." Emphasis is on "learning by doing." For small children this involves working with concrete objects and using the total environment as a classroom through which to learn basic skills and concepts. In discovering relationships for themselves there is not so much need for practice and many children can be working on different levels with the same material. Having done much reading and studying in the field of mathematics over the past ten years, we believe that the Nuffield guides are the best for our use now. We agree with Joseph Featherstone who wrote in one of his articles "A basic comprehension comes best through children's own activities in a classroom designed for permitting choices; and children learn best when they proceed at their own pace." These guides with their excellent foundation in theory are sound in practice and rich in specific suggestions for children's work, but they are not usual in the sense that we know teacher's guides. They demand creativity and choice on the part of the teacher as well. It is in mathematics that the differences between the old and the new methods of learning are most marked. We will no longer allow for technique and mastery of rules alone. We look instead for an understanding of vocabulary and ideas. We explore and use numbers for the real work of counting, measuring, comparing, mapping, graphing and figuring. To do this we need available much equipment: rods, blocks, unifix, games, abaci, sand, water, bottles, scales, nuts, stones, beans to mention only a few items in our ever expanding collections. We want for the most part for children's number work in these early years to be expressive of relevant things around them.

Our beginnings in the fall of 1968 were well publicized throughout our school community. Very quickly we became immersed in the activity of children and in our growing struggle to gain competence in this new way of living with them in school. I would be lying if I said we were happy and successful all of the time. We had some very depressing days and attacks of insecurity. Teachers cannot change overnight and we are impatient with ourselves. Still there were enough successes, there was enough support so that we knew we were not attempting to do an impossible thing but rather needed time to work through our difficulties. Parents were wonderfully patient with us. If they objected they did so silently. Here is another instance where feelings of mutual trust most rewardingly paid off. We had many offers of help from parents.

But because they *were* so interested, they and others needed and wanted to visit us. This almost became our undoing and I would warn others to strictly limit visitors or have none the first year. There were days when I wanted to tear my hair over the mobs, (it seemed to me), that were drifting through the rooms to see the "new method" in operation. It had its funny side too. The children paid them little attention yet it was obvious they felt their presence. One day when my class had a hospital corner in full swing with a staff of doctors and nurses on call to remedy any and all manner of medical problems, a visitor from another school quietly stepped into the doctor's office to get out of our way as we assembled for a group meeting on the rug. Suddenly a figure in apron and hat left us and as she bore down on the visitor I saw her getting her appointment pad ready and heard her say, "The doctor will be with you in a minute. Don't you think you should take off your jacket so he can examine you?" By now I have learned a lesson from the children about involvement and I rarely notice visitors unless they commit the unpardonable sin of participating without being invited.

We were encouraged in November by two things. One; the grade meeting and our parent conferences reassured us that what I have already mentioned about support from them was true. It was obvious from our talks with many that though our methods might seem crazy we did know their children and that the children were happy *and* learning. We also found many parents who wanted to share in our own reading experiences to whom we loaned our books and articles. Their questions often cleared our thinking rather than threatening us. We enjoyed this sharing of our thoughts and work with them. The second was a visit from Roy Illsley who was on this side of the Atlantic to speak at several meetings. He talked with us about our specific problems and helped us see that we should be more patient with ourselves. He reminded us of our favorite saying of the summer: "The truly efficient laborer will not crowd his day with work, but saunter to the task surrounded by a wide halo of ease and leisure." (j) He thought we were making haste too fast and forgetting to enjoy our work! He gave us hints about assignments, reminding us that all things matter equally, not just "work," and that we could do more with building up the arts and music. One particular thing he said at that time was to lead us to serious thought about numbers of children in classes. He said our rooms were too big; that the children didn't have to brush against each other enough or wait or share or help each other enough. This has lead us to increase the size of our classes from 21 to 24 (in 1969). We do feel that more children can live and work together, but that for our school, now, we must limit ourselves. The facilities of the school cannot bear more enlargement without undergoing change. I also feel that we as teachers would have to learn short-cuts in teaching style and reporting were the numbers to increase much more in our school.

A large responsibility of the teacher in this new role is the keeping of records. To understand the children as individuals and be able to plan for their needs, knowing their strengths and weaknesses, the teacher needs to observe. So that these insights will not be lost they must be recorded. In a special notebook the teacher keeps an anecdotal record on each child in her class. At first we attempted to do this reporting each day, but the task is overwhelming if conscientiously attended to along with housekeeping, meetings, and daily planning. Now I find myself more selective. It is not necessary to report everyday, but to include important happenings and learnings, how the child reacts to people and specific situations, as well as one's personal speculations as to what is going on with him. I have developed a good memory for these kinds of details and now know that, instead of writing records, I can go to a concert. A summary at the end of the week is often enough.

Other kinds of records of course have to do with inschool communications and reports to parents. Our reporting has changed because we now want to discuss the whole child in terms of his total school experience, not stratify according to subjects. I can only say that for each school it is important to figure out the best way of doing the most honest and straightforward job of reporting, Parents have a right to answers from teachers. Perhaps one day we will achieve the perfect report — I don't know. Since I have been at Shady Hill, we have changed reporting forms three or four times and are never satisfied with one more than a few years. This is probably healthy in view of changes in education. Still, there are many of us who believe that the confrontation of a conference is far superior to written statements. Nevertheless, we know that in order not to lose the message entirely, it must be written down and filed away. How best to write it down will continue to be a dilemma for teachers not yet on the scene.

During the course of a given year in an open classroom the environment changes many times. The important thing is that the teacher be prepared to be adaptable and allow the children's interests to develop. Then the environment will perforce change because of them. I think of an instance that first year where a child's interest in stones and gems led us from a study, to an exhibit, to making our own museum and to many collecting trips outside the classroom. And another time when spring was bursting all around us when a group moved right out of doors to study buds and twigs and the glories of new life were brought inside and a place made where all could observe, record, and participate. There are times, too, when the teacher will want to create her own interest corner with leads into learning of something historical, topical, or of interest to her. Our study of space and Apollo moon shots derived from my awareness of play in the block corner. I then brought in an exhibit of pictures, added a few items to the play, and held discussions with interested groups. As their interest and knowledge increased, the space needed to play and work it out grew until a large mural, the whole block corner and other areas were devoted to "space" study for a number of weeks. The whole class finally became involved and interest cropped up and on the rest of the year.

At Shady Hill we have long been known for our work in "Central Subject," a name given to the integrated study taken up at any one grade level by a class for the entire year. First graders study Eskimoes or Cave Men, second graders study Indians, third studies Bible or Vikings, fourth studies Greece, fifth, Middle Ages, and so on. These subjects change rarely but vary considerably from year to year because of the teacher involved. English techniques, geographical concepts, historical facts, plus science, music and art are united in a study in depth of a people in time and place. It has proven an excellent technique for arranging curriculum, but, as can be guessed, the teacher is responsible for most of the initial work. She studies and organizes the material to put it in meaningful sequence for her children to learn. All they need to be is receptive. They are easily motivated because if the teacher is at all scholarly, she has done her homework well, and, knowing her age group, she picks out the most appealing bits with which to engage them. Once they are captivated she can use all the techniques of group and individual work to get them going on readings, projects, and discussions. It's fun — it works — it's one of the things I always enjoyed most about my teaching. But our team wasn't sure that that kind of technique of organizing curriculum was what we wanted to impose on this frail new venture of ours where we wanted to emphasize building on children's own interests. We knew that children's play discloses starting points of interest from which the teacher can unfold for them the possibilities of extension, and we wanted to experiment with this way of learning unencumbered by curriculum demands.

Activities are more effective in provoking problems with young children than is discussion, so with the blessing of our Central Subject committee and a promise to report a year hence, we freed ourselves of a set study. It is hard to predict what direction an interest will take. The driving force behind it is the children's own involvement and not the teachers prepared plans or dominating influence, but the teacher is the one who may see the exciting possibilities which unfold only gradually to the children, so she must be ready. A few such topics which arose in our groups that first year were Bridges and Constructions, Printing, Dinosaurs, Space, Undersea Exploration, Hospitals, Restaurants. Some of these had historical implications which were carried as far as both teacher and children felt were appropriate. All had good learning possibilities.

Another way of organizing themes in one's mind is to use the "Study Group" technique. The second year, in addition to centers of interest, we created study groups whenever we recognized an interest expressed by more than a few children. Sometimes we initiated the topics ourselves. Some such "Study Groups" in our combined classes were: Cameras, Animal adaption, Snow and Ice, Islands, Babies or Human Reproduction, Mapping, Poetry, Knights, Birds, Pond Life. Membership overlapped in some of them, bringing together children from two classes. Most of these study groups operated with a teacher as a guide and resource person. We made use of the activity principal foremost, but also, banking on children's curiosity, we were able to raise questions and problems which led them toward academic work, more questions, dramatic play, much art work, writing, and reading.

It was during the second half of this last year (1970) that I elected to try the Central Subject idea in this setting. Believing as I do that there are certain important things that history and grown-ups have to teach children, I felt compelled to see if I could introduce an historical subject which would be appropriate for a vertically grouped class. Motivation by the teacher is important in developing interest in far-away people and times, but too much emphasis by the teacher is not effective at all. Yet there are many benefits to be had from putting oneself in another's moccasins, so to speak. I wanted to see if this kind of teaching would make any difference at all in the class, its operation, its cohesiveness, and its compatability as it had for me with other classes.

Kathleen and I discussed this idea many times during 1969 and became convinced we had to give it a try sometime in order to answer our own questions as well as those being asked us by members of our school community. We decided to take on two aspects of the same problem: would it be better to try this kind of teaching in one class where all the work, reading, and discussion could be contained in one room (as in the past), or could one manage just as well using the study group technique with members of the group coming from two classes and meeting times confined to specific hours and days?

I chose "Eastern Woodland Indians" as the topic to use with my whole class. Kathleen chose "The Charles River" as hers. Membership for her group was to be limited to sixteen six- and seven-year-olds, eight from each of the two other mixed group classes. She had organization problems such as a place to meet and store her materials which could be readily used by both groups and planning a time to meet, which, because it had to be planned for, was therefore limiting. Yet the activity was extremely meaningful to those children who chose to work with that group. They stayed with it for three months, but I have a feeling that, as a teacher, my satisfactions were greater in the end than were Kathleen's, but then we expected just that.

Setting up an "Indian Corner" in my classroom after Christmas was the way I began. It contained books, pictures, maps, an exhibit of artifacts now owned by the second grade, table, chairs, papers, pencils, books, furs birchbark, corn, and questions. For several days no one commented, but there was activity and interest. Finally, one seven-year-old said "Are we going to study Indians like the second grade does?" I asked him if he wanted to; he said, yes, and we dropped the subject. The next week I brought in more reading books about Indians and started reading aloud from "Ride the Wind" (k) at our regular story time at the end of the morning. This is a story of an Indian boy of one of the Algonquin Tribes, the Lenni Lenape, that has long been popular with our young children. My five-year-olds were entranced by the story, the sevens were thoughtful, asking good questions, but it was the six-year-old boys who were captivated immediately and for whom indentification was fast and thorough!

Now, as interest grew and questions led us to find things out together, the children began bringing in things: more furs, beads, arrow heads, costumes, pictures, and books, and our projects began. I can not go into detail here with all we made and did but to conclude: I let this interest and work die its own natural death. It took seven weeks. During the eighth week I put the materials away, though not out of sight. By then everyone had moved off in other directions. It wasn't until three weeks before school closed that one of the older children said at our meeting one day, "Hey, I thought we were going to make an Indian play for the end of school," "Yeah!" came many replies, "Lets!" So out came some of the props; costuming began in earnest again; our dancing, and drumming were recalled and rehearsed; our favorite legend was prepared for dramatization, and a beautiful, haunting Indian song was created by the group. We prepared the whole into a kind of "Ceremony — Play" and presented it for our friends and parents outdoors the day before school closed! Interestingly, I would have felt happy about the Indian Study even without the bang-up ending. I had proven to myself that the material was still good and that the study of mankind is ever interesting to "man." The children had made of it and taken from it what was important to them plus some truths and concepts I wanted to share with them. Then the finish was pure icing on the cake and might never have happened without the older children. They really planned, wrote, and directed the entire operation — another proof to me of their important contribution to a mixed-age group. The whole experience was fun for me too. The interest could easily be reignited another year and, with our background, the possibility of moving West with the Indians or Pioneers, or North to the Eskimoes, could capture our imaginations. However, there's a nice feeling of realizing no pressure, yet knowing that a tiny spark created by the teacher can have such rewarding results and far-reaching implications. But, I do feel entirely satisfied with the activities and learnings of the other study groups and realize that for some children they were the highlight, not the Indians. I would want to be able to have both experiences in my classroom.

I haven't mentioned reading yet. We are often asked questions concerning the teaching of reading in the open classroom situation. People can not believe that it is really possible to teach all children individually and "with all that racket going on." To be honest I wasn't sure myself when I began. What I came to realize after stumbling around a lot was that the same techniques apply, that children want badly to learn to read and that I had to be pretty clear on how best to help each one when the magic moment arrived. Sometimes we group children who need to learn the same thing, sometimes we send them to a special teacher, sometimes we wait and do nothing but watch, sometimes we plan daily individual lessons with a child. All in the interest of supplying the child with the proper "human partner" when he's ready and of steeping him in confidence and rich background. The leads into reading are all around him in the classroom and soon he realizes if he doesn't find out what's on the bulletin board he will be the loser. So he learns the importance of signs and asks questions. One distinct advantage of vertical grouping is that one can always find someone besides the teacher who knows how to do something.

We use any approach to reading that best applies to the individual child. In order to find out how he can best learn we play games, teach him sight words and phonics, and write. Always write. Many of our children have learned the incentive and the idea of reading from their own writing. We want them to write all the time. Any good teacher of young children can learn how to teach reading. It's just more fun in this kind of class. Much of my pleasures in teaching comes from nurturing the school environment to excite and stimulate learning. It is indeed rewarding to be right there with the right material when the child professes an interest to learn something.

Our culture is geared to think of six as the magic age when reading will begin, but all of child development and our own common sense tells us that children develop at different rates and are not all ready at the same time for anything, let alone reading, the hardest task of childhood. How fortunate then that children of three ages can be grouped together for a living and learning experience in which individual readiness is a keynote, competition is at a minimum, and imitation can flourish. We have discovered that among the three ages one can have as wide a range of ability as one has in an average second grade classroom. The difference is that the range looks and feels better to the children in our setting; all the differences are completely acceptable.

One final word on reading — my favorite quote to date on the subject: "If the early teaching of reading and language is human-centered and, if addiction has done its work, there will come a time in childhood when pleasure in reading and in language achieves a certain degree of independence from the human partners who had served as teachers. The dialogue that had originated between the child and his family and the child and his teachers is no longer the indispensable component in learning and in pleasure. The book itself has taken over as a partner and is invested with some of the qualities of a human relationship. In this way literature becomes an extended dialogue." (1)

Evaluation of our new program is a constant ongoing process but can not take the form on paper of more than insight and speculation at this early date. Generally we all agree that our children blend easily into a class of peers at the third grade level and are not behind others in knowledge of basic skills; that they have learned how to manage school time and are particularly inventive and independent in planning for their needs both academically and creatively; that they tend to have a doggedness in pursuing their own interests; and that they are more tolerant of the varying styles and places of learning of their classmates. Parents tell us that their children are showing more initiative at home and that they no longer hear the plaintive "What shall I do now?" from their youngest. Instead many are astonished to hear their children planning and preparing for activities for themselves. They also note that because of the continuous opportunity for communication and socializing all day long in school their youngsters are apt to be more content with solitary activity at home. Many have told us they are pleased to see the balance between work-play situations which the children now exhibit at home as well as in school. With this more realistic rhythm establishing itself, they feel more a part of the child's learning, and we are able to share in our knowledge of and our wishes for a fine balance for their children. Parents have often told me that home now seems as good a place to learn to read as school does. This indicates to us a need to share our resources with parents. It is getting at just what we intended; that children should not categorize and place learning only in the "school slot" but instead grow up knowing that truly the world is everyone's classroom. "He shall seem idle and think he is in sport when he is indeed seriously and well-employed" (m) seems an appropriate thought to remember as we realize that the definitions of work and play are not the children's but imposed upon them by the adult world.

In class we attempt through discussion to talk about "balancing our day" and about "hard-easy" things so that the child may see that life can contain both at any time and place. The child who finds learning to read easy and painting a picture hard should be equally well thought of and helped to achieve at his "hard" thing as the child for whom reading is difficult. We feel that we are beginning to achieve this appreciation among ourselves in class and continue to work on it constantly.

In a world too burdened with technology and conformity we need to be vigilant to bring out in future generations the best they have to offer in independent thought, flexible attitudes, and affectionate understanding. Scientists have determined that the strongest need — and the need most often unfulfilled — is love. "Love has been the most important factor in the evolution of man," says Dr. Ashley Montague. "The love to which I refer is behavior calculated to confer survival benefits on other people in a creatively enlarging manner; in other words, an involvement, a continuing interest and concern in their welfare." He noted: "We were born to live as if to live and love were one. If we fail in loving, then, we fail in living." For this reason, he contended, schools should really be institutes for teaching the art of human relationships, the "theory, art and science of practicing the ability to love." (n) I do not believe that we should replace reading, writing, and arithmetic, but I do believe we can and must emphasize a more humanistic approach to living and learning which involves so much more than academics. I find the "integrated day" the most conducive environment in which to deal with these human values, as well as the basic skills, and to build self-esteem, adequacy, and appreciation.

Though our evaluation is not half begun, we feel positive progress even though we ask ourselves searching questions every week. We feel it is important for everyone involved with us to understand what we are doing and that if we move thoughtfully enough we will make fewer mistakes. As Edward Yoemans says, "There can be no instant Integrated Day. It must come, if it comes at all, as an evolutionary process in which much study and trial-and-error are involved, just as it came in Leicestershire." (o)

We feel we have the ingredients for success in our school. In my mind these consist of teacher readiness and commitment, support from parents and administration for change, an adequate supply of materials with which to keep the environment flexible and exciting, good rapport and communication between staff involved, and, last but not least, a complete understanding on the part of the teacher of her changing role.

With patience, trust, and imagination thrown in one can not fail, for the children love this way of working.

Everyone likes to feel adequate and independent and I do believe that in this setting we can help children with these concepts more than we could before. Through the door of communication which is constantly open, we are ably to show them literally, that they are capable of learning from and through experiences and that it can be a rewarding struggle to "get" something no matter how long it takes. Not all problems are solvable in one class, one day, one week. Children need time to learn, to think, to make mistakes, and to do over again those things they enjoy and can do well. We have been too prone to rush them along, through one class after another, planning at least a problem a day which many will not be able to solve in the little time we allow them. This can be too discouraging. We want children to take time to know what they have learned. We want people for the future who do not fear failure. Mental elasticity and inner-springs would be my gifts to a child, could I give them.

I've talked enough about the advantages of an open classroom, and Integrated Day, a mixed-age group, and it's obvious that I am for this kind of school setting for children. Many changes are going on in other classrooms in our school which indicate that the ideas are spreading. Teachers are offering more freedom of choice activities in their programs, but, better still, they are looking critically at the old traditional ways of doing things and revising and talking and exploring. We want our school to continue to be a place where individual differences among teachers are valued and can flourish as well as among children. We do not seek unanimity, but we look for agreements in philosophy, and we still need a strong central core to belong to. Everyone benefits from innovation in one part of a school. The "ripple effect" reaches out and touches all levels until finally the whole faculty is talking about variations and changes it wishes to make. Then the school has to seize the moment and talk as a whole. New ideas can be honed yet flourish where the conditions are right for change and when the teachers are given as much initiative and responsibility as the children and as much trust and cooperation by the parents as we always had in the past. Let me close with a quote from Roy Illsley. It sticks in my mind because I have applied it to us all as we have been growing inside and changing in our ways of doing things. "Creativity is the growing edge of life and the point at which all improvement, all progress, all novelty comes into being."

Notes

a. "Reflections on a Visit to Leicestershire," *Shady Hill News*, November 1967.

b. Three Articles by Joseph Featherstone in *New Republic,* Autumn, 1967.

c. The Plowden Report of the Central Advisory Council for Education, "Children and Their Primary Schools," *HMSO*, 1967, Vol. 1.

d. Len Sealey, "Looking Back on Leicestershire," *ESI Quarterly Report*, 1966.

e. Edward Yeomans, "The Wellsprings of Teaching," *NAIS*, February 1969, p. 6.

f. Ibid. p. 8.

g. *The Integrated Day in the Primary School*, Brown & Precious Ward Lock Educational, 1968, p. 26.

h. Ibid. p. 30.

i. Nuffield Mathematics Project Teaching Guides available from John Wiley & Sons, Inc., 605 Third Avenue, N.Y., N.Y. 1 - 16 (and Nuffield Junior Science Guides SRA Canada, Ltd., 44 Prince Andrew Place, Don Mills, Ontario.

j. Henry David Thoreau.

k. Ethel Phillips, *Ride the Wind* (Houghton Mifflin Riverside Press, 1933).

l. Selma Frailberg, "Learning to Read and Write," (a paper distributed in 1968).

m. Charles Hoole, a 16th-century schoolmaster.

n. From a reprint in: *Christian Science Monitor*, 28 January 1965; from Coastal Outlook (Half Moon Bay, California).

o. Edward Yeomans, "Education for Initiative and Responsibility," *NAIS*, November 1967, p. 28.   (13)

Open education has its flaws and does not always work perfectly, but, on the whole, it works well, and it is an approach innately self-maximizing, which ideally fosters a very high level of values. Whether someone, with inadequate environmental stimulation or a learning disability, who has not had enough adequate associative learning, can profit from such a setting is not known. Furthermore, England is not America. Homogeniety, a commonly shared tradition, a quiet prevailing politeness, and a social system not nurtured by the American dream are some of the characteristics that help open education function there. It is further essential that the school system in which open education thrives honestly nurture the idea.

There is no approach for all children or for all teachers. In the sense that one has a code of expected behavior, one must pay attention to habit formation. However, without an appreciation of child development, one sails in uncharted waters. The issue that open education raises, however, is an extremely important one: Can we make our institutions *humane, flexible,* and *responsive*?

References to Part 9

1. Bereiter, Carl, and Engelmann, Siegfried, *Teaching Disadvantaged Children in the Preschool* (Englewood Cliffs, N.J.: Prentice-Hall, 1966). By permission.

2. Biber, Barbara, "Integration of Mental Health Principles in the School Setting," in *Prevention of Mental Disorders in Children,*

ed. Gerald Caplan (New York: Basic Books, Inc., 1961), pp. 323-352.

3. *The British Infant School: Report of an International Seminar* (Melbourne, Fla.: Institute for Development of Educational Activities, Inc., 1969).

4. Erikson, Erik, "Identity and the Life Cycle, Psychological Issues," vol. 1, no. 1 (New York: International Universities Press, 1959).

5. Featherstone, Joseph, "The Primary School Revolution in Britain: I. Schools for Children; II. How Children Learn; III. Teaching Children to Think," *The New Republic,* first published August-September 1967, pp. 1-16.

6. Harris, Florence R., *Field Studies of Social Reinforcement in a Preschool* (Durham, N.C.: Durham Education Improvement Program, October 16, 1967), pp. 2-16.

7. Hebb, Donald O., *Organization of Behavior* (New York: John Wiley & Sons, 1949).

8. Kamii, Constance, "Piaget's Interactionism and Development of a Preschool Curriculum" (Revision of a paper read at the November 1970 Conference of the National Association for the Education of Young Children held in Boston, Mass.), mimeographed.

9. _____, "A Sketch of the Piaget-Derived Preschool Curriculum Developed by the Ypsilanti Early Education Program," Ypsilanti Public Schools, Ypsilanti, Mich., August, 1971.

10. Murphy, Lois, et al., *Widening World of Childhood* (New York: Basic Books, Inc., 1962).

11. Piaget, Jean, *The Origins of Intelligence in Children,* trans. Margaret Cook (New York: International Universities Press, 1952).

12. Pines, Maya, *Revolution in Learning: The Years from Birth to Six* (New York: Harper & Row, Publishers, 1966).

13. Prescott, Jane, "Live and Learn," in *Schools Talk to Parents about the Integrated Day* (Boston: National Association of Independent Schools, 1971).

14. Solley, Charles M., and Murphy, Gardner, *Development of the Perceptual World* (New York: Basic Books, Inc., 1960).

Wheel–spoke plan provides
plenty of entrances for rapid
approach and departure.
Play yard is enclosed
and protected by
the building itself.

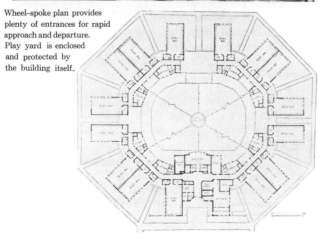

part 10

The Future
Role of Early
Childhood Education
in a Technological
Society

Arguments for the existence of early childhood education as an
entity were not heard until the turn of the nineteenth century.
Those arguments we now take for granted, but originally they were
made with caution. Early childhood education was what occurred
between mother and child at home on the farm. Filled with romantic notions, a formal recognition was given to the fact that children
need nurturance. At that time it was still considered radical to
advocate group care for children with a teacher, if for no other

reason than the dread of spreading diseases. Ironically, when slum nursery schools were propagated at the turn of the twentieth century, it was with the view that optimal health could be promoted in a school setting. Skepticism and lack of proof were swept aside with evangelical fervor. Nursery schools were part of a social movement to correct tenement living conditions in the very best of humanistic tradition.

Early childhood education gained more stature and acceptance as it became allied with the new science of child study. Hope rose that with this new knowledge an environment at home and at school could be so constructed that a child's optimal growth would be fostered. The new science first focused on the child's physical, emotional, and social development; in the late 1950's interest shifted to the young child's cognitive development. Even though the relative influences of nature and nurture on child development were sometimes fiercely debated, no one questioned the fact that science and technology would lead the way. Early childhood education, founded in humanism, was also allied to science and a belief in the perfectability of rational man.

Like all other institutions in the late sixties, early childhood education was caught in the struggles between technology and the new humanism. What values was it to espouse? The earlier questions of how to provide experiences that enhance social competence, cognitive skills, or emotional well being were relegated to a relatively minor position by some who felt society overly valued technical skills. Others held that the skills required ought to at least serve better the interests of the individual or humanity. Efforts at compensatory education for poverty children and enrichment in the sciences for all children lessened in importance as the more crucial issue became humanizing the structures of society. New life styles emerged, particularly those which offered alternatives to the original family.

For the first time the assumption is not universally held that parents are the primary caretakers and educators of young children. Consequently, communes, day care centers, and early childhood educators are assuming greater importance. Who in society will take responsibility for raising its children? There is no clear answer. Urie Bronfenbrenner has been articulate about this problem. A long time student of childrearing practices in both the Soviet Union and the United States, he asks, "Who Cares for America's Children?" (1) He concludes that television and peer groups play an increasingly important role at all socioeconomic levels. Neighborhoods are too frequently devoid of adults, leaving children to their own devices. Bronfenbrenner traces this condition to the pressures families face without adequate sanction or support from society: they cope with their complicated, mobile, fragmented existence by unwittingly absenting themselves from meaningful contact with their children.

from **Who Cares for America's Children**

Urie Bronfenbrenner

... In today's world, parents find themselves at the mercy of a society which imposes pressures and priorities that allow neither time nor place for meaningful activities and relations between children and adults, which downgrade the role of parent and the functions of parent-hood, and which prevent the parent from doing the things he wants to do as a guide, friend and companion to his children.

The frustrations are greatest for the family of poverty, where the capacity for human response is crippled by hunger, cold, filth, sickness and despair. No parent who spends his days in search of menial work and his nights in keeping rats away from the crib can be expected to find the time, let alone the heart, to engage in constructive activities with his children or serve as a stable source of love and discipline. The fact that some families in poverty do manage to do this is a tribute to them, but not to the society or community in which they live.

For families who can get along, the rats are gone but the rat race remains. The demands of a job, or often two jobs, which claim meal-times, evenings and weekends as well as days; the trips and moves one must make to get ahead or simply hold one's own; the ever increasing time spent in commuting; the parties, the evenings out, the social and community obligations; all of the things one has to do if he is to meet his primary responsibilities produce a situation in which a child often spends more time with a passive babysitter than with a participating parent or adult.

Even when the parent is at home, a compelling force cuts off com-munication and response among family members. Although television could, if used creatively, enrich the activities of children and families, it now only undermines them. Like the sorcerer of old, the television set casts its magic spell, freezing speech and action, turning the living into silent statues so long as the enchantment lasts. The primary danger of the television screen lies not so much in the behavior it produces—although there is danger there—as in the behavior it prevents; the talks, the games, the family festivities and arguments through which much of the child's learning takes place and through which his character is

From Urie Bronfenbrenner, "Who Cares for America's Children?" *Young Children*, vol. 26, no. 3 (January 1971). Reproduced with permission from *Young Children*. Copyright © 1971, National Association for the Education of Young Children, 1834 Connecticut Ave., N. W., Washington, D.C. 20009.

formed. Turning on the television set can turn off the process that transforms children into people.

In our modern way of life it is not only parents of whom children are deprived, it is people in general. A host of factors conspire to isolate children from the rest of society: the fragmentation of the extended family, the separation of residential and business areas, the disappearance of neighborhoods, the elimination of small stores in favor of supermarkets, zoning ordinances, occupational mobility, child labor laws, the abolishment of the apprentice system, consolidated schools, television, telephones, the substitution of the automobile for public transportation or just plain walking, separate patterns of social life for different age groups, the working mother, the delegation of child care to specialists; all these manifestations of progress operate to decrease opportunity and incentive for meaningful contact between children and persons older or younger than themselves.

And here we confront a fundamental and disturbing fact: *Children need people in order to become human*. The fact is fundamental because it is firmly grounded both in scientific research and in human experience. It is disturbing because the isolation of children from adults simultaneously threatens the growth of the individual and the survival of the society. The young cannot pull themselves up by their own bootstraps. It is primarily through observing, playing and working with others older and younger than himself that a child discovers both what he can do, and who he can become, that he develops both his ability and his identity. It is primarily through exposure and interaction with adults and children of different ages that a child acquires new interests and skills, and learns the meaning of tolerance, cooperation and compassion.

Hence, to relegate children to a world of their own is to deprive them of their humanity and to deprive ourselves of humanity as well. Yet, this is what is happening in America today. We are experiencing a breakdown in the process of making human beings human. By isolating our children from the rest of society, we abandon them to a world devoid of adults and ruled by the destructive impulses and compelling pressure, both of the age segregated peer group and the aggressive and exploitive television screen. By setting our priorities elsewhere and by putting children and families last, by claiming one set of values while pursuing another, we leave our children bereft of standards and support, and our own lives impoverished and corrupted.

This reversal of priorities, which amounts to a betrayal of our children, underlies the growing disillusionment and alienation among young people in all segments of American society. Those who grew up in settings where children, families, neighborhoods and communities still counted are liable to act out their frustration in positive ways through constructive protest, through participation and through public service. Those who come from circumstances in which the family, the neighborhood and the community could not function—be it in slum or suburb—can only strike out against an environment they have experienced as indifferent, callous, cruel and unresponsive. One cannot condone the destruction and violence manifested by young people in widely disparate and desperate parts of our society. But one can point to the roots of a process which if not reversed will continue to spread.

The failure to reorder our priorities, the insistence on business as usual, and the continued reliance on rhetoric as a substitute for radical reforms can have only one result: the far more rapid and pervasive growth of alienation, apathy, drugs, delinquency and violence among the young and among the not-so-young in all segments of our national life. We face the prospect of a society which resents its own children and fears its youth.

What is needed is a change in our patterns of living which will once again bring people back into the lives of children, and children back into the lives of people. But how? The verse in Isaiah says, "a little child shall lead them." I propose we act upon that text. But perhaps to do so one must speak not in the language of Isaiah, but in the language of our contemporary times.

What I am proposing is the seduction of America by its children. What do I mean? Let me give you some examples, concrete actions we could take at all levels in our society: business, industry, mass media, communities, local, state and Federal governments right down to the local neighborhood; concrete actions that would have the effect of bringing people back into the lives of children, and children back into the lives of people.

One of these suggested actions comes from the USSR, which is not the only country that does this; it's also done in Scandinavia. This is the custom for which there's no English word, so I've used the word "adoption," in which a business or an industry adopts a group of children or a chilldren's program with the aim of becoming friends, of acquainting children with the people who work in the world of work.

My colleague in the Forum Planning Committee, Dr. David Goslin of the Russell Sage Foundation, decided to Americanize this idea, because he felt, as I do, that the values are human rather than parochial. He persuaded the *Detroit Free Press* to try an experiment. Recently that newspaper saw in its composing room, press room, dispatch room, city room and other offices, young children twelve years of age from two schools in the city of Detroit. It was a fascinating thing to watch.

When we first talked to the people at the *Free Press* they said, "Gee! kids? You know we're a newspaper here. What will we do with them, sit there all day and watch them? Besides, you know this is a busy place." As one lady in the advertising section said to me, "Professor, you mean you're going to have kids around here—you really mean that?"

On the last day, that same lady said to me, "Professor, it's going to be so lonely here next week—those kids are easier to talk to than people." They were from two middle schools, one in a slum area, the other in a middle-class area, both black and white. The children were just themselves. They said things like, "This is a place to meet, a way to understand people." "If every kid in Detroit and all around the United States got to do this, I don't think there would be so many problems in the world." It was a two-way street that came alive there. People rediscovered children, and children rediscovered people.

Other Actions can be Taken

Another idea is the notion of encouraging business and industry to place day care centers in or near the place of business—not as the only location for day care and preschool centers, but as one of the options available to parents, so that during the coffee breaks and during the lunch hours, people could visit the kids. Perhaps then children would once again become a subject of conversation in places where children don't get talked about as much as they used to.

We are about to propose that every moderately sized place of business or branch of a business in the country establish a Commission on Children to ask how the policies and practices of that business affect the lives of their employees and their children as family members. On such a commission, obviously the employees as well as the management and the union should participate.

We recommend that business explore and maximize half-time and part-time jobs for comparable rates of pay and status so that those parents who choose to work part-time may do so, instead of having to make the choice between full-time work or full-time no work, or part-time work at a reduced rate of pay, reduced status and reduced job security. We're talking about flexible work schedules so that parents can be at home when the kids arrive at home.

We emphasize especially family-oriented industrial planning and development: so that when plants are established, locations are determined and housing is planned, consideration is given to the fact that employees have families and have to be concerned with how and where they can spend time as families. It should be kept in mind in planning the buildings, the apartments and residences that there will be children and parents living in these places. In short, we are asking for a family-oriented business and industrial policy in America. We speak also of actions to be taken in the realm of the mass media and the advertising industry.

We ask that urgent attention be paid to the creation of an entirely new kind of television programming, one which no longer casts the viewer in the role of a passive and isolated bystander, but which instead involves family members and neighbors in activities with each other. That is, involving children, adults, older kids, younger kids and grandparents in games, conversations and joint creative activity. And we assert that there is nothing inherent in television technology which precludes this kind of possibility.

The community, of course, is the family of families. And it is there, perhaps, more than anywhere else that the family needs support. Because the thesis I am presenting to you is that just as children cannot function unless they have healthy and human parents and caretakers to deal with them, so these caretakers, parents and all those who carry the responsibility for children in our society need the support of the community and of the society in order for them to be able to function effectively in their roles. It is not the family that's breaking down, it is not the staff of people engaged in work with children that is breaking down, it is the support in the society for the family and for those who are faced with the responsibility and the delight of raising a new generation of human beings that is being withdrawn.

There are many other measures we are considering. I will mention one or two, in relation to the schools. We point out the sterility of courses in parent education for junior and senior high school, where there are no children in evidence. We suggest that preschool programs and Head Start centers be located in or near school programs, that school curricula utilize these as learning opportunities and opportunities for responsibility. Then the older children get some notion of what a child is like, what a child's needs are and how much fun a child is, so we do not have a generation of young people who don't discover what a child is until they have one.

These are new kinds of suggestions. They bring difficulties, but they also bring promise. They bring a very important element into the lives of older school-aged children. If one looks at the problems of human development cross-culturally, as I've been privileged to during this past decade, one is struck by the fact that American society is characterized by the inutility of children. We in our country do not give children anything really important to do. We give them duties, not responsibilities. And yet, there are things they could do if we but looked around.

One of the most important responsibilities that the older child can have, both as an individual and as a group, is responsibility for the young. Evidence indicates that older children are very effective as models, as re-inforcers, as praise-givers to the young, but in our age-segregated society such opportunities are seldom given.

Oldsters Offer Vital Assistance

Similarly, there is another group for whom children can be a delight and a genuine help, and who in turn can serve a very important purpose in providing a humanizing experience for children. I refer to older people. The pleasure which a child gets from recognizing how much he's appreciated by an older person is a special kind of pleasure on both sides.

It's perhaps paradoxical that in our discussions and preparation for the White House Conference on a forum which is to deal with children and families, we make very few recommendations to families. Our position is essentially this: that given sun, soil, air and water, a plant does not need to be told how to grow. If America's parents, and those bearing the responsibility for the upbringing of the young, are given the place and the power and the prestige, to enable them to function as guides, companions and sources of love and discipline for children; and to have a decisive role in determining the environments and programs in which our children live and grow, the great majority of these parents and these professional workers will be able to take full advantage of that opportunity to enhance the quality of life both for children and for the nation.

There is but one caution to be borne in mind. The crucial factor, of course, is not how much time is spent with a child, but how the time is spent. A child learns, he becomes human, primarily through participation in challenging activity with those whom he loves and admires. It is the example, challenge and reinforcement provided by people who care that enable a child to develop both his ability and his identity. An everyday example of the operation of this principle is the mother who daily talks with her young child, and usually without thinking much about it, responds more warmly when he uses new words or expressions or new motions. And as he does so, she gradually introduces new and more complex activities in her activity with the child.

So it is this way, in work and in play with children: in games, in projects, in shared responsibilities with parents, adults and older children, that the child develops the skills, motives and qualities of character that enable him to live a life that is gratifying both to himself and to those around him. But this can happen only in a society that lets it happen, and makes it happen, a society in which the needs of families and children become a primary concern, not merely of special organizations and interest groups, but of all the major institutions—government, industry, business, mass media, communities, neighborhoods and individual citizens.

It is the priorities that they set that will determine our children's present and America's future. (2)

Early childhood education may soon be assigned an ever enlarging role in the raising of young children; in fact, teachers of young children may well become potent models of adult behavior. "Not only must she herself function as a motivating model, but *it becomes her responsibility to seek out, organize, develop, and coordinate the activities of other appropriate models and reinforcing agents both within the classroom and outside.*" (1:154) Bronfenbrenner adds: "He must know how to discover, recruit, and utilize individuals and groups outside of school as major adjuncts to the educational process." (1:155) What kinds of values will be perpetuated? How will these values be decided in an age when change occurs so swiftly? This challenge is a formidable one — one that can and must be met anew by both younger and older generations of early educators and parents.

References to Part 10

1. Bronfenbrenner, Urie, *Two Worlds of Childhood: U.S. and U.S.S.R.* (New York: Russel Sage Foundation, 1970).

2. _____, "Who Cares for America's Children?", *Young Children*, 26, no. 3 (January 1971): 157–163. Reproduced with permission from *Young Children*, vol. 26, no. 3, January 1971. Copyright © 1971, National Association for the Education of Young Children, 1834 Connecticut Ave., N. W., Washington, D.C. 20009.

Appendix

**What the Open-Air
Nursery School Is**

Margaret McMillan

No great party has as yet taken the Cause of the Children much to heart. Busy as any party always is, it has had no time to spare for it, and this "busy-ness" — which in itself is no great good thing, for the Devil is busier, we are assured, than anyone else — has brought us to the twentieth century of the Christian era, when in the vanguard nation of the world, the British Empire, there is a percentage of eighty children rickety at the age of two; that is to say: in the poorer quarters about four-fifths of the whole people are damaged for life long before they are old enough to go to school.

The fact would, one might think, give us all pause, startle us, electrify us, make us stand up in horror, and send us breathless into the world to change it all at any cost. It would make, one might suppose, every candidate at every election vow himself to a campaign that would change it all within a year. Every new M.P. would be (one might swear) a new captain in this army. The Press would flame and thunder.

A vain thought! A thousand objects claim the very close attention of the best people in the realm, so that — no! not the cry — rather the silent lapse of the children into lifelong misery and weakness does not touch them.

Five years ago there was a stirring, a doubtful, wondering, "Are you not astonished-to-be-here" kind of movement to put 1,500 London children into Open-air Nursery Schools, and see what would come of it. It was sanctioned if not led by Moderate members of the Children's Care Committee of the L.C.C., who, in justice be it said, did spend £2,300 in extending one existing Open-air Nursery School in this or the following year. The Estimates had provided, however, for an expenditure of £25,000 on this new departure in Education; and thus furnished with mandate and with money four or five members of the L.C.C. set forth in big cars to scour the poorest areas of the great city for open-air sites — a doctor, a clerk going with them to take notes and bear witness.

The Open-air School is on the Statute Book. It was put there in 1918. It is as yet a dead letter.

Dark Slums Where Babies Creep

Down into darkest London did this group of people go — to Bow, to Whitechapel, into the darker parts of St. Pancras, and into the black, stony, roaring wilderness that skirts all Dockland, and makes it a strange dark fringe for the ever-changeful beauty of "sweet Thames." They saw the dark slums where "England's babies are creeping," the dank and noisy hovels where they sleep in coiled heaps; the filthy lanes where they play above the noisome

---

Margaret McMillan, *What the Open-Air Nursery School Is*, 1929, Labour Party Pamphlet, Labour Party, London.

drains, and the great, terrible streets, whose close and heavy traffic they brave, and from which they escape — but not always — as by a miracle. This little group of people saw all that, but they could not, though they looked well, see many places where a site could be found for the planting of a new child-garden. To be sure, the vile rookeries could be pulled down, but where could the sleepers in the "warrens" find shelter? So new is the demand for a decent life that former generations have built over every spot of earth in some of the poorer districts. This is not true of all our slums. Far from true. No place is so unexpected as some of the inner parts of a bad London slum. There are places, such as Deptford (where a sturdy race of seacraft-makers once lived), that have even to-day great tracts of land stretching far behind the roaring streets. Few have seen them. Fewer have looked for them.

The deputation found, in spite of all, some very fair sites. They were all cleared, like oases in the midst of a great rising wall of factories, huge ware-houses, new tenements, and crazy flats. They were all close to slums — hideous slums. These slums teemed with little children. In one house there were over thirty children. The members of the Care Committee, though rather doubtful, and hesitating like a child before a breaking wave, yet made up its mind to have a report, and to remind the Council of the existence of that £25,000. True, the owners of some of the sites made things difficult, quoted old documents, and put up prices. No matter. The report got written. It was sent up to the Education Committee. It reached the full Council. The new proposal was to go forward like a craft in a storm, when crash! The Geddes Axe fell on it. In November, 1921, came a Circular from the Board of Education to declare that the money could not be spent.

The Pioneer Nursery School

The Circular, however, was too late to wreck or hold back for ever the hope of the children. Already the first great worker for the Open-air Nursery School had laid down her life in Deptford. My dear sister, Rachel McMillan, died in 1917, having endured every kind of trial and run every risk to found a sample school of the new order. The school now called by her name was then, thanks to her courage and great insight, fairly at work. She died stricken down at the close of a sad winter. Thus the full price was paid that made the future of the whole movement safe. Five months after her tragic death, on August 3, 1917, Mr. Fisher opened an extension and called the school by her name. In 1918 he placed the Open-air Nursery School on the Statute Book. The L.C.C. gave its first grant to the Rachel McMillan Nursery School in 1920, and now, ere the Geddes Axe had fallen, it had voted about £3,000 for the further extension of this school. The new build-ings were in train, and the L.C.C., thanks largely to the help of Sir Cyril Jackson, were ready to commit themselves (against the advice of some of their chief officers) to the experiment of getting hundreds of little children together in a very new kind of school. It is now possible, years of work having passed, and reports having been made, to give the findings of this school. If I quote from the reports of only one school, it is because there is, alas! no other large Open-air Nursery School in existence.

To begin with, then, you can take a large number of little children together — say three to four hundred — and put them into such conditions that they will throw off their diseases like old garments and step forth in beauty, often in wonderful beauty. For children are made so that if they are well, and well cared for, they are very fair to look on, beautiful, arresting to the eye and heart. You may look all over the world and not meet such a pretty sight as this Open-air Nursery School. On this fair day in June we are in a wide and gay garden, with grass plots and noble trees, with arches covered with roses, and beds full of wandering scent, and soft radiance of flowers.

Children Playing in the Sun

Yet these are only a setting, and a *dim* setting, for the thing that is placed
here. Lo! on the grass twenty girls and boys who have been for years in the
Nursery School, acting and speaking with the charm of real artists. Of these
we must not speak here. They are another story. But see the groups of three-
and four-year-olds round the aviary, or at the rabbit hutches, or calling the
pigeons. Hark! the little two-year-olds, full of life's most vivid joys, patter-
ing warm-footed over the sunny floors or cloistered paths of the shelters.
Look at their silky hair, their sturdy limbs, and radiant eyes. And now try
to remember that you are not in a West-End garden or a manor house
pleasaunce!

No. You are in a *slum*.

The slum is all around you here like a sea. These children were born here—
in stained and foul warrens. Not all, to be sure. For here there are men
and women who make a fair home out of very poor rooms. But not many
people have such great powers. Many sink. In a dark home was born and
lived that child you see here, a boy, still fragile (though no longer deformed
or sullen), and who, when he was found, had been tethered to his bed like
an ox, while his mother went out to earn the bottle of milk she left beside
him. Certainly there shall be no telling of such stories here. They can be
found in any poor dockland or slumland street. Miss Stevinson has written
a book [*The Open-Air Nursery School*] that gives pictures of this world.

Neither shall I describe our shelters, as has been done already a hundred
times. They were designed by one who loved children, and understood their
needs and longings, and this is expressed in everything — in the low fencing
and little gates, the open gables through which the screen of June leaves
rustle, the shadowy covered way where there is always shelter from heat and
rain. It is shown in the warm indoor bath-room, in the wide running space
secured by the oblong form of building, and on the frescoed walls and painted
arches. Tender as the touch of the great Italian artist. In spite of its great
humility of means, love welling from the same deep Fountain of Love as gave
us all our most beautiful buildings is present here. Yes, this is beautiful!
Everyone feels it who comes here. Especially artists — and mothers.

From Schools Like Prisons

Compare it with the forbidding, heavy wall of our prison-like schools and
its hard asphalt, its shadeless space and iron gates! You will no longer doubt
that these last buildings and grounds have another origin. They were an
outburst of the impulse that gave us, not lovely churches, but hideous
factories and satanic mills. My sister Rachel designed the first shelter. It
cost £124, exclusive of the plumbing (which cost nearly £200). The form and
aspect, the whole plan, in fact, has not been improved on by any later building.

The nursery-school day begins not at nine, but at eight o'clock in the morning, and the first hour of the day is the busiest of all, as indeed it ought to be.
Picture one of our 300 mothers turning in at our gate on a bitter January
morning with a toddler in her arms and a four- or three-year-old at her side.
She has not come far, for the children live round our teeming doors and
closeby streets, but this group and others are pinched, cold, and perhaps even
sleepy. Here is welcome: kind hands are stretched out to receive them here.
Young girls of eighteen to twenty-five race down the covered ways eager to
welcome their babies. Grey is the sky. But the camp is bright with blue and
pink overalls and young, rosy faces. The little ones go to their own shelters,
their own indoor bath-room, where is an abundance of hot as well as cold
water. They are quickly overhauled, washed, dressed warmly, but with few
garments, and made entirely comfortable, as every child should be, and is, in
any good private nursery. At nine all sit down to breakfast, and at 9.30 no
one cares a rap either for Jack Frost or his brother, Snow. The toddlers'
camp rings with laughter and the tripping of little feet.

School in the Garden

On the tables and along the walls there is apparatus of varied kinds, coloured discs, coloured balls, insets, colour scales, bright letters to be fitted, pictures and picture-books. Outside there are sliding boards, steps, and rib stalls. All the best apparatus is in the garden. We lose some of it in winter, but not all. The two-year-old works hard. He and she have so much to learn. It is hard to stop him. At twelve there is a two-course dinner, with two-year-old monitors serving, and at 12.30 350 little ones are fast asleep.

There are few days in the year when the Sun God does not come for a while, and always, winter or summer, morning or afternoon, we let Him bring His great healing and joy to our children. That is their birthright. Here it is restored to them. All the afternoon, and on fine mornings, they are playing, working, sleeping where He can find them. This is the great source of our rapid cures. Within a year all our cases of rickets are cured. There is no more anæmia. No more dark threat of death, and of something worse than death. At 5 to 5.30, after the evening meal, a long line of mothers and elder sisters come up the cloisters to fetch the children. With what joy and wonder does many a woman clasp her child, noting the glow of health in cheek and eye, and the passing of every sad and stubborn trace of long weakness and misery.

"No trace of rickets after one year's attendance at this school." This report is open for the public to note if the public wishes to note such things. The public is not much interested as yet, else there would be no local authority in this country who would dare to hesitate in replacing the infant school of to-day by the open-air nursery school of to-morrow.

Revolution in Education

How Carlyle would have thundered over these eighty percent rickety children. He did not know of them, for even in his day the most startling facts lay safe, unearthed, like buried powder under mighty guns. Yet this fact, so terrible and yet so near the surface of things that a bold effort would hunt it out of existence in a year, is, nevertheless, not so simple as it appears. It is related not merely to a part, but to the whole of our educational system. Thus when we want to deal with it we cannot fall back on precedent. We cannot say, "We will build as for the infant school of to-day," for that kind of building is out of date; or, "We shall staff as for the elementary school, but with smaller classes," for that kind of staffing will not do, however we reduce our "classes" (as we call them). In order to do our duty to all rickety toddlers we must think not only of our infant schools but of our secondary schools; and not of our elementary schools alone, but of our colleges and our college system. I hope to write of every one of these places of learning — but not here.

Staffing

The student of to-day loves beauty perhaps more than girls of earlier days. But this love is linked now in some to another. It meets and merges in the rising hope of youth — the hope and desire to find Life's real meaning and mission. She actually wants to find her life work, and to wade right into the middle of her problems as a way of getting to grips with them while she is young. "These sad, anæmic, nurseless little children," she says in her own way, "I am going to deal with them, to cure them, to save them, to give them the fine things that the well-to-do child has already as its right. Not mere lessons, not mere play even, and dismissal into I know not what at 12 o'clock and 4."

In the teacher of yesterday this bold and soaring hope was not born. Or if she knew it she knew it as quenched in the rising, she could not guarantee even the minimum of nurture. It is not quenched now — in all. Our students work two or three hours per day — under trained teachers, and are trained in a new way.

Learning to Teach

Strange! It no sooner becomes clear that they want to save as well as teach than the whole thing brightens. She may still live among rustling trees and riotous roses. These will grow and bloom in any child-garden in the heart of any slum! Neither must we give up scholarship! No! A girl does the work of a nurse for three hours daily in her first terms, just as a doctor works, or as any apprentice to a skilled trade must work. What she learns in the bath-room and nursery gives life and meaning to all her study in psychology, and lends her mind a grasp and vision of reality that the student of yesterday could not reach. There is something one cannot learn from books. Stephenson learned it when he oiled his own engines. We begin to understand that teachers, too, learn only by work. Everyone talks about the "parrot-learning," that takes account only of exams. Here is the real work, the deep, great, human interest that will sweep any girl into higher reaches than the mere desire for poor success can win. And the authorities know it! The Board of Education now pays the same grant for students taking their student course of the first year in a Nursery Training Centre as it pays to the older colleges. We owe much to the Home and Colonial College, which became our first colleague. It takes the Rachel McMillan students for the second year of their Board of Education training courses. The Board of Education finds that this co-operation does not spoil the student's work, but that the student gains by the practical work. Large and stately colleges are not what is needed most to-day. No new college should be too large or take in more than, say, 100. And these new small colleges should be built in the heart of the crowded quarters of the cities — near the swarming streets, close to the homes and life of the children. We are going to build one now (thanks to Lady Astor, who guaranteed £10,000) and train for the country.

Vicarious Motherhood

Even these colleges will not be enough to fill the vast nurseries of the people (who hitherto have had no nurses but overworked, anxious, poor and often over-tired mothers). At the door wait thousands of girls who need not and will not enter the teachers' Trade Union or market, will *not* compete or undersell, but might work with the teacher, learn from her, and enrich even her student days by their friendship. Trades Unionism need not, and should not, cry out before it is threatened or hurt. Many girls do not want to be teachers. They want rather to be nurses, doctors, public health officers, or even mothers. They may be women anxious to serve better in homes or elsewhere. To them the teacher's post will not be given. We have at the head of every Shelter only a trained teacher. It will be part of her work to train and teach those outside helpers. But to say (as some do) that the N. U. T. will not allow the girl from without to learn or to work, that is tyranny and folly also. For without this kind of help the new teacher will herself be helpless. She will have to go back to her classes of fifty or sixty, as the case may be, and let all nurture go again by the board.

Great love and active help has been won for the movement by our Nursery School children. It was the older children, the children who are above five-years-old, and have been through the Nursery School, and left it years ago, who have won the help of many people and the sympathy of other colleges. For these older children (our Camp children) are of striking beauty, and are, according to the Reports of L.C.C. inspectors and of Board of Education inspectors, also of striking intelligence and charm. They are a kind of first fruits of the new order. Plucked as it were in storm, dashed by heavy rain and doubtful weather, unsteady a little, perhaps, in some of their gains, bearing some faint trace of old scars and failures, but very fair, with a strange loveliness, a wistful and triumphant beauty. Having known them it was desired to know how they came to be what they are. The Open-air Nursery School made them. "Then let us make more," cried the Principal of one College. "Let us make so many that the world will be filled with lovely beings." For, after all, the aim of Education Colleges and even Parliament is just this — that the earth may be filled with lovely, happy, and wise people.

These dark, dread slums cannot be wiped out by the building of new houses. *New homes must be built.* Do we not know it well? But the new life that is to grow in the new home must be made ready, too. How can it be made ready? It must live *where it can grow.* What has damned our people in the past is only this — they could not grow. They had no nurseries.

Children Who Could Not Grow

Every slum can become a garden. Every slum child is a power-house of energy. Once given a chance of real growth, this Human Power, inspired by Higher Powers yet, can settle every kind of problem, financial and otherwise. It can change the very nature of the work that has to be done. It offers new duties to everyone — even to Ministers of Health and Labour. There was no money to grow it. The great, the awful blunder of yesterday is that the children were *not allowed to grow up.* They were spent in order that other kinds of wealth should be made and hoarded. And what folly it is even from the low standpoint of material output. For that is not anything like what it should be after all to-day. "But to fit people out like that and make them well, will be a great expense to start with," said a Voice. Why, no. The Open-air Nursery School costs less than the Infant School to-day. The comptroller cannot find out that it costs more than £11 15s. per annum to keep a child there. Even the zealous critic who reminds us that no rent is paid for a part of this school cannot make out his case. Full rent and rates are paid for 120 children who are not on this site at all, and eighty of these are over five years old. If, as we hope, a new shelter can soon be added, the average cost will fall below £11. In Dundee, the Glen Agnes Open-air Nursery School, for which Miss Mabel Brydie laid down her life, the jute worker mothers paid the whole cost of the school, save only the teachers' salaries. Our parents here give us £21 per week. This, an average of 1s. per week — half of the whole cost of the food.

The history of the Scottish pioneer school is much shorter than is the history of the Rachel McMillan Nursery and Training Centre. The latter was a long struggle. It is but four years since the Principal of the Scottish school ended her training at Deptford and began her work in Dundee. In two and a half years the bitter struggle was ended — she died in 1922, a victim to blood poisoning. Yet before she gave her life Mabel Brydie had sent her challenge (heard or unheard) throughout Scotland. Never while a child dies or lives there in a dark cellar, or a fetid yard, will that brave voice be quite silenced. For she not only made these wee Scottish bodies well, she uncovered the strength and valour of their souls. She visited these dens called homes. She told how babies lived and died, only by gas-light, without ever having perhaps seen the sun. She worked with all her failing powers to rouse people to a sense of what this means. She went to the School Board, talked to inspectors, and tried to enlist the people who move things in Dundee and in Scotland, worked and died. No Scotsman can ever read her pamphlet [*A Nursery School in Dundee*] without longing to join the war for new homes and nurseries in Scotland.

Such very precious children are they, too — the handful that is plucked like brands from the fire, typical of the many who are not gathered out of the burning, but are left there. These were not, I say, as English children, fair as the wild rose in the June hedge-rows. They were little Scots, dour and keen to do their own work. "I can do it masel," the refrain always, when help was offered. Looking out at the new world, beyond the gas-lit cavern, with growing astonishment, one little boy, taken for the first time into an omnibus, gazes at the faces of the passengers, with solemn and inquiring eyes. Not chained to work all day then! The world is not all mills and dark rooms. "Why is na everybody in the mills?" he asks in awe-struck tones. Another, having been taken away into the country, in sight of hills and sparkling sea and woodland, fixes great wondering dark eyes on his teacher, looks, but utters no word for a long time. Then, in low, hushed accents, asks a question, "Whaur does God bide?" says he. There are thousands of just such little people in the gas-lit dens of Dundee. Theirs, too, is the metaphysical brain that grapples early with big questions, as distinct from other types, equally precious, but different. If they were nursed, and fed, and washed, and loved, and went forth into the light (as the Nursery School would lead and feed them), they, too, would put forth their native power, would show themselves, like the silver thistles of their own rugged and lovely country — the thistles that are like no other flower of the field. But now they have the same look as the neglected child of any place wears — in Deptford, in Bradford, in Dundee. For misery has one face in early childhood, one dumb and hopeless aspect. In Scot or Saxon it is all the same.

Nurture for All

Neither the English nor the Scottish have yet set out to give nurture to all their children. They have asked for schools and for a certain amount of schooling. And Sir George Newman and others tell us what they have got as the result of fifty-four years' schooling. It is clear that they have got something, but this education, which is now free to all, is always kept down to a certain level; first, because the parents are for the most part too poor to let the children carry on at school long enough to achieve real victory; and also because, long before he goes to school, the child of the people is handicapped by the risks he has run and the losses that have befallen him in his earliest years. Poor children as well as rich children need nurture.

"Well! the mother can give it," cry many hard and careless voices. "If she stays at home she can do all that is needed." This is not true. She cannot do all that is needed. Her well-to-do sister cannot do it. Neither does she attempt it. We are being asked every day to let our trained teacher-nurses go into wealth homes — homes that have every comfort and that are presided over by good mothers.

But we do not want to send them there. Neither do they wish to go. For they have heard the cry of the children and the mothers that have no helpers.

Equality does not begin in the school. It begins in the nursery. The word has gone forth: "Nurture for all." However that voice may be overborne, however long it may be ignored, it will break forth again like a strain of heavenly music. For this the battle-cry of the great lovers who fell; who fell when their work was done.

Bibliography

The Nursery School. Margaret McMillan. (Dent. 7s. 6d. net.)
The Open-Air Nursery School. E. Stevinson. (Dent. 2s. 6d. net.)
Education through the Imagination. Margaret McMillan. (Allen and Unwin.)
The Camp School. Margaret McMillan. (Allen and Unwin.)
Early Childhood. Margaret McMillan. (Allen and Unwin.)
A Nursery School in Dundee. Mabel Brydie. (Dent. 3d.)

from **The Fundamental Needs
of the Child**

Lawrence K. Frank

Every society and every generation uses children for its own purposes. It is significant that today we are beginning to speak of the needs of the child as entitled to consideration in his nurture and education or even as the controlling factor in child care. Contrast this emerging conception of the child's nature and needs with the practices all over the world, among so-called civilized people and so-called primitive people, in which the nurture and education of children are dictated by religious, ethical, and moral ideas, by political and economic requirements, by social class lines, indeed by an extraordinary variety of ideas and purposes all more or less remote from the child himself. The children in all these cultures are molded by the dominant ideas and beliefs and the group purposes into greater or less conformity in which they may sacrifice much or little.

Consider also the variety of practices in regard to the physical make-up or form of children. Among certain Indian tribes, the infant's head is flattened to a board. Among certain African tribes, the lips or ears may be stretched or the neck encased in coils of brass. Every one is familiar with the ancient Chinese practice of binding of the feet of female infants. As children grow older, many peoples have puberty rites involving tattooing, skin incisions, various forms of mutilation of the male and female genitals, and the inculcation of rigidly prescribed motor patterns of action that may involve anatomical deformities. The catalogue of practices that deform, distort, or otherwise manipulate the physical structure is endless, but all are regarded by those who use them as essentially necessary to make over the child into the image prescribed by the culture as the only right form for a man or a woman. In their cultural context these practices and beliefs may be purposeful and valid.

Not only is the physical structure of the child made over into the patterns of the culture, but so are the physiological functions, as we see in the diverse standards imposed upon the young child by different societies. In the matter of nutrition, for example, every group teaches the child to like the food of its traditional choice, which means developing an appetite for an incredible array of foodstuffs, or supposed foodstuffs, and abhorring other foodstuffs of equal or greater nutritive value. Many of these food choices represent a wise, economical use of available animal and vegetable resources, while others are obviously dictated by various beliefs in sympathetic magic, by rigid taboos, and by religious convictions that have little or no relation to the nutritional requirements of the growing child or even of the adult. Every society, again, imposes some kind of training upon children with respect to elimination. In some cultures the requirements are minimal, but in others they may be so severe and so rigorously imposed upon the very young child as to create lifelong impairment of physiological efficiency. Even breathing, in some cultures, is subject to special training, and sleeping patterns, peculiar to each group, are inculcated at an early age.

It is safe to say that most of these traditional patterns of child training and nurture derive from ideas and beliefs and strong convictions that have little or no relevance to the immediate needs of the child. Civilized man in many cases has survived *despite,* not because of, these methods of child care.. . .

Curious as are these practices of physical and physiological training, the variety of practices in psychological training are even more astonishing, since here we find methods and procedures for bringing up children in the most fantastic, distorted patterns of conduct and feeling. The belief in using

From Lawrence Frank, "The Fundamental Needs of the Child," *Mental Hygiene*, vol. 22, July 1938, pp. 353-379. Copyright 1938, by permission of the National Association for Mental Health.

the child for social purposes is revealed here more convincingly than in the realm of physical care, where the organic limits of deformation impose some restraint; whereas in the area of conduct and belief there apparently are no limits to the grotesque, the cruel and brutal, the diabolical ingenuity of man in warping and twisting human nature to cultural patterns which originally may have been useful or even desirable, but which have become rigid and perverse.

When we reflect upon these various beliefs and practices that are imposed upon the child to make him conform to group-sanctioned patterns, we can begin to understand how extraordinarily significant it is today that we are discussing the needs of the child as a basis for his nurture and education. We can also see how questions of education and training become the focus of bitter conflicts, as contending factions in a society struggle to direct the nurture of children in order to control the group life. As we meet today to discuss programs of education for the young child in the home and in the nursery school, we are not concerned merely with questions of technique and procedures, with this or that pedagogical device; we are faced with the major issues of the future of our culture and the direction of our whole social, economic, and political life, since an effective program of early child-hood education based upon the needs of the child will inevitably change our society far more effectively than any legislation or other social action.

We must, therefore, be humble and deliberate in our discussion, not only because of the gravity of the larger social issues involved, but also because we know so little about the needs of the child. It is safe to say that whenever you hear any person or group speaking with strong convictions about specific needs of the child and how to meet them, that person or group is probably sustained more by emotional fervor and loyalty to cultural traditions than by dependable knowledge of actual children.

Any one who is prepared seriously and fairly to consider the question of the child's needs must begin by trying to be honest about his or her own personality bias and beliefs, emotional attitudes, religious loyalties, and social-economic and political leanings, because these often unconscious feelings and values play so large a role in our attitudes toward the child and in our willingness to recognize some of his needs or our strong denial of them. Probably the most general statement that we can make about the child's needs is that he should be protected from distortions, from unnecessary deprivations and exploitations by adults — parents, teachers and nurses, physicians, psychologists, and others engaged in dealing with children.

It is difficult to realize the extent of these often subtle coercions and pressures exerted upon the child.

. . . It is not without reason, therefore, that we stress this primary and inalienable need of the child to be accepted as a unique individual . . . Every child suffers to a greater or less extent from this denial of his own personal, temperamental individuality, because even the most emancipated parents are not wholly free from the desire to see their children conform to the images they have constructed. Moreover, every teacher has these partialities, often unconscious, which incline her toward one child and away from another. Further, the child himself is subject to the strong desire to be like the parents, however out of harmony with his own make-up such an identification may be. It is interesting to see how the recognition of individual differences is resisted even by professionally trained persons, such as teachers, who will accept the fact of such differences with respect to mental capacity, as shown by standardized mental tests, but deny it with respect to personality, temperament, physical maturity, and other obvious characeristics.

The infant, as he grows into childhood and youth, faces a series of life tasks that cannot be evaded or denied. The way in which he meets those life tasks and his attempts to master them give rise to the various needs for which we today believe his nurture and education should provide. It is obvious that we have only a fragmentary knowledge of those needs, since we have studied so briefly the process of growth and development and the life tasks presented by our culture. But it is highly significant, as we suggested earlier, that we are genuinely concerned with understanding child growth and development and are trying to discover the child's needs, as a basis for his education and nurture.

. . . The little child is frequently disturbed physiologically by emotional reactions such as anger, rage, and grief which clamor for expression or release in overt behavior. In a very real sense these physiological disturbances or upheavals seize control of the child and often impel him to act violently and destructively against things and people and even himself. One of the most important of life tasks for the young child is to learn how to manage these emotional reactions and thereby to free himself from this overwhelming experience. It is difficult for adults to conceive or to understand the panic that these emotional reactions may arouse in the child, who finds himself helplessly carried on a tide of feeling so strong that he cannot resist it unaided. If at the same time he meets with a violent response from adults, who strike him or forcibly restrain him, the emotional disturbance may be aggravated cumulatively until terminated by exhaustion. Such an experience teaches the child nothing constructive or helpful, and it may make him so afraid of himself that he begins to be anxious about this behavior and less and less prepared to meet the next provocation. Although the adult may forcibly control the child at the moment, what the child needs is help in controlling the emotional disturbance himself, so that, instead of a persistent conflict within the child between himself and his emotions, he can bring these emotional reactions into the pattern of his own living. The situation is in many respects like that in the case of hunger and elimination, where physiological processes are initially dominant, but are gradually transformed into regulated functional activities over which the individual has, as we say, control, because those functional processes are subject to the culturally sanctioned times, places, and objects.

In other words, the emotional reactions of the child are normal physiological functions that call for regulation and patterning, so that the child may be freed from their urgency and disturbance. They are not, as our tradition teaches, moral or ethical problems, and when handled as such, they only increase the child's guilt and resentment and serve to fixate him at that infantile level, as in toilet training when it is made a moral issue. Anger and rage, like fear, have had a great biological value in the past, but in group living they may, as persistent infantile reactions, seriously interfere with the individual's capacity for peaceful, cooperative adult living, just as persistent incontinence of feces will restrict an individual's activites.

The child, then, needs help in bringing his emotional responsiveness under regulation. Some children are more prone to anger and rage, others to fear and pain, so that each child requires highly individualized help in meeting his peculiar personal reactions. Unfortunately, we have little knowledge of how to provide this help in a constructive, rather than a repressive, manner, because we have treated the problems as moral issues, meeting them with threats, punishment, shame, and often equally violent emotional reactions.

. . . Little children need constant reassurance and simplified enlightenment on questions of sex and procreation if they are to escape prolonged anxiety and possible lifelong unhappiness. In so far as nursery schools and other schools can provide children with an understanding and wholesome attitude here, we can see how the education of children may change our whole culture, for undoubtedly our culture is warped and distorted by our inherited traditions of uncleanliness, obscenity, and wickedness in regard to sex. We cannot expect to dispose of the child's curiosity and concern by purely biological explanations, since, as Otto Rank has pointed out, adults themselves are not satisfied with merely biological answers. Moreover, the exigent questions about sex, for the child and the adult, are not concerned with gestation, but with the uses of sex in living, in feeling, in intimacy and affection.

. . . As we gain more insight into the process of personality development and realize how crucial these preschool sex interests and adjustments are for the subsequent adult life, we can and must work out nursery school procedures designed to help the child to meet these tasks with courage and happiness, free from the distortions and anxieties that are now so prevalent, able and ready to give and to receive affection.

Another life task confronting the child is that of learning to recognize and observe the inviolabilities that every culture establishes with respect to objects, persons, places, and times. We are so accustomed to think of private property in things and animals, of the sanctity of the physical person of individuals, of the great number of special places and days consecrated to particular purposes which must not be profaned, that we fail to realize that private property and the sanctity of the person are not entities or mysterious powers, but learned ways of behaving toward things and persons, taught to children often with severe penalties for evasion or violation. These lessons as to the inviolability of things and persons are painfully learned by the young child as he begins to explore the world about him, seeking occasions for satisfying his needs and expressing his impulses, and being more or less forcibly restrained, rebuffed, and frustrated. He finds that everything and every person is protected by an invisible barrier of inviolability ("don't touch," "don't look," "don't eat," "don't go near," "don't handle") which he may not disregard except in duly sanctioned ways, such as buying and selling and making contracts or agreements. He must also learn to uphold the inviolability of his own person and property.

. . . Besides learning to inhibit his responses to things and persons who are inviolable, the child must also learn to perform those acts which his parents insist upon as the required actions in various situations. These actions include the traditional manners and customs, the etiquette and the moral duties which the parents especially cherish and respect and which they are compelled to teach their children as the essentials of life. These lessons are difficult for the child because, like the inviolability of things and persons, the required conduct has no natural, biological relation to the situations in which it is demanded of the child. He must, therefore, be repeatedly shown what to do, and prompted and compelled to do it, with a greater or less amount of verbal and often physical punishment. The outcome of this training is the establishment of more or less automatic conduct, according to the required pattern, which is always a variation, peculiar to the family, of the general socially approved pattern.

As in the teaching of inviolabilities, parental instruction as to the performance of these required actions involves the exercise of authority, often by the father, who rarely has as close and affectionate a tie with the child as the mother and who, therefore, relies more upon coercion to exact obedience, while the mother relies upon the child's desire for her love and approval. Thus the child experiences authority and coercion for the first time, and only too often it is administered severely and arbitrarily, arousing in the child fear, resentment, and hostility toward the father.

. . . Now if the young child experiences authority for the first time as coercive, severe, and brutal, as something that arouses fear, anxiety, and resentment, his socialization will be compromised. He cannot calmly and gracefully accept that which is expected or demanded, performing acts or refraining from responses, but rather he will feel tension, will resent the parental authority, and will develop a persistent hostility toward the parents, especially the father, and all others who attempt to direct his conduct.

Instead, then, of accepting the inviolabilities or the required performances, the child who has been thus treated will fail to build those conduct patterns into an integrated whole, in which his behavior and his personality are at one. He may outwardly conform to what is demanded or prohibited, but only because of fear and anxiety. The learned conduct, essential to group life, is never assimilated or made wholly automatic, and so the child becomes preoccupied with the conflict between what he must do and not do and what he feels. Often he releases his feelings in misbehavior that is difficult to understand, for it gives the child nothing of value or advantage and usually is wholly incongruous with the situation.

. . . Can we devise experiences in the nursery school that will enable the child to accept authority and to find freedom from the emotional conflicts and resentments that his previous experiences have engendered? The need is for ways of inculcating acceptance of authority without aggravating the already serious conflicts so many children have when they come to nursery schools; and this calls for reformulation of the problem . . . so that the authority will be transferred to the situation and divested of the personal element that evokes the resentment and conflict. Paradoxically, this depersonalization of authority depends upon a personal relation of the parent to the child wherein the exercise of authority is benevolent and helpful, not antagonistic and repressive.

This brings us to another life task of the child, who must create for himself, out of his experiences and the teaching he receives, an image of himself and of the kind of person he would like to be. This ideal of self will embody all the feelings of inadequacy and guilt that the child has experienced and must somehow express. Such feelings may lead to aspirations for constructive achievement, to altruistic, helpful conduct, and to other forms of expiation and atonement which, if not exaggerated into a neurotic drive for perfection, make the individual personality into a friendly, cooperative adult. Or they may lead to hostility and aggression, which take the form of intense competitive striving or coercive conduct; to delinquency, so that the individual striving may obtain punishment; or to mental disorders, in which the individual punishes himself. All these adjustment patterns are exhibited in childhood, when the child already has adopted his "style of life," and if we had enough insight and understanding, these adjustments might be treated in the nursery school group in such a way as to mitigate, if not actually to revise, these personality trends. No one can prescribe a general method or procedure for all children, but undoubtedly the largest single element in the situation is the kind and extent of affectionate personal interest shown by an adult toward the child, who thereby may find much needed help toward a constructive, not a self-defeating, ideal of self. The process of identification, wherein the child strives to emulate an admired and loved adult, makes the teacher-child relationship of crucial importance.

. . . One of the most important problems facing students of personality today is this question whether hostility and aggression are inborn characteristics of all individuals or whether they are the reactions of individuals who, as infants and preschool children, were deprived of needed love and affection and security and so were driven by the unrelieved pressure for socialization to hostile, aggressive, destructive conduct. This question is of the utmost importance socially and educationally, since the answer involves the future of our society and of the civilized world. If man is innately hostile and aggressive, prone to destructive antagonisms and rivalries, then the prospects for a better, more humanly desirable society are not very bright. If human nature, as theological tradition and many of our contemporary students of personality tell us, is born wicked, sinful, and hostile and must be forced to be social, cooperative, and altruistic, the task of education is essentially a coercive one, that of curbing the hostility, of teaching individuals to "handle their aggressiveness." If, on the other hand, human nature is essentially plastic, subject to educational direction toward friendliness, cooperativeness, gentleness, and genuine group or social activity, then the task of education is to prevent the early distortions and unnecessary deprivations that arouse resentment and aggressiveness, by providing as much affectionate reassurance and toleration of individual, temperamental differences as possible for the children who have been ill-treated or neglected by their parents. Here preschool education has an immense opportunity and responsibility for the future course of our culture.

But here we must ask whether we know enough now to meet this issue of resentment and aggressiveness wisely. The policy of restraint and repression in many schools may prevent fighting and disorder for the moment, but it does nothing to release the child from the inner tensions and frustrations of which his aggressions are but symptoms. Perhaps we have to face a mixed answer to the earlier question and realize that tensions and resentment are probably present in all children in the early years, as a necessary consequence of the process of deprivations and coercions they undergo during socialization. . . . No permanent good is achieved by a repressive policy, nor is any constructive end attained by permitting the children to fight it out, with the risk of damage to all concerned. What is needed is an imaginative, insightful handling of conflicts and aggressions on an experimental basis, addressed to the underlying anxiety, guilt, and frustrations and the need for reassurance and security. There is also need for methods of handling situations in such a way that the initial hostility or aggression of the child may be rendered unnecessary by opportunities for friendly, helpful responses. Many children do not know how to act cooperately and need the skillful guidance of an adult to encourage them in friendly conduct and sympathetic actions.

This brings us to the exigent question of freedom and self-expression, over which there has been so much controversy and often hasty action. It may help us to obtain some perspective on this question if we will remember again that the child faces a series of unavoidable life tasks, including the persistent problem of how to get along in an organized group life. To the young child the world around him is indeed precarious and ambiguous. He faces a natural world often dangerous and always puzzling even to adults; his own organism, with its many functions and needs which must conform to parental and social patterning; obscure, often unconscious, impulses that impel him to actions that frequently he cannot understand, and that others usually resent, rebuke, and often retaliate for; a social or cultural world organized into patterns of behavior and regulated by symbols, such as language, that are subtly differentiated and variable; a constellation of human relationships, in the immediate family, the wider kinship group, the neighborhood, and the school, among which he must find personality fulfillment and security despite the capricious and disparate character of all these impinging personalities; and finally an immense body of tradition and folklore, knowledge, skills, and play.

Faced with such a welter of confusing, conflicting adjustments, the young child desperately needs the security of stable, persistently uniform situations, of dependable human relations, and of endless patience and tolerance. The frequent cry against any repression of the child involves a confusion that is often tragic for the child. Every culture involves deprivations and repression, the patterning and regulation of physiological functions and human behavior, which, if wisely handled, are only redirections and modulations of impulses. The young child especially needs a wisely administered regulation or direction because he cannot sustain the immense burden of making individual decisions on all the aspects of life and of learning unaided to manage his impulses. Few adults can do this, as we see in the overwhelming need for guidance, for precepts, for legal, ethical, and religious direction. Moreover, the regularization of hunger and elimination and the respecting of the inviolabilities leaves the individual free for other activities and interests that would not be possible if he were continually driven by hunger, beset by impulses to elimination, and at the mercy of every provocative personal contact or sexual stimulus. These learned patterns and repressions are the chief factors in man's ability to go beyond a purely organic existence. It is not the ordering of life that damages the child, but the distortion, the fears, anxieties, and permanent frustrations and inhibitions that parental and educational practices unnecessarily inflict upon the child in the process of establishing these socially and individually necessary repressions.

It is also the confusion and anxiety and insecurity of capricious, vacillating teaching that damages the personality in search of something stable and constant to build upon. Children love order, regularity, repetition of the same pattern endlessly, and they need consistent adult guidance and help in learning these patterns of what is essential to their adult life and social living. But they do not need, nor can they safely endure, the fears, the anxieties, the feelings of inadequacy and of guilt that so many parents and teachers instill during this socialization process. Indeed, fear seems to be the chief psychological instrument in early child-rearing—either the arousal of fears by cruel and coercive treatment or the inculcation of fears of experience, of people, of living, which cripple the child for life. Fear, and the resentment or hostility it often generates, are indeed the major emotional drives in our social life and give rise to much unsocial and antisocial behavior. What the child needs, but seldom receives, is a clearcut definition of the situation and of the conduct appropriate therein, so that he can and will learn what conduct is permitted and what is not permitted wihout the emotional disturbances he now experiences during these lessons. Practically, this means that the teaching by parents and teachers should stress the desirability or undesirability of the action without imputing blame to the child, so that instead of the usual admonishment, "You are a bad, naughty boy" the statement should be, "That action is not desirable or not kind, not generous or not permissible, and I don't like it." The important difference is in the personal imputation of guilt and the emotional disturbance it creates in the child.

... This question of socialization of the child without distortion and emotional disturbances must be seen in the light of the great individual differences among children in intelligence, temperament, rate of maturation, and need of reassurance, so that each child may be treated individually. The professional urge to standardize, to routinize, to substitute academic training for sympathetic interest and insights into children and to look for uniformities and generalizations that will save thinking, all must be critically reeaxamined by nursery school educators who are aware of these large social responsibilities. Especially is there a need for questioning the well-established principle that nursery school teachers should be impersonal and should repress all affective responses to and from children. This principle came into vogue in the 1920's when behavioristic theories of child-rearing were dominant. The ideal of education was seen as that of almost complete emotional anesthesia and continually rational conduct, which is the ideal of the neurotic who is afraid of life and is seeking to suppress all feelings, of which he is fearful. As we realize how much the child is in need—as indeed all adults are also—of warm personal, human relations, of affectionate interest and real concern, and of opportunities to give and receive affection and to *feel*, we must challenge this old principle as directly contrary to the deepest need of the child and as destructive of human values, which can be preserved only by sensitivity and feeling tones toward people and situations.

Here it is necessary to ask why are we so afraid to recognize that the child needs mothering, not only at home, but in the nursery school, and that nursery school teachers, by the very nature of their work, must be mother surrogates, ready and capable of giving affection and tenderness and warm emotional response to the children and of accepting them from the children. Is it because mothering does not seem scientific that we have tried to exclude it from the nursery schools or because— and I say this is no critical spirit, but as a statement based upon the actual situation—so many of those in nursery school education are unmarried and childless and have unconsciously projected their own personal life adjustment into the training of nursery school teachers? When we reflect upon the number of children in all classes of society who are raised by fear, terror, punishment, and other sadistic methods, with little or no experience of love and affection, we may well ask whether mothering (not smothering) may not be the most important service the nursery school can render to little children. Mothering does not mean babying or pampering, but rather giving a feeling of being liked and wanted, of belonging to some one who cares, and of being guided in the conduct of life with benevolent interest and confidence.

Dr. David Levy, a year or so ago, told this story at a meeting of the American Orthopsychiatric Association. He said that the social workers in the Bureau of Child Guidance were having unusually successful results with problem children, just because they were being maternal to these boys and girls so frequently denied real mothering. But they gave up this procedure because, said he, it did not seem scientific and was so hard to record! Perhaps if the nursery school teacher were to consider her function as not only educational, but clinical, it might be easier to accept what the psychotherapeutic clinician accepts—namely, the role of parent surrogate, who gives the child individual, personal interest and attention and tries to help that child work out a design for living by providing direction and deprivation, but always with interest and helpful concern.

Finally, we must look at the question of socialization in the light of the cultural changes through which we are now living, which are bringing about the destruction of so many of our traditional ideas, beliefs, and older certainties. The men and women of tomorrow will have to live in a shifting, uncertain world, of rapidly changing ideas and conceptions, with few or no absolutes or certainties. What is to guide their lives, to help them find fulfillment and a design for living sanely, wholesomely, and cooperatively? Probably no previous generation has had to face such acute personal problems without help from religion, custom, and tradition. Either they will demand an authoritarian state because they cannot endure uncertainty or tolerate the destructive hostility and aggressions of unhappy individuals, or they will learn to seek in constructive work and recreative play, in the warm human relations of marriage, parenthood ,and the family, a way of life that will permit realization of the enduring human values.

The nursery school, in close and cooperative relationship with the home and parents, is the primary agency for mental hygiene. The opportunity in pre-school education to build wholesome, sane, cooperative, and mature personalities, and to determine the future of our culture, is unlimited. The discharge of that responsibility lies in helping the young child to meet the persistent life tasks and to fulfill his insistent needs. But the nursery school cannot do this alone. It must have collaboration from the kindergarten and the grade schools, and it must find some way of cooperating with the home and the family, desipte the frequent blindness and resistance of the parents. If nursery school teachers were to realize that they are like parents, with their personal peculiarities, their emotional resistance and susceptibilities, their ignorance and rigid convictions—which may be just as undesirable for the child as the home practices they deprecate—perhaps such a realization would make them more tolerant and more willing to seek a basis of collaboration in meeting the fundamental needs of the child. The family can and does provide the child with a place, a status, with "belongingness" and often much needed love and affection. Can the nursery school organize its procedures and prepare its teachers to meet these same needs and also those other educational needs which the family has difficulty in supplying?

The fundamental needs of the child are in truth the fundamental needs of society.

A Social Philosophy
from Nursery School Teaching

James L. Hymes, Jr.

Those of us who work with young children each day see and hear and touch and feel and sometimes even smell things that are unique to our job. They are everyday things, so everyday that the danger is that we will lose sight of them, not seeing because they are so close to us. Yet everyday and simple though they they be, they are our things ... different ... peculiar to us ... not what the butcher or baker or candlestick maker has a chance to learn.

Food is a good example. We count it a good nursery school which makes sure that each child has the food he needs for good living at his level. There is nothing slipshod or casual about this; it is central to what we do. So central that, where we can, we entrust the planning for it only to experts. So central that everywhere we plan without fail regular times for it. In our day with young children this business of getting adequate food into people is highly organized and structuralized with nothing left to chance.

And for good reasons. Because all that we do or have ever done with children has taught us a simple lesson: *food influences behavior.* Small children, wherever we have met them, have pounded into us in unforgettable ways that hungry people are irritable, that they fight more, that they cry easily, that they become destructive—harder for us to live with and harder for them to live with us. Some children we have seen, hungrier still, have told us also that hunger can make people placid, inactive, lethargic, less capable of functioning with the verve and energy that they could otherwise show. Nursery school teachers know these things. They can't escape knowing them.

But not everyone else in the world knows them. Or if they do know, they know dimly. For their experience—the experience of the garage mechanic or the salesman or the bankteller—has not daily pounded these same facts into them. Day by day these other people cannot see irritability or lassitude or combat because people are hungry. Their business is different.

Physical things maybe are easier to see. Think of the child who is out of school today. Yesterday and the day before he was coming down with a cold. You didn't know it for sure then. All you did know was that he was fussy, resistant to what you wanted and resistant to what he wanted, quarrelsome, an angry person. Or perhaps, as sickening children sometimes are, more infantile than usual, more withdrawn, with less energy. Not up to par, you knew; not up to the quality of living of which he was capable. The nursery school worker knows, but not necessarily the dry goods salesman or the postman: *it is harder to organize good group living if all people are not healthy.* Life is meaner, less predictable, less guided by reason and intelligence if good health is not present. The nursery school teacher learns this from children and she learns it every day.

Think of another physical fact. You have only one doll in your room, or one tricycle, or just one ball to bounce or one wagon to pull. What happens? Every person who has worked with young children knows the answer. There is hitting out, yanking, crying, fighting. It is a simple lesson but one with profound implications: *scarcity leads to combat.* When there are just a few of the good things of life, be it a shiny wagon or praise (or good jobs, for that matter), people fight for them and in nasty ways.

There are more subtle things. Think of what happens to a youngster who does a job. Bobby helps set the tables. Mary hangs up her coat. Billy does a finger painting. Tony climbs the incline board for the first time and then he climbs it and he climbs it. Sallie pulls at her mother and pulls until mother takes time to see the clay Sallie has moulded. Jim pours juice; John washes his own face; Bill ties his shoe laces, and Cindy counts to five.

Everyday things to a nursery school teacher. But what happens to the children who do them? Some do them over and over; some get a sparkle in their eye; some smile and some talk proudly of what they can do. But however they show it, there is a good feeling that comes from succeeding, and no nursery school teacher can miss it. A job to do, a chance to succeed, and a little praise for doing both. It has made strong children stronger, and withdrawn children brighter.

Simple friendliness is another such thing: an interest in people, an appreciation of what they are doing, an outgoingness towards them. Nursery school teachers show these every day because they can see the results they bring. They do it with a new child coming into their group (they do it so easily from practice that they sometimes are not aware they are doing anything very special): The greeting to the child, the knowing his name, the admiration for something that is his. And then friendliness carried further so that the child gets a sense of belonging: A locker of his own, a towel and a bib that are his, a doll to hold, a chance to contribute. We know when the child feels "in." We see it in his posture, in his relaxation, in a lessening of tensions, in less fightyness and suspicions. If we have succeeded in being friendly, we know (and we can't forget it because we see it in child after child) that we raise the quality of his living. . . . The child's living—but is it true of children only?

Friendliness, a chance to belong, a job to do, success and someone recognizing it, plenty of life's good things, food, good health . . . teachers see the results of these and even more. They see all these put together, adding up to a fact that is basic to everything a teacher does: they see people change. They see the quiet child talk and the crawling child walk. *They know that people can grow.* They see the fussy child eat and the pale child get color. *They know that people improve.* They see the young child say "Yours" and the aggressive child take turns; they see the hitting child talk things over and the too-accepting child hit back. *They know that people can learn.* These things they know and believe for how, without knowing and believing them, can a teacher work?

If growth is the automatic unfolding of predetermined behavior, it is not teachers who are needed but caretakers and minders of babies. And if the change that comes is the inevitable change, fixed in the genes and with no possibilities for different rates of speed or different directions to be followed, again teachers are not needed but gardeners. No need either for the careful planning of rooms, the stimulation of books, the acceleration of trips, for the praise or the carefully thought-out amount of help in learning. No need for the whole fixing of environment that is the teacher's tool.

But the need *is* there and teachers know it. People can grow; they can improve; they can learn; they can change. And every group we have ever worked with has had in it some who have done all of these things to such an extent that we can't be sure of the limits of change. From withdrawn to aggressive; from silent to loquacious; from dependent to adventuresome; from listless to active; from stolid to participating . . . such change that we are never sure: perhaps that change could have been greater or earlier or in further directions if our techniques had been keen enough.

Is all this important? Do most people know it and accept it and act on it? Or are people what they are because they are? Negroes must be with a small "n" and in their place because they are that way? Criminals are criminals (or are they products)? Wars are inevitable or can there be causes? The railroad tracks are a final division or can the tracks be moved (or the people moved)? Clearly it is not yet universally held that people do change and that people can change. What is perhaps the one most powerfully hopeful fact about human life has remained the privilege of teachers to know.

And not all teachers have known it. And not all who have known it have generalized from it.

. . . What, then, are the jobs for nursery school teachers? The first, clearly, is to so work within their four walls with children that those children have all they need of everything we know to improve living. They must have all that good physical care can do for them: the adequate food, the sufficient quantities of rest and sleep, the stimulus of growth-inducing activity, the correction of every physical defect, and a program of continuous examination so that defects do not occur. They must have all that teaching can mean: the challenge of equipment and companionship, the fullness of books and art and music and science and pets and trips at their level, the help in growing and in the broadening of ideas. They must have all that mental hygiene has taught us children need: belonging, praise, friendliness, participating, success, affection, steadiness.

But this is just one job for teachers: to do the thing. A second job is to know why, to understand what we are doing. It is one approach to have block building as an activity: it is another to know that through the way children can behave while block-building, if they are properly guided, better humans can result. It is one approach to give a routine morning inspection; it is another to work constantly with public health nurses, state nutrition consultants, community immunization clinics, well-baby centers until you are downright sure that no defect will lower a child's performance. It is one thing to have low lockers because all nursery schools do; it is quite another to examine every inch of the day so that in every phase children practice taking as much responsibility for their living as they are able to.

To understand leads only to the third job; we must generalize. This hopeful fact and these good techniques: are they for young children only? Does hunger affect only the behavior of children? Are unwell babies the only bad citizens? Does scarcity of jobs work the way scarcity of toys does? Does the factory worker need a sense of belonging? Do grown-ups flourish under success? Is it only children who can change?

And if we can generalize, we must speak out. So that bankers and butchers and barbers and bat boys and cooks and caterers and carpenters and chauffeurs and druggists and dancers and doctors can know what the teacher knows. And build their adult lives and the national life that is the composite on the basis of this one hopeful fact: *that people can change.* We must be spokesmen to make known those techniques of good teaching—friendliness, belongingness, participation, success, praise, food, health care—to a nation which needs them in all its living.

Spokesmen but not just in general. The need is for people who will know where in society there are the crucial spots that may deny the things teachers know to be true. Teachers must have avenues of information so that they will know the instance in national life where a decision is about to be made that will mean more or less participation. They must have facts so they know who to line up with and against, who wants and who fights all those things in adult life that give people a chance to be enriched. Teachers must know the decisions about to be made—in their community, in their state, and in their nation—so they can support those that inflate people.

To do this teachers must have access to information; not just their professional journals of child development and nursery education but the daily newspapers, the weekly news magazine, the daily news broadcasts, the controversial movie, the liberal journal of opinion. These they must study, not read casually as a disinterested follower of the other fellow's news. For without knowing specifics teachers have no guide as to where to bring their influence.

To experience, first; then, to understand; secondly, to generalize, to have facts and to be active in word and deed. All to the end that these things we learn from children can be widely available, and can pass as they should from the living of children into the living of a nation.

from **The**
Kaiser Child Service Centers

Gwen Morgan

The centers which were operated by the Kaiser Shipbuilding Corporation during World War II were unusual enough to warrant description at some length. The idea that the shipyards provide child care originated with Edgar F. Kaiser, the son of Henry J. Kaiser. Two centers were opened, one at the Swan Island Shipyard and one at the Oregon Shipbuilding Corporation, both in Portland, Oregon. The centers were located directly at the entrance to each shipyard, differentiating them from other federally supported day care centers located throughout the Portland community. They were managed as a department within the industrial company. The centers opened November 8, 1943 and closed September 1, 1945.

Enrollment: Children were enrolled from eighteen months of age to six years of age. On Saturdays, Sundays, and school holidays the Centers also provided care for school-age children. The Centers were open whenever the shipyards were open—seven days a week, twenty-four hours a day, 364 days a year. Children attended during the shift their mother worked. Day shift and swing shift were equally popular . . . Graveyard shift was an exceedingly small service. It tended to be a temporary arrangement used by parents when their plan for home care broke down, and until they could arrange a new plan.

In the beginning, enrollment was slow to build up, because, although all statistics indicated large numbers of children, each family had obviously already made a plan of some kind if the mother was employed. Only Kaiser employees were eligible; and after the centers began to be known, there were instances of people seeking work at the shipyards in order to get the excellent child care. From a very small, slow beginning enrollment, the figures quickly mounted in the first six months of operation until a peak attendance of over one thousand was reached in the first year. The centers served 4,014 different children, many of them not regularly enrolled.

Staff: Each center had a director, and fully qualified teachers and assistant teachers for each group of children. In addition to the educational staff, each had a trained social worker, a nursing staff, and a chief nutritionist.

A total of 292 professionals were employed at the Centers during the twenty-two month period. Teachers were recruited from all over the nation. A good deal of thought and effort went into personnel policies to assure a low turnover and a friendly atmosphere in which staff members would "feel at ease and free to contribute and to participate." (Final Report) Applicants were sent a prepaid railroad ticket; their train was met; they were helped to find housing; and they were made to feel welcomed into a warm social group from the moment of their arrival. Interstaff memos raised questions, offered help and encouragement.

Every effort was made to keep group size to a reasonable minimum, but there were times when the pressures for the employment of women in the yards temporarily exceeded the supply of trained personnel. There were also times, especially after one layoff at the Swan Island Shipyard, when the centers temporarily had more staff than enrollment warranted.

Costs: The United States Maritime Commission provided buildings and equipment of unusually high quality. Parents paid $5 per week for the first child, and $3.75 for siblings. Low fees for certain special services brought in a little additional income. The remaineder of the budget was paid by the company, whose net costs were $2.37 per capita per day. Parents paid only when their children were in attendance, and attendance was roughly eighty

Gwen Morgan, "The Kaiser Child Service Centers," in *A Proposal to Establish a Work-Related Child Development Center*, pp. 68–74, mimeographed 1967, used with permission of the author.

percent. Since the building and equipment were provided, the budget went primarily for staff, some eighty-four percent of expenditures...

The staff made a serious effort to provide a program of very high quality with the least possible expense. This attempt may have reflected a wartime spirit of cooperation with industry, and it also reflected a pioneering spirit and the expectation that such nursery schools were going to continue in peacetime. "One part of our experiment is to discover whether or not large scale nursery education is financially feasible for industries and for communities. This relates to the number of people employed, but also to expenditures for supplies, materials, services, etc." (James L. Hymes, memo)

From a financial point of view, the results of the experiment were inconclusive. According to the Final Report, "*A fair conclusion seems to be that, while most expenses incurred in the operation of the two centers were justified by conditions here, it is not correct to assume that another situation will produce identical conditions leading to an equal financial deficit.*" It was not possible to draw up a final balance sheet on the profit and loss of the operation of the two centers. Against the costs of operation, says the report, must be placed what it has meant to a large number of children to have what was probably the best child care offered in the country. "It probably meant gains to parents and better health and stability for the community and the country." And finally, the report goes on to mention the contribution the centers made in industrial terms, to recruitment, to presentism, to morale on the job, and to public relations. No conclusion is offered about whether the advantages balanced the half-million dollar operating costs...

Relations with the company: A wartime spirit of national cooperation provided outimum conditions for working out a team approach. "The personnel office of the shipyard gave help in publicizing the existence of the centers; posters, loud-speaker announcements and guided tours of the Centers helped in making their existence and facilities and fees known. There was overwhelming evidence that the parents of the children enrolled were extremely grateful to the company for both the service provided and for the high quality of the service. I believe the company felt the service to be among its most useful employee benefits." (James L. Hymes, September 1966 letter)

The Centers tried to fit themselves into the shipyards. In one memo, Dr. Hymes says, "We must do our job in integration with industry, rather than parallel to it or isolated from it. One measure of our success, for example, is the extent to which we make known the resources we ourselves represent, and whether we encourage the shipyard to use our professional skills in every way they can be used." Another measure was the school's use of the resources of the company. Dr. Hymes' Final Report recommends that future centers establish closer working relations with the Personnel Office of the company. "One theoretical danger underlies industrial nursery schools, that the pressure of industry for workers will lead the school to accept a child, who, in the judgment of the professional staff, cannot benefit by group care. It should be stressed that this pressure was not exerted at any time during the twenty-two month period of operation.... Meaningful relationships between the administration of the Child Service Centers and the staff of the Personnel Department... each engaged in employee relations, could be beneficial in the handling of problems and in the development of positive programs to prevent problems."

There is a good deal of evidence that the relations with the shipyard had an effect on the children. They were proud of the ships they saw going by on the river. The Center published a little booklet of anecdotes about the children in November 1944 called "160,874 Children," which contains a good deal of evidence that the adult world impinged on the child world. One such incident, entitled "Their Shipyard" follows:

Almost since the beginning, the Oregon Center has had a group for six- and seven-year-olds on swing shift since few other Centers in Portland care for children this age at night. The six- and seven-year-olds at the Oregon Center were taken one day to see movies about the shipyard which are shown at the Induction Auditorium. When they came back to the Center, they covered the entire floor of their playroom with big blocks and made a huge ship. Out of blocks they also made a whirley. In the midst of their building a minor argument came up so that they all stood around talking back and forth. After about five minutes, Larry, remembering Edgar Kaiser's last words in the movie, pushed up his sleeves and said, "Well, I've got to roll up my sleeves and get to work."

... The attitude of respect for parents and a determination to provide whatever service was needed certainly permeated the philosophy of the Kaiser Centers. It led to a program not conforming to any ideological model, but closely in touch with reality. As time went on, more and more services were added, often for a small fee. In the end these were to comprise a long list.

Besides the special program for preschool children, the Centers were unusual in providing a number of extras:

—Child Care was offered during three shifts. Older children, too, were sometimes able to attend swing and graveyard shifts if necessary...

—Special care was available for nonenrolled children. Parents whose other arrangements for their children temporarily broke down could bring their children on a day-to-day basis. One Center had a Special Services Room for such children; the other integrated them into the regular groups.

—After school care was given school-age children, also Saturdays, holidays, vacations, including summers.

—Children could stay for an extra shift if their parents needed time for overtime work or any other reason, even if only to attend an occasional movie. Day shift children could stay through swing shift supper.

—The program was flexible to allow for individual differences. This was especially true of course with the eighteen months to three-year-old age group.

—Specially built bathtubs made it easy to bathe children. For some living in trailers, this was an important service.

—Food was provided for the children as needed. For example, breakfast was needed for day shift children, who arrived at 6:15 A.M., so it was served. Whatever meal could not be given the children at home easily, was prepared at the Centers. . . .

—Home service food was provided. By ordering in advance, a parent could pick up the evening meal at the Center's kitchen after work.

—Booklets for parents were printed. Informal, unpretentious, and cheerful, these sound, informative pamphlets grew out of discussions at parent meetings, which indicated a need for information on such matters as "Children and War," "Toys to Make," and "Recipes for Foods Children Like."

—Newsletters were also printed, warmly human, letting the parents know more of what their children were doing at school, and news of the staff.

—Nine booklets for teachers were mimeographed. These grew out of staff discussions and were useful enough to be circulated all over the country.

1. *A Social Philosophy from Nursery School Teaching*
2. *Must Nursery School Teachers Plan?*
3. *Who Will Need a Postwar Nursery School?*
4. *Meeting Needs: The War Nursery Approach*
5. *The Role of the Nutritionist in a War Nursery School*
6. *Large Groups in the Nursery School*
7. *Should Children Under Two Be in Nursery School?*

—An infirmary for children who were not seriously ill was part of the service. Dr. Hymes recommended that later centers consider an isolation infirmary for children with contagious diseases.

—Diagnostic tests, immunizations, dietary supplements were given as needed.

—Shipyard facilities were used for equipment construction. A carpenter assigned to the Center constructed some play materials especially designed for their use.

—Close relations were maintained with parents in a spirit of service. Teachers, nurse, nutritionist, and family consultant were available and eager to help. Dr. Hymes recommended that in future centers the mothers be encouraged to visit the centers while in operation, especially in the beginning. . .

—A mending service for mothers was established.

—Shopping service was offered. One shopper did errands for fifty mothers.

—An appointment service was provided. The Centers would make and take children to appointments with dentists, etc.

—Barbers were brought to the school to give haircuts.

—Shoe laces, panties, and other necessities began to be sold at the Centers.

—Photographers were brought in so that Christmas gifts of photographs could be ordered.

—a lending library of books and toys for children was set up. . . .

The wartime spirit of sharing in a job to be done is probably something impossible to recapture in another era. But the remarkable feeling of respect for family needs, and for reality, is an important value developed in the Kaiser Centers, which should not be lost.

Results: The Kaiser Centers helped to improve standards in other child care agencies, contributed to the development of programs by those agencies to better meet the particular needs of shipyard workers, and contributed to increased understanding among the public regarding adequate standards for the care of young children. They demonstrated that a nursery school staff can contribute to the morale of workers on the job, and help them to do a better job with their children. They demonstrated that excellent child care facilities can be operated by industry to the great advantage of children and parents and to the benefit of industry. (Final Report) The hope that this was a pioneering effort which would lead to an increase in child care programs and in meeting family needs, however, was never realized. *Why did the Kaiser Centers and other day care centers die out after the war?* The full answer is probably quite complicated. One part of the reason is that Kaiser Industries and other industries had no further need of the centers in the immediate postwar operations. There was a fire at the Swan Island Shipyards in the late summer of 1945, and the yard never reopened. In September, both yards closed, since the wartime need for ships abruptly stopped, and along with the yards, the Child Service Centers closed their doors.

Their disappearance from the national thinking is quite sudden. During the entire war period there is an element of guilt in the literature which discusses the need for child care to enable mothers to contribute to the war effort. When the war ended, the nation tried to get "back to normal" as quickly as possible, and normal meant that the mother was to be in the home bringing up her own children. In some ways, this postwar period tied women more closely to their homes than they had been before or would be afterward. In spite of the fact that women have been choosing to work in greater and greater numbers during the last few decades, and in spite of the evidence of their economic need to work, the professional fields concerned with children have continued to think of the home-centered mother as the only model for the American family. This may explain why all that was learned in the Kaiser Centers suddenly dropped from sight. The nation, guilty over the war experience, and seeking other values, did not want to hear about the values of the wartime child care experience.

"Another reason, almost surely was the cost." (James L. Hymes, September 1966 letter) The Kaiser Centers were of very high quality and they were expensive. Even with the initial help of the Maritime Commission, the Kaiser shipyard was paying a very high operating cost. This was possible in wartime, when the company was motivated by a determination to get the job done. Wartime industries could not be cost conscious; they had to do whatever was necessary. It may be that a nursery school in those unusual times could be considered a legitimate business expenditure under a government costs-plus-fixed-fee contract. If so, the government indirectly subsidized the schools in full. After the war, it was no longer possible for Kaiser or any other company to survive if it provided an employee benefit of this magnitude. The hope was prevalent in the immediate postwar period that if such services continued to be needed, the community would provide them. But costs, instead of going down as expected, have continued to rise.

Whatever the reason, there is little known today of the Kaiser Centers. The results of a remarkable experiment made by an outstanding group of educators have not had the impact on American education, or on the fields of public health and welfare, that they expected them to have.

Kramer School— Something for Everybody
Bettye M. Caldwell

There is an old journalistic slogan which suggests that the way to write a guaranteed best-seller is to write about God's mother's dog's flag. As each of these topics is in itself appealing, all of them together should be irresistible. In some ways, this formula applies to Kramer School or, more formally, to the Center for Early Development and Education jointly operated by the University of Arkansas and the Little Rock Public Schools. We have come to be known as the Kramer Project because the public school in which our program operates is the Frederick W. Kramer School. We are content with this designation, as the label accurately describes our functional identity even if it does not connote our full range of activities.

Some Background Information

The Kramer Project came into being in 1969 through what was known as the "Special Facilities" grants program of the Children's Bureau. Each funded facility had to have demonstration, research, and training functions, and each had to relate in some way to the goal of improvement of the general welfare of children and families.

The author had previously directed a research-based day care and education program that offered comprehensive services to infants and young children and their families but which lost contact with the children when they reached public school age. During that time her conviction had grown that early childhood education would never significantly have impact on the children of America until it became part of public education. Also she was becoming increasingly aware that the chasm between early childhood education and elementary education had to be bridged. Accordingly, she was resolved to try to help design a new program—a special facility, indeed—that would provide age-appropriate developmental guidance from early infancy through the end of the childhood years.

A move to Little Rock, Arkansas proved to be propitious for the pursuit of that goal, as personnel in the Department of Elementary Education of the University of Arkansas expressed interest in the idea and established contacts with the administrative staff of the Little Rock Public Schools, who pledged cooperation provided outside funding could be secured. An agreement was reached to designate one of the Little Rock elementary schools as the project school for a period of five to seven years. Responsibility for implementing the program in that school would be shared by the director of the project and the principal of the school with the help of guidance offered by an Advisory Council consisting of representatives of the University, the school district, and the State Department of Education. For the better part of a year a planning committee (1) met to work out details of the project, and finally a proposal was submitted to and approved by the Office of Child Development.

Selection of a Project Site

The project school was to be one which: 1) was located in a section of the city likely to have a sizeable proportion of low-income residents; 2) had a racially integrated population; 3) was in reasonably good condition, and 4) had incomplete occupancy which would allow room for the early childhood units. There was really only one school in the community that met all of those criteria (except the one about being in reasonably good condition!)— Kramer School, situated squarely in downtown Little Rock, built in 1895 of an architectural style that can perhaps best be described as "American Ugly." The neighborhood itself is very interesting. Although technically integrated, it really contains assorted pockets of whites and blacks. It is surrounded on two sides by luxury hotels and apartments, and on the other two by a church and reasonably adequate housing. A busy interstate highway officially bisects the community into east and west (and our population into black and white). Moving in another direction we have the main hangout for the local hippie colony and the publication headquarters of the underground newspaper. The neighborhood is varied and interesting with many things to see and do within walking distance of the school.

Kramer contains thirteen classrooms, an auditorium, and a cafeteria and is considered a 300-child school. At the time the project was launched, there were only 150 elementary children in attendance. We have now added to that total approximately 100 children under six. This involves a total of 127 families and two foster homes. In addition to these children who are enrolled in the school on a daily basis, approximately 150 additional families are involved with the project through home visits and other research activities. Thus, altogether, the project touches the lives of approximately 400 children and their families. Of the total number of children, sixty percent are black and forty percent are white. One-third of the children are from families receiving some type of welfare, (AFDC, PA), and only three-fifths of the children reside in two-parent families. Sixty percent of the mothers are employed or in a training program. The modal occupation for both mothers and fathers is semi-skilled. Only thirty-five percent of the mothers and fifty-nine percent of the fathers have a high school education or beyond.

Components of the Program

In Kramer we have blended together a number of program components, each of which in isolation would represent a worthwhile educational endeavor but all of which put together in the right combination represent something more—an exciting program model worthy of consideration for adoption in other communities concerned with designing a school environment capable of meeting the needs of young children and their families.

What are these components that make Kramer a special school? No one in itself is unique, but, at the time the program was launched in 1969 (and even at the time of this writing insofar as the author knows), no school had put them all together in precisely this way.

1. *A comprehensive early childhood program beginning in infancy.* For over a decade now we have been aware of the importance of experience during the early years of life in enabling children to achieve their full developmental potential (Hunt, 1961; Bloom, 1964). During this decade early childhood education, always either a step-child or a petitioner for educational legiti-

macy, has gained a new lease on life. Experimental early enrichment programs (Gordon and Wilkerson, 1966)appeared in a few settings during the
early sixties and, with the launching of Project Head Start in 1965, became
available to large numbers of children in America for the first time. Almost
never, however, have programs for children younger than five been accepted
as an integral part of public education.

Most of the new programs "backed down" gradually from public school
entrance age which, depending on whether the state had public kindergartens, meant either five-year-olds or four-year-olds. An interesting paradox in
this order of program development is that Hunt and Bloom were widely
quoted as having marshaled evidence for the validity of educational intervention in this upper range of the traditional preschool years. Yet, Bloom's
widely cited apothegm reminded us that approximately fifty percent of the
development of a child's intelligence occurred *by* age four, not between four
and five. Similarly, Hunt (1964) speculated that from about eighteen months
onward the social environment was particularly important in shaping the
behavior of the young child. Had we not at that point in history been so
justifiably phobic about the possibly deterious consequences of putting children younger than three into groups, more people would probably have
moved promptly to design programs based on correct inferences from the
data summarized by Hunt and Bloom.

These were especially meaningful in terms of conceptual analyses of early
development of the situation of the young child from underprivileged backgrounds. It is during the early years of life that the child himself has the
least capability of selecting or influencing his environment and is, at least
physically speaking, a prisoner of his home environment. For years it was
assumed that most home environments were equipotential in their pattern of
influence during infancy and that it was only in later years that differential
influence patterns could be detected. The absence of good descriptive data
about the early home environment permitted this stereotype to persist. Now,
however (Caldwell, Heider, and Kaplan, 1966; Wachs, Uzgiris, and Hunt,
1971), we have evidence that, quite apart from any inherent dimension of
"goodness" or "badness," early environments contain as much diversity as is
found in social and physical environments available to older children. It is
in environments that we have come to designate by that curiously misleading
term, "middle class," that those characteristics associated with developmental
acceleration are found with greater consistency and in greater abundance.
Quite apart from any argument as to whether home environments that lack
these characteristics are deficient or simply different, one needs to be concerned with arranging for these characteristics if it can be demonstrated that
young children need them in order to have an opportunity to develop skills
and personality characteristics adaptive in the larger society to which all
subcultural groups within a region belong.

Such is the strategy of the early education component of Kramer School.
It is based on a literal reaction to the lines of evidence that give us a rationale for early intervention programs (see Caldwell, 1970), and that evidence
unmistakably implies that the earlier the intervention the better. Although
at this point in time we do not have *empirical* evidence (Caldwell, 1971)
that enrichment efforts begun in infancy accomplish more than appropriate
intervention begun later in the early childhood period—say at age three or
four—in terms of the *theoretical* rationale for such endeavors the potential
value of beginning during the earliest years cannot be ignored. Accordingly,
Kramer does not involve backing down from first grade but rather moving
forward from birth with activities designed to provide age-appropriate developmental supports.

In the early childhood component of our program, carefully arranged educational experiences are provided young children from early infancy right
up to the age of formal entry into public school. (In Arkansas this is still

age six, as public kindergartens are permissible rather than mandatory and are available largely through private sources or through federally funded programs for children in low-income families.) From the age of six months onward this may be either in the form of home intervention offered on a biweekly basis or in the form of enrollment in the formal educational program offered on the school premises. For those participating in the on-site school program, enrollment may be either for half a day or for the full day, depending on the family employment situation. In terms of the amount of physical space available in the building and the size of the available staff, approximately 100 children can be enrolled in the school program.

One of the things that makes Kramer unique is that these 100 children younger than six go to school right in the same building with their older brothers and sisters. This, of course, has been true for public kindergarten for many years and even for prekindergarten groups (usually just four-year-olds, though occasionally including three-year-olds) since the establishment of Head Start. As Kramer is essentially a big cube holding up an assortment of the turrets and towers and gables considered architecturally stylish in its day, there are no separate wings into which the little ones can be secluded and no partitionable playgrounds that can be assigned separately to older and younger groups. Rather the classes for the younger children are geographically contiguous to those of the older children. The only exception to this arrangement is the contingent of babies, who, because of lack of suitable space in the main building that met fire and safety standards, attend in a portable classroom situated on the school campus. This immediate proximity of younger and older children facilitates many types of cross-age activities which, in a more architecturally ideal physical setting, might be arranged only with difficulty. It means that two or three children from special education can help in the toddler room during snack time or lunch, that several kindergarteners can do the same thing for the babies, that the fifth graders can arrange and give a Valentine party for the three-year-olds, and so on. And, indeed, activities such as these are everyday occurrences at Kramer. It also means that when we have assemblies or special programs, the sixth graders can give the caregivers from Baby House a rest, and feel very grown-up and nurturant at the same time, by holding babies on their laps during the program. And it means that parents who are also encouraged to attend all such programs can gather together all of their young children and participate in the experience as a family group.

In terms of the static aspects of the early childhood part of the program, the children are enrolled in groups that are reasonably homogeneous in terms of developmental level—babies, toddlers, threes, fours, and fives. There are twelve babies and sixteen toddlers in the two youngest groups, and anywhere from twenty to twenty-five in each of the three remaining groups. The adult-child ratio is kept at 1:4 in the two youngest groups, 1:5 in the threes, and 1:6-8 in the two oldest groups. As absenteeism tends to be high in the youngest children, we deliberately over-enroll in both the baby and toddler units in order to avoid underutilization of the facility.

If in our old building we had more open space areas, we would encourage multi-age grouping more than we are now able to do. However, in many ways we had to design our program to fit our building, and our cube is divided into self-contained classrooms. In such a setting, activity and rest cycles correlated with age are hard to ignore, no matter how much one might wish to group children heterogeneously with respect to age. Last year, for example, we found ourselves in a disastrous situation with our infants and toddlers who were together in the same portable classroom. One small bedroom containing six cribs had been partitioned off so that the younger infants in the group would have a separate place to sleep. On paper it should have worked. But what defeated the arrangement was the fact that most of the babies wanted to go to sleep around 11:00 or 11:30 A.M. — which they were permitted to do — whereas the toddlers were not ready for a nap until 12:30 or 1:00 P.M., by which time the infants were ready to get up and begin to play. In the absence of an area large enough to permit separate sleeping areas for both the early and the late resters, these incompatible activity cycles made it necessary to divide the infants and toddlers into separate geographic areas for the major home base assignments. However, in our setting it is easy to find opportunities to bring various groups together for parts of the day. In fact, all of the children except the youngest infants who come to school before 8:00 go into a common receiving area, and all who remain after 3:30 are regrouped into a heterogeneous age group where they remain until their parents come to take them home.

Because our entire educational effort, including our home intervention program, operates out of a public school, we have eschewed the labels "preschool" and "preschoolers." It seems rather foolish to speak of our toddlers as "preschoolers" when they attend school every day, just as their older brothers and sisters do. Also, as part of our conscious effort to unify the entire program and to break down the implicit chasm that all too often appears to separate early childhood education from elementary education, we did not wish to refer to part of the program as "school" and to another part as "not-school" (which is a logical translation of "preschool"). Occasionally, however, it is necessary to refer to that part of the program which deals with children under six, and unless we wanted to remain unified to the point of semantic absurdity we had to come up with a descriptive phrase. Accordingly we refer to the children simply as "younger" and "older" and the program components as "preparatory" and "elementary."

2. *A dynamic elementary program offering continuity of developmental support.* A few years ago many of us who were impassioned advocates for more early education made it sound as though we believed that enough programs would solve all of the problems of poverty, would eliminate school drop-outs, and would make equal educational opportunity more than empty rhetoric. By creative intervention during the early years of life, the child could possibly be changed in such a way as to make him thereafter more receptive to whatever educational fare might be forthcoming. This assumption rested on the translation of what has been called the "critical period hypothesis" into the field of human development (see Caldwell, 1972). As the early years were critical for supporting cognitive and motivational development, corrective programs instituted during this critical period would hopefully produce changes which would sustain the child through any subsequent experiences. When early evidence began to accumulate that it was not that easy (Karnes, 1969; Westinghouse Learning Corporation, 1969), some pushed the panic button and began to claim that the early experience was not critical after all. But, with the wisdom that comes with hindsight, it now seems naive to have assumed that a small slice of enrichment early in the life cycle could have produced permanent changes. If behavior at any point in time is an integrated function of the individual's genetic potential, his pool of accumulated attitudes and skills, and of his current environmental situation, then it is fallacious to assume that one could ever expect the work of the environment to be completed.

The program implications of this point are obvious: no matter how effective an early enrichment program might be, it must be followed by exposure to an environment offering a proper match between the child's previous achievements and the experiences offered in the new environment. If children who do make substantial gains in an early childhood program are placed in an elementary program planned on the basis of previous expectancies rather than on the actual achievements of the children, then the same rate of progress should not be expected.

This continuity is the second major component of the Kramer program. Upon completion of the early childhood program, the child simply goes right on up the educational ladder. By conscious design the kindergarten and the first primary classroom are adjacent to one another, and some children move back and forth between the two areas for part of the day. In our setting this movement made more sense than having the two classrooms duplicate one another in certain respects. For example, there are several children in the kindergarten who, by any standards, are "ready" to learn to read. Likewise, there are a number of children in the primary who need a great deal of readiness work. Rather than either permit each teacher to ignore these indicators of developmental progress in the children or require each one to complicate her teaching strategy to accommodate the children whose deviation from the performance level of the remainder of the group is extreme, we have arranged a simple exchange. The main work period in the kindergarten happens to coincide with the reading period in the primary classroom, so the kindergarten readers and the primary nonreaders simply change places. The teachers on either side of the exchange remain alert to indicators that the arrangement is indeed providing a proper match for the children's continuing development, and change can be made quickly in the event it should be needed.

In limited space, it is not possible to describe all components of our elementary program. The underlying educational philosophy is identical to that which guides the preparatory program. We have referred to our program as representing an ecological model, i.e., one which is concerned with environmental design rather than curriculum development. Our ambitions for that environment are quite expansive. We want it to be one in which the children can develop maximally as integrated social - cognitive - emotional - physical - moral human beings — in short a supportive environment. Furthermore, we want them to be happy in the process, and we want their behavior to be so reinforcing to the teachers and other personnel in the school that their jobs are perceived as rewarding and fulfilling.

We conceptualize the school environment as consisting of *human, physical,* and *temporal* factors, all of which taken together comprise the ecological system of the school.

Human factors involve all the social interactions between adults and children, children and children, and adults with one another. They include the emotional tone of the interactions, the extent to which encounters between children and teachers will be pleasurable rather than painful, and whether they convey mutual respect and love or disdain and hostility. Physical factors include all the teaching materials and equipment and the arrangement of space in the school. Although we think of physical factors as being less important than the human factors in the school, they do indeed set limits for program operation and must be given careful consideration in environmental planning. Temporal factors refer to the organization of events throughout the school day, to the way things are put together. They can thus be consonant or dissonant with the child's needs for activity and rest and with limits of attentiveness set by his own physiological maturity and style of reacting.

The ecological system of the school overlaps and must be coordinated with the ecosystems of the home and the larger community. One of our operating premises is that the greater the consistency among these ecosystems and the greater the extent to which all encourage and support the same patterns of development, the easier will be the developmental task of the children. In all training endeavors, an attempt is made to help staff members think creatively about how these factors can be programmed to help the children progress at their optimal rates.

Our planning for the elementary program has been sensitive to the voices of responsible criticism of public education (e.g., Bruner, 1960; Cremin, 1961; Goodlad, 1966; Schaefer, 1967; Berman, 1968; Silberman, 1970). It may be described as currently lying about midway on a continuum ranging from a highly structured program on the right to a completely open program, and

moving toward the left. Our task in the elementary division has been entirely
different from our early childhood task. The latter program we *developed* and
started; the former we have had to *influence*. It is not easy to change a school,
as thousands of people who have tried in the past will testify.

We have been at the task for about eighteen months at the time of this
writing, and we have many tangible results to show for our efforts. The total
elementary school is now nongraded, and there is considerable movement of
children from one classroom to another for participation in activities that
might more appropriately match their interests and achievements. The old
library has been converted to a Learning Center (similar to what is called a
Media Center in most schools) where remedial work is offered in reading and
math and where children can pursue interests individually. We have added an
exciting and highly appealing physical education program and an art program. We have arranged weekly assemblies during which ethnically relevant
and culturally enriching programs are presented with the children themselves
involved in many of the programs. One classroom has been set up and called
the Alternative Room. The activities of this room are highly fluid and last
only as long as needed to trouble-shoot some particular problem. For example,
for an entire semester it operated as a transition classroom for approximately
half of the early primary children who were not able to respond to instruction
in reading and math within the range appropriate for the remainder of the
class and who were so volatile and impulsive as to need a more carefully
controlled classroom and more behavioral supports in order to show developmental progress. This year the Alternative Room is being used for children
who are simply unable to function in their regularly assigned home classroom, generally because of behavior problems. We find this an extremely
valuable adjunct to the program and now wonder how any school can function
without such a service.

Teaching activities for both elementary and preparatory divisions are
guided by a lengthy list of objectives formulated in the areas of communication (reading and language arts), math, social living (social studies), and
personal development. The objectives are stated in the first person and are
intended to serve as progress reports to children and parents as well as teaching guides for the instructors. The lists of objectives are not considered to be
exhaustive, as it is expected that every creative teacher will permit the children to pursue their own individual interests in every aspect of the curriculum. Nor in many instances are they presumed to have been sequenced perfectly. Most emphatically, a stated objective is *not* expected to carry with it
a prescription of how the objective is to be achieved. Quite the contrary. One
of our instructional premises is that there is no one technique that will work
with every child, and we are organizing a curriculum library around these
objectives to provide hints as to multiple ways of approaching each objective.
Furthermore, it is expected that, insofar as possible, achievement of the objectives should permit the child to take the initiative, with teacher intervention offered only as needed.

As stated above, we still have a long way to go in making our vision for
the elementary division become a full reality. It will be some time before the
full educational impact of the program can be understood. At this time, for
example, we have achievement data on only one group of children who had
participated in at least one year of the preparatory program and who have
gone through at least one level of the elementary program. These children
tested higher on a group IQ test than a comparable group of controls attending another Little Rock school but did not show any substantial acceleration
in reading or math. We are convinced that there are dramatic differences in
the children's attitudes toward adults and toward authority in general.
Almost every visitor comments, for example, on how friendly and loving the
children are to their teachers and other project staff members. As we are
constantly monitoring their development in many areas, we will soon be able
to substantiate what kind of change is occurring, how much and what type

of this change is associated with participation in the early childhood component of the school and how much is due simply to changes being instituted at the elementary level.

One of our most disconcerting problems is that there is less geographic stability in the participating families than we had expected. Recently, the Little Rock Housing Authority took over six square blocks that lie within our attendance boundaries, an act which involved seventy-seven children enrolled in Kramer. An interesting comment on the extent to which the families perceive our program as offering them something of value can be found in the statistic that the families of eighty-three percent of the children under six found ways to continue to bring their children to Kramer, whereas only twenty percent of the elementary children were returned, even though in some instances a family might have been transporting younger children to the school. Granted that there are important reality factors in the situation (wanting children to establish friendship patterns in the new neighborhood, convenience associated with attendance at a school closer to the new address, etc.), we have interpreted this as indicating that as yet we do not have a community image of being an elementary school worth taking extra effort to attend, whereas we apparently do have that image at the preparatory level.

3. *Day care for all children who need this service.* Those who are at all familiar with this author's point of view that day care can most logically and economically be expanded by establishing a liaison with public education (Caldwell, 1971a, 1971b) will not be surprised to learn that Kramer is an extended day school. The school opens at 6:30 A.M. and closes at 5:00 P.M., and all children of whatever age are welcome throughout that period. As would be expected, greatest use of the day care component is made by the parents of the very young children, although a number of primary children remain for the extended day. One of the criteria by which the appeal of the school for the children can be determined is that the great majority of them arrive by 7:30 to 7:45 in the morning, although school does not officially begin until 8:30. Breakfast is served to the early arrivals who indicate that they were not fed at home. In the late afternoon many children who do not actually need after-school care remain in order to participate in the organized playground activities. The boys have had an opportunity to participate in a city Boys' Club intramural sports program, and, because of the expert coaching they receive from their physical education instructors, have walked away with most local sports trophies since the program began.

We had originally planned to use the surplus time in part to strengthen the cognitive program, i.e., offer tutorial help, remedial classes, etc. During our first year we found out what we should have been wise enough to anticipate even without the experience — tutorial help is not what the children want at that time of day. The older children in particular need to be active and free of too much supervision, and we have tried to accommodate those needs while still ensuring safety. The most popular late day activities are organized games and recreation, usually following a seasonal pattern, and art. "Sesame Street" happens to be telecast in our area in the late afternoon, and the younger children who remain late are encouraged to watch that.

The school is licensed as a day care facility by the Arkansas Department of Social and Rehabilitation Services, and all the traditional day care supports are offered as a regular part of the program. In our early days we ran into some interesting problems associated with the fact that Health Department requirements are not identical in school facilities and day care facilities. Sometimes we could meet one but not the other, and, whenever there was any disparity, we were expected to meet the more stringent of the two. Reconciling such differences was actually a fairly easy job, however, and we heartily recommend more unions of this sort.

It has not been a marriage without problems, however. For example, when school holidays come around, it is always hard to remind the staff that the day care facility must stay open in order to be of service to our families.

Similarly, those who must come to work very early can feel resentment when they see other staff members come in later and possibly leave earlier. Also, for the first year of our operation, it was hard to get across the idea that it was all right for the elementary children to remain after the formal school hours. In most of the schools across this nation, there is almost always one staff member whose duty it is to get the children out the door and off the campus as quickly as possible. It is not easy to break up old patterns such as this one.

New ideas usually sell themselves when they are recognized as offering something of value, and the day care component of the program has gradually won converts from among the traditional school personnel in terms of the service it offers. Before the project began, the principal used to come to work and find fifty to seventy-five children standing outside the door wanting to come inside, no matter what the temperature or weather. Similarly, in the afternoon, there were hazards associated with unsupervised play activities on the school grounds. Now the availability of qualified personnel to provide a program for the children early and late so that the regular teachers need not feel either guilty at not responding to the children or frustrated that they cannot plan and get ready because of the premature presence of children in the classrooms has convinced essentially everyone that all schools should offer extended day programs.

One final point should be made about the day care program. Unless their parents work so that there is no one at home to care for them, children are not encouraged to remain at school for the extended day. This applies to the younger as well as the older children. That is, we have as a strong component of our philosophy the importance of strengthening family ties, and we do not wish to encourage dilution of parent-child contacts merely by the availability of the extra school coverage. An occasional exception is made for children who especially need to be in the program whose mothers might decline to enroll them for a half-day only, claiming that it is too much trouble to get them dressed for such a short time!

As stated earlier, admission to Kramer was originally determined solely by geographic residence. Previously the population was well-balanced racially, but during the present year there has been a slight decrease in the proportion of whites in attendance. As we want to keep a population that includes a social class mix as well as a racial mix, we felt the need to enroll a few more middle class white children. Several of our teachers who were securing day care for their own young children elsewhere were very eager to enroll them in Kramer. We saw in their interest an opportunity both to be of further service to our staff and help maintain a racial balance. This is working so well that we would like to evangelize so that the service could be available to all young teachers. There is something very heart-warming about seeing a young mother-teacher go to play with her baby on her break rather than rush to the lounge for a cup of coffee.

4. *A broad research program in child development and education.* Reference was made earlier to the fact that the Kramer project is jointly sponsored by the University of Arkansas and the Little Rock School District. Although the university was obviously interested in the challenge offered by the opportunity to influence public education and participate in the endeavor to design a model school, the opportunity for the conduct of significant research in the setting was an even more powerful determinant of university interest. In this paper it is not possible to give more than a brief description of the many research activities that are part of the project. They range from the macrostudy — the development and evaluation of the impact of the total project concept — to microstudies which may be carried out over fairly short periods of time and which deal with circumscribed questions of relevance for the total project.

The leitmotif of the research program concerns the influence of the environment on the development of the child. More specifically we are concerned with such research topics as: home factors influencing early learning, inter-relations among different types of learning (cognitive, social, emotional), the predictability of early performance, the development of internalized be-havioral controls, naturalistic studies of classroom and home behavior, the relative effectiveness of different types of enrichment models, the develop-ment of a human relations program for the elementary school, the utility of prereading training designed to foster the acquisition of conservation, the development of a language laboratory for two- and three-year-olds, con-sonance and dissonance between values for young children espoused by par-ents and advocated by the school. Different people on the staff are responsible for the direction and conduct of the various studies, and reports will be forthcoming as the projects are completed.

We are especially pleased that our research is conducted as an integral part of the school program, not as an extra feature that has to be grafted on to the regular activities. A possible reason for this is our dedication to a funda-mental policy relating to all research personnel: everyone, including the director, is expected to give some time to working directly with the children in a service capacity. All full-time research staff are required to spend at least one hour per day in such work. This sharing of what the teachers clearly regard as the most demanding part of the work load helps create and main-tain good morale and helps to keep teachers and researchers attitudinally on the same side of the fence. We feel that it helps to avoid the friction that can develop when one group is seen as "doing research" on the other group. This improved camaraderie is essentially a bonus from the policy; it was insti-tuted primarily because of the director's conviction that one learns about children and generates researchable ideas only by interacting with them.

5. *A comprehensive array of supportive family services.* The school is not situated in a part of the city with cohesiveness among the residents and a strong feeling of community. Although the school is racially integrated (as are virtually all of Little Rock's schools, contrary to the national stereotype), the neighborhood is not. Rather it contains areas of white housing and areas of black housing, sections inhabited by stable, long-term residents, and sec-tions where people come and go when the rent is due. In addition to the lack of cohesiveness, it is an area in which most of the mothers work. As the situation changes from time to time, it is difficult to give a definitive figure, but about seventy-five percent of our mothers are employed most of the time. In one of our current classrooms, for example, we have one nonworking mother, and in the Baby House all mothers either work or are in training. These data are mentioned at the outset to make it clear that it has not been easy to develop a dynamic family service program.

The staff assigned primarily to family-oriented work consists of two social workers, one school psychologist, and one aide. Within the project they are referred to collectively as representing "supplementary services." One of the social workers handles the enrollment of children into the program, serving as an information officer who lets the parents know what can be expected in the school, fills vacancies when they occur, makes home visits both to obtain and to give information.

Internal duties involve such things as enrolling children in the program and maintaining contact with families on the waiting list, contacting families of chronically absent children (of whom we have very few), helping acquaint families with community resources that the family might benefit from, ar-ranging for clothing and food distribution to needy families and coordinating periodic rummage sales, maintaining and operating a toy lending library, providing a school guidance service for all children showing learning or be-havior problems, offering individual or group therapy to disturbed children, coordinating coffee hours for all parents — and on and on.

But the supplementary service personnel also have duties which deal with the interface between the community and the families. Monthly meetings are held with a small group of parents who serve in the capacity of a "parent sounding board" (the group was originally designated by the formal title of Community Advisory Council). The purpose of this group is to bring to the attention of the family service worker, who serves as chairman and thence to the project director, any developments within the community that have relevance for the project. Although subtle efforts have been made to encourage concerns with the larger community, most of the topics brought up by this parent group relate to the school — whether the teachers are too easy or too hard on the children, how the groups can be monitored as they walk to or from school, what can be done to improve the playground, etc.

In a program such as we have at Kramer, it is possible for family-oriented activities to touch many families lightly or a few with intensity. Although hopefully there is some impact in even the fairly superficial contacts we have with families in such activities as enrolling a child or checking on an absence, our own perception is that our pattern of significant influence involves a very small number of parents, mainly mothers. Essentially it is the *same* mothers who habitually volunteer to help arrange coffees, who turn up for the parent discussions, who sit on the advisory group, who check out toys for their children. From what we have read (Chilman, 1972) and heard from others engaged in similar ventures, most other programs have the same experience. How to reach the unreachable families remains a big challenge for the future.

6. *A training program for staff and students.* Our training activities may be divided into the traditional preservice and inservice activities. As the school virtually never closes, it is difficult to find a time for the preservice program when *all* staff members can attend. We have managed to find this time in the late summer each year. This is a time when many families are away on vacation and when the need for day care is diminished. At this time the building gets a thorough cleaning and the floors are freshly varnished, and the staff holds a one or two week training workshop. There are always some carry-over personnel and some new personnel, so in these training sessions an attempt is made to give new personnel short courses in the history and philosophy of the project and then have all participants consider together the important planning and learning and preparation that need to be undertaken prior to the fall opening.

The inservice training goes on throughout the year. To be on the staff of Kramer is to assume the attitude of a student — we are all learning all the time. This attitude appears to come rather easily to people in early childhood education, as, having been step-children of formal education for so long anyway, they tend to be a bit self-effacing and to assume that they cannot know anything very important! Facetiousness aside, in the author's experience, most teachers of young children appear to enjoy seeking new knowledge and trying to develop new skills. Our credentialing system makes things somewhat different with our elementary and secondary teachers — they know how to teach, and they have certificates to prove it! And, of course, they are right. They *do* know how to teach, and the educational Cassandras who are crying out that they are doing everything wrong probably have spent precious little time in a classroom and have perhaps not coped without interruption for a single day with a roomful of children.

Even though this author does not consider herself to be a harsh critic of our school system, and though she decries dramatic declarations that our schools are sick, or dead, or are killing our children, the very idea of this project implies that somehow the elementary school must not be doing a good job or there would be no need to try to modify it in order to provide continuity of enrichment for the children who had been in the early childhood program. Thus, it would appear that a social scientist might expect from the outset differences in the attitudes toward the project shown by the preparatory and the elementary teachers. To the one group, the idea of the project translates to the third ear as: "What we do is great. There is not a program in existence that gives enough children exposure to our talents and skills; therefore, we must develop such a program." To the other group the project concept translates more like this: "There is something drastically wrong with the way we are now doing things. If this were not so, the children who go through our classes would not have so much trouble and demonstrate so many learning difficulties. If we were doing things properly, certainly the little children who have the necessary experimental background would continue to make progress and would not develop academic and behavior problems."

These hypothetical messages are elaborated here, as it is our conviction that our aim of developing a unified early childhood-elementary school program was placed in jeopardy from the outset by these different implicit attitudes called forth from personnel in the two divisions. Therefore, one of our major training aims has been to help us all see our task from the same vantage point.

In a day care school this is not as easy as it might sound, as it is virtually impossible ever to get everyone together. Our partial solution has been to arrange movies for the children once a week an hour before regular dismissal time so that the bulk of the staff can get together for a Faculty Forum. Teacher aides and the part-time physical education teachers supervise the children during this time. This does not solve the problem of getting teachers *and* aides together at the same time, but it does at least get the teachers from the lower and upper divisions together.

Topics for this Forum are about evenly divided between sessions in which new ideas are introduced (either by a staff member or an outside speaker) and sessions in which problems are discussed and solutions sought. Because of her own lack of experience in public school settings, the author was unaware of the extent to which this sort of "luxury" was unusual (at least in our community) for elementary teachers. Most schools have faculty meetings only once a month, and these are largely consumed by announcements and discussions of assignments; they are seldom forums for the exchange of ideas. In our meetings we have proceeded from polite listening to a willingness to bring up controversial topics and to be critical of some aspect of the program. (There must still be some feelings of inferiority on the part of the preparatory teachers, for, while I can think of instances in which an elementary teacher criticized something being done in the preparatory division, I cannot recall any instances of reverse criticism.) These sessions in general have been extremely stimulating and rewarding, so much so that they are now being attended by supervisory personnel from the Little Rock School District and by other interested persons in the community. In addition to these large group sessions, many ad hoc training sessions are arranged throughout the week to make new plans or try to work out problems. Finally, staff training includes the provision of training modules of varying dimensions on request, e.g., a four-week unit on behavior modification, a ten-week refresher on methods and materials, a semester course on understanding elementary statistics. It has been our goal to arrange for all staff members who participate in these training sessions to receive appropriate university credits for their involvement; to date, however, this has not been possible. It is easier to influence an elementary school than a university!

Although it unpleasantly suggests a "separate but equal" philosophy, the necessity that someone must always mind the store has mandated a different training program for the teacher aides. This is true only of inservice training, incidentally, for in the annual preservice workshops the entire staff meets as a single body. Our experience has been that, short of having a skilled discussion leader symbolically pull their teeth, the aides will not talk when the training session includes the teachers and other professional staff members. In the Aide's Forum, practical skills have been emphasized, but at the same time they have received an excellent background course in child development. At the time of this writing, the aides themselves are in the process of writing a training manual for others in similar situations.

The remaining major component of our training endeavors involves university students. These are either graduate students who take courses taught by staff members who also hold academic positions in the university, advanced doctoral candidates doing their dissertation research under the guidance of the author, or undergraduate students doing practice teaching. It is only with the last group that our training program is unique and merits description here.

The practice teaching students come to us during their last semester — after having completed all their foundations and methods courses but often with little or no practical experience in working with children (certainly with no sustained experience). All students declare in advance the grade level (though we are nongraded) with which they prefer to work. In addition to their teaching internship, the students also take with us a nondescript course called "Senior Seminar," intended to be an introduction to the world of the professional teacher.

Obviously the most salient feature of Kramer is the wide age range of children participating in the program. What better environment could one find to help give students that often praised but seldom achieved "developmental orientation"? Thus, even though the students had requested a particular level in advance, we wished to expose them to children throughout the available age range. The two major divisions (preparatory and elementary) were each subdivided again, resulting in four quads: babies-toddlers, three's to five's, primary, upper elementary. Each student elects to major in one of these quads and to minor in another, and each is assigned to all four quads for some period of time during the semester. For the first month the students rotate among the quads, getting to know the children and mainly observing the teachers. During the second month they move into their major classrooms for three days a week and spend the remaining two days in their minor quad. Their responsibilities are limited, and they mainly carry out assignments given them by the master teachers. In the third month the major-minor division becomes 4:1, and they are given progressively more responsibility both for planning and execution. Their classroom assignments will, for the most part, be directed toward one or another subgroup of children. In their final month, they are expected to demonstrate their ability to plan daily programs independently, though their plans must still be approved by the master teacher. This gradual build-up of responsibility reaches its culmination during which time they handle the class independently.

Throughout this time an attempt is made in their seminar to relate their classroom experiences to philosophical and theoretical formulations to which they have been exposed previously (or to which they need exposure). They are videotaped twice during the semester in a microteaching situation, and these tapes are critiqued in the seminar. They also participate in the regular Faculty Forum.

An additional feature of the training regimen is that early in the semester, they select one child in the school (not one in their major quad) with whom they form a "big sister" or tutorial relationship. They are expected to get to know this child, meet his family, help him with assigned homework, take him on a special outing, etc. Their experiences with this one child are then written up as a case study — the traditional child development assignment — with inferences drawn from what they learn about that child to the kinds of educational experiences that we need to try to provide for similar children.

We have just completed the first semester in which this training program has been implemented; undoubtedly we will make minor changes in the future. Although the teachers have reservations about its value (they prefer to get a student early in the semester and keep him or her), the students are ecstatic about it. In fact, they are so complimentary that we think something must be wrong — students are just not that prone to approve things these days. We hope to be able to follow the careers of these young people who have had their initial exposure to the world of teaching via this developmental approach. Only then will we be able to know whether it has accomplished our aims for it .

Summary

In this paper I have attempted to present the major features of one prototype of a school for tomorrow which has the good fortune to be in operation today. In the words of my title, it is the kind of school which offers something of value to everybody associated with the endeavor, to the staff no less than to the children and parents. In its program design the school links together early childhood education and elementary education, education and day care, education and research, and the home and the school. Each of these linkages forms a symbiotic relationship in which each component enriches its opposite. Although keeping it all together has not been easy, one could hardly claim that it has been truly difficult.

This description is being written before enough time has elapsed to demonstrate whether the major question posed by the faculty can be answered — can an environment be designed which will provide the experiences necessary to nourish development during the early years and necessary to sustain that development during the years of middle childhood. Therefore, perhaps it would be appropriate to conclude with a paragraph from our original proposal which, better than any we have managed to write since that time, effectively communicates just what it is we are trying to do in the program here described:

"Before being promoted out of the school, it is hoped that each child will have acquired a love of learning, will know how to adapt to group experience, will have mastered thoroughly the rudiments of reading and mathematics, will have experienced a cultural milieu rich enough to enable him to meet all subsequent school experiences without apology, and will have made substantial progress toward becoming a responsible citizen. Similarly it is hoped that each child's family will have realized that education is not something that is done *for* a child *by* a school system but rather is a continuing process in which the child, the parents, the school, and the community work cooperatively toward the goal of further development for all who are involved in the process."

Notes

1. Center for Early Development and Education, College of Education, University of Arkansas, 814 Sherman, Little Rock, Arkansas 72202. The author's work is supported by Grant No. SF-500 from the Office of Child Development, Department of Health, Education, and Welfare. Although this paper carries a single authorship, the project described represents the work and the ideas of many people, at least some of whom the author would like to mention. Important contributions to the original plans for the project were made by Dr. Irvin L. Ramsey and Dr. Robert M. Roelfs of the University of Arkansas, by Mr. John Fortenberry, Mr. David C. Wallace, and Miss Imogene Hines of the Little Rock School District, and Mr. Lowther Penn of the Arkansas State Department of Education. Within the staff special appreciation is expressed to Dr. Phyllis T. Elardo and Dr. Richard Elardo of the Research Services, to Mrs. Elaine Barton and Mrs. Faustenia Bomar, Principal and Vice-Principal, respectively, of the school, and to Mr. Stephen Lehane, Training Coordinator. The author would also like to acknowledge the contributions of former staff members Dr. Jerry D. Perrin, Mrs. Martha Jane Moose, Mrs. Rosanne Gmuer, and Mr. William S. Parker. Most importantly it should be recognized that the project could not operate a single day without the work of the dedicated teachers, aides, research assistants, supplementary service and

clerical personnel. Finally, to the Kramer children and their parents goes my appreciation for remaining such good sports about being visited, interviewed, and innovated. From all of these components has the Kramer model emerged, and without any part the system would break down — "E pluribus unum."

References

Berman, L. M. *New priorities in the curriculum.* Columbus, Ohio: Charles E. Merrill Publishing Co., 1968.

Bloom, B. S. *Stability and change in human characteristics.* New York: John Wiley & Sons, 1964.

Bruner, J. S. *The process of education.* Cambridge, Mass.: Harvard University Press, 1960.

Caldwell, B. M. Impact of interest in early cognitive stimulation. In H. E. Rie (Ed.) *Perspectives in Child Psychopathology.* Chicago: Aldine-Atherton, 1971. 293–334.

Caldwell, B. M. "A timid giant grows bolder." *Saturday Review,* February 20, 1971. 47–49, 65–66.

Caldwell, B. M. "The rationale for early intervention." *Exceptional Children,* 1970, 36: 717–726.

Caldwell, B. M. "The usefulness of critical period hypothesis in the study of filiative behavior." *Merrill-Palmer Quarterly,* 1962, 8, 229–242.

Caldwell, B. M., Heider, J., and Kaplan, B. The inventory of home stimulation. Paper presented at the American Psychological Association Meeting. New York, New York. September 1966.

Chilman, C. S. Programs for disadvantaged parents: some major trends and related research. In B. M. Caldwell and H. Ricciati (Eds.) *Review of Child Development Research,* Vol. III. University of Chicago Press, forthcoming.

Cremin, L. A. *The transformation of the School.* New York: Alfred A. Knopf, 1961.

Goodlad, J. I., with Stoephasius, R., and Klein, M. F. *The changing school curriculum.* New York: Fund for the Advancement of Education, 1966.

Gordon E. W., and Wilkerson, D. A. *Compensatory education for the disadvantaged.* New York: College Entrance Examination Board, 1966.

Hunt, J. McV. *Intelligence and experience.* New York: Ronald Press, 1961.

Hunt, J. McV. The psychological basis for using preschool enrichment as an antidote for cultural deprivation. *Merrill-Palmer Quarterly,* 1964, 10 209–248.

Karnes, M. B. Research and development program on preschool disadvantaged children. Final Report, Project No. 5-1181, Bureau of Research, Office of Education, U. S. Department of Health, Education, and Welfare, 1969.

Schaefer, R. J. *The school as a center of inquiry.* New York: Harper & Row, Publishers, 1967.

Silberman, C. E. *Crisis in the classroom.* New York: Random House, 1970.

Wachs, T., Uzgiris, I., and Hunt, J. McV. Cognitive development in infants of different age levels and from different environmental backgrounds: an exploratory investigation. *Merrill-Palmer Quarterly,* 1971, 17, 283–317.

Westinghouse Learning Corporation/Ohio University. *The impact of Head Start: an evaluation of the effects of Head Start on children's cognitive and affective development.* June, 1969.

Index